Writing Research Papers

A Complete Guide

Twelfth Edition

James D. Lester, Sr.

James D. Lester, Jr.
Clayton College and State University

PEARSON
Longman

New York San Francisco Boston
London Toronto Sydney Tokyo Singapore Madrid
Mexico City Munich Paris Cape Town Hong Kong Montreal

In Memoriam

Dr. James D. Lester passed away on January 10, 2006, at age 70. He was tireless in his publication of scholarly textbooks—42 in all. This is a legacy that has shaped the instruction and understanding of writing and research for the previous four decades. His most successful text was, ironically, his first, *Writing Research Papers: A Complete Guide*. Launched in 1967, it has been used by over three million students at almost every college in America. This life and these accomplishments only begin to touch the true mark of the man and our memories of his love and care for each of us as well as our profession.

It is with pride, loving recollection, and hopeful expectation that I dedicate this twelfth edition of *Writing Research Papers: A Complete Guide* to the memory of my father, J. D. Lester. His guidance, friendship, and professionalism will truly be missed.

Jim Lester

Publisher: Joseph Opiela
Development Editor: Katharine Glynn
Senior Supplements Editor: Donna Campion
Senior Marketing Manager: Sandra McGuire
Production Manager: Bob Ginsberg
Project Coordination, Text Design, and Electronic Page Makeup:
    Electronic Publishing Services Inc., New York City
Senior Cover Design Manager: Nancy Danahy
Cover Photo: © Getty Images, Inc.
Senior Manufacturing Buyer: Dennis J. Para
Printer and Binder: Quebecor World/Taunton
Cover Printer: The Lehigh Press, Inc.

For permission to use copyrighted material, grateful acknowledgment is made to the copyright holders on page C-1, which is hereby made part of this copyright page.

Library of Congress Cataloging-in-Publication Data
Lester, James D.
    Writing research papers : a complete guide / James D. Lester, James D.
Lester. – 12th ed.
        p.   cm.
    Includes bibliographical references and index.
    ISBN 0-321-45798-6 (pbk.) – ISBN 0-321-45799-4 (spiral bound) 1.
Report writing–Handbooks, manuals, etc.   2. Report writing–Handbooks,
manuals, etc.   I. Lester, James D.   II. Title.
    LB2369.L4 2007
    808'.02–dc22

                                                        2006022722

Visit us at www.ablongman.com

ISBN 0-321-45798-6 (paperbound edition)
ISBN 0-321-45799-4 (tabbed edition)

345678910—QWT—09 08

Contents

CHAPTER 12 Writing the Introduction, Body, and Conclusion   199

To the Instructor

Since 1967 this text has kept students and instructors current with academic styles of writing and documentation. Now, the new twelfth edition brings even more updates to assist the student researcher in keeping pace with electronic publishing.

Confirmation of Academic Styles

As with other aspects of our lives, the Internet now plays a major role in research by our students and professional writers which, in turn, forces style guides such as this one to keep pace. The various scholarly associations are also playing catch up with their manuals of style for scholarly writing. *Writing Research Papers: A Complete Guide* conforms in its instructions to these editions:

1. The Modern Language Association of America has greatly expanded coverage on citing electronic sources as well as updates in other areas. It continues to grow in size, from the 30 pages of William Riley Parker's 1951 style sheet to the 361 pages of the sixth edition. The MLA style is the default style for this text with its standards shown in Chapters 1 through 14.

    Gibaldi, Joseph. *MLA Handbook for Writers of Research Papers.* 6th ed. New York: MLA, 2003.

2. The American Psychological Association has a fifth edition in which the staff "took aim at the moving target of electronic referencing and manuscript preparation" (Preface). Like other scholarly guides, the APA manual has grown to 439 pages. This style is explained fully in Chapter 15.

    Publication Manual of the American Psychological Association. 5th ed. Washington: APA, 2001. Fifth Printing, 2002.

3. The University of Chicago Press recognizes the role of electronic research, saying, "Computer technology and the increasing use of the Internet mark almost every chapter" of the new edition because of the "increasing proportion of our users who work with magazines, newsletters, corporate reports, proposals, electronic publications, Web sites, and other nonbook or nonprint documents" (Preface). Now in its 15th edition, this style guide weighs in with 956 pages. This style is featured in Chapter 16.

    The Chicago Manual of Style. 15th ed. Chicago: University of Chicago Press, 2003.

4. The Council of Biology Editors has changed its name to reflect more precisely its role in serving all the sciences—thus, it is now the Council of Science Editors. Its board of directors has published a new edition of its style manual. Thus, the CBE Manual has become the CSE Manual. Researchers now refer to the "CSE style" to respect the new name even though the current standards are based on this book:

> *Scientific Style and Format: The CSE Manual for Authors, Editors, and Publishers.* 7th ed. New York: Rockefeller University Press, 2006.

The details of CSE style are explained in Chapter 17.

Help with Electronic Research and Presentation

Computers and the electronic revolution are so pervasive in research writing today that a single chapter cannot properly encompass such work. Instead, every chapter of the text touches on various aspects of the Internet's effect on topic searches, discovery of source material, gathering notes and drafting the paper, plagiarism and academic integrity, and, of course, documentation of the sources.

Compounding the problem is that the style guides each advance a different method for documenting electronic sources, making a guide of this sort vital to students who move from class to class and thus from one discipline to another. The new CMS guide says the date of access is irrelevant to the documentation, yet MLA, APA, and CSE all think it should be listed. The citing of the URL is standard, but with variations in its presentation.

Nevertheless, *Writing Research Papers: A Complete Guide* takes the students step by step through the various documentation forms of Internet sources. It also spends considerable space in helping students blend electronic citations into their writing. A checklist, "Evaluating Internet Sources," helps students gauge the quality of Internet articles.

Student Papers

Student writing examples show how young writers researched and drafted papers on a wide range of topics. With seven documented manuscripts, more than any other text of this nature, this text demonstrates format, documentation, and the different academic styles. The paper by Norman Berkowitz includes visuals.

Norman Berkowitz "The World's Water Supply: The Ethics of Distribution" (MLA style)

Melinda Mosier "Listening to Hamlet: The Soliloquies" (MLA style)

Valerie Nesbitt-Hall "Arranged Marriages: The Revival is Online" (APA style)

Jamie Johnston "Prehistoric Wars: We've Always Hated Each Other" (CMS style)

Sarah Bemis "Diabetes Management: A Delicate Balance" (CSE style)

Norman Levenson "Annotated Bibliography: Tanning and Tanning Beds" (MLA style)

Kaci Holz "Gender Communication: A Review of the Literature" (MLA style)

Sample abstracts in MLA and APA style are also displayed. Additional sample research papers are available in the *Instructor's Manual, Model Research Papers from Across the Curriculum*, and on the dedicated Web site.

The Writing Process

As in past editions, this text walks with the student through the necessary steps in a natural sequence.

Getting Started. The text explains the reasons for writing a research paper and the ways to discover an academic topic.

Gathering Sources. Special guidance for using Internet sources is given because evidence shows that most students now start their work at a search engine. Filtering the good Internet sources from the bad is a major theme of Chapter 3. Following that, this guidebook takes the student into the library to explain not only the printed materials but additional electronic sources that can be accessed only through their identification number for library access. Then Chapter 5 explains field research and encourages students to conduct interviews, surveys, and other techniques for gathering empirical evidence. Appendix B provides, by academic discipline, the best printed references in the library and the academically sponsored Internet sites.

Plagiarism. Before the student goes any further, academic integrity is discussed. Chapter 6 shows what must be done when borrowing from sources and gives the researcher the basic rules to follow in order to avoid all forms of plagiarism.

Critical Reading. Writing Research Papers discusses at length the methods for finding sources that are reliable and worthy of paraphrase or quotation.

Getting Organized. Chapters 8 and 9 direct the student in methods of organizing the paper and taking notes so that the paper will meet the demands of academic form and style.

Blending the Sources. Three chapters, 10 through 13, are devoted to the most difficult task of all—drafting a manuscript that displays the student's voice while blending sources effectively into the narrative flow.

Writing in the Academic Styles. Our students drift from class to class and from one discipline to another, meeting along the way a variety of requirements in research paper formats. Chapters 14 through 17 address these needs, helping students format their papers for four basic styles: MLA, APA, CMS, and CSE. Appendix A provides a glossary to the rules and techniques for preparing a manuscript.

Preparing Electronic Research Papers. Developed to meet the needs of modern researchers in preparing electronic research papers, Chapter 18 begins with the easiest way to present your research findings, putting a word-processed research paper on a disk for your instructor, and moves to the most difficult, designing a Web site and releasing the paper onto the Internet.

Reference Works by Topic

The list of references in Appendix B, "Finding Reference Works for Your General Topic," provides a user-friendly list of sources for launching your research project. Arranged into ten general categories, as listed on pages A-9 to A-15, Appendix B allows a student who is examining an issue in health, fitness, or athletics to have quick access to relevant library books, library databases, and Internet sites.

Navigable Design

Again with this edition, *Writing Research Papers* is printed with four-color text and artwork to make the information easier to find and more pleasing to read. It brings strong, visual elements to the instruction. "Where to Look" boxes, signaled with an eyeglass icon, make the many cross-references in this comprehensive textbook easier to spot. A globe icon directs the researcher to a Web site that supports and expounds on the text.

The spiral-bound version of *Writing Research Papers* has cardboard tabs to divide the text and make information easier to find. Printed on one side of each tab are suggested Web sites for additional and appropriate information. The other side of the tab features a table of contents to that section of the book.

The Ancillary Package

The publication package includes these additional features:

- **Companion Website.** The Companion Website <www.ablongman.com/lester12e> provides activities specific to each chapter's content, such as using key words to find and narrow a topic, using listserv archives as potential research areas, and evaluating different kinds of Web materials. A Web icon within the text signals to students (and instructors) that a Web activity is available.
- **E-mail access to the author.** The author is available to students and instructors to answer questions on style and format and to accept suggestions for improvement of the book's content.
- **Instructor's Manual.** This handy guide contains chapter-by-chapter classroom exercises, research assignments, quizzes, and duplication masters. Available to instructors upon request.

Acknowledgments

The preface would not be complete without the recognition of many key people who served in the development of *Writing Research Papers: A Complete Guide,* Twelfth Edition.

As you will see in the text and the ancillary material, thanks is extended to several students: Norman Berkowitz, Sarah Bemis, Jamie Johnston, Valerie Nesbitt-Hall, Melinda Mosier, Kaci Holz, and Norman Levenson.

For editorial assistance that kept us focused, special thanks are extended to the Longman group headed by Joe Opiela, vice president and publisher. Sincere appreciation must go to Katharine Glynn, development editor; and Lisa Kinne, production editor. Finally we want to recognize a great group of reviewers who offered penetrating and perceptive suggestions for this new edition: Jeanne Bickford, PhD., University of California-Irvine; Christine Caver, Ph.D., University of Texas at San Antonio; Ann Cobb, Coppin State University; Dr. Janice Corbett, Delaware Valley College; Sarah Dye, Elgin Community College; Amy Flint, North Idaho College; Matthew S. Hartman, Ball State University; Michael Hricik, Westmoreland County Community College; Mary Lang, Wharton County Jr. College; Christina McCaslin, University of Wisconsin Marathon County; Cynthia Mitchell, University of Northern Colorado; Derek P. Royal, Texas A&M University-Commerce; Marian K. Salwierak, St. Gregory's University; and Cynthia M. VanSickle, McHenry County College.

Heartfelt appreciation is also extended to the members or our family: Martha, Mark, Debbie, Caleb, and Sarah. Their love and patience made this project possible.

JAMES D. LESTER, JR.

To the Student

As a member of the academic community you will be asked by instructors to write "researched" essays. The emphasis on research means quite simply that you must go beyond what you know and think personally to find information from a variety of sources, and incorporate the ideas and words of others in your manuscript. Thus, you will soon need to access the Internet, check out books from the library, and perhaps interview knowledgeable people. You will absorb the words and opinions of the experts and bring them to bear on your topic. You will also become a facilitator, one who pulls together and makes sense of divergent views.

A research assignment may take various forms, such as these:

- Write a paper that explores the former Berlin Wall as a symbol for the rise and fall of communism in the Soviet Union.
- What are you curious about? Find a problem, question, or issue that piques your interest and that requires research.
- Defend the contributions to American society of a famous but controversial person, such as Martin Luther King, Jr. or Alexander Hamilton.
- Conduct a survey of students and faculty on the problems of campus parking. Discuss the implications of your findings. Submit the report in APA style.

These four examples merely touch the surface of possible assignments, but they demonstrate an important point: a research assignment may be open-ended or highly specific. Whatever kind of assignment you receive, you will need to follow a logical procedure for developing the paper. That is what *Writing Research Papers: A Complete Guide* is all about. We have designed it to carry you step by step to a finished research project.

Frequently Asked Questions and Where to Find Answers

- Why do research at all? Chapter 1 explains why we do research and report our findings.
- Need to find a research topic? Chapter 2 tells how to find a topic that will interest you and your readers.
- Need to find information? Chapters 3–5 show you how to find information in the library, on the Internet, and in the real world through interviews, observation, and questionnaires.
- What about plagiarism and publishing on a Web site? Chapter 6 addresses matters of integrity and honesty in reporting, especially in this electronic age when downloading the words of others is so easy.

- Which sources are reliable and worth citing? Chapter 7 helps you judge the sources to know which to cite in your paper and which to dismiss.
- Time to get organized? Chapter 8 helps you organize your notes and ideas for a focused paper.
- Need guidelines for taking notes? Chapter 9 shows how to write effective notes that will transfer easily into your text.
- What about blending the sources and drafting the manuscript? Chapters 10–13 help give your writing an academic style, one that blends sources effectively into your prose and encourages strength and purpose in your introduction, body, and conclusion.
- What happens when the instructor says, "Use APA style" or "Reference your sources with footnotes"? Chapters 14–17 provide detailed instruction and examples of four academic styles—MLA (English), APA (social sciences), CMS (humanities), and CSE (sciences).
- How can I most effectively submit or present my research findings? Developed to meet the needs of modern researchers in preparing electronic research papers, Chapter 18 begins with the easiest way to present your research findings, putting a word-processed research paper on a disk for your instructor, and moves to the most difficult, designing a Web site and releasing the paper onto the Internet.
- What about all the little details about formatting, numbering, ellipsis points, and so forth? Appendix A provides a glossary to the rules and techniques for preparing a manuscript, and Chapter 13 explains the format for a paper in the MLA style.
- Need a list of the best scholarly sources? Appendix B, "Finding Reference Works for Your General Topic," provides a user-friendly list which will enable you to select rather quickly a few basic references from one of ten general categories. Here are the ten sections and the page number that begins each:
    1. Historic Issues of Events, People, and Artifacts, A-9
    2. Scientific Issues in Physics, Astronomy, and Engineering, A-10
    3. Issues of Health, Fitness, and Athletics, A-11
    4. Social and Political Issues, A-11
    5. Issues in the Arts, Literature, Music, and Language, A-12
    6. Environmental Issues, Genetics, and the Earth Sciences, A-12
    7. Issues in Communication and Information Technology, A-12
    8. Issues in Religion, Philosophy, Psychology, A-14
    9. Issues in Business and Economics, A-14
    10. Popular Culture, Current Events, and Modern Trends, A-15

Now in its twelfth edition, this text has served millions of students, like you, by giving detailed up-to-date information on the methods of scholarly research and writing from sources. Early editions encouraged students to write with the computer, later editions advocated research on the Internet, and this edition motivates students like you to publish the paper in an electronic form, not merely on paper. We welcome any thoughts and suggestions you may have on this text as you work through it. We wish you well!

JAMES D. LESTER, JR.

Hint boxes throughout the text offer practical advice and insight on important elements of the research and writing process.

HINT: Learn the special language of the academic discipline and use it. Every field of study, whether sociology, geology, or literature, has words to describe its analytical approach to topics, such as the *demographics* of a target audience (marketing), the *function* of loops and arrays (computer science), the *symbolism* of Maya Angelou's poetry (literature), and *observation* of human subjects (psychology). Part of your task is learning the terminology and using it appropriately.

Your Research Project exercises offer guidance and practice in applying the general principles of each chapter to your own research project.

YOUR RESEARCH PROJECT

1. Make a list of your personal interests and items that affect your mental and physical activities, such as homework, hiking, or relations with your family. Examine each item on the list see if you can find an academic angle that will make the topic fit the context of your research assignment. See Section 2a, pages 12–17, for more help.
2. Ask questions about a possible subject, using the list on pages 16–17.
3. Look around your campus or community for subjects. Talk with your classmates and even your instructor about campus issues. Focus on your hometown community in search of a problem, such as the demise of the Main Street merchants. Investigate any environmental concerns in your area, from urban sprawl to beach erosion to waste disposal. Think seri-

Where to Look boxes help to locate additional information and related material in other parts of the text.

Research teaches the basic ingredients of argument. In most cases, a research paper requires you to make a claim and support it with reasons and evidence. For example, if you argue that "urban sprawl has invited wild animals into our backyards," you will learn to anticipate challenges to your theory and to defend your assertion with evidence.

Making a claim and establishing a thesis: **1c**, pages 3–4

Checklists summarize and review key concepts within each chapter.

CHECKLIST

Narrowing a General Subject into a Scholarly Topic

Unlike a general subject, a scholarly topic should:

- Examine one narrowed issue, not a broad subject.
- Address knowledgeable readers and carry them to another plateau of knowledge.
- Have a serious purpose—one that demands analysis of the issues, argues from a position, and explains complex details.
- Meet the expectations of the instructor and conform to the course requirements.

Writing from Research

Communication begins when we make an initial choice to speak or to record our ideas in writing. When we speak, our words disappear quickly, so we are often lax about our grammar because no record of what we say remains. The written word, however, creates a public record of our knowledge, our opinions, and our skill with language, so we try to make our writing accurate, forceful, and honest. A piece of writing—whether it is a history paper, a field report, or a research project—commits our personal concerns to public knowledge. Many people can examine our written document and then make judgments about our beliefs. That scrutiny is intimidating.

Regardless of the writer's experience or the instructor's expert direction, writing is a demanding process that requires commitment. Discovering a well-focused topic, and more importantly a reason for writing about it, begins the process. Choosing a format, exploring sources through critical reading, and then completing the writing task with grace and style are daunting tasks.

Despite this, writing is an outlet for the inquisitive and creative nature in each of us. Our writing is affected by the richness of our language, by our background and experiences, by our targeted audience, and by the form of expression that we choose. With perceptive enthusiasm for relating detailed concepts and honest insights, we discover the power of our own words. The satisfaction of writing well and relating our understanding to others provides intellectual stimulation and insight into our own beliefs and values.

As a college student, you will find that your writing assignments will extend past personal thoughts and ideas to explore more complex aspects of academic studies. Writing will make you confident in your ability to find information and present it effectively in all kinds of ways and for all sorts of projects, such as:

- A theme in a freshman composition course on the value of Web logs, online journals, and other online discussion groups.
- A paper in history on Herbert Hoover's ineffectual policies for coping with the Great Depression of the early 1930s.
- A report for a physical fitness class on the benefits of Jujitsu as exercise and as personal protection.
- A sociological field report on free and reduced-cost lunches for school-aged children.
- A brief biographical study of a famous person, such as labor leader César Chávez.

All of these papers require some type of "researched writing." Papers similar to these will appear on your schedule during your first two years of college and increase in frequency in upper-division courses. This text takes off the pressure—it shows you how to research "online discussion groups" or "the Great Depression," and it demonstrates the correct methods for documenting the sources.

We conduct informal research all the time. We examine various models and their options before buying a car, and we check out another person informally before proposing or accepting a first date. We sometimes search the classified ads to find a summer job, or we roam the mall to find a new tennis racket, the right pair of sports shoes, or the latest CD. Research, then, is not foreign to us. It has become commonplace to use a search engine to explore the Internet for information on any subject—from personal concerns, such as the likely side effects of a prescribed drug, to complex issues, such as robotics or acupuncture.

In the classroom, we begin thinking about a serious and systematic activity, one that involves the library, the Internet, or field research. A research paper, like a personal essay, requires you to choose a topic you care about and are willing to invest many hours in thinking about. However, unlike a personal essay or short report, you will develop your ideas by gathering an array of information, reading sources critically, and collecting notes. As you pull your project together, you will continue to express personal ideas, but now they are supported by and based on the collective evidence and the opinions of experts on the topic.

Some instructors prefer the description *research*ed *writing,* for this type of writing grows from investigation, and the research is used in different ways, in different amounts, and for different purposes. Each classroom and each instructor will make different demands on your talents. The guidelines here are general; your instructors will provide the specifics.

This text therefore introduces research as an engaging, sometimes exciting pursuit on several fronts—your personal knowledge, ideas gleaned from printed and electronic sources, and research in the field.

Each classroom and each instructor will make different demands on your talents, yet all stipulate *researched writing*. Your research project will advance your theme and provide convincing proof for your inquiry.

- *Researched writing* grows from investigation.
- *Researched writing* establishes a clear purpose.
- *Researched writing* develops analysis for a variety of topics.

With the guidance of your instructor, you are making inquiry to advance your own knowledge as well as increase the data available for future research by others.

Writing Research Papers introduces research as an engaging, sometimes exciting pursuit on several fronts—your personal knowledge, ideas gleaned from printed and electronic sources, and research in the field.

1a   Why Do Research?

Instructors ask you to write a research paper for several reasons:

Research teaches methods of discovery. Explanation on a topic prompts you to discover what you know on a topic and what others can teach you. Beyond reading, it often expects you to venture into the field for interviews, observation, and experimentation. The process tests your curiosity as you probe a complex subject. You may not arrive at any final answers or solutions, but you will come to understand the different views on a subject. In your final paper, you will synthesize your ideas and discoveries with the knowledge and opinions of others.

Research teaches investigative skills. A research project requires you to investigate a subject, gain a grasp of its essentials, and disclose your findings. The exercise teaches important methods for gaining knowledge on a complex topic. Your success will depend on your negotiating the various sources of information, from reference books in the library to computer databases and from special archival collections to the most recent articles in printed periodicals. The Internet, with its vast quantity of information, will challenge you to find reliable sources. If you conduct research by observation, interviews, surveys, and laboratory experiments, you will discover additional methods of investigation.

> Finding material on electronic sources and the Internet: Chapter 3, pages 33–54.

Research develops inquiry-based techniques. Some instructors prefer the description "researched writing," to signal that this type of writing grows from investigation, and the research is used in different ways, in different amounts, and for different purposes. Each classroom and each instructor will make different demands on your talents. With the guidance of your instructor, you are making inquiry to advance your own knowledge as well as increase the data available for future research by others.

Research teaches critical thinking. As you wade through the evidence on your subject, you will learn to discriminate between useful information and unfounded or ill-conceived comments. Some sources, such as the Internet, will provide timely, reliable material but may also entice you with worthless and undocumented opinions.

Research teaches logic. Like a judge in the courtroom, you must make perceptive judgments about the issues surrounding a specific topic. Your decisions, in effect, will be based on the wisdom gained from research of the subject. Your paper and your readers will rely on your logical response to your reading, observation, interviews, and testing.

Research teaches the basic ingredients of argument. In most cases, a research paper requires you to make a claim and support it with reasons and evidence. For example, if you argue that "urban sprawl has invited wild animals into our backyards," you will learn to anticipate challenges to your theory and to defend your assertion with evidence.

> Making a claim and establishing a thesis: 1c, pages 4–5.

1b Learning Format Variations

Scholarly writing in each discipline follows certain conventions—that is, special forms are required for citing the sources and for designing the pages. These rules make uniform the numerous articles written internationally by millions of scholars. The society of language and literature scholars, the Modern Language Association, has a set of guidelines generally known as MLA style. Similarly, the American Psychological Association has its own APA style. Other groups of scholars prefer a footnote system, while still others use a numbering system. These variations are not meant to confuse; they have evolved within disciplines as the preferred style.

What is important for you, right now, is to determine which format to use. Many composition instructors will ask you to use MLA style, as explained in Chapters 11–14, but they are just as likely to ask for APA style (Chapter 15) if your topic concerns one of the social sciences. In a like manner, your art appreciation instructor might expect the footnote style but could just as easily request the APA style. Ask your instructor early which style to use and organize accordingly.

> MLA Style, pages 248–299
> APA Style, pages 300–336
> Chicago (CMS) Style, pages 337–365
> CSE Style, pages 366–385

1c Understanding a Research Assignment

Beyond selecting an effective subject, you need a reason for writing the paper. Literature instructors might expect you to make judgments about the structure of a story or poem. Education instructors might ask you to examine the merits of a testing program. History instructors might want you to explore an event—perhaps the causes and consequences of the 2003 U.S. war on Iraq.

Your inquiry can be a response to a question, such as "What about Hamlet and his long-winded speeches?" Prompted by her own question, Melinda Mosier developed a paper on Hamlet's soliloquies, which is reproduced on pages 226–235. Another student, Valerie Nesbitt-Hall, noticed a cartoon on the Internet that tickled her fancy and caused her to wonder about and then investigate online matchmaking services and chat rooms. Her research helped her develop a paper entitled "Arranged Marriages: The Revival Is Online" (see pages 336–347). Thus, different kinds of topics and questions can motivate you to explore your own thoughts and discover what others are saying.

Understanding the Terminology

Assignments in literature, history, and the fine arts will often require you to *interpret, evaluate,* and *perform causal analysis.* Assignments in education, psychology, political science, and other social science disciplines will usually require *analysis, definition, comparison,* or a search for *precedents* leading to a *proposal.* In the sciences, your experiments and testing will usually require a discussion of the *implications* of your findings. The next few pages explain these assignments.

Evaluation

To evaluate, you first need to establish clear criteria of judgment and then explain how the subject meets these criteria. For example, student evaluations of faculty members are based on a set of expressed criteria—an interest in student progress, a thorough knowledge of the subject, and so forth. Similarly, you may be asked to judge the merits of a poem, an art show, or a new MP3 player. Your first step should be to create your criteria. What makes a good movie? How important is a poem's form and structure? Is space a special factor in architecture? You can't expect the sources to provide the final answers; you need to experience the work and make your final judgments on it.

Let's see how evaluation develops with one student, Sarah Bemis, who was asked to examine diabetes. At first, Sarah worked to define the disease and its basic attack on the human system. However, as she read the literature she shifted her focus from a basic definition to evaluate and examine the methods for controlling diabetes. Her paper, "Diabetes Management: A Delicate Balance," appears on pages 375–385.

The same evaluative process applies to other subjects. For example, student Jamie Johnston conducted his inquiry on how prehistoric tribes were not the noble savages that some historians thought them to be. His study evaluated recent sources to learn that, in truth, war has long been a part of human history. His paper, "Prehistoric War: We Have Always Hated Each Other," is located on pages 352–365.

In many ways, every research paper is an evaluation.

Interpretation

To interpret, you must usually answer, "What does it mean?" You may be asked to explain the symbolism in a piece of literature, examine a point of law, or make sense of test results. Questions often point toward interpretation:

What does this passage mean?
What are the implications of these results?
What does this data tell us?
Can you explain your reading of the problem to others?

For example, your instructor might ask you to interpret the 1954 Supreme Court ruling in *Brown v. Board of Education*; interpret results on pond water testing at site A, in a secluded country setting, and site B, near a petrochemical plant; or interpret a scene from Henrik Ibsen's *An Enemy of the People*.

In her paper on Internet dating, Nesbitt-Hall found herself asking two interpretive questions: What are the social implications of computer dating? and What are the psychological implications?

Definition

Sometimes you will need to provide an extended definition to show that your subject fits into a selected and well-defined category. Note these examples:

1. A low-fat diet reduces the risk of coronary disease.
   You will need to define "low-fat" by describing foods that make up a low-fat diet and naming the benefits from this type of diet.
2. Title IX has brought positive changes to college athletic programs.
   You will need to define the law in detail and specify the changes.
3. The root cause of breakups in relationships is selfishness.
   This topic will require a definition of selfishness and examples of how it weakens relationships.
4. Are modern-day heroes limited to athletes and entertainers?
   This topic will require a definition of who a modern-day hero is and the characteristics that illustrate their influence.

These examples demonstrate how vague and illusive our language can be. We know what a "hero" is in general, but the term needs a careful analysis to solicit examples of a *modern-day hero*. The writer will need to work carefully to reach agreement with the reader about the terminology. What's more, the writer will need to define in some detail the term *public servant*.

A good definition usually includes three elements: the subject (modern-day hero); the class to which the subject belongs (public servant); and the differences between others in this class (firefighters and police officers). The writer must establish that firefighters are public servants. If the writer can associate the firefighter with heroic deeds, then the argument might have merit.

Definition will almost always become a part of your work when some of the terminology is subjective. If you argue, for example, that medical experiments on animals are cruel and inhumane, you may need to define what you mean by *cruel* and explain why *humane* standards should be applied to animals that are not human. Thus, definition might serve as your major thesis.

Definition is also necessary with technical and scientific terminology, as shown by Sarah Bemis in her paper on diabetes. The paper needed a careful, detailed definition of the medical disorder in addition to the methods for managing it. By her inquiry, she reached her conclusion that medication in harmony with diet and exercise were necessary for victims of the disease.

Thus, most writers build their paper on an issue that gives them a reason for inquiry and investigation of their own attitudes and beliefs as well as ideas from written sources, interviews, observation, and other research methods.

Proposal

This type of argument says to the reader, "We should do something." It often has practical applications, as shown by these examples:

1. To maintain academic integrity, college administrators must enact stringent policies and punishments for cheating and plagiarism.
2. A chipping mill should not be allowed in our town because its insatiable demand for timber will strip our local forests and ruin the environment.
3. It is time to cease the fanciful and costly enterprise of space exploration and resolve our most desperate plight on earth—poverty.

As shown by these examples, the proposal argument calls for action—a change in policy, a change in the law, and, sometimes, an alteration of accepted procedures. Again, the writer must advance the thesis and support it with reasons and evidence.

In addition, a proposal demands special considerations. First, writers should convince readers that a problem exists and is serious enough to merit action. In the example above about chipping mills, the writer will need to establish that, indeed, chipping mills have been proposed and perhaps even approved for the area. Then the writer will need to argue that they endanger the environment: They grind vast amounts of timber of any size and shave it into chips that are reprocessed in various ways. As a result, lumberjacks cut even the immature trees, stripping forests into barren wastelands. The writer presumes that clear-cutting damages the land.

Second, the writer must explain the consequences to convince the reader that the proposal has validity. The paper must defend the principle that clear-cutting damages the land, and it should show, if possible, how chipping mills in other parts of the country have damaged the environment.

Third, the writer will need to address any opposing positions, competing proposals, and alternative solutions. For example, chipping mills produce chip board for decking the floors of houses, thus saving trees that might be required for making expensive plywood boards. Without chipping mills, we might run short on paper and homebuilding products. The writer will need to note opposing views and consider them in the paper.

In its own way, Sarah Bemis's paper on diabetes offers a proposal, one that people with this disorder might use to manage it—a balance of medication, exercise, and diet.

Causal Argument

Unlike proposals, which predict consequences, causal arguments show that a condition exists because of specific circumstances—that is, something has caused or created this situation, and we need to know why. For example, a student's investigation uncovered reasons why schools in one state benefit greatly from a lottery but do not in another.

Let's look at another student who asked the question, "Why do numerous students, like me, who otherwise score well on the ACT test, score poorly in the math section of the test and, consequently, enroll in developmental courses that offer no college credit?" This question merited his investigation, so he gathered evidence from his personal experience as well as data drawn from interviews, surveys, critical reading, and accumulated test results. Ultimately, he explored and wrote on a combination of related issues—students' poor study skills, bias in the testing program, and inadequate instruction in grade school and high school. He discovered something about himself and many things about the testing program.

Student Norman Berkowitz uses causal analysis to build his paper, "The World's Water Supply: The Ethics of Distribution" (see pages 236–247). He traces the causes of water shortages, identifies key areas approaching a desert status, and discusses the consequences, saying that people with water must be willing to help those without.

In addition, Valerie Nesbitt-Hall (see pages 323–336) uses causal argument in her essay about online romance, showing that availability, privacy, and low cost are forces that drive this new type of dating. Sarah Bemis (see pages 375–385) uses a similar kind of causal argument in her essay on diabetes management; she traces the causes for the disease and then examines the methods for controlling it: medication, diet, and exercise.

Comparison, Including Analogy

An argument often compares and likens a subject to something else. You might be asked to compare a pair of poems or to compare stock markets—Nasdaq with the New York Stock Exchange. Comparison is seldom the focus of an entire paper, but it can be useful in a paragraph about the banking policy of Andrew Jackson and that of his congressional opponents.

An analogy is a figurative comparison that allows the writer to draw several parallels of similarity. For example, the human circulatory system is like a transportation system with a hub, a highway system, and a fleet of trucks to carry the cargo.

Valerie Nesbitt-Hall (pages 323–336) uses comparison in her essay. She describes online matchmaking as similar to the practice of prearranged marriages. When families arrange a marriage, they cautiously seek a good match in matters of nationality, economics, political alliances, and so forth. In comparison, says Nesbitt-Hall, couples on the Internet can seek a good match on similar grounds.

Precedence

Precedence refers to conventions or customs, usually well established. In judicial decisions, it is a standard set by previous cases, a *legal precedent*. Therefore, a thesis statement built on precedence requires a past event that establishes a rule of law or a point of procedure. As an example, let's return to the argument against the chipping mill. If the researcher can prove that another mill in another part of the country ruined the environment, then the researcher has a precedent for how damaging such an operation can be.

Norman Berkowitz, in his study of the world's water supply (see pages 236–247), examines the role of a commodity, such as timber and oil resources, and its precedence in the case of water. If water is a commodity, nations can buy and sell. The courts in Canada are currently resolving that issue.

Implications

If you conduct any kind of test or observation, you will probably make field notes in a research journal and tabulate your results at regular intervals. At some point, however, you will be expected to explain your findings, arrive at conclusions, and discuss the implications of your scientific inquiry. Lab reports are elementary forms of this task. What did you discover, and what does it mean?

For example, one student explored the world of drug testing before companies place the products on the market. His discussions had chilling implications for consumers. Another student examined the role of mice as carriers of Lyme disease. This work required reading as well as field research and testing to arrive at final judgments. In literature, a student examined the recurring images of birds in the poetry of Thomas Hardy to discuss the implications of the birds in terms of his basic themes.

In review, fit one or more of these argument types to the context of your project:

- Evaluation
- Interpretation
- Definition
- Proposal
- Causal argument
- Analogy
- Precedence
- Implications

1d   Establishing a Schedule

The steps for producing a research paper have remained fundamental for many years. You will do well to follow them, even to the point of setting deadlines on the calendar for each step. In the spaces below, write dates to remind yourself when deadlines should be met.

_____ *Topic approved by the instructor*. The topic must have a built-in question or argument so you can interpret an issue and cite the opinions found in the source materials.

_____ *Reading and creating a working bibliography*. Preliminary reading establishes the basis for your research, helping you discover the quantity and quality of available sources. If you can't find much, your topic is too narrow. If you find far too many sources, your topic is too broad and needs narrowing. Chapters 3 and 4 explain the processes of finding reliable, expert sources online and in the library.

_____ *Organizing*. Instructors will require different types of plans. For some, your research journal will indicate the direction of your work. Others ask for a formal outline. In either case, see Chapter 8.

_____ *Creating notes*. Begin entering notes in your computer or in a research journal, if you prefer. Write plenty of notes and collect a supply of photocopied pages, which you should carefully label. Some notes will be summaries, others will need carefully drawn quotations from the sources, and some will be paraphrases written in your own voice. Chapter 9 explains these various techniques.

_____ *Drafting the paper*. During your writing, let your instructor scan the draft to give you feedback and guidance. He or she might see further complications for your exploration and also steer you clear of any simplistic conclusions. Drafting is also a stage for peer review, in which a classmate or two looks at your work. Section 13a, pages 218–220 gives more details on peer review. The instructor may also have classroom workshops that offer in-class review of your work in progress. Chapters 10, 11, and 12 explain matters of drafting the paper.

_____ *Formatting the paper*. Proper manuscript design places your paper within the required design for your discipline, such as the number system for a scientific project or the APA style for an education paper. Chapters 14–17 provide the guidelines for the various disciplines.

_____ *Writing a list of your references*. You will need to list in the proper format the various sources used in your study. Chapters 14–17 provide documentation guidelines.

_____ *Revision and proofreading*. At the end of the project, you should be conscientious about examining the manuscript and making all necessary corrections. With the aid of computers, you can check spelling and some aspects of style. Chapter 13 gives tips on revision and editing. Appendix A is a glossary of terms to explain aspects of form and style.

_____ *Submitting the manuscript*. Like all writers, you will need at some point to "publish" the paper and release it to the audience, which might be your instructor, your classmates, or perhaps a larger group. Plan well in advance to meet this final deadline. You may publish the paper in a variety of ways—on paper, on a disk, on a CD-ROM, or on your own Web site.

2 Finding a Topic

Instructors usually allow students to find their own topics for a major writing assignment; thus, choose something of interest so you won't get bored after a few days. At the same time, your chosen topic will need a scholarly perspective. To clarify what we mean, let's take a look at how two students launched their projects.

- Valerie Nesbitt-Hall saw a cartoon about a young woman saying to a man, "Sorry—I only have relationships over the Internet. I'm cybersexual." Although laughing, Valerie knew she had discovered her topic—online romance. Upon investigation, she found her scholarly angle: Matching services and chat rooms are like the arranged marriages from years gone by. You can read her paper on pages 323–336.
- Norman Berkowitz, while watching news reports of the Iraqi War of 2003, noticed dry and barren land, yet history had taught him that this land between the Tigris and the Euphrates rivers was formerly a land of fruit and honey, perhaps even the Garden of Eden. What happened to it? His interest focused, thereafter, on the world's water supply, and his scholarly focus centered on the ethics of distribution of water. You can read his paper on pages 236–247.

As these examples show, an informed choice of subject is crucial for fulfilling the research assignment. You might be tempted to write from a personal interest, such as "Fishing at Lake Cumberland"; however, the content and the context of your course and the assignment itself should drive you toward a serious, scholarly perspective: "The Effects of Toxic Chemicals on the Fish of Lake Cumberland." This topic would probably send you into the field for hands-on investigation (see Chapter 5 for more on field research).

Look for a special edge or angle. The topic "Symbolism in Hawthorne's Fiction" has no originality, but "Hester Prynne in the Twenty-First Century" does. Similarly, "The Sufferings of Native Americans" could be improved to "Urban Sprawl in Morton County: The Bulldozing of Indian Burial Grounds." Melinda Mosier, on page 227, entitles her paper "Listening to Hamlet: The Soliloquies," but her special focus is the setting within which Hamlet performs—that is, the events prior to, during, and after each of his speeches.

In another example, you might be tempted by the topic "Computer Games," but the research assignment requires an evaluation of issues, not a description. It also requires detailed definition. A better topic might be "Learned Dexterity with Video and Computer Games," which requires the definition of learned dexterity and how some video games promote it. Even in a first-year composition class, your instructor may expect discipline-specific topics, such as:

Education	Differentiated Instruction: Options for Classroom Participation
Political Science	Conservative Republicans and the Religious Right
Literature	Kate Chopin's *The Awakening* and the Women's Movement
Health	The Effects of Smoking during Pregnancy
Sociology	Parents Who Lie to Their Children

A scholarly topic requires inquiry, like those above, and it sometimes requires problem solving. For example, Sarah Bemis has a problem—she has diabetes—and she went in search of ways to manage it. Her solution—a balance of medication, monitoring, diet, and exercise—gave her the heart and soul of a good research paper. (See pages 375–385 for "Diabetes Management: A Delicate Balance.")

Thus, your inquiry into the issues or your effort to solve a problem will empower the research and the paper you produce. When your topic addresses such issues, you have a reason to:

- Examine with intellectual curiosity the evidence found in the library, on the Internet, and in the field.
- Share your investigation of the issues with readers, bringing them special perspectives and enlightening details.
- Write a meaningful conclusion that discusses the implications of your study rather than merely presenting a summary of what you said in the body.

This chapter will help you mold a general subject into a workable topic. It explains how to:

- Relate your personal ideas to a scholarly problem (see 2a).
- Talk with others to refine the topic (see 2b).
- Use online sources to refine your topic (see 2c).
- Examine the library's electronic databases and printed sources for topics discussed in the academic literature (see 2d and 2e).

Narrowing a General Subject into a Scholarly Topic

Unlike a general subject, a scholarly topic should:

- Examine one narrowed issue, not a broad subject.
- Address knowledgeable readers and carry them to another plateau of knowledge.
- Have a serious purpose—one that demands analysis of the issues, argues from a position, and explains complex details.
- Meet the expectations of the instructor and conform to the course requirements.

2a Relating Your Personal Ideas to a Scholarly Problem

Try to make a connection between your interests and the inherent issues of the subject. For instance, a student whose mother became seriously addicted to the Internet developed a paper from the personal experiences of her dysfunctional family. She worked within the sociology discipline and consulted journals of that field. Another student, who worked at Wal-Mart, developed a research project on discount pricing and its effect on small-town shop owners. She worked within the discipline of marketing and business management, reading appropriate literature in those areas. Begin with two activities:

1. Relate your experiences to scholarly problems and academic disciplines.
2. Speculate about the subject by listing issues, asking questions, engaging in free writing, and using other idea-generating techniques.

Connecting Personal Experience to Scholarly Topics

You can't write a personal essay and call it a research paper, yet you can choose topics close to your life. Use one of the techniques described below:

1. Combine personal interests with an aspect of academic studies:

Personal interest:	Skiing
Academic subject:	Sports medicine
Possible topics:	"Protecting the Knees"
	"Therapy for Strained Muscles"
	"Skin Treatments"

2. Consider social issues that affect you and your family:

Personal interest:	The education of my child
Social issue:	The behavior of my child in school
Possible topics:	"Children Who Are Hyperactive"
	"Should Schoolchildren Take Medicine to Calm Their Hyperactivity?"

3. Consider scientific subjects, if appropriate:

Personal interest:	The ponds and well water on the family farm
Scientific subject:	Chemical toxins in the water
Possible topic:	"The Poisoning of Underground Water Tables"

4. Let your cultural background prompt you toward detailed research into your heritage, your culture, or the mythology of your ethnic background:

Ethnic background:	Native American
Personal interest:	History of the Apache tribes
Possible topic:	"The Indian Wars from the Native American's Point of View"

Ethnic background:	Hispanic
Personal interest:	Struggles of the Mexican child in an American classroom
Possible topic:	"Bicultural Experiences of Hispanic Students: The Failures and Triumphs"

HINT: Learn the special language of the academic discipline and use it. Every field of study, whether sociology, geology, or literature, has words to describe its analytical approach to topics, such as the *demographics* of a target audience (marketing), the *function* of loops and arrays (computer science), the *symbolism* of Maya Angelou's poetry (literature), and *observation* of human subjects (psychology). Part of your task is learning the terminology and using it appropriately.

Speculating about Your Subject to Discover Ideas and to Focus on the Issues

At some point you may need to sit back, relax, and use your imagination to contemplate the issues and problems worthy of investigation. Ideas can be generated in the following ways:

Free Writing

To free write, merely focus on a topic and write whatever comes to mind. Do not worry about grammar, style, or penmanship, but keep writing nonstop for a page or so to develop valuable phrases, comparisons, personal anecdotes, and specific thoughts that help focus issues of concern. Below, Jamie Johnston comments on violence and, perhaps, finds his topic.

> The savagery of the recent hazing incident at Glenbrook North High School demonstrates that humans, men and women, love a good fight. People want power over others, even in infancy. Just look at how siblings fight. And I read one time that twins inside the womb actually fight for supremacy, and one fetus might even devour or absorb the other one. Weird, but I guess it's true. And we fight vicariously, too, watching boxing and wrestling, cheering at fights during a hockey game, and on and on. So personally, I think human beings have always been blood thirsty and power hungry. The French philosopher Rousseau might claim a "noble savage" once existed, but personally I think we've always hated others.

This free writing set the path for this writer's investigation into the role of war in human history. He found a topic for exploration. (To see the completed paper, go to pages 353–365.)

Listing Keywords

Keep a list of words, the fundamental terms, that you see in the literature. These can help focus the direction of your research. Jamie Johnston built this list of terms:

prehistoric wars	early weapons	noble savages
remains of early victims	early massacres	slaves
sacrificial victims	human nature	power
limited resources	religious sacrifices	honor

These key words can help in writing the rough outline, as explained below.

Arranging Keywords into a Preliminary Outline

Writing a rough outline early in the project might help you see if the topic has substance so you can sustain it for the length required. At this point, the researcher needs to recognize the hierarchy of major and minor issues.

Prehistoric wars

    Evidence of early brutality

        Mutilated skeletons

Evidence of early weapons

    Clubs, bows, slings, maces, etc.

    Walled fortresses for defense

Speculations on reasons for war

    Resources

    Slaves

    Revenge

    Religion

Human nature and war

    Quest for power

    Biological urge to conquer

This initial ranking of ideas would grow in length and mature in depth during Johnston's research (see pages 353–365 for his paper).

Clustering

Another method for discovering the hierarchy of your primary topics and subtopics is to cluster ideas around a central subject. The cluster of related topics can generate a multitude of interconnected ideas. Here's an example by Jamie Johnston:

Narrowing by Comparison

Comparison limits a discussion to specific differences. Any two works, any two persons, any two groups may serve as the basis for a comparative study. Historians compare Robert E. Lee and Ulysses S. Grant. Political scientists compare conservatives and liberals. Literary scholars compare the merits of free verse and those of formal verse. Jamie Johnston discovered a comparative study in his work, as expressed in this way:

Ultimately, the key questions about the cause of war, whether

ancient or current, centers on one's choice between biology and culture. One the one side, society as a whole wants to preserve its culture, in peace if possible. Yet the biological history of men and women suggests that we love a good fight.

That comparative choice became the capstone of Johnston's conclusion (see pages 362–363).

Asking Questions

Research is a process of seeking answers to questions. Hence, the most effective researchers are those who learn to ask questions and seek answers. Raising questions about the subject can provide clear boundaries for the paper. Stretch your imagination with questions to develop a clear theme.

1. General questions examine terminology, issues, causes, etc. For example, having read Henry Thoreau's essay "Civil Disobedience," one writer asked:

    What is civil disobedience?
    Is dissent legal? Is it moral? Is it patriotic?
    Is dissent a liberal activity? Conservative?
    Should the government encourage or stifle dissent?
    Is passive resistance effective?

    Answering the questions can lead the writer to a central issue or argument, such as "Civil Disobedience: Shaping Our Nation by Confronting Unjust Laws."

2. Rhetorical questions use the modes of writing as a basis. One student framed these questions:

Comparison:	How does a state lottery compare with horse racing?
Definition:	What is a lottery in legal terms? in religious terms?
Cause/Effect:	What are the consequences of a state lottery on funding for education, highways, prisons, and social programs?
Process:	How are winnings distributed?
Classification:	What types of lotteries exist, and which are available in this state?
Evaluation:	What is the value of a lottery to the average citizen? What are the disadvantages?

3. Academic disciplines across the curriculum provide questions, as framed by one student on the topic of sports gambling.

Economics:	Does sports gambling benefit a college's athletic budget? Does it benefit the national economy?
Psychology:	What is the effect of gambling on the mental attitude of the college athlete who knows huge

sums hang in the balance on his or her performance?

History: Does gambling on sporting events have an identifiable tradition?

Sociology: What compulsion in human nature prompts people to gamble on the prowess of an athlete or team?

4. Journalism questions explore the basic elements of a subject: Who? What? Where? When? Why? and How? For example:

Who?	Athletes
What?	Illegal drugs
When?	During off-season training and also on game day
Where?	Training rooms and elsewhere
Why?	To enhance performance
How?	By pills and injections

The journalist's questions direct you toward the issues, such as "win at all costs" or "damaging the body for immediate gratification."

5. Kenneth Burke's *pentad* questions five aspects of a topic: act, agent, scene, agency, purpose.

What happened (the act)?	Crucifixion scene in *The Old Man and the Sea.*
Who did it (agent)?	Santiago, the old fisherman.
Where and when (scene)?	At the novel's end.
How did it occur (the agency)?	Santiago carries the mast of his boat up the hill.
What is a possible motive for this event (purpose)?	Hemingway wanted to make a martyr of the old man.

Example from a journal entry as based on these questions and answers:

> The crucifixion scene in Hemingway's *The Old Man and the Sea* shows Santiago hoisting the mast of his boat on his shoulder and struggling up the Cuban hillside. Hemingway suggests Christian connotations with this scene, so I wonder if, perhaps, he has used other Christian images in the novel.

This researcher can now search the novel with a purpose—to find other Christian images, rank and classify them, and determine if, indeed, the study has merit.

2b   Talking with Others to Refine the Topic

Personal Interviews

Like some researchers, you may need to consult formally with an expert on the topic or explore a subject informally while having coffee or a soda

---

CHECKLIST

Exploring Ideas with Others

- Consult with your instructor.
- Discuss your topic with three or four classmates.
- Listen to the concerns of others.
- Conduct a formal interview (see pages 77–79).
- Join a computer discussion group.
- Take careful notes.
- Adjust your research accordingly.

with a colleague, relative, or work associate. Ask people in your community for ideas and for their reactions to your general subject. For example, Valerie Nesbitt-Hall knew about a couple who married after having met initially in a chat room on the Internet. She requested an interview and got it.

Nesbitt-Hall's interview, pages 78–79; the interview in the finished paper, pages 329–330.

Casual conversations that contribute to your understanding of the subject need not be documented. However, the conscientious writer will credit a formal interview if the person approves. The interviewed subjects on pages 77–79 preferred anonymity.

Online Discussion Groups

What are other people saying about your subject? You might use the computer to share ideas and messages with other scholars interested in your subject. Somebody may answer a question or point to an interesting aspect that has not occurred to you. With discussion groups, you have a choice:

- Classroom e-mail groups that participate in online discussions of various issues.
- Online courses that feature a discussion room.
- MUD and MOO discussion groups on the Internet.
- Real-time chatting with participants online—even with audio and video, in some cases.

More on discussion groups on the Internet, 3g, pages 48–49.

For example, your instructor may set up an informal classroom discussion list and expect you to participate online with her and your fellow students. In other cases, the instructor might suggest that you investigate a specific site, such as

alt.religion

for a religious subject or

alt.current-events.usa

for a paper on gun control laws. You can find many discussion groups, but the manner in which you use them is vital to your academic success. Rather than chat, solicit ideas and get responses to your questions about your research.

2c   Using the World Wide Web to Refine Your Topic

The Internet provides a quick and easy way to find a topic and refine it to academic standards. Chaper 3 discusses these matters in greater detail. For now, use the subject directories and keyword searches.

Internet searches, Chapter 3, pages 33–54.

Using an Online Subject Directory

Many search engines have a directory of subjects on the home page that can link you quickly to specific topics. With each mouse click, the topic narrows. For example, one student studying Thomas Jefferson consulted AltaVista's subject categories and clicked on Reference where she found Archives, then Early American Archives, and eventually *Early American Review,* a journal that featured an article entitled "Jefferson and His Daughters." The search occurs quickly—in seconds, not minutes.

However, the Internet has made it difficult to apply traditional evaluations to an electronic article: Is it accurate, authoritative, objective, current, timely, and thorough in coverage? Some Internet sites are advocates to special interests, some sites market products or sprinkle the site with banners to commercial sites and sales items, some sites are personal home pages, and then many sites offer objective news and scholarly information. The answers:

1. Go to the reliable databases available through your library, such as Info-Trac, PsychInfo, UMI ProQuest, Electric Library, and EBSCOhost. These are monitored sites that give information filtered by editorial boards and peer review. You can reach them from remote locations at home or the dorm by connecting electronically to your library.
2. Look for articles on the Internet that first appeared in a printed version. These will have been, in most cases, examined by an editorial board.
3. Look for a reputable sponsor, especially a university, museum, or professional organization.
4. Go to Chapter 3, which discusses the pros and cons of Internet searching, and also look at the Web site accompanying this book for additional tips on methods for evaluating Internet sources, with examples, at <http://ablongman.com/lester/>.

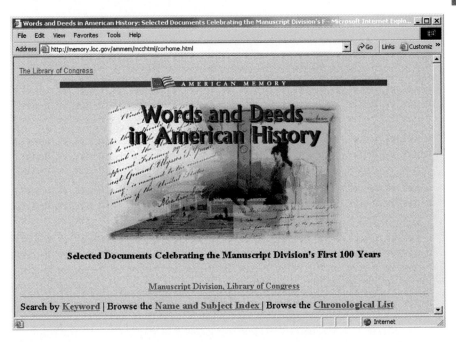

File   Edit   View   Favorites   Tools   Help

Address http://memory.loc.gov/ammem/mcchtml/corhome.html   Go   Links Customiz »

The Library of Congress

AMERICAN MEMORY

Words and Deeds in American History

Selected Documents Celebrating the Manuscript Division's First 100 Years

Manuscript Division, Library of Congress

Search by Keyword | Browse the Name and Subject Index | Browse the Chronological List

Internet

FIGURE 2.1 A Library of Congress site "Words and Deeds in American History," found by using a keyword search for American history manuscripts.

Using an Internet Keyword Search

To find sites quickly, enter the keywords for a topic you wish to explore. For example, entering "American history manuscripts" at one of the browsers such as Google will produce a page like that shown in Figure 2.1. It has links to search the files by keyword, name, subject, and chronological list. From there you can search for comments on the Puritans, the Jeffersonian years, the Andrew Jackson administration, and so forth.

Internet search engines will force you to narrow your general subject. For example, one student entered "Internet + addiction," and the computer brought up thousands of sources. By tightening the request to the phrase "Internet addiction," enclosed within quotation marks, she cut the list considerably and discovered other keywords: cyber-wellness, weboholics, and netaddiction. She realized she had a workable topic.

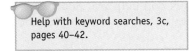

Help with keyword searches, 3c, pages 40–42.

2d   Using the Library's Electronic Databases to Find and Narrow a Subject

College libraries have academic databases not found on general search engines, such as InfoTrac, Silverplatter, and UMI-ProQuest. These database

Evaluating Internet Sources, pages 36–37, and also this book's Web site at http://www.ablongman.com/lester12e.

files are reliable because they refer you to thousands of articles that have been peer reviewed by experts or filtered through editorial processes. For now, examine various titles as you search for your own topic. If you see one of interest, click on it for more information. Follow these steps:

1. **Select a database.** Some databases, such as InfoTrac and UMI-ProQuest, are general; use them to find a subject. Other databases focus on one discipline; for example, PsycINFO searches psychological sources, ERIC indexes educational sources, and Health & Wellness describes itself. These databases will move you quickly to a list of articles on your topic.

2. **List keywords or a phrase to describe your topic, enclosed within quotation marks.** Avoid using just one general word. For example, the word *forestry* on the EBSCOhost database produced 6,000 possible sites. The two-word phrase "forestry conservation" produced a manageable 31 sites. Here is one of 31 entries: "Timberrr!" *Audubon,* Jan/Feb2006, Vol. 108 Issue 1, p58, 6p <u>Full Text</u>.

3. **Examine the various entries for possible topics.** Look for relevant articles, browse the descriptions, read the abstracts, and—when you find something valuable—print the full text, if it's available.

2e   Using the Library's Electronic Book Catalog to Find a Topic

Instructors expect you to cite information from a few books, and the library's book index will suggest topics and confirm that your subject has been treated with in-depth studies in book form, not just on the Internet or in magazines. Called by different names at each library (e.g., Acorn, Felix, Access), the electronic index lists all books housed in the library, plus film strips, videotapes, and similar items. It does not index articles in magazines and journals, but it will tell you which periodicals are housed in the library and whether they are in printed form or on microforms. Like the electronic databases described in 2d, the index will help you find a workable topic by guiding you quickly from general subjects to subtopics and, finally, to specific books.

Pages 58–59 describe the process in great detail with examples. For now, enter your subject, such as *food, nutrition, allergies,* to see what titles are available in the library. The titles, such as *Children and Food Allergies, Environmental Poisons in Our Food,* or *Living with Something in the Air,* will suggest a possible topic, perhaps "Special Diets to Control Allergic Reactions to Food." If you go into the stacks to find a book, take the time to examine nearby books on the same shelf, for they will likely treat the same subject.

With your working topic in hand, do some exploratory reading in books to enhance your understanding of the topic. Look to see how your subject is discussed in the literature. Carefully read the **titles** of books and chapter titles, noting any key terms:

The Lessons of the French Revolution
Napoleon's Ambition and the Quest for Domination
"Perspectives: Napoleon's Relations with the Catholic Church"

These titles provide several keywords and possible topics for a research paper: *Napoleon's ambition, Napoleon and the church, the French Revolution.*

Inspect a book's **table of contents** to find topics of interest. A typical history book might display these headings in the table of contents:

The French Revolution
The Era of Napoleon
Reaction to Napoleon and More Revolutions
The Second Empire of France

If any of these headings look interesting, go to the book's **index** for additional headings, such as this sample:

Napoleon
    becomes Emperor, 174–176
    becomes First Consul, 173
    becomes Life Consul, 174
    and the Catholic Church, 176–178
    character of, 168–176
    and codes of law, 178–179
    defeated by enemies, 192–197
    defeats Austrians, 170
    encounters opposition, 190–191
    extends empire in Europe, 180–189
    seizes power for "One Hundred Days" 198
    sent to Elba, 197
    sent to St. Helena, 199

If you see something that looks interesting, read the designated pages to consider the topic further. For example, you might read about Napoleon's return from Elba to his beloved France for a few additional days of glory before the darkness of confinement at St. Helena.

HINT: Topic selection goes beyond choosing a general category (e.g., "single mothers"). It includes finding a research-provoking issue or question, such as "The foster parent program seems to have replaced the orphanage system. Has it been effective?" That is, you need to take a stand, adopt a belief, or begin asking questions.

2f Expressing a Thesis Sentence, Enthymeme, or Hypothesis

One central statement will usually control an essay's direction and content, so as early as possible, begin thinking in terms of a controlling idea. Each has a separate mission:

- A **thesis sentence** advances a conclusion the writer will defend: *Contrary to what some philosophers have advanced, human beings have always participated in wars.*
- An **enthymeme** uses a *because* clause to make a claim the writer will defend: *There has never been a "noble savage," as such, because even prehistoric human beings fought frequent wars for numerous reasons.*
- A **hypothesis** is a theory that must be tested in the lab, in the literature, and/or by field research to prove its validity: *Human beings are motivated by biological instincts toward the physical overthrow of perceived enemies.*

Let us look at each type in more detail.

Thesis

A thesis sentence expands your topic into a scholarly proposal, one that you will try to prove and defend in your paper. It does not state the obvious, such as "Langston Hughes was a great poet from Harlem." That sentence will not provoke an academic discussion because your readers know that any published poet has talent. The writer must narrow and isolate one issue by finding a critical focus, such as this one that a student considered for her essay:

> Langston Hughes used a controversial vernacular language that paved the way for later artists, even today's rap musicians.

This sentence advances an idea the writer can develop fully and defend with evidence. The writer has made a connection between the subject, *Langston Hughes,* and the focusing agent, *vernacular language.* Look at two other writers' preliminary thesis statements:

THESIS: Chat rooms and online matching services enable people to meet only after a prearranged engagement by e-mail.

THESIS: Hamlet's character is shaped, in part, by Shakespeare's manipulation of the stage setting for Hamlet's soliloquies.

In the first, the writer will defend online romance as similar to prearranged marriages of the past. In the second, the writer will discuss how various shifts in dramatic setting can affect the message of the primary character.

Depending on the critical approach, one topic might produce several issues from which the writer might pick:

Biological approach: Functional foods may be a promising addition to the diet of those who wish to avoid certain diseases.

Economic approach: Functional foods can become an economic weapon in the battle against rising health care costs.

Historic approach: Other civilizations, including primitive tribes, have known about food's healing properties for centuries. Why did we let modern chemistry blind us to its benefits?

Each statement above will provoke a response from the reader, who will demand a carefully structured defense in the body of the paper.

Your thesis anticipates your conclusion by setting in motion the examination of facts and pointing the reader toward the special idea of your paper. Note below how three writers developed different thesis sentences even though they had the same topic, "Santiago in Hemingway's *The Old Man and the Sea.*" (This novel narrates the toils of an old Cuban fisherman named Santiago, who desperately needs the money to be gained by returning with a good catch of fish. On this day he catches a marlin. After a long struggle, Santiago ties the huge marlin to the side of his small boat. However, during the return in the darkness, sharks attack the marlin so that he arrives home with only a skeleton of the fish. He removes his mast and carries it, like a cross, up the hill to his home.)

> **THESIS:**   Poverty forced Santiago to venture too far and struggle beyond reason in his attempt to land the marlin.

This writer will examine the economic conditions of Santiago's trade.

> **THESIS:**   The giant marlin is a symbol for all of life's obstacles and hurdles, and Santiago is a symbol for all suffering humans.

This writer will examine the religious and social symbolism of the novel.

> **THESIS:**   Hemingway's portrayal of Santiago demonstrates the author's deep respect for Cuba and its stoic heroes.

This writer takes a social approach in order to examine the Cuban culture and its influence on Hemingway.

Enthymeme

Your instructor might want the research paper to develop an argument expressed as an enthymeme, which is a claim supported with a *because* clause. Examples:

> **ENTHYMEME:**   Hyperactive children need medication because ADHD is a medical disorder, not a behavioral problem.

The claim that children need medication is supported by the stated reason that the condition is a medical problem, not one of behavior. This writer will need to address any unstated assumptions—for example, that medication alone will solve the problem.

> **ENTHYMEME:**   Because people are dying all around the globe from water shortages, the countries with an abundance of water have an ethical obligation to share it.

The claim that countries with water have an ethical obligation to share is, of course, the point of contention.

Hypothesis

As a theory, the hypothesis requires careful examination to prove its validity, and sometimes that doesn't happen. The proof isn't there, so the writer must present negative results—and that's okay. Disproving a theory is just as valid as proving it. Here are the various types of hypotheses.

The Theoretical Hypothesis:

> Discrimination against young women in the classroom, known as "shortchanging," harms the women academically, socially, and psychologically.

Here the student will produce a theoretical study by citing literature on "shortchanging."

The Conditional Hypothesis:

> Diabetes can be controlled by medication, monitoring, diet, and exercise.

Certain conditions must be met. The control will depend on the patient's ability to perform the four tasks adequately to prove the hypothesis valid.

The Relational Hypothesis:

> Class size affects the number of written assignments by writing instructors.

This type of hypothesis claims that as one variable changes, so does another, or it claims that something is more or less than another. It could be tested by examining and correlating class size and assignments, a type of field research (see pages 84–86).

The Causal Hypothesis:

> A child's toy is determined by television commercials.

This causal hypothesis assumes the mutual occurrence of two factors and asserts that one factor is responsible for the other. The student who is a parent could conduct research to prove or disprove the supposition. A review of the literature might also serve the writer.

In effect, your work as based on a hypothesis might be a theoretical examination of the literature, but it might also be an actual visit to an Indian burial ground or a field test of one species of hybrid corn. Everything is subject to examination, even the number of times you blink while reading this text.

2g Drafting a Research Proposal

A research proposal is presented in one of two forms: (1) a short paragraph to identify the project for yourself and your instructor, or (2) a formal, multipage report that provides background information, your rationale for conducting the study, a review of the literature, your methods, and the conclusions you hope to prove.

The Short Proposal

A short proposal identifies five essential ingredients of your work:

- The specific topic.
- The purpose of the paper (explain, analyze, argue).
- The intended audience (general or specialized).
- Your voice as the writer (informer or advocate).
- The preliminary thesis sentence or opening hypothesis.

For example, here is the proposal of Norman Berkowitz (see his paper on pages 236–247):

> The world is running out of fresh water while we sip our Evian. However, the bottled water craze signals something—we don't trust our fresh tap water. We have an emerging crisis on our hands, and some authorities forecast world wars over water rights. The issue of water touches almost every facet of our lives, from religious rituals and food supply to disease and political instability. We might frame this hypothesis: Water will soon replace oil as the economic resource most treasured by nations of the world. However, that assertion would prove difficult to defend and may not be true at all. Rather, we need to look elsewhere, at human behavior, and at human responsibility for preserving the environment for our children. Accordingly, this paper will examine (1) the issues with regard to supply and demand, (2) the political power struggles that may emerge, and (3) the ethical implications for those who control the world's scattered supply of fresh water.

This writer has identified the basic nature of his project and can now go in search of evidence that will defend the argument.

The Long Proposal

Some instructors may assign the long proposal, which includes some or all of the following elements:

1. A *cover page* with the title of the project, your name, and the person or agency to whom you are submitting the proposal:

Arranged Marriages: The Revival Is Online

By Valerie Nesbitt-Hall

Submitted to

Dr. Lee Ling and

The University Committee on Computers

2. An *abstract* that summarizes your project in 50 to 100 words (see pages 222–223 for additional information).

> Arranged marriages are considered old-fashioned or a product of some foreign cultures, but the Internet, especially its online dating services and chat rooms, has brought arranged marriages into the twenty-first century. The Internet provides an opportunity for people to meet, chat, reveal themselves at their own pace, and find, perhaps, a friend, lover, and even a spouse. Thus, computer matchmaking has social and psychological implications that have been explored by psychologists and sociologists. The social implications affect the roles of both men and women in the workplace and in marital relations. The psychological implications involve online infidelity, cybersexual addiction, and damage to self-esteem; yet those dangers are balanced against success stories. Those persons who maintain an anonymous distance until a true romance blossoms are anticipating, in essence, a carefully arranged date that might become a marriage.

3. A *purpose statement* with your *rationale* for the project. In essence, this is your thesis statement or hypothesis, along with your identification of the audience that your work will address and the role you will play as investigator and advocate.

> This project was suggested by Dr. Lee Ling to fulfill the writing project for English 2100 and also to serve the University Committee on

---

CHECKLIST

Addressing the Reader

Identify your audience. Have you visualized your audience, its expertise, and its expectations? Your perception of the reader will affect your voice, style, and choice of words.

Identify your discipline. Readers in each discipline will bring differing expectations to your paper with regard to content, language, design, and documentation format.

Meet the needs of your readers. Are you saying something worthwhile? something new? Do not bore the reader with known facts from an encyclopedia. (This latter danger is the reason many instructors discourage the use of an encyclopedia as a source.)

Engage and even challenge your readers. Find an interesting or different point of view. For example, a report on farm life can become a challenging examination of chemical contamination because of industrial sprawl into rural areas, and an interpretation of a novel can become an examination of the prison system rather than a routine discourse on theme or characterization.

Computers, which has launched a project on Student Internet Awareness. This paper, if approved, would become part of the committee's *Student Booklet on Internet Protocol.*

4. A *statement of qualification* that explains your experience and, perhaps, the special qualities you bring to the project. Nesbitt-Hall included this comment in her proposal:

I bring first-hand experience to this study. I have explored the Internet like many other students. I joined a service, entered my profile, and began looking at photographs and profiles. It was exciting at first, but then I became bored; it seemed that everything and everybody blended into a fog of indifference. Then when some jerk sent a vulgar message I withdrew my profile and user name. I'll just remain old-fashioned and start my dates with a soda at the student center.

If you have no experience with the subject, you can omit the statement of qualification.

5. A *review of the literature,* which surveys the articles and books that you have examined in your preliminary work (see page 119 for an explanation and another example).

Limited research is being done in the area of online romance. My search of the literature produced a surprisingly short list of journal articles. Maheu (1999) has discussed methods of helping clients, even to the point of counseling in cyberspace itself, which would establish professional relationships online. Schneider and Weiss (2001) describe it but offer little psychoanalysis. Cooper (2002) has an excellent collection of articles in his guidebook for clinicians, and he has argued that online dating has the potential to lower the nation's divorce rate. Kass (2003) has identified the "distanced nearness" of a chat room that encourages "self-revelation while maintaining personal boundaries" (cited in Rasdan, 2003, p. 71). Epstein (2003) has argued that many arranged marriages, by parents or by cyberspace, have produced enduring love because of rational deliberation performed before moments of passionate impulse. In addition, Schneider and Weiss (2001) have listed some of the advantages to online romance: It links people miles apart; impressions are made by words, not looks; there is time to contemplate a message; there is time to compose a well-written response; and messages can be reviewed and revised before transmission (p. 66).

6. A *description of your research methods,* which is the design of the *materials* you will need, your *timetable,* and, where applicable, your *budget.* These elements are often a part of a scientific study, so see Chapters 15 and 17 for work in the social, physical, and biological sciences. Here is Nesbitt-Hall's description:

This paper will examine online dating as a forum for arranging dates and even marriages. The Method section will explore the role of Match.com and other dating services as a testing board for people with similar interests to form communication lines that might last one minute or one year. The Subjects section will examine the people who participate, from the modest person to one who is aggressive, and from high-profile people like Rush Limbaugh to those with low profiles and quiet lifestyles. The Procedures section examines the process so common to the services: to bring two compatible people together on the Web. There they can e-mail each other, participate in IM chats, send attachments of favorite songs or personal photographs, and eventually exchange real names, phone numbers, and addresses. The various services provide not only lists of available people but also personality

Explaining Your Purpose in the Research Proposal

Research papers accomplish several tasks:

- They explain and define the topic.
- They analyze the specific issues.
- They persuade the reader with the weight of the evidence.

1. Use *explanation* to review and itemize factual data. Sarah Bemis explains how diabetes can be managed (see pages 375–385), and Jamie Johnston explains the nature of prehistoric wars (see pages 353–365).

2. Use *analysis* to classify various parts of the subject and to investigate each one in depth. Melinda Mosier examines Hamlet's soliloquies (pages 226–235) and Valerie Nesbitt-Hall analyzes Internet romance (pages 323–336).

3. Use *persuasion* to question the general attitudes about a problem and then to affirm new theories, advance a solution, recommend a course of action, or—in the least—invite the reader into an intellectual dialog. Norman Berkowitz argues for ethical distribution of the world's water supply (pages 236–247).

tests, detailed profiles of subjects, and even nightclubs with calling cards for patrons to share with others whom they find interesting. The Results section explains the obvious—that online romance can prove productive for some people, interesting for the lurking voyeur, and an absolute disaster for the gullible and careless. The Case Study provides a success story for online dating.

The Discussion section explores the social and psychological implications for men and women, especially for those captured by cybersexual addiction.

YOUR RESEARCH PROJECT

1. Make a list of your personal interests and items that affect your mental and physical activities, such as homework, hiking, or relations with your family. Examine each item on the list see if you can find an academic angle that will make the topic fit the context of your research assignment. See Section 2a, pages 13–18, for more help.

2. Ask questions about a possible subject, using the list on pages 17–18.

3. Look around your campus or community for subjects. Talk with your classmates and even your instructor about campus issues. Focus on your hometown community in search of a problem, such as the demise of the Main Street merchants. Investigate any environmental concerns in your area, from urban sprawl to beach erosion to waste disposal. Think seriously about a piece of literature you have read, perhaps Fitzgerald's *The Great Gatsby*. If you are a parent, consider issues related to children, such as finding adequate child care. Once you have a subject of interest, apply to it some of the narrowing techniques described on pages 13–18, such as clustering, free writing, or listing keywords.

4. To determine if sufficient sources will be available and to narrow the subject even further, visit the Internet, investigate the library's databases (e.g., InfoTrac), and dip into the electronic book catalog at your library. Keep printouts of any interesting articles or book titles.

Finding and Filtering Electronic Sources

Electronic sources are now a major source of research information, and we know that many students start their research on the World Wide Web. That's okay. You may start your research on the Web, but don't you dare stop there! Let's review immediately the good, the bad, and the ugly on matters of using electronic sources and the Internet. First, the ugly: You can buy a canned research paper and submit it as your own. However, just because you buy a research paper does not mean you own it and can put your name on it. You always have the obligation of identifying the source, and the author or publisher retains rights to the content, whether in printed form or an electronic format. This is considered plagiarism and can result in your failing the course or even being expelled. Also ugly, and also considered **plagiarism,** is downloading Internet material into your paper without citation and documentation, thereby making it appear to be your own work.

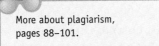

More about plagiarism, pages 88–101.

Second, the bad: You will find articles that are not worthy of citation in your research paper. You must filter personal opinion pieces that are unsubstantiated in any way. These will pop up on your browser list and may be nothing more than a home page. You must also filter commercial sites that disguise their sales pitch with informative articles. In other cases, you will encounter advocacy pages with a predetermined bias that dismisses objective analysis of an issue in favor of the group's position on the environment, gun control, immigration, and so forth. This chapter will help you identify these sites. (See also the Checklist, pages 36–37, "Evaluating Online Sources.")

Third, the good: The Internet, if you know where to look, is loaded with absolutely marvelous material that was unattainable just a few years ago. It offers instant access to millions of computer files relating to almost every subject, including articles, illustrations, sound and video clips, and raw data. Much of it meets basic academic standards, yet you should keep in mind that the best academic material is available only through databases at your college library, such as InfoTrac and PsycINFO. That is, you can rest assured that scholarly articles found through the library's databases are far more reliable than those you might find by general access through Google or Yahoo!

Therefore, this chapter will help you with two tasks: (1) to become an efficient searcher for academic information on the Web, and (2) to

---

CHECKLIST

Using Online Rather Than Print Versions

Online versions of articles offer advantages, but they also present problems. On the plus side, you can view them almost instantly on the monitor rather than searching, threading, and viewing microfilm or microfiche. You can save or print an abstract or article without the hassle of photocopying, and you can even download material to your disk and, where appropriate, insert it into your paper. However, keep these issues in mind:

- The text may differ from the original printed version and may even be a digest. Therefore, cite the Internet source to avoid giving the appearance of citing from the printed version. There are often major differences between the same article in *USA Today* and in *USA Today DeskTopNews*. Cite the correct one in your Works Cited.

- Online abstracts may not accurately represent the full article. In fact, some abstracts are not written by the author at all but by an editorial staff. Therefore, resist the desire to quote from the abstract and, instead, write a paraphrase of it—or, better, find the full text and cite from it (see also pages 67-68).

- You may need to subscribe (at a modest cost) to some sites. A company has the right to make demands before giving you access. However, your school library can often provide you with access to the sites most suitable for your research.

---

become accomplished at evaluating and filtering the complex web of Internet sites.

3a   Beginning an Online Search

To trace the good and the bad, let's follow the trail of one student, Sherri James, who has decided, because she is a competitive swimmer, to investigate the use of drugs for enhancing one's performance in the pool—not that she wants to try drugs but rather to educate herself and produce a research paper at the same time. Remember, we said to find topics that affect you personally.

Probably the first thing most of you do, like Sherri James, is visit your favorite browser, such as one of these:

About.com	http://www.about.com
AltaVista	http://www.altavista.com/
Excite	http://www.excite.com
Go.com	http://www.go.com

Google	http://www.google.com/
Hotbot	http://www.hotbot.com
Dogpile	http://www.dogpile.com
Webcrawler	http://webcrawler.com
Yahoo!	http://www.yahoo.com

At the search window, Sherri James typed "fitness and drugs." Immediately, she was directed to Beachbody.com, healthandfitness.com, and truly huge.com. Notice that all three sites are commercial sites (*.com*). Also, they each want to sell something—Power 90 supplements, a carb-electrolyte drink, and cybergenics nutritional products and instructional videos. One site advertised steroids for sale, such as Epogen and Erythropoietin. For Sherri James, these Internet locations offered no information, except to suggest this note that she jotted into her research journal:

> With supplements, drugs, and even steroids readily available on Web sites, it's no wonder so many athletes get caught in the "quick-fix" bodybuilding trap.

Next, Sherri James found two articles about swimming: "Three Steps to Swimming Success" and "Beat Fatigue in Long Meets." These were written by Rick Curl, a noted swim coach who has trained Olympic champions. Curl advocates three elements in training: in-pool workouts, out-of-pool training, and nutrition. For nutrition, the article encourages swimmers to "refuel their muscles with a sports drink containing plenty of carbohydrates." And guess what? The articles are promoting and selling two sports drinks. Sherri James noticed that the site, Powering Muscles, is sponsored by PacificHealth Laboratories, the makers of ACCELERADE sports drink and Eudurox Recovery drink. This site, too, was a *.com* site. Thus, Sherri James wrote a note to position the good instruction from the swim coach within the context of the site:

> Despite promoting two commercial supplements for swimmers, successful swim coach Rick Curl goes beyond pitching the nutritional products to offer valuable advice on in-pool techniques as well as out-of-pool aerobic training, stretching, and calisthenics.

At this point, Sherri James decided to try the browser's directory. In Yahoo! she found hyperlinks to:

Business and Economy
Computer and Internet
News and Media
Entertainment
Recreation and Sports

She clicked on the last one and found another list, which contained what she was looking for: a hyperlink to Drugs in Sports. At this site she found 13 links, among them:

Doping and Sports—collective expert assessment on doping by bicyclists

Drugs in Sport—provides information on performance-enhancing drugs in sport, the latest articles on the subject, reports, resources, and useful Web sites

Findlaw: Drug Use in Sports—includes a story archive and background information on testing, prevention, policies, and commonly used drugs.

NCAA Drug Testing—information on the association's drug testing policy

PlayClean—promotes anti-doping policies and preventing youth drug use through sports; from the Office of National Drug Control Policy

Sherri had now found site domains other than commercial ones, such as *.org*, *.gov*, *.net*, and *.edu*. At NCAA.org she was able to print out the NCAA (National Collegiate Athletic Association) Drug-Testing Program and use portions of the rules in her paper. Here is one of her notes:

> The NCAA clearly forbids blood doping. It says, "The practice of blood doping (the intravenous injection of whole blood, packed red blood cells or blood substitutes) is prohibited and any evidence confirming use will be cause for action consistent with that taken for a positive drug test" (Bylaw 31.1.3.1.1).

At Playclean, Sherri found a link to www.whitehousedrugpolicy.gov and an article entitled "Women and Drugs" by the Office of National Drug Control Policy. She was now finding material worthy of notetaking:

> A study by scientists at Columbia University has found the signals and situations of risk are different for girls and that "girls and young women are more vulnerable to abuse and addiction: they get hooked faster and suffer the consequences sooner than boys and young men" ("Women and Drugs").

Sherri James has begun to find her way to better sources on the Internet, but she will still need to examine the academic databases by logging on at her college library (see pages 55–76, where we will again watch Sherri search for sources). She will also need to consider doing field research, such as interviewing fellow athletes or developing a questionnaire (see pages 77–79 and 83–84).

CHECKLIST

Evaluating Online Sources

The Internet and other online sources supply huge amounts of material, some of it excellent and some not so good. You must make judgments about the validity and veracity of these materials. In addition to your commonsense judgment, here are a few guidelines:

1. Prefer the *.edu* and *.org* sites. Usually, these are domains developed by an educational institution, such as Ohio State University, or by a

professional organization, such as the American Psychological Association. Of course, *.edu* sites also include many student papers, which can include unreliable information.

2. The ".gov" (government) and ".mil" (military) sites are generally considered to be reliable, but look closely at any information that involves politically sensitive materials.

3. The ".com" (commercial) sites are generally developed by for-profit organizations. Keep in mind that: (a) they are selling advertising space, (b) they often charge you for access to their files, (c) they can be ISP sites (Internet Service Provider) that people pay to use and to post their "material." Although some .com sites contain good information (for example, reputable newspaper and magazine sites), use these sites with caution unless you can verify their reliability.

4. Look for the *professional* affiliation of the writer, which you will find in the opening credits or an e-mail address. Search for the writer's home page: Type the writer's name into a search engine to see how many results are listed. Also, type the writer's name into Amazon.com for a list of his or her books. If you find no information on the writer, you will need to rely on a sponsored Web site. That is, if the site is not sponsored by an organization or institution, you should probably abandon the source and look elsewhere.

5. Look for a bibliography that accompanies the article, which will indicate the scholarly nature of this writer's work.

6. Usenet discussion groups offer valuable information at times, but some articles lack sound, fundamental reasoning or evidence to support the opinions.

7. Look for the timeliness of the information on the site. Check dates of publication and how often the information is updated.

8. Treat e-mail messages as "mail," not scholarly articles. A similar rule applies to "chat."

9. Does the site contain hypertext links to other professional sites or to commercial sites? Links to other educational sites serve as a modern bibliography to more reliable sources. Links to commercial sites are often attempts to sell you something.

10. Learn to distinguish from among the different types of Web sites, such as advocacy pages, personal home pages, informational pages, and business and marketing pages. One site provides evaluation techniques: http://www.widener.edu/Tools_Resources/Libraries/Wolfgram_Memorial_Library/Evaluate_Web_Pages/659/.

11. Your skills in critical thinking can usually determine the validity of a site. For more help in critical thinking and Internet evaluation, visit http://www.virtualsalt.com.

3b   Reading an Online Address

Following is some information to help you understand online addresses. In the library, you must employ a book's call number to find it. On the Internet, you employ a Uniform Resource Locator (URL), like this one: http://www.georgetown.edu/library_catalogues.html

- The *protocol* (http://) transmits data.
- The *server* (www, for World Wide Web) is the global Internet service that connects the multitude of computers and the Internet files.
- The *domain* (georgetown.edu) names the organization feeding information into the server with a *suffix* to label the type of organization: *.com* (commercial), *.edu* (educational), *.gov* (government), *.mil* (military), *.net* (network organization), and *.org* (organization).
- The *directory/file* (library_catalogues) finds one of the server's directories and then a specific file.
- The *hypertext markup language* (html) names the computer language used to write the file.

Often, knowing just the protocol and the server.domain will get you to a home site from which you can search deeper for files. The URL http://lcweb.loc.gov/homepage will take you to the Library of Congress (see Figure 3.1), where you can examine a specific directory, such as Thomas: Congress

FIGURE 3.1 The home page for the Library of Congress.

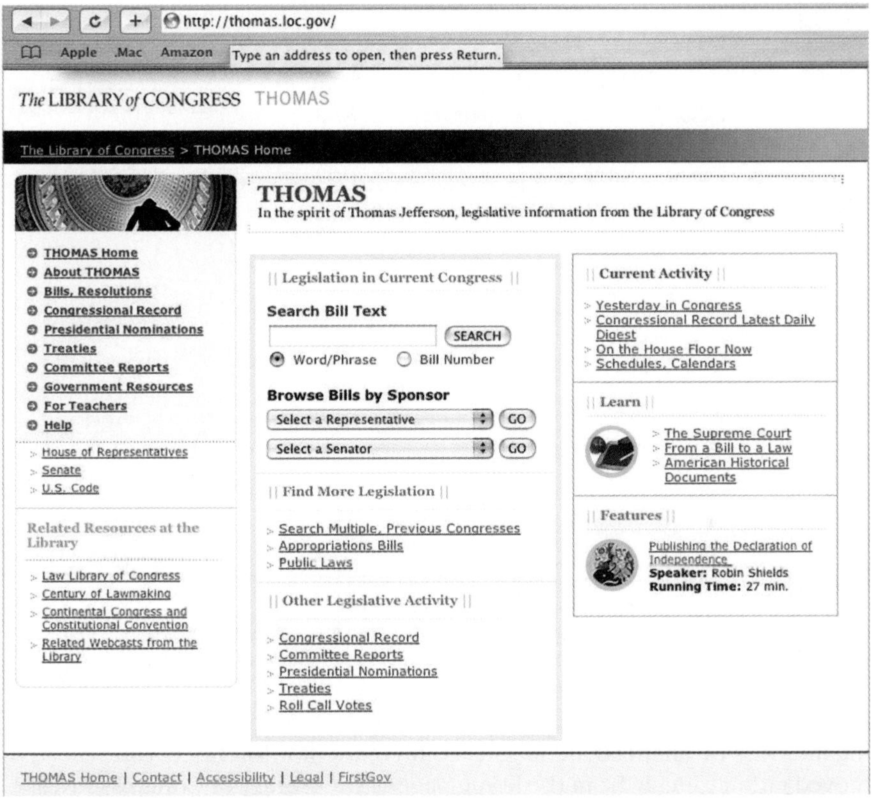
http://thomas.loc.gov/
Apple .Mac Amazon
Type an address to open, then press Return.
The LIBRARY of CONGRESS THOMAS
The Library of Congress > THOMAS Home
THOMAS
In the spirit of Thomas Jefferson, legislative information from the Library of Congress
THOMAS Home
About THOMAS
Bills, Resolutions
Congressional Record
Presidential Nominations
Treaties
Committee Reports
Government Resources
For Teachers
Help
House of Representatives
Senate
U.S. Code
Related Resources at the Library
Law Library of Congress
Century of Lawmaking
Continental Congress and Constitutional Convention
Related Webcasts from the Library
Legislation in Current Congress
Search Bill Text
SEARCH
Word/Phrase
Bill Number
Browse Bills by Sponsor
Select a Representative
GO
Select a Senator
GO
Find More Legislation
Search Multiple, Previous Congresses
Appropriations Bills
Public Laws
Other Legislative Activity
Congressional Record
Committee Reports
Presidential Nominations
Treaties
Roll Call Votes
Current Activity
Yesterday in Congress
Congressional Record Latest Daily Digest
On the House Floor Now
Schedules, Calendars
Learn
The Supreme Court
From a Bill to a Law
American Historical Documents
Features
Publishing the Declaration of Independence
Speaker: Robin Shields
Running Time: 27 min.
THOMAS Home | Contact | Accessibility | Legal | FirstGov

FIGURE 3.2 The home page for Thomas, the congressional site for the Library of Congress.

at Work (see Figure 3.2). In Thomas, you have access to legislation of both the House and Senate, with links to many other sites and a search engine for finding specific information.

You can search the current Congress for the text of bills. At the Thomas search engine, enter a word or phrase, such as "student financial aid," and the site will take you to a list of resolutions, bills, and acts, like the five listed here:

1. Responsible Student Financial Assistance Assurance Act of 2003 (Introduced in House) [H.R.696.IH]
2. Hazing Prohibition Act of 2003 (Introduced in House) [H.R.1207.IH]
3. To express the support and commitment of the U.S. House of Representatives for the troops serving to protect and defend the United States of America by encouraging actions to extend . . . (Introduced in House) [H.RES.158.IH]
4. To express the sense of the House of Representatives that the maximum Pell Grant should be increased to $5,800. (Introduced in House) [HRES.144.I]
5. Educational Excellence for All Learners Act of 2003 (Introduced in Senate) [S.8.IS]

At this point, you have the option of reading the House bills, the resolution, or the Senate bill by clicking on the colored links. The House bill on haz-

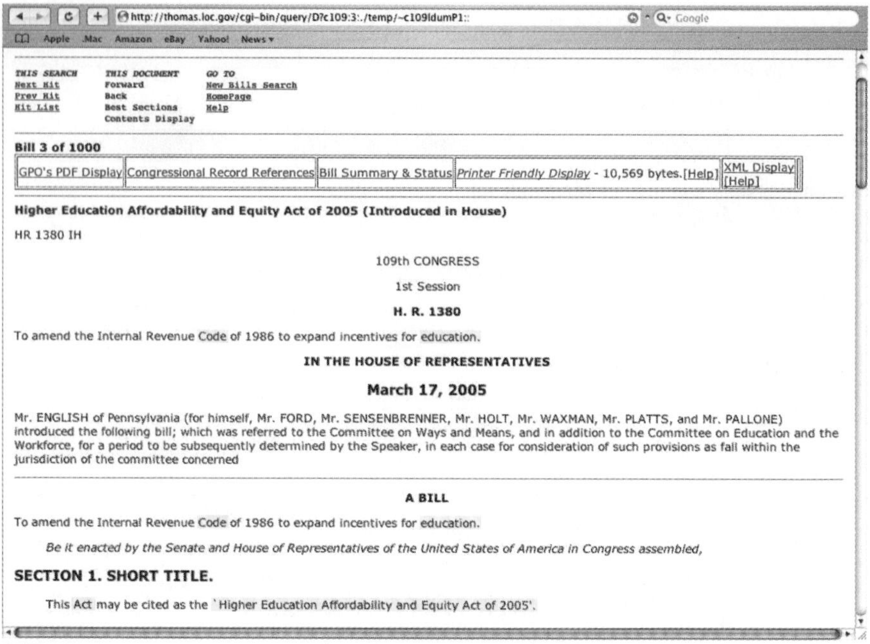
http://thomas.loc.gov/cgi-bin/query/D?c109:3:./temp/~c109ldumP1::

THIS SEARCH
Next Hit
Prev Hit
Hit List

THIS DOCUMENT
Forward
Back
Best Sections
Contents Display

GO TO
New Bills Search
HomePage
Help

Bill 3 of 1000

GPO's PDF Display | Congressional Record References | Bill Summary & Status | Printer Friendly Display - 10,569 bytes.[Help] | XML Display [Help]

Higher Education Affordability and Equity Act of 2005 (Introduced in House)

HR 1380 IH

109th CONGRESS

1st Session

H. R. 1380

To amend the Internal Revenue Code of 1986 to expand incentives for education.

IN THE HOUSE OF REPRESENTATIVES

March 17, 2005

Mr. ENGLISH of Pennsylvania (for himself, Mr. FORD, Mr. SENSENBRENNER, Mr. HOLT, Mr. WAXMAN, Mr. PLATTS, and Mr. PALLONE) introduced the following bill; which was referred to the Committee on Ways and Means, and in addition to the Committee on Education and the Workforce, for a period to be subsequently determined by the Speaker, in each case for consideration of such provisions as fall within the jurisdiction of the committee concerned

A BILL

To amend the Internal Revenue Code of 1986 to expand incentives for education.

Be it enacted by the Senate and House of Representatives of the United States of America in Congress assembled,

SECTION 1. SHORT TITLE.

This Act may be cited as the `Higher Education Affordability and Equity Act of 2005'.

FIGURE 3.3 H.R.1207.I, a bill in the House of Representatives on hazing.

ing and loss of financial aid is shown in Figure 3.3. In effect, you will have moved rather quickly from the home page of the Library of Congress to a specific piece of legislation you might wish to use in your paper.

3c Using a Search Engine

By this point in your career, you probably have a favorite search engine and know how to use it. So this section merely lists the types and the way they perform. Keep in mind that search engines change often, and more are added each year while others disappear. Also, search with more than one browser, because one cannot catalog even half the sites available. In addition, we can't stress enough the importance of using the educational search engines as listed on pages 42–43; with those, you can have confidence that the articles have a scholarly basis, not a commercial one.

Subject Directory Search Engines

These search engines are human compiled and indexed to guide you to general areas that are then subdivided to specific categories. Your choices control the list.

About.com	http://www.about.com
Go.network	http://www.go.com
Lycos	http://www.lycos.com
Yahoo!	http://www.yahoo.com

1. Type a keyword into the Search field.
2. Use Advanced Search to refine date, language, or number of results.
3. Click on hyperlinks for specific types of information—auctions, maps, movies, and so forth.
4. Use the subject directory to move quickly from a general subject to specific categories and specific articles.
5. For current events, click on hyperlinks to news, sports, and events.

Yahoo! is an edited site with plenty of directories and subdirectories. Figure 3.4 shows the opening page from Yahoo! with circled numbers to its features keyed to the numbered comments below the screen shot. You can make a keyword search or click on one of the categories, such as Health, to go deeper into the Web directories and, eventually, the articles.

Robot-Driven Search Engines

Another set of engines responds to a keyword by electronically scanning millions of Web pages. Your keywords will control the size of the list.

AltaVista	http://www.altavista.com
Ask	http://www.ask.com
Excite	http://www.excite.com
Google	http://www.google.com
Go.com	http://www.go.com

Hotbot	http://www.hotbot.com
InferenceFind	http://www.inference.com
Webcrawler	http://www.webcrawler.com

Metasearch Engines

A metasearch examines your topic in several of the search engines listed above. Thus, you need not search each engine separately. For example, when you enter a query at the Mamma.com Web site, the engine simultaneously queries about ten of the major search engines, such as Yahoo!, Webcrawler, and Google. It then provides you with a short, relevant set of results. You will get fewer results than might appear at one of the major search engines. For example, the request for "chocolate + children" produced 342,718 results on AltaVista but only fifty on Mamma.com. The claim is that a metasearch engine gives you the more relevant sites. This claim is based on the fact that the metasearch engine selects the first few listings from each of the other engines under the theory that each engine puts the most relevant sites at the top of its list; however, some commercial sites are able to buy their way to the top of various lists. Listed next are four metasearch engines:

Dogpile	http://dogpile.com
Mamma.com	http://mamma.com
Metacrawler.com	http://metacrawler.com
Metafind.com	http://metafind.com

Specialized Search Engines

Other search engines specialize in one area, such as WWWomen (women's studies), TribalVoice (Native American Studies), and Bizweb (business studies). In addition, many Web sites, such as the Library of Congress and New York Times Online, have search engines just for themselves. Even the sites for local newspapers have search engines to their own archives (see pages 46–47).

To discover any specialized search engine, go to one of the major sites, such as AltaVista, and ask, "Where can I find a search engine on journalism?" or "Where can I find a search engine on the environment?" The computer will name specialized search engines, such as these two:

www.journalism.net
www.biodiv.org (Convention on Biological Diversity)

Educational Search Engines

Educational search engines provide subject indexes to the various disciplines (humanities, sciences) and to subtopics under those headings (history, literature, biochemistry, and so on). Try several, because they will take you to academic material, not commercial sites with advertising banners popping up all over the screen.

Argus Clearinghouse	http://www.clearinghouse.net
English Server	http://eserver.org
Internet Public Library	http://ipl.org/
ProQuest K-12	http://www.proquestk12.com/
Library of Congress	http://www.loc.gov/
Discovery Channel	http://dsc.discovery.com/
SearchEDU	http://www.searchedu.com
SearchGOV	http://www.searchgov.com
SearcheBOOKS	http://www.searchebooks.com
SearchMIL	http://www.searchmil.com
Voice of the Shuttle	http://vos.ucsb.edu/

Returning once again to Sherri James and her investigations, we find her entering the phrase "blood doping" at the SearchEDU engine, which directed her to the United States Olympic Committee at http://www.usoc.org/.

What Is Doping?

Currently national anti-doping agencies around the world are working to harmonize the definition of doping. For USADA testing, each athlete is responsible for his/her International Federation's (IF) definition of doping since USADA looks to IF definitions. The Olympic Movement Anti-Doping Code (OMADC), published by the International Olympic Committee (IOC) in late 1999, set forth one definition of doping as follows:

> "The presence of a substance, defined as a prohibited substance under the Olympic Movement Anti-Doping Code (OMADC), in a competitor's sample or the use of a prohibited method under OMADC".

Doping does not necessarily mean that performance is enhanced. The ethics of both sport and medical science are breached when someone dopes. It is important to remember that a doping violation can happen regardless of whether an athlete deliberately uses a prohibited substance, or unknowingly uses a product containing a prohibited substance. The presence of a prohibited substance or evidence of the use of prohibited method in your sample constitutes a doping violation, irrespective of how it got there.

The bottom line is that you are responsible for any substance that you ingest—it is your responsibility to ensure that any product you take does not contain a prohibited substance.

Why Is Doping Prohibited?

Doping is prohibited to protect your rights to compete on a level playing field without the use of prohibited substances or prohibited methods. There are other reasons to prohibit doping, including the fact that doping can cause:

- **Harm to athletes who dope.** Most sports carry a certain amount of risk. Many prohibited substances and methods may add serious risks of harm to those that use them. Clean and ethical sport does not require that athletes take unnecessary risks.

- **Harm to athletes who do not dope.** Athletes who dope ruin fair sport for all athletes who do not dope. Clean athletes may perceive the need to dope in order to compete with other athletes they suspect are doping. This senseless cycle of doping can bring about personal devastation through health and safety risks, and the destruction of sport.

Sherrie James can draw several ideas from this source.

Educational Search Engines Maintained by Libraries

Here's a list of excellent sites that provide valuable academic information.

BUBL Link	http://bubl.ac.uk/
Internet Public Library	http://www.ipl.org/ref
Librarians Index to the Internet	http://lii.org
Scout Select	http://scout.wisc.edu/
	Projects/PastProjects/
	toolkit/bookmarks/

HINT: Most Web programs include a Bookmark or Favorites tool to save addresses for quick access. When you find a file you want to access later, create a bookmark so you can revisit it with just a click of the mouse. For example, in Netscape, simply click on Bookmarks, then click on Add Bookmark. This will automatically add the URL to the list of bookmarks. In Microsoft Internet Explorer, use the button bar marked Favorites to make your bookmarks. *Note:* If you are working at a university computer laboratory, do not add bookmarks to the hard drive. Instead, save the bookmarks to your disk by using Save As in the File menu.

3d   Searching for Articles in Journals and Magazines

The Internet helps you find articles in online journals and magazines. *Note:* The *best* source for academic journals is your library's database collection.

Online Journals

You can find online journals in one of three ways:

- First, access your favorite search engine and use a keyword search for "journals" plus the name of your subject. For example, one student accessed AltaVista and used a keyword search for "journals + fitness." The search produced links to 20 online journals devoted to fitness, such as *Health Page, Excite Health*, and *Physical Education*. Another student's search for "women's studies + journals" produced a list of relevant journals, such as *Feminist Collections, Resources for Feminist Research*, and *Differences*. By accessing one of these links, the student can examine abstracts and articles.

- Second, access a search engine's subject directory. In Yahoo!, for example, one student selected Social Science from the key directory, clicked on Sociology, clicked on Journals, and accessed links to several online journals, such as *Edge: The E-Journal of Intercultural Relations* and *Sociological Research Online*.
- Third, if you already know the name of a journal, go to your favorite search engine to make a keyword query, such as "Psycholoquy," which will link you to the social science journal of that name.

Many of the online periodicals offer keyword searches to their articles. In addition, they often provide full-text articles that you may download; however, some online journals charge a fee or require you to join an association before they permit access.

Online Magazines

Several directories exist for discovering articles in magazines

NewsDirectory.Com   http://www.newsdirectory.com/new/

This search engine directs you to magazine home pages where you can begin your free search in that magazine's archives. Under "current events," for example, it will send you to *Atlantic Monthly* at <theatlantic.com>, *Harper's* at <Harpers.org>, and *Newsweek* at <Newsweek.com>.

Highbeam Library Research   http://www.highbeam.com/
                            library/index.asp

This site has a good search engine, but it requires membership (which is free for one month). Remember to cancel your membership after you finish research, or charges will accrue.

Pathfinder   http://pathfinder.com/

This site gives you free access to *Time* magazine; it has a good search engine with links to thousands of archival articles.

ZD Net   http://www.zdnet.com/

This search engine provides excellent access to industry-oriented articles in banking, electronics, computers, management, and so on. It offers two weeks of free access before charges begin to accrue.

Another way to access online magazines is through a search engine's directory. For example, one student accessed AltaVista, clicked on Health and Fitness in the directory on the home page, clicked on Publications, then

Magazines. The result was a list of 40 magazines devoted to various aspects of health and fitness, such as *Healthology* and *The Black Health Net.*

3e   Searching for Articles in Newspapers and Media Sources

First, to find almost any newspaper in the United States, even the local weeklies, consult:

www.newspapers.com

This site takes you to the *Aspen Times* or the *Carbondale Valley Journal* or one of 800-plus newspapers. In most cases, the online newspaper has its own internal search engine that enables you to examine articles from its archives. Figure 3.5 shows the opening page of the online site for a local newspaper in Los Angeles, California. Notice especially the hyperlink at the upper left, **Archives,** a feature that enables you to find articles from past issues.

Most major news organizations maintain Internet sites. Consult one of these:

The Chronicle of Higher Education   http://www.chronicle.com

This site requires a paid subscription, so access it through your library at no cost.

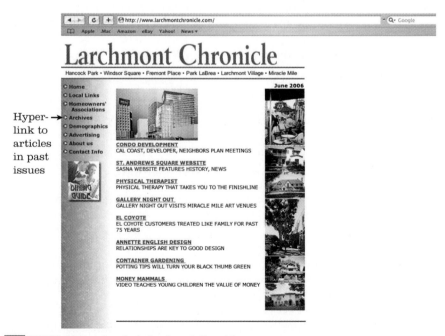

FIGURE 3.5 Los Angeles's *Larchmont Chronicle.*

CNN Interactive   http://www.cnn.com

CNN maintains a good search engine that takes you quickly, without cost, to transcripts of its broadcasts. It's a good source for research in current events.

C-SPAN Online   http://www.c-span.org

This site focuses on public affairs and offers both a directory and a search engine for research in public affairs, government, and political science.

Fox News   http://www.foxnews.com

This site provides articles from its own network and also from news services such as Reuters and the Associated Press.

London Times   http://www.thetimes.co.uk/
                                        news/pages/Times/
                                        frontpage.html

The *Times* provides directories and indexes, but not a search engine, so improve your search for articles in the *Times* with searchuk.com.

National Public Radio Online   http://www.npr.org

NPR provides audio articles via RealPlayer or some other audio engine. Be prepared to take careful notes.

The New York Times on the Web   http://www.nytimes.com

You can read recent articles for free. However, if you search the 365-day archive, be prepared with your credit card. Articles cost $2.50. After purchase, they appear on the monitor for printing or downloading.

USA Today DeskTopNews   http://www.usatoday.com

This site has a fast search engine that provides information about current events.

U.S. News Online   http://www.usnews.com

This magazine site has a fast search engine and provides free, in-depth articles on current political and social issues.

Wall Street Journal   http://www.wsj.com

This business-oriented site has excellent information, but it requires a subscription.

The Washington Times   http://www.washingtontimes.com/

Look here for up-to-the-minute political news.

    To find other newspapers and online media, search for "newspapers" on Yahoo! or AltaVista. Your college library may also provide LEXIS-NEXIS, which searches news sources for you.

3f Accessing E-books

One of the best sources of full-text online books is the Online Books Page at the University of Pennsylvania: http://digital.library.upenn.edu/books/. This site indexes books by author, title, and subject. It has a search engine that will take you quickly, for example, to the full text of Thomas Hardy's *A Pair of Blue Eyes* or to Linnea Hendrickson's *Children's Literature: A Guide to the Criticism*. This site adds new textual material almost every day, so consult it first. Understand, however, that contemporary books, still under copyright protection, are not included. That is, you can freely download an Oscar Wilde novel but not one by John Updike. JSTOR is another site for accessing books in a photocopied format (see page 63). *Caution*: Other sites offer e-books, but they are commercial and require a subscription.

3g Using Listserv, Usenet, and Chat Groups

E-mail discussion groups have legitimacy for the exchange of academic ideas when everybody in the group has the same purpose, project, or course of study. Chat rooms seldom have academic value. Let's look at each briefly.

E-mail News Groups

The word **listserv** is used to describe discussion groups that correspond via e-mail about a specific educational or technical subject. For example, your literature professor might ask everybody in the class to join a *listserv* group on Victorian literature. To participate, you must have an e-mail address and subscribe to the list as arranged by your instructor.

In like manner, online courses, which have grown in popularity, usually have a discussion area where students are expected to participate by responding to general questions for the group or corresponding with each other about assignments, issues, and other topics. On the Blackboard system, for example, online students have a Discussion Board with any number of Forums where they may participate or where they are required to participate.

> Usenet.com   http://www.usenet.com
> Search the main directory of Usenet.com for more than 2 million articles and 120,000 mailing lists.

> Tile.Net   http://www.tile.net/
> This site provides access to lists, usenet newsgroups, and other sites.

At some point you may wish to join a list, and each site will explain the procedure for subscribing and participating via e-mail in a discussion. However, you are advised to use extreme caution if you visit the usenet groups via the commercial search engines. Student Sherri James visited the Yahoo! site for listserv groups in swimming, but she abandoned the search because the groups, by their very titles, seemed obscene (e.g., "See Girls in Their Speedos").

A few additional aspects of *listserv* and *usenet* are FAQ, lurking, and moderated and unmoderated lists.

- *FAQs* (frequently asked questions) provide answers to questions by new members.
- *Lurking* is to watch messages on the list without participating.
- A *moderated list* has an editor who screens messages before they are posted to the list.
- *Unmoderated lists* have an automatic process that distributes any message that comes through.

Real-Time Chatting

Usenet and chat groups use Internet sites with immediate messaging rather than e-mail. To access usenet, go to <dogpile.com> or <metacrawler.com> and click the People & Chat button before launching the search. Typing "fitness" might take you, under a fictional name, to a reasonable discussion, but probably not. Another way to find discussion groups is through a keyword search for "List of online chat groups" at one of the search engines. If you want a commercial site that requires a monthly fee, try Usenet.com. However, *you cannot cite from these anonymous sources*, so they are best avoided for your academic work.

3h   Examining Library Holdings via Online Access

Most major libraries now offer online access to their library catalog. This allows you to search their collections for books, videos, dissertations, audio tapes, special collections, and other items. However, you must open an account and use your identification to log in, just as you do with your college library. You may sometimes order books online through interlibrary loan. Additionally, some libraries now post full-text documents, downloadable bibliographies, databases, and links to other sites.

If you need identification of all books on a topic, as copyrighted and housed in Washington, DC, consult:

Library of Congress   http://www.loc.gov
This site allows you to search by word, phrase, name, title, series, and
  number. It provides special features, such as an American Memory
  Home Page, full-text legislative information, and exhibitions, such
  as the various drafts of Lincoln's "Gettysburg Address."

For an Internet overview of online libraries, their holdings, and addresses, consult:

LIBCAT   http://www.librarysites.info
This site gives you easy access to almost 3,000 online library catalogs.

LIBWEB   http://lists.webjunction.org/libweb

This site takes you to home pages of academic, public, and state
libraries. You will be prompted for a public-access login name, so
follow the directions for entering and exiting the programs.

Another kind of online library is:

IngentaConnect   http://www.ingentaconnect.com

This site provides a keyword search of 17,000 journals by author, title,
or subject. Copies of the articles can be faxed to you, usually
within the hour, for a small fee.

3i   Finding an Internet Bibliography

You can quickly build a bibliography on the Internet in two ways: by using
a search engine or by visiting an online book store.

Search Engine

At a search engine on the Internet, such as AltaVista, enter a descriptive
phrase, such as "Child Abuse Bibliographies." You will get a list of bibliographies, and you can click the mouse on one of them, such as:

Child Abuse
Child Abuse. Child Abuse Articles. Child Abuse Reports.
http://www.childwelfare.com

Clicking with the mouse on the hypertext address will carry you to a
list:

Child Abuse Articles
Child Abuse Reports
Child Sexual Abuse
Substance Abuse

Clicking on the first item will produce a set of hypertext links to articles you
might find helpful, such as this one:

Little, Michael, Amelia Kohm, and Ronald Thompson. "The Impact of
Residential Placement on Child Development: Research and Policy
Implications." International Journal of Social Welfare 14.3
(2005): 200–209.

Online Bookstore

Use the search engines of Amazon.com and BarnesandNoble.com to gain a
list of books currently available. In most cases, the books on the list will be available in your library. For example, one student searched BarnesandNoble.com for

FIGURE 3.6 A page from the Barnes & Noble Internet site listing books on the topic "fad dieting."

books on "fad dieting." She received the list as shown in Figure 3.6, which gave her the beginnings of a complete bibliography.

3j Conducting Archival Research on the Internet

The Internet has made possible all kinds of research in library and museum archives. You may have an interest in this type of work. If so, consider several ways to approach the study.

Go to the Library

Go physically into a library and ask about the archival material housed there, or use the library's electronic catalog. Most libraries have special collections. The Stanford University Library, for example, offers links to antiquarian books, old manuscripts, and other archives. It also provides ways to find material by subject, by title, and by collection number. It carries the researcher to a link, such as the London (Jack) Papers, 1897–1916 at the Online Archive of California. These can be accessed by Internet if the researcher has the proper credentials for entering and using the Stanford collection.

Go to an Edited Search Engine

An edited search engine, such as Yahoo!, may give you results quickly. For example, requesting "Native American literature + archives" produced such links as:

American Native Press Archives
Native American History Archive
Native Americans and the Environment
Indigenous Peoples' Literature
Sayings of Chief Joseph

One or more of these collections might open the door to an interesting topic and enlightening research.

Go to a Metasearch Engine

A metasearch engine such as dogpile.com offers a way to reach archival material. Make a keyword request, such as "Native American literature + archives." Dogpile will list such sites as Reference Works and Research Material for Native American Studies, which is located at www.stanford.edu. There, the Native American Studies Collections offers several valuable lists:

Native American Studies Encyclopedias and Handbooks.
Native American Studies Bibliographies.
Native American Studies Periodical Indexes.
Native American Biography Resources.
Native American Studies Statistical Resources.
Links to other Native American sites on the Internet.
Links to usenet discussion groups related to Native Americans.

Thus, the researcher would have a wealth of archival information to examine.

Use Search Engine Directories

Use the directory and subdirectories of a search engine and let them take you deeper and deeper into the files. Remember, this tracing goes quickly. Here are examples of links at several engines:

Excite Guide	Lifestyle: Cultures and Groups: Native Americans: Literature
Lycos	Entertainment: Books: Literature: Native American Literature
AltaVista	Society: History: Indigenous People: Native Americans: Art

The latter site, for example, carried one researcher to the Red Earth Museum in Oklahoma City (see Figure 3.7, page 53).

FIGURE 3.7 The home page to the Red Earth Museum, where a student might find archival information on Native Americans.

Go to a Listserv or Usenet Group

Using a search engine, simply join your topic with the word listserv: "Native American literature + listserv." The search engine will produce such links as Native-L: Native Literature listserv and archives. By following the proper procedures, you can log on and begin corresponding. Participants might quickly point you in the direction of good topics and sources for developing the paper.

Go to Newspaper Archives

Use www.newspapers.com to locate a newspaper of interest, and then use the newspaper's search engine to explore its archives of articles. See page 46 for more information on this valuable resource.

YOUR RESEARCH PROJECT

1. To look for an online discussion group on your topic, go to a metasearch engine (see page 42); however, before entering your subject, select the

button for searching newsgroups rather than the Web. Explore the choices. You may also search the lists described in 3g, pages 48–49.

2. Voice of the Shuttle is a large and powerful search engine for educational information. Enter this URL, http://vos.ucsb.edu/, and search for your topic. If unsuccessful, try one of the other educational search engines listed on page 43.

3. When you have found an Internet article directly devoted to your subject, apply to it an evaluation as described on pages 36–37. Ask yourself, "Does this site have merit?" Apply that same test to other Internet articles as you find them.

4. Practice using the Bookmark feature of your browser. That is, rather than print an article from the Internet, bookmark it instead for future reference (see page 44).

5. As you would with library sources, begin making bibliography entries and writing notes about promising Internet sources. Begin building a computer file of promising sources, develop a folder of printouts from the Internet, and save pertinent information you will need for your bibliography entries later on (see pages 57–59 for more information on a working bibliography, and see pages 278–288 for examples of the bibliography for Internet sources).

4 Gathering Data in the Library

The library should be the center of your research, whether you access it electronically from your dorm room or go there in person. As the repository of the best books and periodicals, it is the highest quality resource you can access. You cannot ignore it.

Why is the library a better source than the Internet? Scholarship, that's why! The articles you access through the library are, in the main, written by scholars and published in journals only after careful review by a board of like-minded scholars.

Also, in today's modern electronic libraries, the material can be accessed just as easily as the Internet. In fact, many of the library's databases are part of the Web. Logged in at the library, you can download articles to your computer, print files, and read some books online. But you also need to visit the library in person to soak up the atmosphere of academia as well as consult books in the reference room and visit the stacks to find and check out books.

4a Launching the Search

Your research strategy in the library should include four steps, with adjustments for your individual needs.

1. **Conduct a preliminary search for relevant sources.** Scan the reference section of your library for its electronic sources as well as the abundance of printed indexes, abstracts, bibliographies, and reference books. Search the library's electronic book catalog and dip into the electronic networks, such as InfoTrac's Academic Index or Silverplatter. Remember that there are numerous meta-search engines such as dogpile.com that can provide valuable resources. This preliminary work will serve several purposes:
   - It shows the availability of source materials with diverse opinions.
   - It provides a beginning set of reference citations, abstracts, and full-text articles.
   - It defines and restricts your subject.
   - It gives you an overview of the subject by showing how others have researched it.

   Your preliminary search should include a survey of the entire library if orientation classes have not given you an overview.

55

2. **Refine the topic and evaluate the sources.** On this first trip to the library or on later visits, narrow your topic to something you believe will be manageable. As soon as you refine the topic, you can spend valuable time reading abstracts, articles, and pertinent sections of books. Most instructors will expect you to cite from the library's scholarly sources, so a mix of journal articles and books should accompany your online articles and field research.

3. **Take shortcuts.** First, consult Appendix B of this book, "Finding Reference Works for Your General Topic" (pages A-9–A-15), which lists appropriate electronic and printed sources. It sends you to key sources in psychology, art, literature, and most other disciplines. For example, if your work is on an education topic, it sends you to ERIC (online), *Current Index to Journals in Education,* and Edweb (online), but it sends computer science students to INSPEC (online) or to *Computer Literature Index.*

   In addition, you will need to access a variety of computer sources in the library, such as the electronic book catalog (see pages 58–59) and the electronic services like InfoTrac and Silverplatter (see pages 73–74). Without leaving the computer workstation in the reference room of the library, you can develop a working bibliography, read a few abstracts and full-text articles, and, in general, make substantive advances before you ever enter the library stacks.

   Note: As you probably know, many of these sources can be accessed from your dorm room or home computer.

4. **Read and take notes.** Examine books, articles, essays, reviews, computer printouts, and government documents. Whenever possible, write complete notes as you read so you can transcribe them or paste them into your text. Don't delay the writing task until you face a huge, imposing pile of data.

5. **Consult with a reference librarian:** If your topic does not initially generate a number of sources, confer with a reference librarian. This step can assist your research efforts by narrowing or expanding the topic. A reference librarian may suggest more appropriate words or phrases for the subject; this can be a critical step when you feel that you might be stuck.

HINT: Just as we learn proper Internet behavior, we learn basic library etiquette, such as talking softly out of respect for others and not bringing in food or drinks. Also, the best researchers do not reshelve books and periodicals; they leave them at the reshelving bins so librarians can return them to the correct place. They rewind microfilm and leave it in the reshelving bin. They avoid breaking down the spines of books in attempts to copy the pages. At the computer station, they analyze sources and then print; they do not randomly print everything. (See pages 36–37 for methods of analyzing a source.)

4b   Developing a Working Bibliography

Because the research paper is a major project involving many papers and notes, organization is crucial. That means keeping a copy of every abstract, article, and downloaded file with full publication information and the URLs of Internet materials. Your final manuscript will require a bibliography page listing all your sources, so now is the time to start accumulating the data.

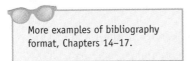

More examples of bibliography format, Chapters 14–17.

If you want to be fully organized—and your instructor may require this—write as an ongoing project a working bibliography. This list of the sources may be kept on cards or, more efficiently, on a computer file. Either way, producing a set of bibliography entries has three purposes:

1. It locates articles and books for notetaking purposes.
2. It provides information for the in-text citations, as in this example in MLA style:

   > The healing properties of certain foods have been noted by Milner (682–88) and Hasler (6–10).

3. It provides information for the final reference page (see Chapters 14–17). If you keep your entries current in a computer file, you can easily insert them into your Works Cited page at the end of your manuscript.

Whether you keyboard your sources or make handwritten notes for easy access, each working bibliography entry should contain the following information—with variations, of course, for books, periodicals, and government documents:

1. Author's name
2. Title of the work
3. Publication information
4. Library call number
5. (Optional) A personal note about the location or contents of the source
6. The URL for online sources

Bibliography Entry for a Book (MLA style):

> F2546.M587
>
> Millard, Candice. The River of Doubt: Theodore Roosevelt's Darkest Journey. New York: Doubleday, 2005.
>
> Books level 3

Bibliography Entry for a Journal Article (MLA style):

> McCann, Thomas M., and Larry R. Johnson. "The Role and Responsibility of the Experienced Teacher." English Journal 95 (Nov. 2005): 52–57.

Bibliographic Entry for a Magazine Article (MLA style):

> Shea, William. "Winter Battle: Pea Ridge and the Civil War in the West." <u>Hallowed Ground</u>. Winter 2005: 23–30.

Bibliographic Entry for an Article Found on an Academic Database (MLA style):

> Davis, Sandra K. "The Politics of Water Scarcity in the Western States." <u>The Social Science Journal</u> 38 (2002): 527–529. <u>Expanded Academic ASAP</u>. InfoTrac. Vanderbilt U, Heard Lib. 9 Nov. 2005 <http://www.galegroup.com/>.

Bibliography Entry for an Online Article (MLA style):

> Soraghan, Mike. "Mining Measure Modified, but Foes Still Not Mollified." Denver Post Online. 13 Dec. 2005. 14 Dec. 2005 <http://www.denverpost.com/nationworld/ci_3303770>.

4c Finding Books on Your Topic

The library is no longer a repository of printed materials only. It has gone high-tech like the business world. Thus, much of your research will be conducted on the library's electronic network with call numbers to its own books and with links to sources around the world.

Using Your Library's Electronic Book Catalog

Your library's computerized catalog to its holdings probably has a special name, such as LIBNET, FELIX, ACORN, UTSEARCH, and so forth. In theory, it includes every book in the library filed by subject, author, and title. Begin your research at the catalog by using a *keyword search* to a subject, such as "Fitness." You will get a list of books on the monitor, and you can click the mouse on each one to gather more information. The list will look something like this:

Search Results

Blink: The Power of Thinking without Thinking. Malcolm Gladwell. 2005.

The Success Principles: How to Get from Where You Are to Where You Want to Be. Jack Canfield and Janet Switzer. 2004.

Driven from Within. Michael Jordan. 2005.

The electronic card catalog, in effect, has provided a bibliography that lists a variety of available books on a particular subject. The next procedure is to click on one, such as *Driven from Within,* to get the full details with call number and availability, as shown in the example below. You can print the information and use it to find the book in the stacks and to write your working bibliography. The entry at your library will be similar to the following example.

> *The Success Principles: How to Get from Where You Are to*
> *Where You Want to Be* / Jack Canfield and Janet Switzer.
> By Jack Canfield and Janet Switzer.
> New York: HarperCollins, 2004
> Subjects: Self-improvement—Self-help—Success—
>   Relationships
> Description: 473 p.; ill.; 34 cm.
> Series: Self-help and improvement
> COPY / HOLDING INFORMATION
>
> | Location | Collection | Call No. | Status |
> |----------|-----------|----------|--------|
> | Woodward Library | General Book Collection, Level 3 | TE331.A8 D75 2004 | Available |

The card catalog will also help you find subject-specific bibliographies. For instance, one student entered *bibliographies + women's studies.* The catalog provided a large list of sites, each appearing as a hypertext link to full data on the source. Here's an example of four items from a list of 30 or more:

- Bibliographies on Native American Women's Theatre (2000)
- Bibliography: Gender and Technology (2004)
- Women Immigrants 1945 to the Present: A Bibliography (2002)
- Black American Feminism: A Multidisciplinary Bibliography (2003)

HINT: Many college libraries as well as public libraries are now part of library networks. The network expands the holdings of every library because one library will loan books to another. Therefore, if a book you need is unavailable in your library, ask a librarian about an interlibrary loan. Understand, however, that you may have to wait several days for its delivery. Periodical articles usually come quickly by fax.

Using the Library's Printed Bibliographies

You may need to supplement your computer printouts with old-fashioned searching of printed reference guides, bibliographies, and indexes.

Searching the General Bibliographies

When ordering its research databases, the library subscribes to electronic versions or print versions. You will need to determine which are available. Three general works provide page numbers to many books and journals that contain bibliographies on numerous subjects.

> *Bibliographic Index: A Cumulative Bibliography of Bibliographies.* New
>   York: Wilson, 1938–date. Available both in print and online within
>   your library's network.

Prehistoric War

LeBlanc, Steven A. *Constant Battles: The Myth of the Peaceful, Noble Savage.* New York: St. Martin's, 2003 p 247–64

FIGURE 4.1 Example from *Bibliographic Index*, 2003.

Hillard, James, and Bethany J. Easter. *Where to Find What: A Handbook to Reference Service.* 4th ed. Metuchen, NJ: Scarecrow, 2000.

Balay, Robert, et al. *Guide to Reference Books.* 11th ed. Chicago: ALA, 1996.

These guides will also give you a list of books relating to your subject. Figure 4.1 shows how *Bibliographic Index* will send you to bibliographic lists that are hidden inside books; these are sources you might not find otherwise. Entries will look something like this to show that a bibliography will be found in LeBlanc's book on pages 247-64. Such a list could be a valuable resource in the early stages of research.

If the book fits your research, you will probably want to write a bibliography entry for this source. Then you can examine the text as well as the bibliography on pages 247-64 of LeBlanc's book, where you might find additional articles on this topic. Here is a student's bibliography notation:

LeBlanc, Steven A. <u>Constant Battles: The Myth of the Peaceful, Noble

Savage</u>. New York: St. Martin's, 2003. Bibliography on pages

247-64.

Using the Trade Bibliographies

Trade bibliographies, intended primarily for use by booksellers and librarians, can help you in three ways:

1. Discover sources not listed in other bibliographies or in the card catalog.
2. Locate facts of publication, such as place and date.
3. Determine if a book is in print.

Search this work for your topic:

Subject Guide to Books in Print (New York: Bowker, 1957–date).

Note: Online, this source may appear as Books in Print.

Use this work for its subject classifications, any one of which will provide a ready-made bibliography to books. Figure 4.2 shows a sample found with the keyword "education."

The following trade bibliographies may also lead you to valuable sources available online or in printed versions:

Books in Print lists by author and title all books currently in print.

Publishers' Weekly offers the current publication data on new books and new editions.

```
1 — Foster, Charles R., et al. Educating Clergy:
2 — Teaching Practices and the Pastoral Imagination.
                                                    — 4
3 — LC 2005-024316. xx, 435p. 2005.                 — 5
                                                    — 7
6 — 40.00 (0787977446) Wiley Pub.                   — 8
```

▮▮▮ **FIGURE 4.2 From *Subject Guide to Books in Print*, 2005**
1. Author   2. Title   3. Library of Congress number   4. Number of pages   5. Date of publication
6. Price   7. International Standard Book Number (used when ordering)   8. Publisher

Paperbound Books in Print locates all paperback books on one topic; these are usually books available at local bookstores.

Cumulative Book Index provides complete publication data on one book but will also locate *all* material in English on a particular subject.

Library of Congress Catalog: Books, Subject provides a ready-made bibliography to books on hundreds of subjects.

Ulrich's International Periodicals Directory helps you locate current periodicals, both domestic and foreign, and to order photocopies of articles.

Using the Bibliographies in Appendix B

Go to Appendix B of this book, pages A-9–A-15. It furnishes a guide to important reference works—some in print at the library, some online in the library's electronic network, and others available on the World Wide Web. Reference sources are listed for nine major categories (see page A-9). Here are three examples of titles to reference works that you will find under the heading "Issues in the Arts, Literature, Music, and Language." The first is a printed source in the library, the second is available on the library's electronic network, and the third is available on the World Wide Web.

MLA International Bibliography of Books and Articles on the Modern Languages and Literatures. New York: MLA, 1921–present. The best overall index to major literary figures, literary issues, and language topics. Online and in print.

MLA International Bibliography of Books and Articles on the Modern Languages and Literatures. New York: MLA, 1921–date. This reference work indexes major literary figures, literary issues, and language topics; may be listed on the library's network as *MLA Bibliography*.

Netlibrary http://www.netlibrary.com. This site provides a vast collection of full-text stories, poems, novels, and dramas; search by title or author and then read the text online or print it out; must create a membership account.

Searching for Bibliographies in Encyclopedias

Search for specialized encyclopedias in your field at the electronic book catalog. Entering "encyclopedia of psychology" might give you a list that looks like this:

BF31.E52 2000
Encyclopedia of psychology

BF31. E52 2001
The Corsini encyclopedia of psychology and behavioral science

BF 31 .B25 1999
Baker encyclopedia of psychology and counseling

Click on one, scan an article, and look especially at the end of the article for a bibliography. It might point you to additional sources, like the one shown in Figure 4.3 at the bottom of the page.

Examining the Bibliography at the End of a Book

When you get into the stacks, look for bibliographies at the end of books. Jot down titles on cards or photocopy the list for further reference. An example is shown in Figure 4.4 on the next page.

Searching for Bibliographies at the End of Journal Articles

Look for bibliographies at the end of articles in scholarly journals. For example, students of history depend on the bibliographies in various issues of *English Historical Review,* and students of literature find bibliographies in *Studies in Short Fiction.* In addition, the journals themselves provide subject indexes to their own contents. If your subject is "Adoption," you will discover that a majority of your sources are located in a few key

See also "Citation Searching," pages 106–107.

FURTHER REFERENCES

Clarke, E., & Dewhurst, K. *An illustrated history of brain function.*
Clarke, E., & O'Malley, C.D. *The human brain and spinal cord.*
Ferrier, D. *The functions of the brain.*
Finger, S., & Stein, D.G. *Brain damage and recovery: Research and clinical perspectives.*
McHenry, L.C., Jr. *Garrison's history of neurology.*

FIGURE 4.3 Sample bibliography from the end of an article in *Encyclopedia of Psychology.*

SECONDARY SOURCES

Abbott, Edith. "The Civil War and the Crime Wave of 1865–70."
    Social Service Review, 1977.
Amis, Moses N. *Historical Raleigh,* 1913.
Andrews, Marietta M. *Scraps of Paper.* 1929.
Badeau, Adam. *Military History of U. S. Grant.* 1885.
Bailey, Mrs. Hugh. "Mobile's Tragedy: The Great Magazine
    Explosion of 1865."*Alabama Review,* 1968.
Bakeless, John. "The Mystery of Appomattox."
    Civil War Times Illustrated, 1970.

FIGURE 4.4 A portion of a bibliography list at the end of N. A. Trudeau's book,
Out of the Storm.

journals. In that instance, going straight to the annual index of one of
those journals will be a shortcut.

4d Finding Articles in Magazines and Journals

An index furnishes the exact page number(s) of specific sections of books
and of individual articles in magazines, journals, and newspapers. The library's
online index of databases not only directs you to articles in magazines, it also
gives an abstract of the article, and more and more often, it provides the full
text. Thus, at the library's computer terminals, you might download several
articles without going into the stacks at all.

Searching the General Indexes to Periodicals

The library network gives you access to electronic databases. Here are
just a few of the many that will be available to you:

AGRICOLA	Agriculture, animal and plant sciences
America: History and Life	U.S. history
American Chemical Society Publications	Chemistry
BioOne	Biological, ecological, and environmental sciences
CINAHL	Nursing, public health, and allied health fields
ERIC	Education and mass communication
GPO	Government publications on all subjects

HighWire	Science, technology, and medicine
InfoTrac	All subjects
JSTOR	Social sciences
Lexis-Nexis Academic	News, business, law, medicine, reference
MLA Bibliography	Literature, linguistics, and folklore
Music Index	Music
ProjectMUSE	Social sciences, arts, humanities
PsycINFO	Psychology, medicine, education, social work
Westlaw	Legal subjects, including laws and cases

One of these databases will usually guide you to several sources, provide an abstract, and often provide a full-text version of the article, as shown in Figure 4.5 at the bottom of this page.

The Journal of Nutrition, January 2006, 136:277S-280S.

Amino Acids and Muscle Loss with Aging.

Full Text: COPYRIGHT 2006 American Society for Nutrition

Byline: Satoshi Fujita and Elena Volpi

Aging is associated with a progressive loss of muscle mass (sarcopenia), which increases the risks of injury and disability. Although the mechanisms of sarcopenia are not clearly elucidated, age-associated alterations in the muscle anabolic response to nutritional stimuli and a decline in protein intake may be significant contributing factors. The most recent findings regarding the role of nutritional intake on protein metabolism in the elderly will be reviewed. Specifically, aging is associated with changes in the muscle protein metabolism response to a meal, likely due to alterations in the response to endogenous hormones. Nonetheless, the older muscle is still able to respond to amino acids, mainly the essential and BCAAs, which have been shown to acutely stimulate muscle protein synthesis in older individuals. It is likely that this stimulatory effect of essential and BCAA is due to the direct effect of leucine on the initiation of mRNA translation, which is still present in older age, although it appears to be attenuated in aged animals. Recent data suggest that excess leucine may be able to overcome this age-related resistance of muscle proteins to leucine. For this reason, long-term essential amino acid supplementation may be a useful tool for the prevention and treatment of sarcopenia, particularly if excess leucine is provided in the supplement.

FIGURE 4.5 InfoTrac printout with abstract

Finding Indexes by Topic in Appendix B

Appendix B in this textbook, pages A-9–A-15, lists many indexes to periodical articles. The list is organized by topic, so you can find the best references for your field. Shown below are a few of the entries for Music:

Bibliographic Guide to Music. Boston: Hall, 1976–present. Annually. This reference work provides an excellent subject index to almost every topic in the field of music. It will give you the bibliographic data to several articles on most topics in the field.

Music Article Guide. Philadelphia: Information Services, 1966–present. This reference work indexes music education and instrumentation in such journals as *Brass and Wind News, Keyboard, Flute Journal,* and *Piano Quarterly.*

Music Index. Warren, MI: Information Coordinators, 1949–date. This reference work indexes music journals such as *American Music Teacher, Choral Journal, Journal of Band Research, Journal of Music Therapy.*

The New Grove Dictionary of Music and Musicians. Ed. Stanley Sadie and John Tyrrell. 29 vols. New York: Grove, 2001. This mammoth work will provide you with information on almost every topic related to music. A good place to find technical definitions.

RILM Abstracts of Music Literature. Online and in print. This massive collection provides you with brief descriptions to help you in selecting appropriate works for you bibliography.

Using the H.W. Wilson Indexes

For many years, the Wilson Company in Minneapolis has provided excellent indexes to periodical literature. The tradition continues, and the indexing firm has kept its lists current by making its indexes available online as well as in printed versions. The index topics will send you to articles in a wide variety of periodicals in many disciplines.

Readers' Guide to Periodical Literature

The *Readers' Guide to Periodical Literature* (online and in print) indexes important reading for the early stages of research in magazines such as:

Aging	*Foreign Affairs*	*Psychology Today*
American Scholar	*Foreign Policy*	*Scientific Review*
Astronomy	*Health*	*Science Digest*
Bioscience	*Negro History*	*Science*
Business Week	*Oceans*	*SciQuest*
Earth Science	*Physics Today*	*Technology Review*

An entry from *Readers' Guide to Periodical Literature* will look something like this:

> My whole soul is in it. (Smithsonian Bookshelf).
> *Smithsonian* January 2006 v36 i10 p48(8)
> <u>Text with graphics</u> / <u>Library holdings</u>

This entry identifies the title, the magazine, the publication information, and provides a hyperlink to the full text and to any library holdings of *Smithsonian*. Make a bibliographic entry to the source if it looks promising:

"My Whole Soul Is in It." <u>Smithsonian</u> Jan. 2006: 48+.

Note: Writing the pages as "48 + ." means page 48 and discontinuous pages thereafter.

Social Sciences Index

The *Social Sciences Index* (online and in print) indexes journal articles for 263 periodicals in these fields:

anthropology	geography	political science
economics	law and criminology	psychology
environmental science	medical science	sociology

Humanities Index

The *Humanities Index* (online and in print) catalogs 260 publications in several fields:

archeology	folklore	performing arts
classical studies	history	philosophy
language and literature area studies	literary	religion
	political criticism	theology

Other Indexes

Other indexes of importance include:

Applied Science and Technology Index for articles in chemistry, engineering, computer science, electronics, geology, mathematics, photography, physics, and related fields.

Biological and Agricultural Index for articles in biology, zoology, botany, agriculture, and related fields.

Education Index for articles in education, physical education, and related fields.

Business Periodicals Index for articles in business, marketing, accounting, advertising, and related fields.

Recently Published Articles for articles in history and related fields.

In addition to these major indexes, you should examine the reference work for your topic as listed in Appendix B of this book, pages A-9–A-15.

Searching for an Index to Abstracts

An abstract is a brief description of an article, usually written by the author. An index to abstracts can accelerate your work by allowing you to read the abstract before you assume the task of locating and reading the entire work. You may find them at the electronic book catalog by entering the keyword "abstracts," which will produce a list with great variety. It will look something like this:

Show detail	Abstracts of current studies
Show detail	Dissertation abstracts international
Show detail	Social work abstracts
Show detail	Women studies abstracts

A more specific keyword search will include your discipline, such as "psychology abstracts." This will produce a reference, most likely, to PyscINFO, the searchable database produced by the American Psychological Association. It will give you the type of entry shown in Figure 4.6.

Record 1 of 34 in PsycINFO 1999-2001/01

1 —— AN: 2000-15373-006

2 —— DT: Journal-Article

3 —— TI: Evaluating an electronic monitoring system for people who wander.

4 —— AU: Altus,-Deborah-E; **Mathews,-R.-Mark**; Xaverius,-Pamela-K; Engelman,-Kimberely-K; Nolan,-Beth-A-D

5 —— SO: American-Journal-of-Alzheimer's Disease. 2000 Mar-Apr; Vol 15(2): 121-125

6 —— PB: US: Prime National Publishing Corp.

7 —— IS: 0182-5207

8 —— PY: 2000

9 —— AB: Wandering away from home, or elopement, is a behavior that places persons with dementia at risk of serious injury and may lead family caregivers to place their loved ones in institutions or to severely restrict their independence. This study evaluated the Mobile Locator, an electronic device designed to help caregivers quickly locate a person who has eloped. This 6 month pilot study included case studies of 7 users and an opinion survey of family caregivers, professional caregivers, and search and rescue workers. The survey results showed that respondents were positively impressed by the device, only identifying cost as a potential drawback. Case studies revealed that the equipment was easy to use, effective, and helpful to caregivers' peace of mind. These results suggest that the Mobile Locator is a valuable tool deserving of further study. (PsycINFO Database Record © 2000 APA, all rights reserved)

▬▬ **FIGURE 4.6 Sample entry from PsycINFO.**
(1) AN = accession number; (2) DT = document type; (3) TI = title of the article; (4) AU = author; (5) SO = source; (6) PB = publisher; (7) IS = ISSN number; (8) PY = publication year; (9) AB = abstract of the article.

Searching for Abstracts of Dissertations

You may also wish to examine the abstracts to the dissertations of graduate students in *Dissertation Abstracts International,* which you can access from the Internet via the ProQuest software platform under *ProQuest Dissertations & Theses* or find in a printed version in the library's reference room. In the printed versions, you will need to look for issue no. 12, Part 11, of each volume, for it contains the cumulated subject and author indexes for Issues 1–12 of the volume's two sections—A: *Humanities and Social Sciences,* and B: *Sciences and Engineering.* For example, an online search of *ProQuest Dissertations & Theses* for 2004–2005 listed the following three entries under the heading "Novels":

Novels

1— Hawthorne and the travelling eye: Nineteenth-century tourism and American literary culture (Nathaniel Hawthorne). By Baraw,
2— Charles Eaton, PhD
3— YALE UNIVERSITY, 2005, 265 pages —— *4*
5— AAT 3168856

American regionalist modernism: Willa Cather, William Faulkner, Oscar Zeta Acosta, and Sandra Cisneros. By Alumbaugh, Heather Anne, PhD
NEW YORK UNIVERSITY, 2005, 269 pages
AAT 3157808

Native domesticity: Eighteenth-century representations of the multiracial family in the Americas. By Bush, Shannon Alma, PhD
UNIVERSITY OF CALIFORNIA, RIVERSIDE, 2005, 245 pages
AAT 3179365

FIGURE 4.7 Findings for an online search of *ProQuest Dissertations & Theses* (1) title of dissertation, (2) author, (3) affiliation, (4) number of pages, (5) publication number.

The abstract of Charles Eaton Baraw's dissertation is shown in Figure 4.8 on page 69.

You may cite the abstract in your paper, but inform your readers you are citing from the abstract, not the actual dissertation. If you need the full dissertation and have time, order a copy of the complete work from Bell & Howell Information and Learning Company. Address your request to Bell & Howell Information and Learning Company, 300 North Zeeb Road, Ann Arbor, MI 48106-1346 USA. Telephone (734) 761-7400; info@bellhowell.infolearning.com; http://www.bellhowell.infolearning.com.

4e Searching for a Biography

When you wish to examine the life of a person, you will find biographies in both books and articles and in print versions as well electronic versions.

AAT 3157808

Hawthorne and the travelling eye: Nineteenth-century tourism and American literary culture (Nathaniel Hawthorne).

By Baraw, Charles Eaton, PhD
YALE UNIVERSITY, 2005, 265 pages

This dissertation presents a new account of nineteenth-century American literary culture by elucidating the crucial and unacknowledged role aesthetic tourism played throughout the paradigmatic career of Nathaniel Hawthorne. The theoretical basis for this study is the assumption that nineteenth-century tourism, as a hybrid social form that combines the pictorialism and perspectivism of the visual arts, the textuality and narrativity of literature, and the performativity of ritual and drama, becomes a new epistemology that I call "the travelling eye," a portable subject position applicable to both literary practice and tourism itself. Using this new conceptual frame, I suggest how Hawthorne's professional travels, following those of Irving, Cooper, and Hale and anticipating those of James, Howells, and Jewett, illustrate the intimate connection between the structures of tourism and the basis of literary authorship in the United States. Throughout the century, aesthetic tourism animated the invention of authorial personae, the construction of the reader, and the creation of literary form. Chapter One outlines this process, taking Washington Irving's invention of Geoffrey Crayon as a central model, and then reading Hawthorne's abandoned book, *The Itinerant Story-teller*, as his own sophisticated revision of his predecessors. Chapter Two reads all of Hawthorne's professional utterances—letters, prefaces, first-person fictions and sketches—as performances of a fictive (and in Hawthorne's case, a touristic) character and demonstrates how Hawthorne transposes the structure of his epistolary relations with the critic Evert Duyckinck to the imagined relation between the Author as tour-guide and the reader as tourist. Chapter Three, an extended reading of *The Blithedale Romance*, looks at the narrative errancy, disturbances of memory, and verbal repetition that characterize the narrator's touristic representation of both the utopian community and the new urban sensorium. My interpretations of Hawthorne's later novels demonstrate how the "traveling eye" shapes their form on the levels of verbal style, figuration, and narrative structure. Chapter Four integrates the methodological strategies of previous chapters in a study of the conception, composition, and reception of *The Marble Faun*, a novel that is experimental in its approach to narrative, description, and characterization and a celebrated attraction on the Anglo-American tour of Rome. Together these chapters introduce both a new version of Hawthorne's work and a new conceptual model for understanding the links between the aesthetics of social practice and the transatlantic production of American literature.

FIGURE 4.8 From *ProQuest Dissertations & Theses*, 2004–2005
(1) Publication number, (2) title of dissertation, (3) author, degree earned, school, and date, (4) total number of pages of the dissertation, (5) the abstract.

The electronic card catalog will usually provide multiple sources if you enter the keywords "biography + index."

Show detail   Black biography, 1790–1950
Show detail   Index to literary biography
Show detail   Index to artistic biography
Show detail   Biography index

Several electronic indexes, like InfoTrac and ProQuest, will provide you with abstracts to some biographies and even full-text biographies, such as these:

Biography Reference Bank
Current Biography: 1940–Present
Current Biography Illustrated
Marquis Who's Who Online
Wilson Biographies Plus Illustrated

Other indexes, in print and online, also have value for finding biographies.

Biography Index

The *Biography Index,* in its printed form, has long been a starting point for studies of famous persons. It will lead you to biographical information for people of all lands. See Figure 4.9 on this page for the type of information it provides.

Current Biography Yearbook

Current Biography Yearbook provides a biographical sketch of important people. Most articles are three to four pages in length, and they include references to other sources at the end. It is current, thorough, and has international scope.

Contemporary Authors

Contemporary Authors provides a biographical guide for current writers in fiction, nonfiction, poetry, journalism, drama, motion pictures, television,

FIGURE 4.9 From *Biography Index*, 2005
(1) Subject, (2) dates of subject's birth and death, (3) subject's profession, (4) author of the biography, (5) title of the biography, (6) contains portraits, (7) publisher, (8) specific pages, (9) publication date.

and a few other fields. It provides a thorough overview of most contemporary writers, giving a list of writings, biographical facts (including a current address and agent), a list of writings, sidelights, and, in many cases, an interview by the editors of the guide with the author. Most entries include a bibliography of additional sources about the writer. It has good coverage of major writers and stays current with updates on the important authors.

Dictionary of Literary Biography

Dictionary of Literary Biography provides profiles of thousands of writers in over 100 volumes under such titles as these:

American Humorists, 1800–1950
Victorian Novelists after 1885
American Newspaper Journalists, 1926–1950

4f Searching for Articles in the Newspaper Indexes

For many years, searching for newspaper articles was difficult, if not impossible. There were no indexes capable of doing the task. Now the electronic networks enable you to find newspaper articles from across the nation. Your library may have a newspaper search engine on its network, or you may need to go to the World Wide Web and access newspapers.com. It will take you quickly to over 800 newspapers, from the *Aspen Times* to the *Carbondale Valley Journal.* In most cases, online newspapers have their own internal search engine that enables you to examine articles from the archives. See pages

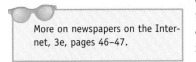

More on newspapers on the Internet, 3e, pages 46–47.

46-47 for a full discussion and image of a hometown newspaper. In addition, several indexes are helpful:

Bell and Howell's Index to the Christian Science Monitor
The New York Times Index
Official Index [to *The London Times*]
Wall Street Journal Index

4g Searching the Indexes to Pamphlet Files

Librarians routinely clip items of interest from newspapers, bulletins, pamphlets, and miscellaneous materials and file them alphabetically by subject in loose-leaf folders.

Vertical File Index

Make the pamphlet file a regular stop during preliminary investigation. Sometimes called the *vertical file,* it will have clippings on many topics, such as:

"Asbestos in the Home"
"Carpel Tunnel Syndrome"

"Everything Doesn't Cause Cancer"
"Medicare and Coordinated Care Plans"

The *Vertical File Index* gives a description of each entry, the price, and how to order the pamphlet. Check at your library's electronic card catalog to see if your librarians have created an online index to local pamphlets.

Social Issues Resources Series *(SIRS)*

Also important to you are published pamphlets that feature articles on a common topic. *Social Issues Resources Series* (SIRS), online and in print, collects articles on special topics and reprints them as one unit on a special subject, such as abortion, AIDS, prayer in schools, or pollution. With *SIRS,* you will have 10 or 12 articles readily available in one booklet.

The CQ Researcher

Like *SIRS, The CQ Researcher,* online and in print, devotes pamphlets to one topic, such as "Energy and the Environment." The pamphlet will examine central issues on the topic, give background information, show a chronology of important events or processes, express an outlook, and provide an annotated bibliography. In one place, you have material worthy of quotation and paraphrase as well as a list of additional sources. Figure 4.10 shows one of numerous sources on this topic as listed in *The CQ Researcher*'s bibliography:

HINT: For the correct citation forms to articles found in *SIRS* or *The CQ Researcher,* see page 271.

Ochoa, George, Jennifer Hoffman, and Tina Tin. *Climate: The Force That Shapes Our World and the Future of Life on Earth,* **Emmaus, PA: Rodale, 2005.**

Climate describes the marvelous and complex workings of Earth's climate systems, from its primordial atmosphere to today's extreme changes in weather, ecology, and environment. Climate systems around the world are being transformed by rising temperatures. Every continent is undergoing alarming changes: melting glaciers, deadly droughts, severe storms, and loss of habitat for plants and animals—and humans.

FIGURE 4.10 An annotated bibliography from *The CQ Researcher*

4h Searching for Government Documents

All branches of the government publish massive amounts of material. Many of these documents have great value for researchers, so investigate the following source if your topic is one that government agencies might have investigated.

GPO on Silverplatter on your library's network or
GPOAccess on the Internet

Either of these sites will take you to the files of the Government Printing Office. The database list includes *Congressional Bills, Congressional Record, Economic Indicators, Public Laws,* the *U.S. Constitution,* and much more. A keyword search will provide an entry similar to that shown in Figure 4.11 at the bottom of this page.

A working bibliography entry to the source shown in Figure 4.11, a Senate hearing, should look like this:

United States. Congress. House. Committee on the Judiciary. "Border

Protection, Anti-terrorism, and Illegal Immigration Control Act of

2005." Report. 109th Cong., 1st sess. H Hearing 109–345, part I.

Washington: GPO, 2005.

Other works that provide valuable information on matters of the government are:

Monthly Catalog of the United State Government Publications. The printed version of GPO.

Record 5 of 366 in GPO on SilverPlatter 1976-2000/10
1 — AN: 99053103
2 — SU: Y 4.AG 4:S.HRG.106-444
3 — CA: United States. Congress. Senate. Special Committee on Aging.
4 — TI: Nursing home residents: short-changed by staff shortages : forum before the Special Committee on Aging, United States Senate, One Hundred Sixth Congress, first session, Washington, DC, November 3,1999.
5 — SO: Washington: U.S. G.P.O.: For sale by the U.S. G.P.O., Supt. of Docs. Congressional Sales Office, 1999 [i.e. 2000].
6 — SE: United States. Congress. Senate. S. hrg.; 106-444.
7 — IT: 1009-B-01 1009-C-01 (MF)

FIGURE 4.11 From GPO on Silverplatter.
(1) AN = accession number, (2) SU = document number, (3) CA = corporate author, (4) TI = title, (5) SO = source, (6) SE = series, (7) IT = GPO item number.

Public Affairs Information Service Bulletin (PAIS), online and in print. This work indexes articles and documents published by miscellaneous organizations. It's a good place to start because of its excellent index.

Congressional Record, online and in print. This daily publication features Senate and House bills, documents, and committee reports.

Public Papers of the Presidents of the United States, online and in print. This work is a publication of the Executive Branch, which includes not only the president but also all members of the cabinet and various agencies.

The U.S. Code, online and in print. The Supreme Court regularly publishes decisions, codes, and other rulings, as do appellate and district courts. State courts also publish rulings and court results on a regular basis.

Bibliography citations for government documents, pages 276–278.

4i   Searching for Essays within Books

Some essays get lost in collections and anthologies. You can find essays listed by subject on this database at your library:

Essay and General Literature Index on Silverplatter

The print version is:

Essay and General Literature Index, 1900-1933. New York: H. W. Wilson, 1934. Supplements, 1934–date.

This reference work helps you find essays hidden in anthologies. It indexes material of both a biographical and a critical nature. The essay listed in the example on the next page might easily have been overlooked by any researcher.

King, Martin Luther, 1929–1968
Raboteau, A.J. Martin Luther King and the tradition of black religious protest. (*In* Religion and the life of the nation; ed. by R.A. Sherrill, p. 46-65).

Your electronic book catalog will give you the call number to Sherrill's book.

4j   Using the Microforms

Online sources are gradually replacing microforms, but your library may have magazines and newspapers converted to a small, single sheet of film called *microfiche* (flat sheet of film) or *microfilm* (roll). Your library will specify in the cardex files (the list of periodicals) how journals and magazines are housed—whether they are in bound printed volumes or microforms.

Your library may also house guides to special microform holdings with titles such as *American Culture 1493-1806: A Guide to the Microfilm*

Collection or perhaps *American Periodicals 1800–1850: A Guide to the Microfilm Collection.* Every library has its own peculiar holdings of microfilm and microfiche materials; if you need assistance, the librarian can help you.

YOUR RESEARCH PROJECT

1. If you have not already done so with an orientation group, take the time to stroll through your library. Identify its various sections and the types of information available there. Especially learn about the reference room, the stacks, and the printed periodical articles. Pick up a bound volume of a journal, open it, and notice how it contains 12 issues (or 6) of one year's publications.

2. At the library, sit down at one of the computer terminals and investigate its options. Make up a topic for the moment and search for books or articles at the terminal. Try to find an abstract or a full-text article and then print it.

3. Go to the reference desk and ask the librarian for a specialized bibliography on your topic—that is, say something like this: "Do you have a specialized bibliography on global warming?"

4. Locate the library's holdings of *The CQ Researcher* and *Social Issues Resources Series.* Page through the various booklets to note how they provide several penetrating articles on a common topic. In the indexes, search to see if your favorite topic has been treated in a special issue.

5. To test the resources of the library, go in search of information about the day you were born. Don't limit yourself to major events of the day; go also in search of hometown news. Look at the advertisements to see what people were wearing and what things cost back then.

CHECKLIST

The Library Search

When you start your research on a topic, you will need to switch between the computer terminals, the library stacks of books and periodicals, and the printed bibliographies and indexes, according to the resources in your library. Start, perhaps, with the sources on this list.

To find books:

electronic book catalog with keyword

online with keywords "bibliographies + [your discipline]"

To find periodical articles:

    an electronic database with a keyword

    online with keywords "indexes + [your discipline]"

    the Wilson indexes

To find an abstract:

    online with keywords "abstracts + [your discipline]"

To find biographies in books and periodicals:

    online with keywords "biography + indexes"

    Biography Index, online or in print

To find newspaper articles:

    Internet at http://www.newspapers.com

    electronic database under keyword "newspapers"

To find pamphlet files:

    online with the library's network to *SIRS* and *The CQ Researcher*

    Ask your librarian for local files

To find government documents:

    online with the library network to GPO on Silverplatter

    Internet access to GPOAccess

To find essays within books:

    Essay and General Literature Index, online or in print

To find microforms:

    online with the library network to ERIC

5 Conducting Research Outside the Library

Field research refers, in general, to any studies conducted outside the library, such as digging at an archeology site, measuring a sinkhole fault, observing student behavior at a parking lot, or surveying a selected group with a questionnaire. This type of work is not beyond the realm of first-year students, and you should consider it an important ingredient in your research plans. Therefore, converse with people by letter or e-mail, and if time permits it, conduct personal one-on-one interviews or use a questionnaire. Watch television specials, visit the courthouse archives, and conduct research by observation under the guidance of an instructor (see pages 83–86).

Set up your field research in an objective manner in order to control subjective feelings. Student Odette Ogburn (see her letter on pages 79–80) had strong personal feelings about her own daughter's condition as she researched attention deficit hyperactivity disorder, so she had to force herself to look objectively for viable evidence. Questionnaires and observations that are slanted to get a desired report should be avoided. Allow your instructor to review your methods and apparatus before launching the study. All writers get deeply involved in their subject, but they must couple that involvement with the skill of detachment. What are the facts? What conclusions do they support? Conduct the test, get results, and then discuss their implications.

Build a table, graph, or chart with the evidence collected and make it part of your study. Your instructor may ask you to place evidence of your research—field notes, interview transcripts, survey data—in an appendix at the end of your paper. You may also be asked to design your finished paper with the scientific paradigm, in which you establish a hypothesis, discuss your design and method, reveal the results of your study, and then discuss their implications (see pages 85–86 for more information).

5a Investigating Local Sources

Interviewing Knowledgeable People

Talk to people who have experience with your subject. Personal interviews can elicit valuable in-depth information. Interviews provide information that few others will have. Look to organizations for knowledgeable experts. For example, if writing on folklore, you might contact the county historian, a senior citizens' organization, or the local historical society. If necessary, post a notice soliciting help: "I am writing a study of local folklore. Wanted: People who have a knowledge of regional tales." Another way to accomplish this task is to join an e-mail discussion group to invite commentary from a group interested in the same topic (see pages 18–19 for more details). Try using the discussion board if yours is an online class. For accuracy, save files or record the interview with a tape recorder (with permission of the person interviewed, of course). When finished, make a bibliography entry just as you would for a book:

> Thornbright, Mattie Sue. E-mail interview. 15 Jan. 2006.

Note: For a paper written in APA style, you should document an e-mail interview in the text only, not in the references. To maintain the anonymity of the source, write this in-text citation: (Anonymous interview, April 6, 2006). The APA style requires that you omit from the References items that are not retrievable, such as e-mail messages, interviews, personal letters, memos, or private papers.

In addition to the checklist of guidelines listed on page 83 you need to remember several vital matters. First, be prepared for interviews, which means that you know your interviewee's professional background and that you have a set of pertinent questions, with followups. Second, keep your focus on the principal issue. Subjects may wish to wander toward tangential ideas, so you need to bring them back to the central subject with an appropriate question. Third, maintain an ethical demeanor that honors with accuracy the statements of the subject.

Student Valerie Nesbitt-Hall researched the role of matching services and chat rooms in promoting online romance. Because she was acquainted with a couple that had met online and eventually married, she decided to request an interview—online, of course. These were her questions and, in brief form, the responses of the subjects, Stephen of Scotland and Jennifer of the United States. (See Nesbitt-Hall's paper on pages 323–336):

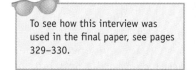

To see how this interview was used in the final paper, see pages 329–330.

1. When did you first meet online? Answer: *September of 1996*
2. What prompted you to try an online matching service? Answer: *We didn't really try online matching services. We chatted in a chat room, became friends there, and met in person later.*
3. Who initiated the first contact? Answer: *Stephen initiated the first online chat.*
4. How long into the relationship did you correspond by e-mail before one of you gave an address and/or phone number? Who did it first, Steve or Jennifer? Answer: *We chatted and corresponded by e-mail for nine months before Jennifer shared her phone number.*
5. How long into the relationship did you go before sharing photographs? Answer: *At nine months we began to share written correspondence and photographs.*

6. Who initiated the first meeting in person? Where did you meet? How long were you into the relationship before you met in person? Answer: *Stephen first requested the meeting, and Jennifer flew from the States to Glasgow, Scotland. This was about a year into the relationship.*

7. How much time elapsed between your first online meeting and your marriage? Answer: *One and a half years after our first chat, we were married.*

8. Did you feel that online romance enabled you to prearrange things and protect your privacy before meeting in person? Answer: *Yes. We were cautious and at times reluctant to continue, but we kept coming back to each other, online, until we knew the other well enough to trust in the relationship. Once we got offline into what we might call real-time dating, the love blossomed quickly.*

9. Did you feel, when you finally met in person, that you really knew the other person—Spiritually? Emotionally? Intellectually? Answer: *Yes.*

10. Not to put you on the spot, but do you feel as a couple that the relationship has been excellent to this point? Answer: *Yes, super.*

11. Has the difference in nationalities been a problem? Answer: *Yes, but only in relation to sorting out immigration matters. Also, Jennifer's parents were concerned that she was going to another country to see someone she had never met.*

12. Finally, would you recommend online matching services or chat rooms to others who are seeking mates? Answer: *Yes, in the right circumstances. We were lucky; others might not be.*

Writing Letters and Corresponding by E-mail

Correspondence provides a written record of research. As you would in an interview, ask pointed questions so correspondents respond directly to your central issues. Tell the person who you are, what you are attempting to do, and why you have chosen to write to this particular person or set of persons. If germane, explain why you have chosen this topic and what qualifies you to write about it.

Odette Ogburn
1551 Grayside Road
Topeka, KS 66612

Ms. Evelyn Casasola, Principal
Parkview Elementary School
Topeka, KS 66612

Dear Ms. Casasola:

I am a college student conducting research into methods for handling hyperactive children in the public school setting. I am surveying each elementary school principal in Shawnee County. I have contacted the central office also, but I wished to have perspectives from those of you on the front lines. I have a child with ADHD, so I have a personal as well as a scholarly reason for this research. I could ask specific questions on policy, but I have gotten that from the central office. What I would like from you is a brief paragraph that describes your policy and procedure when one of your teachers reports a hyperactive child. In particular, do you endorse the use of medication for calming the child? May I quote you in my report? I will honor your request to withhold your name.

I have enclosed a self-addressed, stamped envelope for your convenience. You may e-mail me at oogburn@washburn.edu.

Sincerely,

Odette Ogburn

If Ogburn decided to build a table or graph from the nine replies of the various principals, she would need to document the survey in a Works Cited entry as shown on page 84.

This letter makes a fairly specific request for a minimum amount of information. It does not require an expansive reply. Should Ogburn use a quotation from the reply, she should provide a bibliography entry on her Works Cited page.

Casasola, Evelyn. Principal of Parkview Elementary School, Topeka, KS.

E-mail to the author. 5 Apr. 2006.

Reading Personal Papers

Search out letters, diaries, manuscripts, family histories, and other personal materials that might contribute to your study. The city library may house private collections, and the city librarian can usually help you contact the county historian and other private citizens who have important documents. Obviously, handling private papers must be done with the utmost decorum and care. Again, make a bibliography entry for such materials:

Joplin, Lester. "Notes on my visits to the Robert Penn Warren family

home and museum in Guthrie, Kentucky." Unpublished paper.

Nashville, 2005.

Attending Lectures and Public Addresses

Watch bulletin boards and the newspaper for featured speakers who might visit your campus. When you attend a lecture, take careful notes and, if it is available, request a copy of the lecture or speech. Remember, too, that many lectures, reproduced on video, will be available in the library or in departmental files. Always make a bibliography entry for any words or ideas you use.

> Petty-Rathbone, Virginia. "Edgar Allan Poe and the Image of Ulalume."
>
> Lecture. Heard Library, Vanderbilt U., 25 Jan. 2006.

5b Investigating Government Documents

Documents are available at four levels of government—city, county, state, and federal. As a constituent, you are entitled to examine many kinds of records on file at various agencies. If your topic demands it, you may contact the mayor's office, attend and take notes at a city council assembly, or search out printed documents.

Local Government

Visit the courthouse or county clerk's office, where you can find facts on elections, censuses, marriages, births, and deaths. These archives include wills, tax rolls, military assignments, deeds to property, and much more. Therefore, a trip to the local courthouse can be rewarding, helping you trace the history of the land and its people.

State Government

Contact by phone or online a state office that relates to your research, such as Consumer Affairs (general information), Public Service Commission (which regulates public utilities such as the telephone company), and the Department of Human Services (which administers social and welfare services). The agencies may vary by name in your state. Remember, too, that the state will have an archival storehouse whose records are available for public review. Figure 5.1 on page 82 shows the type of information readily available to a student conducting research on a city's population and demographics.

Federal Government

Your United States senator or representative can send you booklets printed by the Government Printing Office (GPO). A list of these materials, many of which are free, appears in a monthly catalog issued by the Super-intendent of Documents: *Monthly Catalog of United States Government Publications,* Washington, DC 20402. This list is also available with an excellent search engine at www.access.gpo.gov/. In addition, you can gain access to the National Archives Building in Washington, DC, or to one of the regional branches in Atlanta, Boston, Chicago, Denver, Fort Worth, Kansas City, Los Angeles, New York, Philadelphia, and Seattle. Their archives contain court records and government documents, which you can review in

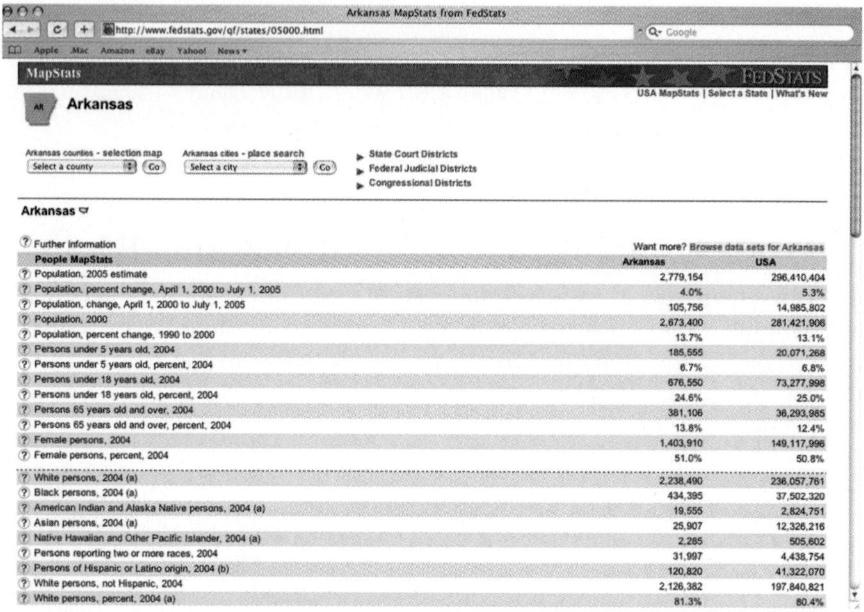

People MapStats	Arkansas	USA
Population, 2005 estimate	2,779,154	296,410,404
Population, percent change, April 1, 2000 to July 1, 2005	4.0%	5.3%
Population, change, April 1, 2000 to July 1, 2005	105,756	14,985,802
Population, 2000	2,673,400	281,421,906
Population, percent change, 1990 to 2000	13.7%	13.1%
Persons under 5 years old, 2004	185,555	20,071,268
Persons under 5 years old, percent, 2004	6.7%	6.8%
Persons under 18 years old, 2004	676,550	73,277,998
Persons under 18 years old, percent, 2004	24.6%	25.0%
Persons 65 years old and over, 2004	381,106	36,293,985
Persons 65 years old and over, percent, 2004	13.8%	12.4%
Female persons, 2004	1,403,910	149,117,996
Female persons, percent, 2004	51.0%	50.8%
White persons, 2004 (a)	2,238,490	236,057,761
Black persons, 2004 (a)	434,395	37,502,320
American Indian and Alaska Native persons, 2004 (a)	19,555	2,824,751
Asian persons, 2004 (a)	25,907	12,326,216
Native Hawaiian and Other Pacific Islander, 2004 (a)	2,285	505,602
Persons reporting two or more races, 2004	31,997	4,438,754
Persons of Hispanic or Latino origin, 2004 (b)	120,820	41,322,070
White persons, not Hispanic, 2004	2,126,382	197,840,821
White persons, percent, 2004 (a)	81.3%	80.4%

FIGURE 5.1 Population and demographics: Fort Smith, Arkansas.

two books: *Guide to the National Archives of the United States* and *Select List of Publications of the National Archives and Record Service* (see http://www.archives.gov.) You can borrow some documents on microfilm if you consult the *Catalog of National Archives Microfilm Publications*. One researcher, for example, found the table shown in Figure 5.1 (page 82) while looking for information on shifts in population.

The researcher also made a bibliography entry to record the source of this table.

FedStats. "MapStats: Arkansas." 21 June 2006. 8 Aug. 2006. <http://www.fedstats.gov/qf/states/05000.html>.

5c Examining Audiovisual Materials, Television, and Radio

Important data can be found in audiovisual materials: films, filmstrips, music, CDs, slides, audio cassettes, video cassettes and DVDs. You will find these sources both on and off campus. Consult such guides as *Educators Guide* (film, filmstrips, and tapes), *Media Review Digest* (nonprint materials), *Video Source Book* (video catalog), *The Film File*, and *International Index*

Interviews, Letters, Private Papers, Courthouse Documents

- Set up appointments in advance.
- Consult with experienced persons. If possible, talk to several people in order to weigh their different opinions. Telephone and e-mail interviews are acceptable.
- Be courteous and on time for interviews.
- Be prepared in advance with a set of focused, pertinent questions for initiating and conducting the interview.
- Handle private and public papers with great care.
- For accuracy, record the interview with a tape recorder (with permission of the person interviewed, of course).
- Double-check direct quotations with the interviewee or the tape.
- Get permission before citing a person by name or quoting his or her exact words.
- Send helpful people a copy of your report, along with a thank-you note.

---

to Recorded Poetry. Television, with its many educational channels, such as *The History Channel,* offers invaluable data. With a VCR, you can record a program for detailed examination. Again, write bibliography entries for any materials that contribute to your paper.

Alvarez, Manny. "Holidays Blues." Interview. Fox News. 8 Dec. 2005.

5d Conducting a Survey with a Questionnaire

Questionnaires can produce current, firsthand data you can tabulate and analyze. Of course, to achieve meaningful results, you must survey a random sample—that is, each one must represent the whole population in terms of age, sex, race, education, income, residence, and other factors. Various degrees of bias can creep into the questionnaire unless you remain objective. Thus, use the formal survey only when you are experienced with tests and measurements as well as with statistical analysis or when you have an instructor who will help you with the instrument. Be advised that most schools have a Human Subjects Committee that sets guidelines, draws up consent forms, and requires anonymity of participants for information gathering that might

---

CHECKLIST

Using Media Sources

- Watch closely the opening and closing credits to capture the necessary data for your bibliography entry. The format is explained on page 298.
- Your citations may refer to a performer, director, or narrator, depending on the focus of your study.
- As with live interviews, be scrupulously accurate in taking notes. Try to write with direct quotations because paraphrases of television commentary can unintentionally be distorted and colored by bias.
- Plan carefully the review of a media presentation, even to the point of preparing a list of questions or a set of criteria to help with your judgment.

An informal survey gathered in the hallways of campus buildings lacks credibility in the research paper. If you build a table or graph from the results, see "Using Visuals," pages 168–170, for examples and instructions. Label your survey in the bibliography entry:

Castor, Diego, and Carmen Aramide. "Child Care Arrangements of

Parents Who Attend College." Questionnaire. Coeur d'Alene, Idaho:

North Idaho College, 2006.

Unlike interview questions (see pages 77–79), which are meant to elicit a response from one person or a couple, questionnaires are designed for multiple responses from many people, from 25 or 30 up to several thousand. Design them for ease of tabulation with results you can arrange in graphs and charts.

5e   Conducting Experiments, Tests, and Observation

Empirical research, usually performed in a laboratory, can determine why and how things exist, function, or interact. Your paper will explain your methods and findings in pursuit of a hypothesis (your thesis). An experiment thereby becomes primary evidence for your paper.

Observation is field research that occurs outside the lab—"in the field"— which might be a child care center, a movie theater, a parking lot, or the counter of a fast food restaurant. The field is anywhere you can observe, count,

CHECKLIST

Conducting a Survey

- Keep the questionnaire short, clear, and focused on your topic.
- Write unbiased questions. Let your professor review the instrument before using it.
- Design a quick response to a scale (Choose A, B, or C), to a ranking (first choice, second choice, and so on), or to fill the blanks.
- Arrange for an easy return of the questionnaire, even to the point of providing a self-addressed, stamped envelope.
- Retain e-mail responses until the project is complete.
- Provide a sample questionnaire and your tabulations in an appendix.
- Tabulate the results objectively. Even negative results that deny your hypothesis have value.

count, and record behavior, patterns, or systems. It might also include observing and testing the water in a stream, the growth of certain wildflowers, or the nesting patterns of deer. We seldom notice the careful study conducted by retail merchandisers who want to know our buying habits or the analysis by a basketball coach on the shot selections by members of his team. Gathering data is a way of life—by television networks, politicians, and thousands of marketing firms.

Most experiments and observations begin with a *hypothesis*, which is similar to a thesis sentence (see pages 24–27). The hypothesis is a statement assumed to be true for the purpose of investigation. *Hummingbirds live as extended families governed by a patriarch* is a hypothesis needing data to prove its validity. *The majority of people will not correct the poor grammar of a speaker* is a hypothesis that needs testing and observation to prove its validity.

However, you can begin observation without a hypothesis and let the results lead you to conclusions. Assignment 1, page 87, asks you to conduct a double-entry observation for one week and to write a short reflection about what you learned by keeping the field notes. This could be your introduction to field research.

Generally, a report on an experiment or observation follows an expected format featuring four distinct parts: introduction, method, results, discussion. Understanding these elements will help you design your survey:

Introduction to explain the design of your experiment:
- Present the point of the study.
- State the hypothesis and how it relates to the problem.

- Provide the theoretical implications of the study.
- Explain the manner in which this study relates to previously published work.

Method to describe what you did and how you conducted the study:
- Describe the subjects who participated, whether human or animal.
- Describe the apparatus to explain your equipment and how you used it.
- Summarize the procedure in execution of each stage of your work.

Results to report your findings:
- Summarize the data you collected.
- Provide the necessary statistical treatment of the findings with tables, graphs, and charts.
- Include findings that conflict with your hypothesis.

Discussion that explains the implications of your work:
- Evaluate the data and its relevance to the hypothesis.
- Interpret the findings as necessary.
- Discuss the implications of the findings.
- Qualify the results and limit them to your specific study.
- Make inferences from the results.

Your experiment and the writing of the report will require the attention of your instructor. Seek his or her advice often. *Note*: This paradigm can also be used for a fully developed proposal. In fact, instructors often ask for proposals that will never be implemented as research toward a completed report.

Consult the Lester Web site, http://www.ablongman.com/lester12e, for additional information, examples, and links to sites that discuss in greater detail the matters of experiment and observation.

CHECKLIST

Conducting an Experiment or Observation

- Express a clear hypothesis.
- Select the proper design for the study—lab experiment, observation, or the collection of raw data in the field.
- Include a review of the literature, if appropriate.
- Keep careful records and accurate data.
- Don't let your expectations influence the results.
- Maintain respect for human and animal subjects. In that regard, you may find it necessary to get approval for your research from a governing board. Read your college's rules and regulations on research that requires the use of humans and animals.

YOUR RESEARCH PROJECT

1. Select an event or object from nature to observe daily for one week. Record field notes in a double-entry format by using the left side of the page to record and the right side of the page to comment and reflect on what you have observed. Afterwards, write a brief paragraph discussing your findings.

Record:	*Response:*
Day 1	
10-minute session at window, three hummingbirds fighting over the feeder	Is the male chasing away the female, or is the female the aggressor?
Day 2	
10-minute session at window, saw eight single hummingbirds and one guarding feeder by chasing others away	I did some research, and the red-throated male is the one that's aggressive.

2. Look carefully at your subject to determine if research outside the library will be helpful for your project. If so, what kind of research: correspondence? local records? the news media? a questionnaire? an observation or experiment?

3. Work closely with your instructor to design an instrument that will affect your research and your findings. In fact, most instructors will want to examine any questionnaire that you will submit to others and will want to approve the design of your experiment or observation.

4. Follow university guidelines on testing with humans and animals.

6 | Understanding and Avoiding Plagiarism

You probably know that turning in someone else's research paper as your own work is plagiarism of the worst kind. But do you really understand what is plagiarism and what isn't? Are you comfortable that you understand when to document (cite) sources and when it's okay not to? Do you know what criteria to use? Most problems related to plagiarism arise in college writing because students lack clear and confident answers to these questions—and not because students want to cheat the system. In this chapter, we'll define plagiarism, explore the ethical and community standards for writing in an academic environment, and provide examples of the worst and best of citations.

Plus, here's the newest problem: The Internet makes it easy to copy and download material and paste it into a paper—which in itself is not a problem *unless* the writer fails to acknowledge the source with an in-text citation of some sort and a bibliography entry at the back of the paper.

Colleges now have stringent policies concerning plagiarism and the use of a paper that is purchased or copied from an online site. Programs such as Turnitin.com and even a simple Web search can detect plagiarism, whether deliberate or accidental. Making an average grade is better than an F on a paper, failing the course, or facing the consequences of violating the academic code of conduct. You must resist the temptation to take shortcuts. Don't plagiarize!

Let's look at it this way: Intellectual property has value just like the cash drawer at the local McDonald's. Yet words are not hard currency, and they can't be confined to somebody's cash box. In fact, ideas and theories must be shared if they are to multiply and grow. What's more, the law gives students limited rights to copy from sources. Nevertheless, the word *plagiarism* raises red flags and frightens some students to the point of stifling their research. The purpose of this chapter is to make you comfortable with and knowledgeable about the ethics of research, especially about these matters:

- Using sources to enhance your credibility
- Using sources to place your work in its proper context
- Honoring property rights
- Avoiding plagiarism
- Sharing credit and honoring it in collaborative projects

- Honoring and crediting sources in online classrooms
- Seeking permission to publish material on your Web site

6a Using Sources to Enhance Your Credibility

What some students fail to realize is that citing a source in their papers, even the short ones, signals something special and positive to your readers—that you have researched the topic, explored the literature about it, and have the talent to share it. Research is something you need to share, not hide. Research writing exercises your critical thinking and your ability to collect ideas. You will discuss not only the subject matter, such as water pollution in the Delaware River, but also the *literature* of the topic, such as articles from the Internet and current periodicals found at your library's databases. By announcing clearly the name of a source, you reveal the scope of your reading and thus your credibility, as in this student's notes:

> Americans consume an average of 300 plus liters of water per day per capita while the average person needs only 20 to 40 liters, according to O'Malley and Bowman.

> Sandra Postel says water is "a living system that drives the workings of a natural world we depend on" (19).

> Postel declares: "A new water era has begun" (24). She indicates that the great prairies of the world will dry up, including America's. Hey, when folks in America notice the drought, then maybe something will happen.

These notes, if transferred into the paper, will enable readers to identify the sources used. The notes give clear evidence of the writer's investigation into the subject, and they enhance the student's image as a researcher. You will get credit for displaying the sources properly. The opposite, plagiarism, presents the information as though it were your own:

> The great prairies of the world will soon dry up, and that includes America's, so a new water era has begun.

That sentence borrows too much. If in doubt, cite the source and place it within its proper context.

6b Placing Your Work in Its Proper Context

Your sources will reflect all kinds of special interests, even biases, so you need to position them within your paper as reliable sources. If you must use a biased or questionable source, tell your readers up front. For example, if you are writing about the dangers of cigarette smoke, you will find different opinions in a farmer's magazine, a health and fitness magazine, and a trade journal sponsored by R.J. Reynolds. You owe it to your readers to scrutinize Internet sites closely and examine printed articles for:

- Special interests that might color the report.
- Lack of credentials.
- An unsponsored Web site.
- Opinionated speculation, especially that found in chat rooms.
- Trade magazines that promote special interests.
- Extremely liberal or extremely conservative positions.

Here's an example: Norman Berkowitz, in researching articles on the world's water supply, found an article of interest but positioned it with a description of the source, as shown in this note.

> Earth First, which describes itself as a radical environmental journal, features articles by an editorial staff that uses pseudonyms, such as Sky, Jade, Wedge, and Sprig. In his article "The End of Lake Powell," Sprig says, "The Colorado River may soon be unable to provide for the 25 million people plumbed into its system" (25). The danger, however, is not limited to Lake Powell. Sprig adds, "This overconsumption of water, compounded with a regional drought cycle of 25 years, could mean that Lake Powell and every other reservoir in the upper Colorado River area will be without water" (24-25).

Not only does Berkowitz recognize the source with name, quotation marks, and page numbers, he identifies the nature of the magazine for his readers.

6c   Honoring Property Rights

If you invent a new piece of equipment or a child's toy, you can get a patent that protects your invention. You now own it. If you own a company, you can register a symbol that serves as a trademark for the products produced. You own the trademark. In like manner, if you write a set of poems and publish them in a chapbook, you own the poems. Others must seek your permission before they can reproduce the poems, just as others must buy your trademark or pay to produce your toy.

The principle behind the copyright law is relatively simple. Copyright begins at the time a creative work is recorded in some tangible form—a written document, a drawing, a tape recording. It does not depend on a legal registration with the copyright office in Washington, DC, although published works *are* usually registered. Thus, the moment you express yourself creatively on paper, in song, on a canvas, that expression is your intellectual property. You have a vested interest in any profits made from the distribution of the work. For that reason, songwriters, cartoonists, fiction writers, and other artists guard their work and do not want it disseminated without compensation. Recent attempts to prevent the downloading of music onto private computers is a demonstration of this concern.

Scholarly writing is not a profitmaking profession, but the writers certainly deserve recognition. We can give that recognition by providing in-text citations and bibliography entries. As a student, you may use copyrighted material in your research paper under a doctrine of *fair use* as described in the U.S. Code, which says:

> The fair use of a copyrighted work . . . for purposes such as criticism, comment, news reporting, teaching (including multiple copies for classroom use), scholarship, or research is not an infringement of copyright.

Thus, as long as you borrow for educational purposes, such as a paper to be read by your instructor, you should not be concerned. Just give the source the proper recognition and documentation, as explained next in section 6d. However, if you decide to *publish* your research paper on a Web site, then new considerations come into play (see 6g, "Seeking Permission to Publish Material on Your Web Site").

6d Avoiding Plagiarism

There are a number of steps you can take to avoid plagiarizing. First, develop personal notes full of your own ideas on a topic. Discover how you feel about the issue. Then, rather than copy sources one after another onto your pages of text, try to express your own ideas while synthesizing the ideas of the authorities by using summary, paraphrase, or direct quotation, which are explained fully on pages 148–156. Rethink and reconsider ideas gathered during your reading, make meaningful connections, and, when you refer to the ideas or exact words of a source—as you inevitably will—give the other writer full credit.

To repeat, *plagiarism* is offering the words or ideas of another person as one's own. Major violations, which can bring failure in the course or expulsion from school, are:

- The use of another student's work.
- The purchase of a "canned" research paper.
- Copying whole passages into a paper without documentation.
- Copying a key, well-worded phrase into a paper without documentation.
- Putting specific ideas of others into your own words without documentation.
- Inadequate or missing citation.
- Missing quotation marks.
- Incomplete or missing Works Cited entry.

Whether deliberate or not, these instances all constitute forms of plagiarism.

Closely related, but not technically plagiarism, is to fabricate information knowingly—that is, just make it up off the top of your head. Some news reporters have lost their jobs because of fabrication.

In addition, a gray area of plagiarism exists: errors caused by carelessness. For example:

- The writer fails to enclose quoted material within quotation marks, yet he or she provides an in-text citation with name and page number.
- The writer's paraphrase never quite becomes paraphrase—too much of the original is left intact—but he or she provides a full citation to name and page.

In these situations, instructors must step in and help the beginning researcher, for although these cases are not flagrant instances of plagiarism, they can mar an otherwise fine piece of research.

What's more, double standards exist. Magazine writers and newspaper reporters offer citations to quotations and paraphrases that seldom show academic documentation. For example, the magazine might say:

Randall Hicks, in his essay "A Lesson for the Future," says "young people's ability to think about the future is not very well developed and their images tend to be pessimistic."

That's it—no page number and no bibliography at the end of the magazine article. The magazine citation gives minimal information, but usually enough that a reader could go in search of the full essay by Hicks.

However, as an academic writer, you must document fully any borrowed ideas and words. The academic citation—author, page number, and bibliography entry—establishes two things beyond your reliability and credibility:

1. A clear trail for other researchers to follow if they also want to consult the source
2. Information for other researchers who might need to replicate (reproduce) the project

When you provide an academic citation, you've made it clear *who* you've read, *how* you used it in your paper, and *where* others can find it.

Even then, scholarly documentation differs from field to field—that is, literary papers are written in a different style from a scientific paper. In the social sciences, a paraphrase does not require a page number. In the applied sciences, a number replaces the authority's name, the year, and even the page number. So you will find that standards shift considerably as you move from class to class and from discipline to discipline. The good writer learns to adapt to the changes in the academic standards. Thus, this book devotes separate chapters to MLA, APA, CSE, and CMS styles.

Common Knowledge Exceptions

Common knowledge exceptions exist under several circumstances:

1. **Local knowledge.** You and your reader might share local or regional knowledge on a subject. For example, if you attend Northern Illinois University,

Documenting Your Sources

- Let the reader know when you begin borrowing from a source by introducing the quotation or paraphrase with the name of the authority.
- Enclose within quotation marks all quoted materials—both key phrases and sentences.
- Use an indented block for quotations of four lines or more.
- Make certain that paraphrased material has been rewritten in your own style and language. The simple rearrangement of sentence patterns is unacceptable.
- Provide specific in-text documentation for each borrowed item, but keep in mind that styles differ for MLA, APA, CSE, and CMS standards.
- Provide a bibliography entry in the Works Cited for every source cited in the paper, including sources that appear only in content footnotes or an appendix.

you need not cite the fact that Illinois is known as the Land of Lincoln, that Chicago is its largest city, or that Springfield is the capital city. Information of this sort requires *no* in-text citation, as shown in the following example.

> The flat rolling hills of Illinois form part of the great Midwestern Corn Belt. It stretches from its border with Wisconsin in the north to the Kentucky border in the south. Its political center is Springfield in the center of the state, but its industrial and commercial center is Chicago, that great boisterous city camped on the shores of Lake Michigan.

However, a writer in another place and time might need to cite the source of this information. Most writers would probably want to document this next passage.

> Early Indian tribes on the plains called themselves *Illiniwek* (which meant strong men), and French settlers pronounced the name *Illinois* (Angle 44).

2. **Shared experiences.** Coursework and lectures will give you and members of your class a similar perspective on the subject. For example, students in a literary class studying African American writers would share

common information, so the student might write, without documentation, something like this:

> Langston Hughes, an important poet in the 1920s and 1930s, became a leader of the Harlem Renaissance, and like so many writers, he took great pride in his African American heritage. He was not afraid to use the vernacular black dialect, and I would say that he is one of the fathers of today's rap music.

If the student shifts to nongeneral information, then a citation is in order:

> Hughes has been described by Gerald Early as the major artistic link between the revolutionary poet Paul Lawrence Dunbar and the radical poet Amiri Baraka (246).

3. **Common facts.** Common factual information that one might find in an almanac, fact book, or dictionary need not be cited. Here is an example:

> President George Herbert Walker Bush launched the Desert Storm attack in 1991 against Iraq and its leader, Saddam Hussein, with the support of allies and their troops from several nations. His son, President George W. Bush, launched a similar attack in 2003 against the same dictator and his army.

CHECKLIST

Common Knowledge Exceptions

- Do not document the source if an intelligent person would and should know the information, given the context of both writer and audience.

- Do not document terminology and information from a classroom environment that has become common knowledge to all members of the class.

- Do not document the source if you knew the information without reading it in an article or book.

- Do not document almanac-type information, such as date, place of birth, occupation, and so on.

- Do not document information that has become general knowledge by being reported repeatedly in many different sources (i.e., Michael Jordan holds several National Basketball Association [NBA] scoring records).

The passage needs no documentation, but the farther we move in history from that time and place, the more likely will be the need for documentation. Of course, provide a citation for analysis that goes beyond common facts.

The elder Bush demonstrated great mastery in his diplomatic unification of a politically diverse group of allies (Wolford 37).

Correctly Borrowing from a Source

The next examples in MLA style demonstrate the differences between the accurate use of a source and plagiarism. First is the original reference material that discusses methods for solving the world's water shortage; it is followed by the student versions that use the passage, along with discussions of their failures and merits.

Original Material:

> The impulse to memorialize the Civil War dead does not stop with southerners. In 1964, roughly a century after Gettysburg, when the Civil Rights movement had brought new battles and more bloodshed to the southern countryside, the quintessential Yankee poet Robert Lowell celebrated the Confederacy's ancient opponents in his own elegy, "For the Union Dead." Instead of a confederate graveyard, Lowell contemplates the famed monument to Col. Robert Gould Shaw and the 54th Massachusetts Volunteers that stands on the Boston Common. Shaw was a Boston Brahmin, Lowell's relative by marriage, who led a regiment of African American soldiers in the assault on Fort Wagner in South Carolina and was buried with them in a common grave when their attack failed. Like Tate, Lowell admires his subject's courage and contrasts it to his own feckless complicity in modern urban society, choked with automobiles and parking garages, where warfare has been degraded to the mass horror of the mushroom cloud, and even Hiroshima has become and advertising image. Harry L. Watson, "Front Porch," *Southern Cultures*, (Summer 2005): 3.

STUDENT VERSION A (A case of deliberate plagiarism that is ethically and morally wrong)

The impulse to memorialize the Civil War dead does not stop with southerners. In 1964, roughly a century after Gettysburg, when the Civil Rights movement had brought new battles and more bloodshed to the southern countryside, the quintessential Yankee poet Robert Lowell celebrated the Confederacy's ancient opponents in his own elegy, "For the Union Dead." Instead of a confederate graveyard, Lowell contemplates the famed monument to Col. Robert Gould Shaw and the 54th Massachusetts Volunteers that stands on the Boston Common.

This passage reads well, and the unsuspecting reader will probably think so as well. However, the writer has borrowed the entire passage from Watson, so it is plagiarism of the first order. The writer implies to the reader that these sentences are an original creation when, actually, the sentences are stolen.

STUDENT VERSION B (Plagiarism that steals the ideas of another)

> Proper respect and ardor is needed in our modern society for remembering the dead of the American Civil War. Poet Robert Lowell's elegy, "For the Union Dead" commemorates the brave accomplishments of the 54th Massachusetts Volunteers, a regiment of African American soldiers who were led by the white commander Colonel Robert Gould Shaw. Their blood was shed together in a futile attempt to take Fort Wagner in South Carolina, and their burial is in a common grave.

This version borrows extensively from the original with paraphrasing. The writer has stolen the keys ideas of the original without credit of any sort. The words might belong to the student writer, but the ideas belong to Watson.

STUDENT VERSION C (Plagiarism that paraphrases improperly and offers a vague citation)

> Memorializing the fallen dead of the American Civil War is sadly a thing of the past. The celebrations of the first few generations after the end of the Civil war have been replaced by modernization and the fickleness of American society; we live in a world that is more consumed by individual consumption and driving a fancy automobile than remembering the bloodshed that preserved the rights and privileges we now possess (Watson 3).

This version is somewhat better. It provides a reference to Watson, but readers cannot know that the paraphrase contains far too much of Watson's language—words that should be enclosed within quotation marks. Also, the citation to Watson is ambiguous; when does the borrowing begin? The next version handles these matters in a better fashion.

STUDENT VERSION D (An acceptable version with a proper citation to a block quotation)

> The commemoration of the fallen dead of the American Civil War has diminished with our modern generation. While the parades, poetry, and memorials do not hold the same significance as they once did, the heroes are still held in reverence by many in

the South. According to Harry L. Watson, Director of the Center for
the Study of the American South, the desire to honor the Civil War
dead is not unique to southerners only:

> Yankee poet Robert Lowell celebrated the Confederacy's
> ancient opponents in his own elegy, "For the Union
> Dead." Instead of a confederate graveyard, Lowell
> contemplates the famed monument to Col. Robert Gould
> Shaw and the 54th Massachusetts Volunteers that stands
> on the Boston Common. (3)

This version represents a satisfactory handling of the source material. The
source is acknowledged at the outset of the borrowing, the passage has been
quoted as a block of material, and a page citation closes the material. Let's
suppose, however, that the writer does not wish to quote an entire passage.
The following example shows a paraphrased version.

STUDENT VERSION E (An acceptable version with a citation to the
source)

> Once honored with parades, poetry, and memorials, the heroic
> deeds of the fallen dead of the American Civil War have been
> forgotten. Our current generation is consumed with self-
> gratification and individualism that has no time for moldy
> monuments under the leaves of mighty oaks. According to Harry L.
> Watson, Director of the Center for the Study of the American
> South, the previous generation's remembrance of the past has been
> replaced by a "feckless complicity in modern urban society, choked
> with automobiles and parking garages, where warfare has been
> degraded to the mass horror of the mushroom cloud, and even
> Hiroshima has become and advertising image" (3).

This version also represents a satisfactory handling of the source material. In
this case, a direct quotation is employed, the author and the authority are
acknowledged and credited, and an introduction presented in the student's
own language precedes Watson's ideas.

6e Sharing Credit in Collaborative Projects

Joint authorship is seldom a problem in collaborative writing, especially
if each member of the project understands his or her role. Normally, all
members of the team receive equal billing and credit. However, it might serve

---

Required Instances for Citing a Source

1. An original idea derived from a source, whether quoted or para-phrased. This next sentence requires an in-text citation and quota-tion marks around a key phrase

   > Genetic engineering, by which a child's body shape and intellectual ability is predetermined, raises for one source "memories of Nazi attempts in eugenics" (Riddell 19).

2. Your summary of original ideas by a source

   > Genetic engineering has been described as the rearrangement of the genetic structure in animals or in plants, which is a technique that takes a section of DNA and reattaches it to another section (Rosenthal 19–20).

3. Factual information that is not common knowledge within the con-text of the course

   > Genetic engineering has its risks: a nonpathogenic organism might be converted into a pathogenic one or an undesirable trait might develop as a result of a mistake (Madigan 51).

4. Any exact wording copied from a source

   > Kenneth Woodward asserts that genetic engineering is "a high-stakes moral rumble that involves billions of dollars and affects the future" (68).

you well to predetermine certain issues with your peer group and the instructor:

- How will the project be judged and grades awarded?
- Will all members receive the same grade?
- Can a nonperformer be dismissed from the group?
- Should each member write a section of the work and everybody edit the whole?
- Should certain members write the draft and other members edit and load it onto a CD or onto the Web?

- Can the group work together via e-mail rather than meeting frequently for group sessions?

Resolving such issues at the beginning of a project can go a long way toward eliminating entanglements and disagreements later on. *Note*: Electronic publishing of your collaborative project on the Web raises other legal and ethical questions (see section 6g, page 100).

6f Honoring and Crediting Sources in Online Classrooms

A rapidly growing trend in education is the Web-based course or online course via e-mail. In general, you should follow the fair use doctrine of printed sources (see pages 90–91)—that is, give proper credit and reproduce only limited portions of the original.

The rules are still emerging, and even faculty members are often in a quandary about how to transmit information. For educational purposes, the rules are pretty slack, and most publishers have made their texts or portions thereof available on the Web. Plus, the copyrights of many works have expired, are now in the public domain, and are therefore free. In addition, many magazines and newspapers have made online versions of their articles available for free.

What you send back and forth with classmates and the instructor(s) has little privacy and even less protection. Rules are gradually emerging for electronic communication. In the meantime, abide by a few commonsense principles:

1. Credit sources in your online communications just as you would in a printed research paper, with some variations:
   - The author, creator, or Webmaster of the site
   - The title of the electronic article
   - The title of the Web site
   - The date of publication on the Web
   - The date you accessed the site
   - The address (URL)
2. Download to your file only graphic images and text from sites that have specifically offered users the right to download them.
3. Non-free graphic images and text, especially an entire Web site, should be mentioned in your text, even paraphrased and quoted in a limited manner, but not downloaded into your file. Instead, link to them or point to them with URL addresses. In that way, your reader can go find the material and count it as a supplement to your text.
4. Seek permission if you download substantive blocks of material. See section 6g on the next page if you wish to publish your work on the Web.
5. If in doubt, consult by e-mail with your instructor, the moderator of a listserv, or the author of an Internet site.

6g Seeking Permission to Publish Material on Your Web Site

If you have your own home page and Web site, you might wish to publish your papers on the Web. However, the moment you do so, you are *publishing* the work and putting it into the public domain. That act carries responsibilities. In particular, the *fair use* doctrine of the U.S. Code refers to the personal educational purposes of your usage. When you load onto the Internet borrowed images, text, music, or artwork, you are making that intellectual property available to everybody all over the world.

Short quotations, a few graphics, and a small quantity of illustrations to support your argument are examples of fair use. Permission is needed, however, if the amount you borrow is substantial. The borrowing cannot affect the market for the original work, and you cannot misrepresent it in any way. The courts are still refining the law. For example, would your use of three Doonesbury comic strips be substantial? Yes, if you reproduce them in full. Would it affect the market for the comic strip? Perhaps. Follow these guidelines:

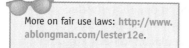

More on fair use laws: http://www.ablongman.com/lester12e.

- Seek permission for copyrighted material you publish within your Web article. Most authors will grant you free permission. The problem is tracking down the copyright holder.
- If you make the attempt to get permission and if your motive for using the material is *not for profit,* it's unlikely you will have any problem with the copyright owner. The owner would have to prove that your use of the image or text caused him or her financial harm.
- You may publish without permission works that are in the public domain, such as a section of Hawthorne's *The Scarlet Letter* or a speech by the president from the White House.
- Document any and all sources that you feature on your Web site.
- If you provide hypertext links to other sites, you may need permission to do so. Some sites do not want their address clogged by inquiring students. However, right now the Internet rules on access are being freely interpreted.
- Be prepared for people to visit your Web site and even borrow from it. Decide beforehand how you will handle requests for use of your work, especially if it includes your creative efforts in poetry, art, music, or graphic design.

YOUR RESEARCH PROJECT

1. Begin now to maintain a systematic scrutiny of what you borrow from your sources. Remember that direct quotation reflects the voice of your source and that paraphrase reflects your voice. Just be certain, with paraphrase, that you don't borrow the exact wording of the original.

2. Look at your college bulletin and the student handbook. Do they say anything about plagiarism? Do they address the matter of copyright protection?

3. Consult your writing instructor whenever you have a question about your use of a source. Writing instructors at the freshman level are there to serve you and help you avoid plagiarising (among other responsibilities).

4. If you think you might publish your paper on the Web and if it contains substantial borrowing from a source, such as five or six cartoons from the *New Yorker* magazine, begin now to seek permission for reproducing the material. In your letter or e-mail, give your name, school, the subject of your research paper, the material you want to borrow, and how you will use it. You might copy or attach the page(s) of your paper in which the material appears.

7 Finding and Evaluating Sources

The research paper assignment requires you to bring outside sources into your paper, so it only makes good sense to choose the most reliable and well-written sources you can find. We discussed this matter in Chapters 3 and 4, but further review is certainly in order.

With your research and writing, you will enter the intellectual discussions found in numerous places, but questions will arise quickly during your reading:

- How do I find and evaluate the best, most appropriate sources?
- How can I evaluate a source by analyzing its parts?
- How do I respond to it?

One answer to all three questions is this: Be skeptical and cautious. Don't accept every printed word as the truth. Constantly review and verify to your own satisfaction the words of your sources, especially in this age of electronic publication. It is wise to consider every article on the Internet as suspect until you verify its sponsoring organization and scholarly intent (see especially pages 36–37 for guidelines on judging the value of Internet articles).

Your task is twofold: (1) You must read and personally evaluate the sources for your own benefit as a writer, and (2) you must present them to your reader in your text as validated and authentic sources. This chapter offers a few tips on those two responsibilities.

> **HINT:** Some student researchers photocopy entire journal articles and carry an armload of books from the library. Such diligence is misplaced. The quality of your citations and the way you position them far outweigh the quantity of your source materials.

7a Finding Reliable Sources

Several resources are readily at hand to guide you in finding reliable sources.

Your instructors. Do not hesitate to ask your instructor for help in finding sources. Instructors know the field, know the best writers, and can provide a brief list to get you started. Sometimes instructors will even pull books from their office shelves to give you a starting point.

102

Librarians. Nobody knows the resources of the library like the professionals. They are evaluated on how well they meet your needs. If you ask for help, they will often walk into the stacks with you to find the appropriate reference books or relevant journal articles.

The library. The college library provides the scholarly sources—the best books, certainly, but also the appropriate databases and the important journals—in your field of study. As we discussed in Chapter 3, the library databases are grounded in scholarship and, in general, they are not available to the general public on the Web. Your access is by your student identification. A public library may have, but seldom does have, the scholarly resources of an academic library.

The date. Try to use recent sources. A book may appear germane to your work, but if its copyright date is 1975, the content has probably been replaced by recent research and current developments. Scientific and technical topics *always* require up-to-date research. Learn to depend on monthly and quarterly journals as well as books.

Choices. An inverted pyramid shows you a progression from excellent sources to less reliable sources. The pyramid chart does not ask you to dismiss items at the bottom, but it indicates that sources at the top are generally more reliable and therefore preferred.

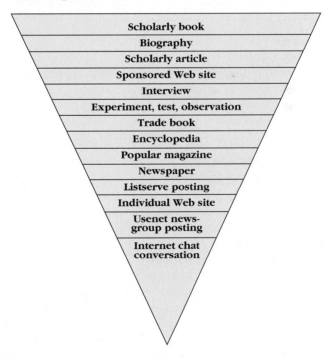

Scholarly Book

A college library is a repository for scholarly books—technical and scientific works, doctoral dissertations, publications of university presses, and textbooks. These sources offer in-depth discussions and careful documentation of the evidence. Two works will help you evaluate a book:

Book Review Digest provides an evaluation of several thousand books each year. Arranged alphabetically, it features summaries and brief quotations from the reviews to uncover the critical reception of the work.

The Booklist, a monthly magazine that reviews new books for librarians, includes brief summaries and recommendations.

Book reviews hidden within magazines and journals can be found by using these sources:

Book Review Index will send you to reviews in 225 magazines and journals.

Index to Book Reviews in the Humanities indexes book reviews in history, philosophy, literature, art, and similar fields.

Index to Book Reviews in the Social Sciences provides book reviews in education, psychology, political science, and similar fields.

Current Book Review Citations gives an author-title index to book reviews in more than 1,000 periodicals.

Another quick source of the review is the computer. One student in Caribbean Studies used her library to access Project Muse to find a review on the writer Jamaica Kincaid. Using the site's search mechanism, she found this listing:

Reviews
Forbes, Curdella.
Writing the Autobiography of My Father (review) [<u>Access article in HTML</u>] [<u>Access article in PDF</u>] *Subjects:*
Kincaid, Jamaica. Mr. Potter.
Chauffeurs—Fiction.

Clicking on the access link took the student to the book review by Curdell Forbes on Jamaica Kincaid's book *Mr. Potter.* A portion of the review is reproduced below to show you that book reviews can provide penetration into the essence of a text.

Writing the Autobiography of My Father
Curdella Forbes
Mr. Potter, **Jamaica Kincaid.** New York: Farrar, Strauss and Giroux, 2002. ISBN: 0374214948

A man, hungry, unable to read or write, curses God. He dies violently, still cursing, howling at history. His offspring, unacknowledged, perpetuate their father's bequest of material and mental poverty. Out of this erasure of history emerges one son who, not being able to read or write or (therefore) reflect on his own being, "has a line drawn through him." He nevertheless produces a daughter, who writes his story. By shaping him in terms of the written word, she grants him recognition, names him with a name, invites us to "Hear Mr. Potter! Touch Mr. Potter! See Mr. Potter"—reference to whom now begins every sentence of his own (unknown to him) redacted memoir.

Rendered in stunningly compelling prose, Jamaica Kincaid's *Mr. Potter* recalls music and song—fugue, religious litany, (parodic) biblical enunciation of genealogies, Nordic lament, children's nursery rhyme, the *Weltanschauung* of T. S. Eliot's *Wasteland. Mr. Potter* is also elegy and revenge code; history (auto/biography) and myth; a project of identification and the deliberate negation of identity; a discourse about writing and the erasure of sentences.

The hologrammatic "portrait" that this matrix of discursive possibilities overlays is Kincaid's father, who "has been the central figure in [her] life without either of [them] knowing it." The book is the latest in the cycle of autobiographical and putatively fictional writings about Kincaid's relations with her family, writings through which Kincaid has sought to work through the problematics of a personal, literary, and historical (West Indian) identity. These texts represent a series of journeys that paradoxically end where they begin: with the conviction that a radical form of self-empowerment is necessary and capable of achievement only through the rejection of antecedents— that is to say, through the credo of a new self in imperative disjunction from the histories from which it was produced. With *My Brother,* the motif of the mother as the point of severance began to be mediated; with *Mr. Potter,* which might well have been subtitled *The Autobiography of My Father,* the paternal connection is examined.

Biography

The librarian can help you find an appropriate printed biography from among the thousands available. Short biographies appear in such works as *Contemporary Authors, Dictionary of American Negro Biography,* and *Who's Who in Philosophy.* Longer critical biographies are devoted to the life of one person, such as Richard Ellmann's *Oscar Wilde,* a study of the British poet and playwright, and Alf Mapp's *Thomas Jefferson: A Strange Case of Mistaken Identity,* which interprets the life and times of the former president. To find a critical biography, use the electronic card catalog at the library. You can also find biographies on the Internet. Most notable figures have several Web sites devoted to them that include articles by and about them.

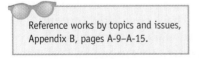
Reference works by topics and issues, Appendix B, pages A-9–A-15.

Refer to biography for these reasons:

1. To verify the standing and reputation of somebody you want to paraphrase or quote in your paper.

2. To provide biographical details in your introduction. For example, the primary topic may be Carl Jung's psychological theories of the unconscious, but information about Jung's career might be appropriate in the paper.
3. To discuss a creative writer's life in relation to his or her work. That is, Jamaica Kincaid's personal life may shed some light on your reading of her stories or novels.

Scholarly Article

A scholarly article usually appears in a journal you access through the library's databases. With a journal article, you may feel confident in its authenticity because the authors of journal articles write for academic honor, they document all sources, and they publish through university presses and academic organizations that use a jury to judge an article before its publication. Thus, a journal article about child abuse found in *Child Development* or in *Journal of Marriage and the Family* should be reliable, but an article about child abuse in a popular magazine may be less reliable in its facts and opinions. Usually, but not in every case, you can identify a journal in these ways:

1. The journal does not have a colorful cover; in fact, the table of contents is often displayed on the cover.
2. No colorful drawings or photography introduce each journal article, just a title and the name of the author(s).
3. The word *journal* often appears in the title (e.g., *The Journal of Sociology*).
4. The yearly issues of a journal are bound into a book.
5. Usually, the pages of a journal are numbered continuously through all issues for a year (unlike magazines, which are paged anew with each issue).

Yet some magazines are noted for their quality—*Atlantic Monthly, Scientific Review, Psychology Today,* and many others. The major newspapers—*New York Times, Chicago Sun-Times, Wall Street Journal,* and others—hire the best writers and columnists, so quality articles can be found in both printed newspapers and newspapers online.

Sometimes you may face a bewildering array of articles, and you will wonder which are the best. One way to evaluate a set of articles is with *citation searching,* which will search for authors who have been cited repeatedly in the literature. For example, Norman Berkowitz, while researching for sources on the world's water supply, saw repeated references to Sandra Postel and S. Postel, in these four citations:

> Postel, S. 1997. *Last Oasis: Facing Water Scarcity.* 2 ed. New York: W. W. Norton.
> Postel, Sandra. *Dividing the Waters: Food Security, Ecosystem Health, and the New Politics of Scarcity.* Washington (DC): Worldwatch Institute.
> Postel, S., Carpenter S. 1997. Freshwater ecosystem services. Pages 195–214 in Daily, G.C., ed. *Nature's Services: Societal Dependence on Natural Ecosystems.* Washington (DC): Island Press.

Postel, S., Daily, G.C., Ehrlich, P.R. 1996. Human appropriation of renew-able freshwater. *Science* 271: 785–788.

Common sense told Berkowitz to search out something by Postel; that she is respected in this field was evident in these numerous citations in the literature. As a result, he cited from two works by Postel in his paper (see pages 236–247).

Three reference books provide citation indexes:

Arts and Humanities Citation Index (AHCI) 1977–date
Science Citation Index (SCI) 1961–date
Social Sciences Citation Index (SSCI) 1966–date

Sponsored Web Site

Online article, annotated by a student, page 115.

The Internet supplies both excellent information and some that is questionable in value. You must make judgments about the validity of these materials. On that note, see section 3b for a set of guidelines. Ask yourself a few questions about any article from a Web site:

Is it appropriate to my work?
Is it reliable and authoritative?
Is it sponsored by an institution or organization?

Usually, just the name of a Web site offers clues about its validity. For exam-ple, how would you rank the following sites as most reliable for information?

Spank! Youth Culture Online: An Ezine for Youth and Teens
Project Muse: Scholarly Journals Online
www.factmonster.com
CBC News: Canada's Online Information Service
Thomas: Legislative Information on the Internet, sponsored by the Library of Congress

Probably you picked Project Muse and Thomas first, with CBC News third—all good choices.

Interview

Interviews with knowledgeable people provide excellent information for a research paper. Whether conducted in person, by telephone, or by e-mail, the interview brings a personal, expert perspective to your work. The key element, of course, is the expertise of the person. For full details about con-ducting an interview, see section 5a, pages 77–79. For one student's use of an interview, see Valerie Nesbitt-Hall's research paper, pages 329–330.

Experiment, Test, or Observation

Gathering your own data for research is a staple in many fields, especially the sciences. An experiment will bring primary evidence to your paper as you explain your hypothesis, give the test results, and discuss the implications of your findings. For a full discussion on conducting scientific investigation, with guidelines and details on format, see section 5e, pages 84–86.

Trade Book

CNC Robotics: Build Your Own Workshop Bot and *A Field Guide to Industrial Landscapes* are typical titles of nonfiction trade books to be found in bookstores and some public libraries, but not usually in a college library. Designed for commercial consumption, trade books seldom treat with depth a scholarly subject. Trade books have specific targets—the cook, the gardener, the antique dealer. In addition, trade books, in general, receive no rigorous prepublication scrutiny like that of scholarly books and textbooks. For example, if your topic is "dieting" with a focus on "fad diets," you will find plenty of diet books at the local bookstore and on commercial Web sites. However, pass them by in favor of serious discussions backed by careful research that you will find by searching your library's databases.

Encyclopedia

By design, encyclopedias contain brief surveys of well-known persons, events, places, and accomplishments. They will serve you well during preliminary investigation, but most instructors prefer that you go beyond encyclopedias in order to cite from scholarly books and journal articles. Encyclopedias seldom have the critical perspective you can gain from books and journal articles. There are some exceptions, of course, because specialized encyclopedias (see page 62) often have in-depth articles by noted scholars.

Popular Magazine

Like trade books, magazines have a targeted audience—young women, wrestling fans, computer connoisseurs, travelers. The articles are written rather quickly and seldom face critical review by a panel of experts. Therefore, exercise caution when reading a popular commercial magazine. However, some magazines target an intellectual audience and thereby have a superior quality with academic merit; these include *Atlantic Monthly, Scientific Review, Astronomy, Smithsonian, Discover, Harper's,* and the *New Yorker.* In general, college libraries house the intellectual magazines, but they can also be found at most chain bookstores, such as Borders and Barnes & Noble.

Newspaper

Some newspaper articles are not carefully researched or peer reviewed, but major newspapers such as the *New York Times*, the Los Angeles *Times*, and the *Wall Street Journal* offer carefully fact-checked information and rigorously researched stories. Generally, newspapers offer an excellent source of information, especially of local information that may not be found elsewhere.

Listserv

E-mail information via listserv deserves consideration when it focuses on an academic issue, such as British Romantic literature or, more specifically, Shelley's poetry. In many cases, listservs originate from a college or scholarly organization. In fact, many instructors establish their own listserv sites for individual classes. Online courses usually feature a listserv site for exchange of ideas and peer review. These listservs can be a great way to seek out possible topics and learn what literature teachers or sociologists are talking about these days. Caution: Use the listserv to generate ideas, not as a source for facts to use in quotations.

Individual Web Site

A person's home page provides a publication medium for anybody who presumes to a knowledge they do or do not possess. You can't avoid home pages because they pop up on search engines, but you *can* approach them with caution. For example, one student, investigating the topic "fad diets," searched the Web, only to find mostly commercial sites that were blatant in their commercial attempts to sell something and home pages that described personal battles with weight loss. Caution is vital. On this point see 3a, pages 34–37.

Usenet

Usenet newsgroups post information on a site. Like call-in radio shows, they invite opinions from a vast cross section of people, some reliable and some not. In most cases, participants employ a fake pseudonymous username, rendering their ideas useless for a documented paper.

Internet Chat Conversations

Chat rooms have almost no value for academic research. In most cases, you don't even know who you are chatting with, and the conversations are seldom about scholarly issues.

7b Selecting a Mix of Primary and Secondary Sources

Primary sources include novels, speeches, eyewitness accounts, interviews, letters, autobiographies, and the results of original research. Feel free to quote often from a primary source if it has direct relevance to your discussion. If you examine a poem by Dylan Thomas, you must quote the poem. If you examine President George W. Bush's domestic policies on healthcare, you must quote from White House documents.

Secondary sources are writings *about* the primary sources, *about* an author, or *about* somebody's accomplishments. Examples of secondary sources are a report on a presidential speech, a review of new scientific findings, and an analysis of a poem. A biography provides a secondhand view of the life of a notable person. A history book interprets events. These

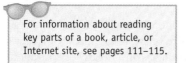

For information about reading key parts of a book, article, or Internet site, see pages 111–115.

evaluations, analyses, or interpretations provide ways of looking at primary works, events, and lives.

Do not quote liberally from secondary sources. Be selective. Use a well-worded sentence, not the entire paragraph. Incorporate a key phrase into your text, not eight or nine lines.

The subject area of a research paper determines in part the nature of the source materials. Use the following chart as a guide:

Citing from Primary and Secondary Sources

	Primary Sources	*Secondary Sources*
Literature	Novels, poems, plays, short stories, letters, diaries, manuscripts, autobiographies, films, videos of live performances	Journal articles, reviews, biographies, critical books about writers and their works
Government, Political Science, History	Speeches, writings by presidents and others, the *Congressional Record,* reports of agencies and departments, documents written by historic figures	Newspaper reports, news magazines, political journals and newsletters, journal articles, history books
Social Sciences	Case studies, findings from surveys and questionnaires, reports of social workers, psychiatrists, and lab technicians	Commentary and evaluations in reports, documents, journal articles, and books
Sciences	Tools and methods, experiments, findings from tests and experiments, observations, discoveries, and test patterns	Interpretations and discussions of test data as found in journals and books (scientific books, which are quickly dated, are less valuable than up-to-date journals)
Fine Arts	Films, paintings, music, sculptures, as well as reproductions and synopses of these designed for research purposes	Evaluations in journal articles, critical reviews, biographies, and critical books about the authors and their works

	Primary Sources	*Secondary Sources*
Business	Market research and testing, technical studies and investigations, drawings, designs, models, memorandums and letters, computer data	Discussion of the business world in newspapers, business magazines, journals, government documents, and books
Education	Pilot studies, term projects, sampling results, tests and test data, surveys, interviews, observations, statistics, and computer data	Analysis and evaluation of educational experimentation in journals, pamplets, books, and reports

7c   Evaluating Sources

Confronted by several books and articles, many writers have trouble determining the value of material and the contribution it will make to the research paper. To save time, you must be selective in your reading. To serve your reader, cite only carefully selected material that is pertinent to the argument. To void the loss of your own voice, do not dump large blocks of quotation into the paper.

Evaluating the Key Parts of an Article

Look closely at these parts of any article that looks promising.

1. The **title.** Look for the words that have relevance to your topic before you start reading the article. For example, "Children and Parents" may look ideal for child abuse research until you read the subtitle: "Children and Parents: Growing Up in New Guinea."
2. An **abstract.** Reading an abstract is the best way to ascertain if an essay or a book will serve your specific needs. Some are available at the beginning of printed articles; others are provided by abstracting services (e.g., *Psychological Abstracts*). Most articles found through the library's databases will feature an abstract that you should read before printing or downloading the entire article. Save a tree, read before printing.
3. The **opening paragraphs.** If the opening of an article shows no relevance to your study, abandon it.
4. The topic sentence of each paragraph of the body. These first sentences, even if you scan them hastily, will give you a digest of the author's main points.
5. The **closing paragraph(s).** If the opening of an article seems promising, skim the closing for relevance.
6. **Author credits.** Learn something about the credentials of the writer. Magazine articles often provide brief biographical profiles of authors.

Journal articles and Internet home pages generally include the author's academic affiliation and credentials.

Read an entire article only if a quick survey encourages you to further investigation. Student Norman Berkowitz scanned an article for his paper on the world's water supply. Figure 7.1 shows how he highlighted key phrases with

Voice: The Tide Is Rising and the World Is Coming to Your Front Door

Ray Dasmann as Interviewed by David Kupfer

When an environment has become unbalanced, polluted, or devastated to the point where it is no longer healthy or able to sustain life, restoration becomes necessary. Then you must ask, what is it you are trying to restore?

This writer and the magazine are environmentally sensitive and conservative.

Ecosystems are always changing, whether you are doing anything or not: What direction are they going in, and why? These basic questions have to be kept in mind from the start. Most restoration aims to regain the condition existing when the Indians inhabited this land prior to the Euro-Caucasians. The question is, is that what you want? Native Americans also deliberately managed the environment.

Nature changes all the time. So what do we want from it?

We are at the point where we have to think globally. There is no option. The tide is rising and the world is coming to your front door. It used to seem rather simple: just create a national Park. But that is only the beginning. You must get people involved—not just local people, but all people interested in the place. Here in California, I see an opportunity for restoring the land to the condition in which the Euro-Americans "inherited" it from the Native Americans. But we must consider how we want to restore the land.

We must think globally about conditions elsewhere that will affect us in time.

I believe the biggest challenge will be restoring nearshore marine ecosystems. This is one area that is receiving considerable damage. If you're looking for biodiversity, that is where you will find it. Marine systems are far more diverse than terrestrial ones in that there is a tremendous amount of life we are affecting, a lot of which we cannot even see. And of course climate change is hitting the oceans particularly hard. So we can sit around and watch Manhattan gradually sink into the water or we can do something about it. If you're living on a Pacific island, that's no joke.

We must restore the marine ecosystems.

He uses scare tactics to excite anybody living on one of the coasts or an island.

We know how to solve these problems, without a doubt. To begin with, I believe we must restore a sense of individual responsibility and involvement, and get away from the idea that conservation is the responsibility of somebody else—the federal government, the state, the corporations, the rich. We must each face up to the need to develop an ecologically sustainable way of living; we need to look at our patterns of

We need to restore individual responsibility and involvement.

(continued)

■■■ **FIGURE 7.1**
Article with highlighting and marginal comments on items that the student considered important to his thesis.
Source: Earth Island Journal 18 (2003): 48.

consumption and behavior, and shed those practices that contribute to the continuing destruction of nature.

An essential individual change is the need to stop thinking of living beings as things to be exploited or manipulated and recognize that they are partners in a community of fellow beings. We must start to develop that reverence for life that Albert Schweitzer called for long ago. We need to lose some of our much-vaunted objectivity, which is useful only for certain purposes, and develop a greater subjectivity, empathy, feeling. This does not mean we stop using plants or animals for food, but it begins to prevent gross excess.

A third step for those who are in a position to do it—and not everybody is—is finding like-minded people and developing ecologically sustainable communities that can unhook themselves from the waste- and pollution-producing systems that prevail in the society at large.

These are only beginnings, but they are essential beginnings. Other things must happen also. The government, corporations, industries, and consumer society are still there. They have to be influenced. Throughout the nation what is needed is an increasing degree of local and regional self-sufficiency, leading to self-sufficiency for the nation as a whole. There is no need to give up trade and commerce, or to cease consumption of things that are produced elsewhere, but there *is* a need to get out of a state of dependence on the exploitation of other people, places, and communities.

> We must realize that we are partners with the animals and all elements of nature. Somehow, we must develop ecologically sustainable communities that avoid any systems that cause pollution.
>
> We need self-sufficiency of the nation as a whole.
>
> Somehow, we must stop the exploitation of people, places, and communities locally and worldwide.

■■■■ **FIGURE 7.1** *(continued)*

marginal comments that were germane to his study. Note that he recognizes the bias expressed throughout the environmental magazine *Earth Island Journal*.

Reading the Key Parts of a Book

A **book** requires you to survey several items beyond those listed on page 111 for articles:

1. The **table of contents.** A book's table of contents may reveal chapters that pertain to your topic. Often, only one chapter is useful. For example, Richard Ellmann's book *Oscar Wilde* devotes one chapter, "The Age of Dorian," to Wilde's *The Picture of Dorian Gray*. If your research focuses on this novel, then the chapter, not the entire book, will demand your attention.
2. The **book jacket,** if one is available. For example, the jacket to Richard Ellmann's *Oscar Wilde* says:

   Ellmann's *Oscar Wilde* has been almost twenty years in the work, and it will stand, like his universally admired *James Joyce,* as the definitive life. The book's emotional resonance, its riches of authentic color and conversation, and the subtlety of its critical illuminations give dazzling life to this portrait of the complex man, the charmer, the great play-wright, the daring champion of the primacy of art.

Such information can stimulate the reading and notetaking from this important book.

3. The **foreword, preface,** or **introduction.** An author's *preface* or *introduction* serves as a critical overview of the book, pinpointing the primary subject of the text and the particular approach taken. For example, Ellmann opens his book *Oscar Wilde* by saying:

> Oscar Wilde: we have only to hear the great name to anticipate that what will be quoted as his will surprise and delight us. Among the writers identified with the 1890s, Wilde is the only one whom everyone still reads. The various labels that have been applied to the age—Aestheticism, Decadence, the Beardsley period—ought not to conceal that fact that our first association with it is Wilde, refulgent, majestic, ready to fall.

This introduction describes the nature of the book: Ellmann will portray Wilde as the dominating literary figure of the 1890s. A *foreword* is often written by somebody other than the author. It is often insightful and worthy of quotation.

4. The **index.** A book's index lists names and terms with the page on which they are mentioned within the text. For example, the index to *Oscar Wilde* lists about eighty items under *The Picture of Dorian Gray,* among them:

> homosexuality and, 312, 318
> literature and painting in, 312–131
> magazine publication of, 312, 319, 320
> possible sources for, 311
> underlying legend of, 314–315
> W's Preface to, 311, 315, 322, 335
> W's self-image in, 312, 319
> writing of, 310–314

An index, by its detailed listing, can determine the relevance of the book to your research.

Evaluating the Key Parts of an Internet Article

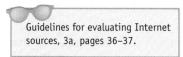

Guidelines for evaluating Internet sources, 3a, pages 36–37.

The techniques listed above for evaluating periodical articles (page 111) apply also to Internet articles. In addition, examine:

1. The **home page,** if there is one. Prefer sites sponsored by universities and professional organizations. You may have to truncate the URL to find the home page where such information is featured. For example, this URL: **www.theatlantic.com/unbound/wordpolice/three/** can be truncated to www.theatlantic.com/, which is the magazine's home page.

2. The **hypertext links** to other sites whose quality can again be determined by the domain tags *.edu, .org, .gov.* Be wary of sites that have the tag *.com.*

Figure 7.2 on the next page displays a sponsored Web site Norman Berkowitz discovered in his search for sources about conservation and the world's water supply. It shows an online article by David Western accompanied by the student's marginal notes to key ideas. Examine your Internet articles in like manner.

Spring 2000

The Delicate Balance: Environment, Economics, Development

DAVID WESTERN

Conservation in a Human-Dominated World

Forging a tangible connection among environment, development, and welfare is a formidable challenge, given the complex global interactions and slow response times involved. The task is made all the harder by quickening change, including new ideas about conservation and how it can best be done. Present policies and practices, vested in government and rooted in a philosophy that regards humanity and nature as largely separate realms, do little to encourage public participation or to reinforce conservation through individual incentives and civil responsibility. The challenge will be to make conservation into a household want and duty. This will mean moving the focus of conservation away from central regulation and enforcement and toward greater emphasis on local collaboration based on fairness, opportunity, and responsibility. Given encouragement, such initiatives will help reduce extinction levels and the isolation of parks by expanding biodiversity conservation in human-dominated landscapes.

    The problems that beset current conservation efforts are daunting. Three factors in particular threaten steady economic and social progress as well as conservation: poverty, lack of access rights linked to conservation responsibilities, and environmental deterioration. Poverty and lack of access rights, especially in Africa, will keep populations growing and will fuel Rwandan-like emigration and political unrest. With short-term survival as its creed, poverty accelerates environmental degradation and habitat fragmentation. The peasant lacking fuel and food will clear the forest to plant crops or will poach an elephant if there is no alternative. So, for example, tropical forests–home to half the world's species–are being lumbered, burned, grazed, and settled. Forest destruction precipitates local wrangles between indigenous and immigrant communities over land and squabbles between North and South over carbon sinks and global warming.

    We cannot rely on the trickle-down effect of economic development and liberalism to eradicate poverty, solve access problems, or curb environmental losses–at least not soon. It was, after all, unfettered consumerism in the West that killed off countless animal species, stripped the forests, and polluted the air and water. And the same consumer behavior and commercial excesses are still evident, depleting old-growth forests and fighting pollution legislation every step of the way.

Western addresses the problems of effective conservation.

Instead of expecting the government to handle conservation, people must do it on their own as a civic responsibility.

Poverty must be controlled.

He says consumer behavior has destroyed the environment, and it's human behavior that must change.

FIGURE 7.2 Online article from Issues in Science and Technology Online.

7d Outlining a Source

You can frame an outline to capture an author's primary themes by listing statements that reveal the major issues and any supporting ideas. A quick outline of the Dasmann article, pages 112–113, might look like this:

> Restoration becomes necessary when the environment becomes polluted.
>
> We must think globally because the entire earth has become unbalanced.
>
> The land needs restoration.
>
> Marine ecosystems need immediate attention.
>
> Three steps are necessary for reviving the environment.
>
> Restore individual responsibility and involvement.
>
> Stop manipulating and exploiting natural resources.
>
> Develop communities that sustain the ecology.
>
> Develop local and regional self-sufficiency to end exploitation of our natural resources.

This quickly drawn outline by Norman Berkowitz provides an overview of the article with the issues clearly labeled. Now Berkowitz can go in search of other sources that address these issues.

7e Summarizing a Source

A summary condenses into a brief note the general nature of a source. Writing a summary forces you to grasp the essence of the material. You might even use the summary in your paper, and it could serve as the heart of an annotated bibliography, which is a citation with a summary attached (see pages 117–119). Here is Norman Berkowitz's summary of the Dasmann article (see pages 112–113).

> Ray Dasmann offers his views on environmental damage and what each of us can do to correct it. He says we must think in terms of the entire earth, not just our little neighborhood, and three events must occur. We must each accept individual responsibility for the environment and get involved in protecting it. We must change our attitude about exploiting the natural resources and develop communities that will sustain the ecological balance. And we must have local self-sufficiency that will lead to national awareness for the protection of people, places, and communities.

That summary can serve the researcher as he develops the paper, and it can become a part of the paper as part of the review of the literature (see pages 120–126).

Responding to a Source

- Read and make marginal notes on your sources. See pages 111–115 for details and an example.
- Search out scholarly materials—books and journals—by accessing your college library's resources. Don't depend entirely on the Internet.
- If appropiate, use a mix of quotations from primary sources, such as a novel, as well as paraphrases and quotations from secondary sources. See pages 109–111 for a list of both types.
- Assess the nature of the source for any bias it might contain. See page 102 and pages 171–173 for details.
- Read and highlight the key parts of the source, whether it be an article, book, or Internet site. See pages 111–115 for further details.
- Outline key ideas to identify the issues. See page 116 for an example.
- Write a summary that captures the essence of the article. See pages 116–117 for an example.

7f Preparing an Annotated Bibliography

An *annotation* is a summary of the contents of a book or article. A *bibliography* is a list of sources on a selected topic. Thus, an annotated bibliography does two important things: (1) it gives a bibliographic list of a selection of sources, and (2) it summarizes the contents of each book or article. Writing an annotated bibliography may at first appear to be busywork, but it will help you evaluate the strength of your sources.

The annotated bibliography that follows summarizes a few sources on the issue of tanning, tanning beds, lotions, and the dangers of skin cancer.

Levenson 1

Norman Levenson

Professor Davidson

English 1020

24 January 2006

Annotated Bibliography

Cohen, Russell. "Tanning Trouble: Teens Are Using Tanning Beds in

Record Numbers." <u>Scholastic Choices</u> 18 (2003): 23–28. Cohen warns that tanning beds "can be just as dangerous as the sun's rays" (23). The writer explains that tanning salons are not well regulated, so the amount of exposure can be really dangerous. The writer also explains how skin type affects tanning and the dangers of cancer.

Conforth, Tracee. "Tanning Booths: Are They Worth the Risk?" Women's Health. 17 Jan. 2006 <http://womenshealth.about.com/cs/ azhealthtopics/a/tanboothworthit.htm>. This site raises the central question of whether tanning booths are less dangerous than obtaining a tan from the sun. Most laypeople agree that solar radiation is damaging to our skin. The fact is that they expect their skin to pass through these damaging changes. For these individuals, a deep, golden glow offsets the risk of skin cancer.

Geller, Alan C., et al. "Use of Sunscreen, Sunburning Rates, and Tanning Bed Use Among More than 10,000 U. S. Children and Adolescents." Pediatrics 109 (2002): 1009–15. The objective of this study was to examine the psychosocial variables associated with teens seeking suntans. It collected data from questionnaires submitted by 10,079 boys and girls 12 to 18 years old. It concluded that many children are at risk for skin cancer because of failure to use sunscreen.

"Skin Care for Your Skin Type." Harvard Medical School. 1 Apr. 2005. 18 Jan. 2006 <http://www.intelihealth.com/IH/ihtIH?d= dmtContent&c=283481&p=~br,IHW|~st,24479|~r,WSIHW000|~b,*|>. This site features Harvard Medical School's Consumer Health Information. In this article, information is given about the three main types of skin cancers as well as advice about tanning, including the use of sunscreen of SPF 15 or higher, use of suntan lotions, the effects of the sun, and the dangers of skin cancer.

"Skin Protection—My Teen Likes to Tan." St. Louis Children's Hospital. Mar. 2005. 17 Jan. 2006. This site quotes Susan Mallory, the director of dermatology at St. Louis Children's Hospital, and Registered Nurse Ann Leonard, who both offer warning against the use of tanning beds. Rather than damaging the skin with sun

or tanning beds, the two experts suggest the use of tanning
sprays or lotions.

"Sunny Days." <u>Health Watch</u>. The U of Texas Southwestern Medical
Center at Dallas. 2006. 21 Jan. 2006. This article warns against
sun worship and skipping sunscreen. Experts suggest more public
education and warnings, for tanning damages the structure of the
skin and promotes sagging skin and wrinkles in later life. Dr.
Sarah Weitzul, a UT Southwestern dermatologist, says proper
sunscreen use is the key to saving your skin from the sun.

Zazinski, Janic. "A Legion of Ladies' Lesions." <u>Research Briefs</u>. Boston
U. 15 May 2003. 18 Jan. 2006. This article cites Dr. Marie-France
Demierre, a professor of dermatology, who laments the use of
tanning beds by young women. In truth, women are joining men
in contracting and dying of melanoma, in great part because of
tanning beds. Demierre and Zazinski warn youngsters against
addiction to tanning beds and sun worship.

7g Preparing a Review of the Literature on a Topic

The *review of literature* presents a set of summaries in essay form for two purposes:

1. It helps you investigate the topic because it forces you to examine and then describe how each source addresses the problem.
2. It organizes and classifies the sources in some reasonable manner for the benefit of the reader.

Thus, you should relate each source to your central subject, and you should group the sources according to their support of your thesis. For example, the brief review that follows explores the literature on the subject of gender communication. It classifies the sources under a progression of headings: the issues, the causes (both environmental and biological), the consequences for both men and women, and possible solutions.

You also will need to arrange the sources according to your selected categories or to fit your preliminary outline. Sometimes this task is as simple as grouping those sources that favor a course or action and those that oppose it. In other cases—let's say, in a paper on F. Scott Fitzgerald's *The Great Gatsby*—you may need to summarize sources on critics who examine Gatsby's character, others who study Daisy, and still others who write about Nick Carraway.

Like Kaci Holz in the paper below, you may wish to use headings that identify your various sections.

Kaci Holz

Dr. Bekus

April 23, 2006

English 1010

Gender Communication:

A Review of the Literature

Several theories exist about different male and female communication styles. These ideas have been categorized below to establish the issues, show causes for communication failures, the consequences for both men and women, and suggestions for possible solutions.

The Issues

Deborah Tannen, Ph.D., is a professor of sociolinguistics at Georgetown University. In her book <u>You Just Don't Understand: Men and Women in Conversation</u>, 2001, she claims there are basic gender patterns or stereotypes that can be found. Tannen says that men participate in conversations to establish "a hierarchical social order," while women most often participate in conversations to establish "a network of connections" (Tannen, <u>Don't Understand</u> 24–25). She distinguishes between the way women use "rapport-talk" and the way men use "report-talk" (74).

In similar fashion, Susan Basow and Kimberly Rubenfeld in "'Troubles Talk': Effects of Gender and Gender Typing," explore in detail the sex roles and how they determine and often control the speech of each gender. They notice that "women may engage in 'troubles talk' to enhance communication; men may avoid such talk to enhance autonomy and dominance" (186).

In addition, Kawa Patel asserts that men and women "use conversation for quite different purposes." He provides a "no" answer to the question in his title, "Do Men and Women Speak the Same Language?" He claims that women converse to develop and maintain connections, while men converse to claim their position in the hierarchy they see around them, Patel asserts that women are less likely to speak publicly than are men because women often perceive such speaking as putting oneself on display. A man, on the other hand, is usually comfortable with speaking publicly because that is how he establishes his status among others (Patel).

Similarly, masculine people are "less likely than androgynous individuals to feel grateful for advice" (Basow and Rubenfeld 186).

Julia T. Wood's book <u>Gendered Lives</u> claims that "male communication is characterized by assertion, independence, competitiveness, and confidence [while] female communication is characterized by deference, inclusivity, collaboration, and cooperation" (440). This list of differences describes why men and women have such opposing communication styles.

In another book, Tannen addresses the issue that boys, or men, "are more likely to take an oppositional stance toward other people and the world" and "are more likely to find opposition entertaining-to enjoy watching a good fight, or having one" (Tannen, <u>Argument</u> 166). Girls try to avoid fights.

Causes

Two different theories suggest causes for gender differences-the environment and biology.

<u>Environmental Causes</u>. Tammy James and Bethan Cinelli mention, "The way men and women are raised contributes to differences in conversation and communication..." (41).

Another author, Susan Witt, in "Parental Influence on Children's Socialization to Gender Roles," discusses the various findings that support the idea that parents have a great influence on their children during the development of their self-concept. She states, "Children learn at a very early age what it means to be a boy or a girl in our society" (253). She says that parents "[dress] infants in gender-specific colors, [give] gender-differentiated toys, and [expect] different behavior from boys and girls" (Witt 254).

Patel notices a cultural gap, defining culture as "shared meaning." He goes on to comment that problems come about because one spouse enters marriage with a different set of "shared meanings" than the other. The cultural gap affects the children. Patel also talks about the "Battle of the Sexes" as seen in conflict between men and women. Reverting back to his "childhood gender pattern" theory, Patel claims, "Men, who grew up in a hierarchical environment, are accustomed to conflict. Women, concerned more with relationship and connection, prefer the role of peacemaker."

Like Patel, Deborah Tannen also addresses the fact that men and women often come from different worlds and different influences. She says, "Even if they grow up in the same neighborhood, on the same block, or in the same house, girls and boys grow up in different worlds of words" (Tannen, Don't Understand 43).

Biological Causes. Though Tannen often addresses the environmental issue in much of her research, she also looks at the biological issue in her book The Argument Culture. Tannen states, "Surely a biological component plays a part in the greater use of antagonism among men, but cultural influence can override biological inheritance" (Tannen, Argument 205). She sums up the nature versus nurture issue by saying, "the patterns that typify women's and men's styles of opposition and conflict are the result of both biology and culture" (207).

Lillian Glass, another linguistics researcher, has a 1992 book called He Says, She Says: Closing the Communication Gap Between the Sexes. Glass addresses the issue that different hormones found in men's and women's bodies make them act differently and therefore communicate differently. She also discusses how brain development has been found to relate to sex differences.

Judy Mann says, "Most experts now believe that what happens to boys and girls is a complex interaction between slight biological differences and tremendously powerful social forces that begin to manifest themselves the minute the parents find out whether they are going to have a boy or a girl" (qtd. in McCluskey 6).

Consequences of Gender Differences

Now that we have looked at different styles of gender communication and possible causes of gender communication, let us look at the possible results. Morgan and Coleman relate that divorce is one of the most stressful events a person can experience. They expound upon this point by stating, "The decision to divorce is typically made with ambivalence, uncertainty and confusion. It is a difficult step. The family identity changes, and the identities of the individuals involved change as well."

Through various studies, Tannen has concluded that men and women have different purposes for engaging in communication. In the open forum that Deborah Tannen led in 2004 (on compact disc), she explains the different ways men and women handle communication throughout the day. She explains that a man constantly talks during his workday in order to impress those around him and to establish his status in the office. At home he wants peace and quiet. On the other hand, a woman is constantly cautious and guarded about what she says during her workday. Women try hard to avoid confrontation and avoid offending anyone with their language. So when a woman comes home from work she expects to be able to talk freely without having to guard her words. The consequence? The woman expects conversation, but the man is tired of talking (Tannen, He Said).

Solutions

Answers for better gender communication seem elusive. What can be done about this apparent gap in communication between genders? In his article published in Leadership, Jeffrey Arthurs offers the obvious suggestion that women should make an attempt to understand the male model of communication and that men should make an attempt to understand the female model of communication.

However, in his article "Speaking Across the Gender Gap," David Cohen mentions that experts didn't think it would be helpful to teach men to communicate more like women and women to communicate more like men. This attempt would prove unproductive because it would go against what men and women have been taught since birth. Rather than change the genders to be more like one another, we could simply try to "understand" each other better.

In addition, Carolyn Crozier makes this observation, "The idea that women should translate their experiences into the male code in order to express themselves effectively...is an outmoded, inconsistent, subservient notion that should no longer be given credibility in modern society." She suggests three things we can change: 1.) Change the norm by which leadership success is judged, 2.) Redefine what we mean by power, and 3.) Become more sensitive to the places and times when inequity and inequality occur (Crozier). Similarly, Patel offers advice to help combat "cross-cultural" fights. He suggests: 1.) Identify your fighting style, 2.) Agree on rules of engagement, and 3.) Identify the real issue behind the conflict (Patel).

McCluskey claims men and women need honest communication that shows respect, and they must "manage conflict in a way that maintains the relationship and gets the job done" (5). She says, "To improve relationships and interactions between men and women, we must acknowledge the differences that do exist, understand how they develop, and discard dogma about what are the 'right' roles of women and men" (5).

Obviously, differences exist in the way men and women communicate, whether caused by biological and/or environmental factors. We can consider the possible causes, the consequences, and possible solutions. Using this knowledge, we should be able to more accurately interpret communication between the genders.

Holz 6

Works Cited

Arthurs, Jeffrey. "He Said, She Heard: Any Time You Speak to Both Men and Women, You're Facing Cross-Cultural Communication." Leadership 23.1 (Winter 2002): 49. Expanded Academic. Austin Peay State U, Woodward Lib. 19 Apr. 2006 <http://www. galegroup.com/search>.

Basow, Susan A., and Kimberly Rubenfeld. "'Troubles Talk': Effects of Gender and Gender Typing." Sex Roles: A Journal of Research (2003): 183– . Expanded Academic. Austin Peay State U., Woodward Lib. 19 Apr. 2006.

Cohen, David. "Speaking Across the Gender Gap." New Scientist 131.1783 (1991): 36. Expanded Academic. Austin Peay State U, Woodward Lib. 18 Apr. 2006.

Crozier, Carolyn Y. "Subservient Speech: Women Need to be Heard." 8 Aug. 2005. 15 Apr. 2006.

Glass, Lillian. He Says, She Says: Closing the Communication Gap Between the Sexes. New York: G. P. Putnam's Sons, 1992.

James, Tammy, and Bethann Cinelli. "Exploring Gender-Based Communication Styles." Journal of School Health 73 (2003): 41–42.

McCluskey, Karen Curnow. "Gender at Work." Public Management 79.5 (1997): 5–10.

Morgan, Marni, and Marilyn Coleman. "Focus on Families: Divorce and Adults." 12 Aug. 2005. 17 Apr. 2006.

Patel, Kawa. "Do Men and Women Speak the Same Language?" 14 Nov. 2005. 18 Apr. 2006 <http://www.cssu.edu/~kpatel/eng/ paper_one.htm>.

Tannen, Deborah. The Argument Culture: Moving From Debate to Dialogue. New York: Random House, 1998.

---. He Said, She Said: Exploring the Different Ways Men and Women Communicate. CD. New York: Barnes & Noble, 2004.

---. You Just Don't Understand: Women and Men in Conversation. New York: HarperCollins, 2001.

Witt, Susan D. "Parental Influence on Children's Socialization to

   Gender Roles." <u>Adolescence</u> 32 (1997): 253.

Woods, Julia T. <u>Gendered Lives</u>. 6th ed. San Francisco: Wadsworth,

   2004.

■ YOUR RESEARCH PROJECT

1. Examine your sources to test the validity of the list against the pyramid on page 103. Do you have enough sources from the upper tier of scholarly works? If not, go in search of journal articles and scholarly books to beef up the list. Do not depend on Internet articles entirely, even if every one is from a sponsored Web site.

2. Conduct a citation search (see pages 106–107 for details) on your topic, which will help you identify key people who have written on the subject several times and for several publications.

3. Examine the chart of primary and secondary sources on pages 110–111. Look for your discipline—literature, government, history—and then determine if you are using a mix of primary and secondary sources.

4. Respond to one of your sources by writing two items: (1) a rough outline of the contents of the source (see page 116), and (2) a brief summary of the source (see pages 116–117).

8 Organizing Ideas and Setting Goals

Initially, research is haphazard, and your workspace will be cluttered with bits of information scattered through your notes and on sheets of photocopied material or printouts from the Internet. After the initial search to confirm the availability of sources, you should organize your ideas so that reading and notetaking will relate directly to your specific needs. Careful organization and the presentation of evidence will augment your voice and give it a touch of authority, which will invite readers to share your position. Gathering, organizing, and notetaking occur simultaneously, so use this chapter in harmony with the next chapter, "Writing Notes," as you gather more and more material.

Your needs become clear when you draw plans such as a research proposal, a list of ideas, a set of questions, or a rough outline. In addition, the design of your study should match an appropriate organizational model, called a *paradigm*. You may also be required to create a final outline to keep your manuscript well ordered. The organizational ideas in this chapter should help you find your way through the maze.

8a Charting a Direction and Setting Goals

Instead of plunging too quickly into notetaking, first decide *what* to look for and *why* you need it. One or more of these exercises will help your organization:

- Chart the course of your work with a basic order.
- Revisit your research proposal, if you developed one, for essential issues.
- List keywords, ideas, and issues that you must explore in the paper.
- Rough out an initial outline.
- Ask a thorough set of questions.
- Use modes of development (e.g., definition or cause/effect) to identify key issues.
- Search issues across the curriculum (e.g., economics, psychology, biology).
- Let your thesis statement point you toward the basic issues.

Each of these techniques is explored on the following pages.

Using a Basic, Dynamic Order to Chart the Course of Your Work

Your finished paper should trace the issues, defend and support a thesis, and provide dynamic progression of issues and concepts that point forward to the conclusion. The paper should provide these elements:

Identification of the problem or issue.
A review of the literature on the topic.
Your thesis or hypothesis.
Analysis of the issues.
Presentation of evidence.
Interpretation and discussion of the findings.

In every case, you must generate the dynamics of the paper by (1) building anticipation in the introduction, (2) investigating the issues in the body, and (3) providing a final judgment. In this way, you will satisfy the demands of the academic reader, who will expect you to:

- Examine a problem.
- Cite pertinent literature on it.
- Offer your ideas and interpretation of it.

All three are necessary in almost every instance. Consequently, your early organization will determine, in part, the success of your research paper.

Using Your Research Proposal to Direct Your Notetaking

Your research proposal, if you developed one, introduces issues worthy of research. For example, the last sentence of this research proposal names four topics:

> I want to address this paper to everybody who thinks water is plentiful and will always be here. I'm afraid that water might soon replace oil as an economic resource most treasured by nations. We already have legal battles about the sharing of water, and we may one day have wars over it. Preliminary reading has shown that a growing world population faces a global water supply that is shrinking. Accordingly, this paper will examine some of the issues with regard to supply and demand, the political power struggles that are emerging, and the ethical and perhaps even moral implications engulfing the world's scattered supply of fresh water.

This writer will search the literature and write notes to build an environmental examination on those who have good supplies of water and those who don't.

Note: For a discussion and directions for completeing the research proposal, see Chapter 2, pages 27–31.

Another writer sketched the following research proposal, which lists the types of evidence necessary to accomplish her project:

> This paper will study organ and tissue donation. It will expose the myths that prevail in the public's imagination and, hopefully, dispel them. It will explore the serious need of and benefits derived from donated organs and tissue. It will also itemize the organs and their use to rehabilitate the diseased and wounded. It will evaluate, but it will also be a proposal: Sign the donor card!

Listing Keywords and Phrases to Set Directions for Notetaking

Follow two fairly simple steps: (1) Jot down ideas or words in a rough list, and (2) expand the list to show a hierarchy of major and minor ideas. Student Norman Berkowitz started listing items that are affected by and depend on the world's water supply:

> wildlife survival
>
> sanitation and hygiene
>
> irrigation of farms and the food supply
>
> bioscience issues
>
> water distribution
>
> global warming
>
> the Ogallala aquifer

Berkowitz could begin notetaking with this list and label each note with one of the phrases.

> **HINT:** What you are looking for at this point are terms that will speed your search on the Internet and in the library's indexes.

Writing a Rough Outline

As early as possible, organize your key terminology in a brief outline, arranging the words and phrases in an ordered sequence, as shown in this next example. Jamie Johnston began research in the matter of prehistoric wars. He soon jotted down this rough outline:

> Prehistoric wars
>
> > Evidence of weapons
> >
> > Evidence from skeletal remains

Evidence of soldiers and fortresses

Reasons for early fighting

Resources

Slaves, concubines, and sacrificial victims

Gold, silver, bronze, copper

Revenge

Defend honor

Cause for human compulsion to fight

Biology

Culture

This outline, although sketchy, provides the terminology needed for keyword searches on the Internet and in your library's databases. Also, it's not too early to begin writing notes for the items on the list.

Using Questions to Identify Issues

Questions can invite you to develop answers in your notes. (See also section 2a, "Asking Questions," pages 17–18.) Early in her work, one student made this list of questions:

What is a functional food?

How does it serve the body in fighting disease?

Can healthy eating actually lower health care costs?

Can healthy eating truly prolong one's life?

Can we identify the components of nutritional foods that make them

work effectively?

What is an antioxidant? a carcinogen? a free radical? a triglyceride?

She then went in search of answers and built a body of notes. One question might lead to others, and an answer to a question (Are nutritional foods new?) might produce a topic sentence for a paragraph:

Although medical professionals are just beginning to open their

minds and eyes to the medicinal power of food, others have known

about food's healthful properties for centuries.

Setting Goals by Using Organizational Patterns

Try to anticipate the kinds of development, or organizational patterns, you will need to build effective paragraphs and to explore your topic fully. Then base your notes on the modes of development: *definition, comparison and contrast, process, illustration, cause and effect, classification, analysis,* and *description.* Here's a list by one student who studied the issues of organ and tissue donation.

Define tissue donation.

Contrast myths, religious views, and ethical considerations.

Illustrate organ and tissue donation with several examples.

Use statistics and scientific data.

Search out causes for a person's reluctance to sign a donor card.

Determine the consequences of donation with a focus on saving the lives of children.

Read and use a case study on a child's death and organ donation by the public.

Explore the step-by-step stages of the process of organ donation.

Classify the types and analyze the problem.

Give narrative examples of several people whose lives were saved.

With this list in hand, a writer can search for material to develop as *contrast, process, definition,* and so forth.

> **HINT:** Try developing each important item on your list into a full paragraph. Write a definition paragraph. Write a paragraph to compare and contrast the attitudes expressed by people about organ donation. Then write another paragraph that gives four or five examples. By doing so, you will be well on your way to developing the paper.

One student recorded this note that describes the subject:

> Organ and tissue donation is the gift of life. Each year, many people confront health problems due to diseases or congenital birth defects. Organ transplants give these people the chance to live a somewhat normal life. Organs that can be successfully transplanted include the heart, lungs, liver, kidneys, and pancreas (Barnill 1). Tissues that can be transplanted successfully include bone, corneas, skin, heart valves, veins, cartilage, and other connective tissues (Taddonio 1).

Using Approaches across the Curriculum to Chart Your Major Ideas

Each scholarly field gives a special insight into any given topic. Suppose, for example, that you wish to examine an event from U.S. history, such as the

Battle of Little Big Horn. Different academic disciplines will help you approach the topic in different ways.

Political science:	Was Custer too hasty in his quest for political glory?
Economics:	Did the government want to open the western lands for development that would enrich the nation?
Military science:	Was Custer's military strategy flawed?
Psychology:	Did General Custer's ego precipitate the massacre?
Geography:	Why did Custer stage a battle at this site?

These approaches can also produce valuable notes as the student searches out answers in the literature, as shown in this example:

> The year 1876 stands as a monument to the western policies of Congress and the President, but Sitting Bull and Custer seized their share of glory. Custer's egotism and political ambitions overpowered his military savvy (Lemming 6). Also, Sitting Bull's military tactics (he told his braves to kill rather than show off their bravery) proved devastating for Custer and his troops, who no longer had easy shots at "prancing, dancing Indians" (Potter 65).

Using Your Thesis to Chart the Direction of Your Research

Often, the thesis statement sets the direction of the paper's development.

Arrangement by Issues

The thesis statement might force the writer to address various issues and positions.

THESIS:	Misunderstandings about organ donation distort reality and set serious limits on the availability of those persons who need an eye, a liver, or a healthy heart.
ISSUE 1.	Many myths mislead people into believing that donation is unethical.
ISSUE 2.	Some fear that as a patient they might be terminated early for their body parts.
ISSUE 3.	Religious views sometimes get in the way of donation.

The outline above, though brief, gives this writer three categories that require detailed research in support of the thesis. The notetaking can be focused on these three issues.

Arrangement by Cause/Effect

In other cases, the thesis sentence suggests development by cause/effect issues. Notice that the next writer's thesis on television's educational values points the way to four very different areas worthy of investigation.

Formulating an effective thesis, 2f, pages 24–27.

THESIS:	Television can have positive effects on a child's language development.
CONSEQUENCE 1.	Television introduces new words.
CONSEQUENCE 2.	Television reinforces word usage and proper syntax.
CONSEQUENCE 3.	Literary classics come alive verbally on television.
CONSEQUENCE 4.	Television provides the subtle rhythms and musical effects of accomplished speakers.

The outline above can help the writer produce a full discussion on television viewing.

Arrangement by Interpretation and Evaluation

Evaluation will evolve from thesis sentences that judge a subject by a set of criteria, such as your analysis of a poem, movie, or museum display. Notice how the next student's thesis sentence requires an interpretation of Hamlet's character.

THESIS: Shakespeare manipulates the stage settings for Hamlet's soliloquies to uncover his unstable nature and forecast his failure.

1. His soul is dark because of his mother's incest.
2. He appears impotent in comparison with the actor.
3. He is drawn by the magnetism of death.
4. He realizes he cannot perform cruel, unnatural acts.
5. He stands ashamed by his inactivity in comparison.

Arrangement by Comparison

Sometimes a thesis sentence stipulates a comparison on the value of two sides of an issue, as shown in one student's preliminary outline:

THESIS:	Discipline often involves punishment, but child abuse adds another element: the gratification of the adult.
COMPARISON 1:	A spanking has the interest of the child at heart but a beating or a caning has no redeeming value.

COMPARISON 2:   Time-outs remind the child that relationships are important and to be cherished but lock-outs in a closet only promote hysteria and fear.

COMPARISON 3:   The parent's ego and selfish interests often take precedence over the welfare of the child or children.

CHECKLIST

Evaluating Your Overall Plan

1. What is my thesis? Will my notes and records defend and illustrate my proposition? Is the evidence convincing?
2. Have I found the best plan for developing the thesis with elements of argument, evaluation, cause/effect, or comparison?
3. Should I use a combination of elements—that is, do I need to evaluate the subject, examine the causes and consequences, and then set out the argument?

8b   Using Academic Models (Paradigms)

A paradigm is a universal outline, one that governs most papers of a given type. It is not content-specific; rather, it provides a general model, a broad scaffold, and a basic academic pattern of reasoning for all papers with a certain purpose. In contrast, a traditional outline, with its specific detail on various levels of subdivision, is useful for only one paper. Therefore, we recommend that you start with a paradigm, an ideal pattern for many papers, and finish with an outline, a content-oriented plan for one paper only—your paper.

A General All-Purpose Model

If you are uncertain about the design of your paper, start with this bare-bones model and expand it with your material. Readers, including your instructor, are accustomed to this sequence for research papers. It offers plenty of leeway.

Identify the subject.
    Explain the problem.
    Provide background information.
    Frame a thesis statement.
Analyze the subject.
    Examine the first major issue.

Examine the second major issue.
Examine the third major issue.
Discuss your findings.
Restate your thesis and point beyond it.
Interpret the findings.
Provide answers, solutions, or a final opinion.

To the introduction you can add a quotation, an anecdote, a definition, or comments from your source materials. Within the body, you can com-
pare, analyze, give evidence, trace historical events, and handle other matters. In the conclusion, you can challenge an assumption, take exception to a prevailing point of view, and reaffirm your thesis. Flesh out each section, adding subheadings as necessary, to create an outline.

Developing introductions, bodies, and conclusions, Chapter 12.

Paradigm for Advancing Your Ideas and Theories

Writing theory in APA Style, Chapter 15.

If you want to advance a theory in your paper, use this next design, but adjust it to eliminate some items and add new elements as necessary.

Introduction:
Establish the problem or question.
Discuss its significance.
Provide the necessary background information.
Introduce experts who have addressed the problem.
Provide a thesis sentence that addresses the problem from a fresh perspective, if at all possible.
Body:
Evaluate the issues involved in the problem.
Develop a past-to-present examination.
Compare and analyze the details and minor issues.
Cite experts who have addressed the same problem.
Conclusion:
Advance and defend your theory as it grows out of evidence in the body.
Offer directives or a plan of action.
Suggest additional work and research that is needed.

Paradigm for the Analysis of Creative Works

If you plan to analyze musical, artistic, or literary works, such as an opera, a set of paintings, or a novel, adjust this next paradigm to your subject and purpose.

Introduction:
Identify the work.

Give a brief summary in one sentence.

Provide background information that relates to the thesis.

Offer biographical facts about the artist that relate to the specific issues.

Quote and paraphrase authorities to establish the scholarly traditions.

Write a thesis sentence that establishes your particular views of the literary work.

Body:

Provide evaluative analysis divided according to such elements as imagery, theme, character development, structure, symbolism, narration, and language.

Conclusion:

Keep a fundamental focus on the artist of the work, not just the elements of analysis as explained in the body.

Offer a conclusion that explores the contributions of the artist in accord with your thesis sentence.

Paradigm for Argument and Persuasion Papers

If you write persuasively or argue from a set position, your paper should conform in general to this next paradigm. Select the elements that fit your design.

Introduction:

In one statement, establish the problem or controversial issue your paper will examine.

Summarize the issues.

Define the key terminology.

Make concessions on some points of the argument.

Use quotations and paraphrases to clarify the controversial nature of the subject.

Provide background information to relate the past to the present.

Write a thesis to establish your position.

Body:

Develop arguments to defend one side of the subject.

Analyze the issues, both pro and con.

Give evidence from the sources, including quotations as appropriate.

Conclusion:

Expand your thesis into a conclusion that makes clear your position, which should be one that grows logically from your analysis and discussion of the issues.

Paradigm for Analysis of History

If you are writing a historical or political science paper that analyzes events and their causes and consequences, your paper should conform, in general, to the following plan.

Introduction:
> Identify the event.
> Provide the historical background leading up to the event.
> Offer quotations and paraphrases from experts.
> Give the thesis sentence.

Body:
> Analyze the background leading up to the event.
> Trace events from one historic episode to another.
> Offer a chronological sequence that explains how one
>> event relates directly to the next.
> Cite authorities who have also investigated this event
>> in history.

Conclusion:
> Reaffirm your thesis.
> Discuss the consequences of this event, explaining how it
>> altered the course of history.

Paradigm for a Comparative Study

A comparative study requires that you examine two schools of thought, two issues, two works, or the positions taken by two persons. The paper examines the similarities and differences of the two subjects, generally using one of three arrangements for the body of the paper.

Introduction:
> Establish A.
> Establish B.
> Briefly compare the two.
> Introduce the central issues.
> Cite source materials on the subjects.
> Present your thesis.

Body (choose one):

Examine A.	Compare A and B.	Issue 1
Examine B.	Contrast A and B.	Discuss A and B.
Compare and	Discuss the central	Issue 2
contrast A and B.	issues.	Discuss A and B.
		Issue 3
		Discuss A and B.

Conclusion:
> Discuss the significant issues.
> Write a conclusion that ranks one side over the other, or
> Write a conclusion that rates the respective genius of each side.

Remember that the models provided above are general guidelines, not iron-clad rules. Adjust each as necessary to meet your special needs.

8c Writing a Formal Outline

Not all papers require a formal outline, nor do all researchers need one. A short research paper can be created from keywords, a list of issues, a rough outline, and a first draft. As noted earlier in this chapter, rough or informal outlines will help you to make sure you cover the key points and guide your research. However, a formal outline can be important because it classifies the issues of your study into clear, logical categories with main headings and one or more levels of subheadings. An outline will change miscellaneous notes, computer drafts, and photocopied materials into an ordered progression of ideas.

> **HINT:** A formal outline is not rigid and inflexible; you may, and should, modify it while writing and revising. In every case, treat an outline or organizational chart as a tool. Like an architect's blueprint, it should contribute to, not inhibit, the construction of a finished product.

You may wish to experiment with the Outline feature of your computer software, which will allow you to view the paper at various levels of detail and to highlight and drop the essay into a different organization.

Using Standard Outline Symbols

List your major categories and subtopics in this form:

I. _____		First major heading
A. _____		Subheading of first degree
1. _____		Subheadings of second degree
2. _____		
a. _____		Subheadings of third degree
b. _____		
(1) _____		Subheadings of fourth degree
(2) _____		
(a) _____		Subheadings of fifth degree
B. _____		Subheading of first degree

The degree to which you continue the subheads will depend, in part, on the complexity of the subject. Subheads in a research paper seldom carry beyond subheadings of the third degree, the first series of small letters.

An alternative form, especially for papers in business and the sciences, is the *decimal outline,* which divides material by numerical divisions:

```
1. _____
   1.1. _____
        1.1.1. _____
        1.1.2. _____
        1.1.3. _____
   1.2. _____
        1.2.1. _____
        1.2.2. _____
2. _____
```

Writing a Formal Topic Outline

If your purpose is to arrange quickly the topics of your paper without detailing your data, build a topic outline of balanced phrases. The topic outline may use noun phrases:

III. The senses

    A. Receptors to detect light

        1. Rods of the retina

        2. Cones of the retina

It may also use gerund phrases:

III. Sensing the environment

    A. Detecting light

        1. Sensing dim light with retina rods

        2. Sensing bright light with retina cones

And it may also use infinitive phrases:

III. To use the senses

    A. To detect light

        1. To sense dim light

        2. To sense bright light

No matter which grammatical format you choose, you should follow it consistently throughout the outline. Student Sarah Bemis's topic outline follows. Her paper appears on pages 375–385.

I. Diabetes defined

    A. A disease without control

        1. A disorder of the metabolism

        2. The search for a cure

    B. Types of diabetes

        1. Type 1, juvenile diabetes

        2. Type 2, adult-onset diabetes

II. Health complications

    A. The problem of hyperglycemia

        1. Signs and symptoms of the problem

        2. Lack of insulin

    B. The conflict of the kidneys and the liver

        1. Effects of ketoacidosis

        2. Effects of arteriosclerosis

III. Proper care and control

    A. Blood sugar monitoring

        1. Daily monitoring at home

        2. Hemoglobin test at a laboratory

    B. Medication for diabetes

        1. Insulin injections

        2. Hypoglycemia agents

    C. Exercise programs

        1. Walking

        2. Swimming

        3. Aerobic workouts

    D. Diet and meal planning

        1. Exchange plan

        2. Carbohydrate counting

IV. Conclusion: Balance of all the factors

Writing a Formal Sentence Outline

The sentence outline requires full sentences for each heading and subheading. It has two advantages over the topic outline:

1. Many entries in a sentence outline can serve as topic sentences for paragraphs, thereby accelerating the writing process.
2. The subject/verb pattern establishes the logical direction of your thinking (for example, the phrase "Vocabulary development" becomes "Television viewing can improve a child's vocabulary").

Consequently, the sentence outline brings into the open any possible organizational problems rather than hiding them as a topic outline might do. The time invested writing a complete sentence outline, like writing complete, polished notes (see Chapter 9, pages 144–156), will pay off when you write the rough draft and revise it.

Jamie Johnston's sentence outline is shown below. Turn to pages 353–365 to see the complete paper. As shown below, the thesis sentence should appear as a separate item in the outline. It is the main idea of the entire paper, so try not to label it as Item I in the outline. Otherwise, you may search fruitlessly for parallel ideas to put in II, III, and IV. (See also pages 199–200 on using the thesis in the opening.)

Outline

Thesis: Prehistoric humans were motived by biological instincts toward warfare rather than cultural demands for a share of limited resources.

I. The conflict of "noble savage" versus prehistoric warriors has surfaced in recent literature.

    A. Some literature has advocated the existence of harmony and peace among early tribes.

        1. Rousseau argued for a noble savage in the 1700s.

        2. The Bible speaks of the Garden of Eden.

    B. Recent research suggests that wars have existed since the dawn of life.

        1. LaBlanc cites evidence from the Southwest Indians.

        2. Yates reports on Chinese weapons from 28,000 BC.

        3. Ferrill has examined cave paintings.

II. The evidence points clearly to the existence of prehistoric wars.

    A. Anthropologists have uncovered skeletal remains of captives who were executed.

        1. Victims were skinned alive.

        2. Victims were decapitated.

        3. Massacres occurred in Europe, North and South America, Japan, and other parts of the world.

    B. Weapons of mass destruction (on their terms) have been unearthed along with fortifications.

        1. Clubs, slings, daggers, spears, and bows give testimony to early fighting.

        2. Fortress cities prove that villagers attempted to protect themselves from ravaging hordes.

III. Many reasons for prehistoric fighting have been advanced.

    A. Some fought to capture resources of various kinds.

        1. Humans were captured to serve as slaves, concubines, and sacrificial victims of religious ceremonies.

        2. Food, water, and cattle were targets of desperate tribes during famines.

        3. Gold, silver, bronze, and copper were prized commodities and worthy of a good battle.

        4. Trade routes and key locations were subject to dispute.

B. Some fought for personal reasons and points of honor.

   1. Revenge was often a motivating factor for attacks on a village.

   2. Religion motived warriors to search out not only religious icons but sacrificial victims.

   3. Defending the tribe's honor was sometimes motivation for desperate battles.

IV. At issue is the primary motivating factor that prompted mass carnage at the dawn of civilization.

   A. Some argue that society as a whole wants to preserve its culture and will fight to maintain it.

   B. Others argue that human beings by nature are aggressive and love a good fight in the search for power over others.

Using a Research Journal to Enrich Your Organizational Plan

If you have kept a research journal, you have probably developed a number of notes in addition to the collection of printouts and photocopies. Therefore, review the collection and assign each piece to a section of your outline. Do this by making a note, such as "put in the conclusion," or by assigning an outline number, "use in II.A.1." Do the same thing with your other materials. Then assign them to a spot in your outline, as shown in this brief example from an outline:

A. Television viewing can improve the vocabulary of children.

   1. Negative views
     Cite Powell; cite Winkeljohann.

   2. Positive views
     Cite Rice and Woodsall; cite Singer; cite Postman.

In the next chapter, we discuss methods for building notes from the various pieces you have collected.

 **YOUR RESEARCH PROJECT**

1. Sketch out an outline for your project. List your general thesis and, below that, establish several divisions that will require careful and full development. Test more than one plan. Do you need several criteria of

judgment? causal issues? arguments? evidence from field research? Which seems to work best for you?

2. Select one of the paradigms, as found on pages 134–137, and develop it fully with the information in your sketch outline (see #1 immediately above).

3. If you are familiar about the design of Web pages, you probably realize that the hierarchical ideas have value because readers can click on links that will carry them deeper into the files. Test your outline by constructing a plan like the one below, filling the blanks downward from the large block (thesis) to major issues (medium blocks) to evidence (small blocks). The chart, which you can redraw on a sheet of paper, looks something like this:

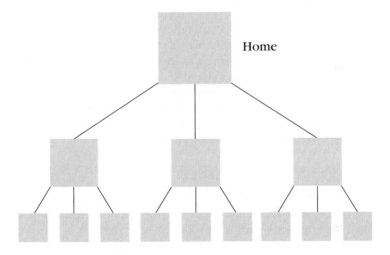

9 Writing Effective Notes

The primary reason for writing from research is to announce and publicize new findings. A botanist explains the discovery of a new strain of ferns in Kentucky's Land between the Lakes. A medical scientist reports the results of her cancer research. A sociologist announces the results of a two-year pilot study of Native Americans in the Appalachian region.

Similarly, you will be asked to explain your findings from a geology field trip, disclose research on animal imagery in Robert Frost's poetry, or discuss the results of an investigation into overcrowding of school classrooms. The accurate notes from your personal research will join with your carefully paraphrased notes from experts on the topic to form the support for your thesis. Your goal is to share verifiable information, but others can verify your work only if good records are kept and reported.

Gathering Printouts, Photocopies, Scanned Images, and Downloaded Data

Today's technology makes it fairly easy to collect material quickly and in volume. You can print online articles or save them to a file. You can use a scanner to make digital images of graphics as well as text. Plus, photocopy machines enable you to carry home a few sheets of paper instead of an entire book.

Yet this convenience comes at a price: You will have a nice collection of articles and copied chapters from books, plus notes you have made along the way in your research journal, but *you must somehow make sense of it all*. Therefore, consult Chapter 8 often for tips on organizing and outlining the material.

Read each piece you have, make marginal notes on it, and assign it a place in your organization chart—be it an outline, a paradigm, or even a general list of issues. Identify a location for it in the overall layout. Then you have a choice: You can write notes from it now or wait to borrow from it during the drafting of the paper.

All this material will gradually make sense as you arrange it and use it. Warning: Keep *everything*. You will need to cite the source in the text and in a bibliography entry, so don't throw away a note, printout, or a photocopy.

Writing Notes of High Quality

Keeping accurate records and writing notes of high quality are essential steps in the research process. As you write, you will depend heavily on your notes. In like manner, your reader will rely on the precision of your information. For example, the inventor Thomas Edison built on documented research by others. How fortunate he was that his predecessors recorded their experiments and kept good notes.

Thus, notetaking is the heart of research. If you write notes of high quality, they may need only minor editing to fit the appropriate places in your first draft. Prepare yourself to write different types of notes—quotations for well-phrased passages by authorities but also paraphrased or summarized notes to maintain your voice.

- *Personal notes* (9b), which express your own ideas or record data from field research.
- *Quotation notes* (9c), which preserve the wisdom and distinguished syntax of an authority.
- *Paraphrase notes* (9d), which interpret and restate what the authority has said.
- *Summary notes* (9e), which distill factual data that has marginal value; you can return to the source later if necessary.
- *Précis notes* (9f), which capture the essence of one writer's ideas in capsule form.
- *Field notes* (9g), which record interviews, questionnaire tabulations, laboratory experiments, and other types of field research.

9a Creating Effective Notes

Whether you write notes on a computer or by hand, you should keep in mind some basic rules, summarized in the checklist on page 146.

Honoring the Conventions of Research Style

Your notetaking will be more effective from the start if you practice the conventions of style for citing a source, as advocated by the Modern Language Association (MLA), American Psychological Association (APA), Council of Science Editors (CSE), or Chicago Manual of Style (CMS), and as shown briefly below and explained later in this book.

MLA: Lawrence Smith states, "The suicidal teen causes severe damage to the psychological condition of peers" (34).

APA: Smith (1997) has commented, "The suicidal teen causes severe damage to the psychological condition of peers" (p. 34).

> **CHECKLIST**
>
> ### Writing Effective Notes
>
> 1. Write one item per note to facilitate the shuffling and rearranging of the data as you develop your paper during all stages of organization. Several notes can be kept in a computer file if each is labeled clearly.
> 2. List the source with name, year, and page to be ready for in-text citations and/or bibliographic entries.
> 3. Label each note (for example, "objectivity on television").
> 4. Write a full note in well-developed sentences to speed the writing of your first draft.
> 5. Keep everything (photocopy, scribbled note) in order to authenticate dates, page numbers, and full names.
> 6. Label your personal notes with "my idea" or "personal note" to distinguish them from the sources.

CMS footnote: Lawrence Smith states, "The suicidal teen causes severe damage to the psychological condition of peers."[3]

CSE number: Smith (4) has commented, "The suicidal teen causes severe damage to the psychological condition of peers."

Using a Computer for Notetaking

The computer affects notetaking strategies in several ways:

1. You can enter your notes into the word processor using one of two methods:

   a. Write each note as a separate temporary file in a common directory so each can be moved later into the appropriate section of your draft via the Copy and Paste commands.

   b. Write all notes in a single file. Begin each new note with a code word or phrase. When you begin the actual writing of the paper, you can begin writing at the top of the file, which will push the notes down as you write. As necessary, search out and bring up specific notes as you need them. In other situations, you might employ a split screen or use two windows so your draft is in one window and your notes are in another.

   Note: It might be wise to keep a copy of the original file(s) in case anything is lost or deleted while arranging materials.

2. You can record the bibliography information for each source you encounter by listing it in a BIBLIO file so that you build the necessary list

Identifying sources, 177–178

Darrel Abel in his third volume of <u>American</u>

Underscoring, A-19

<u>Literature</u> narrates the hardships of the Samuel Clemens

family in Hannibal, yet Abel asserts that "despite such

Using lower case after that, 195–196

hardships and domestic grief, which included the deaths

of a brother and sister, young Sam Clemens [Mark Twain]

Interpolations, 199–200

had a happy and reasonably carefree boyhood" (11–12).

Single quotation marks 191

Page citations, 177–178

Abel acknowledges the value of Clemens's "rambling

reminiscences dictated as an 'Autobiography' in his old

Punctuation with quotations, 188–191

age" (12). Of those days Clemens says, "In the small

Ellipses points, 196–199

town . . . <u>everybody</u> [my underlining] was poor, but didn't

know it; and everybody was comfortable, and did know it"

(qtd. in Abel 12). Clemens felt at home in Hannibal with

Signaling your underscoring of another's words, 200

One source quotes another, 182–184

everybody at the same level of poverty.

FIGURE 9.1 Conventions of style for writing notes.

of references in one alphabetical file. Chapters 14, 15, 16, and 17 give you the correct forms.

HINT: Notetaking programs, such as *Take Note!*, and bibliography organizers, such as *Endnote,* can serve you well in this stage of developing your paper. Later, formatting software such as *StyleEase* can help you format the paper as you write it.

Developing Handwritten Notes

Handwritten notes should conform to these additional conventions:

- Write in ink, because penciled notes blur after repeated shuffling.
- Keep notes and the working bibliography separate.
- Write on one side of a sheet because information written on the back may be overlooked. Use the back side, if at all, for personal notes and observations, but mark the front with "OVER."
- Staple together two or more notes that document one item.

9b Writing Personal Notes

The content of a research paper is not a collection of ideas transmitted by experts in books and articles; it is an expression of your own ideas as supported by the scholarly evidence. Readers are primarily interested in *your* thesis statement, *your* topic sentences, and *your* personal view of the issues. Therefore, during your research, record your thoughts on the issues by writing plenty of personal notes in your research journal, or in your computer files. Personal notes are essential because they allow you to:

- Record your discoveries.
- Reflect on the findings.
- Make connections.
- Explore another point of view.
- Identify prevailing views and patterns of thought.

Personal notes should conform to these three standards:

1. The idea on the note is yours.
2. The note is labeled with "my idea," "mine," or "personal thought" so that later you can be certain it has not been borrowed.
3. The note is a rough summary, a sketch of ideas, or, preferably, a complete sentence or two.

A sample of a personal note follows:

Personal thought

———

For me, organ donation might be a gift of life, so I have signed my donor card. At least a part of me will continue to live if an accident claims my life. My boyfriend says I'm gruesome, but I consider it practical. Besides, he might be the one who benefits, and then what will he say?

9c Writing Direct Quotation Notes

Quoting the words of another person is the easiest type of note to write. Quotation notes are essential because they allow you to:

- Capture the authoritative voice of the experts on the topic.
- Feature essential statements.
- Provide proof that you have researched the subject carefully.
- Offer conflicting points of view.
- Show the dialog that exists about the topic.

In the process, you will need to follow basic conventions:

1. Select quoted material that is important and well-phrased, not something trivial or something that is common knowledge. NOT "John F. Kennedy was a Democrat from Massachusetts" (Rupert 233) BUT "John F. Kennedy's Peace Corps left a legacy of lasting compassion for the down-trodden" (Rupert 233).
2. Use quotation marks. Do not copy the words of a source into your paper in such a way that readers will think *you* wrote the material.
3. Use the exact words of the source.
4. Provide an in-text citation to author and page number, like this (Henson 34–35), or give the author's name at the beginning of the quotation and put the page number after the quotation, like this example in MLA style:

    Barnill says, "More than 400 people each month receive the gift

    of sight through yet another type of tissue donation—corneal

    transplants. In many cases, donors unsuitable for organ donation are

    eligible for tissue donation" (2).

5. The in-text citation goes *outside* the final quotation mark but *inside* the period.
6. Try to quote key sentences and short passages, not entire paragraphs. Find the essential statement and feature it; do not force your reader to fumble through a long quoted passage in search of the relevant statement. Make the brief quotation a part of your sentence, in this way:

    Many Americans, trying to mend their past eating habits, adopt

    functional foods as an essential step toward a more health-conscious

    future. This group of believers spends "an estimated $29 billion a year"

    on functional foods (Nelson 755).

7. Quote from both primary sources (the original words by a writer or speaker) and secondary sources (the comments after the fact about original works). The two types are discussed immediately below.

Quoting Primary Sources

Quote from primary sources for four specific reasons:

1. To draw on the wisdom of the original author
2. To let readers hear the precise words of the author
3. To copy exact lines of poetry and drama
4. To reproduce graphs, charts, and statistical data

Cite poetry, fiction, drama, letters, and interviews. In other cases, you may want to quote liberally from a presidential speech, cite the words of a

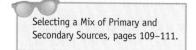

Selecting a Mix of Primary and Secondary Sources, pages 109–111.

businessman, or reproduce original data. As shown in the next example, quote exactly, retain spacing and margins, and spell words as in the original.

Images of Frustration Have a Prominent Role in Eliot's "Prufrock":

For I have known them all already,

known them all:—

Have known the evenings, mornings,

afternoons,

I have measured out my life with

coffee spoons;

I know the voices dying with a

dying fall

Beneath the music of a farther room.

So how should I presume?

Quoting Secondary Sources

Quote from secondary sources for three specific reasons:

1. To display excellence in ideas and expression by experts on the topic
2. To explain complex material
3. To set up a statement of your own, especially if it spins off, adds to, or takes exception to the source as quoted

The overuse of direct quotation from secondary sources indicates either (1) that you did not have a clear focus and copied verbatim just about everything related to the subject, or (2) that you had inadequate evidence and used numerous quotations as padding. Therefore, limit quotations from secondary sources by using only a phrase or a sentence, as shown here:

The geographical changes in Russia require "intensive political

analysis" (Herman 611).

If you quote an entire sentence, make the quotation a direct object. It tells *what* the authority says. Headings on your notes will help you arrange them.

Geographic Changes in Russia

In response to the changes in Russia, one critic notes, "The

American government must exercise caution and conduct intensive

political analysis" (Herman 611).

More examples of handling quoted materials, Chapter 11, pages 174–198.

Blend two or more quotations from different sources to build strong paragraphs, as shown here:

> Functional foods are helping fight an economic battle against rising health care costs. Clare Hasler notes, "The U.S. population is getting older," which means more people are being diagnosed and treated for disease (68). These individuals are putting a huge financial strain on the health care system with their need for expensive antibiotics and hospital procedures. Dr. Herbert Pierson, director of the National Cancer Institute's $20 million functional food program, states, "The future is prevention, and looking for preventive agents in foods is more cost effective than looking for new drugs" (qtd. in Carper xxii).

9d Writing Paraphrased Notes

A paraphrase is the most difficult note to write. It requires you to restate, in your own words, the thought, meaning, and attitude of someone else. With *interpretation*, you act as a bridge between the source and the reader as you capture the wisdom of the source in approximately the same number of words. Use paraphrase for these reasons:

- To maintain your voice in the paper.
- To sustain your style.
- To avoid an endless string of direct quotations.
- To interpret the source as you rewrite it.

Keep in mind these five rules for paraphrasing a source:

1. Rewrite the original in about the same number of words.
2. Provide an in-text citation of the source (the author and page number in MLA style).
3. Retain exceptional words and phrases from the original by enclosing them within quotation marks.
4. Preserve the tone of the original by suggesting moods of satire, anger, humor, doubt, and so on. Show the author's attitude with appropriate verbs: "Edward Zigler condemns . . . defends . . . argues . . . explains . . . observes . . . defines."
5. To avoid unintended plagiarism, put the original aside while paraphrasing to avoid copying word for word. Compare the finished paraphrase with the original source to be certain the paraphrase truly restates the original and uses quotation marks with any phrasing or standout words retained from the original.

> **HINT:** When instructors see an in-text citation but no quotations marks, they will assume that you are paraphrasing, not quoting. Be sure their assumption is true.

Here are examples that show the differences between a quotation note and a paraphrased one.

Quotation:

Heredity   Hein 294

Fred Hein explains, "Except for identical twins, each person's heredity is unique" (294).

Paraphrase:

Heredity   Hein 294

Fred Hein explains that heredity is special and distinct for each of us, unless a person is one of identical twins (294).

Quotation (more than four lines):

Heredity   Hein 294

Fred Hein clarifies the phenomenon:

> Since only half of each parent's chromosomes are
> transmitted to a child and since this half represents a
> chance selection of those the child could inherit, only
> twins that develop from a single fertilized egg that
> splits in two have identical chromosomes. (294)

As shown above, MLA style requires a 10-space indention.

Paraphrase:

Heredity   Hein 294

Hein specifies that twins have identical chromosomes because they grow from one egg that divides after it has been fertilized. He affirms that most brothers and sisters differ because of the "chance selection" of chromosomes transmitted by each parent (294).

As shown in the example above, place any key wording of the source within quotation marks.

9e Writing Summary Notes

You may write two types of summary notes: a quick sketch of material, as discussed here, and the more carefully drawn *précis*, as explained next in section 9f.

The *summary note* describes and rewrites the source material without great concern for style or expression. Your purpose at the moment will be quick, concise writing without careful wording. If the information is needed, you can rewrite it later in a clear, appropriate prose style and, if necessary, return to the source for revision. Use summary notes for these reasons:

- To record material that has marginal value.
- To preserve statistics that have questionable value for your study.
- To note an interesting position of a source speaking on a closely related subject but not on your specific topic.
- To reference several works that address the same issue, as shown in this example:

> The logistics and cost of implementing a recycling program have been examined in books by West and Loveless and in articles by Jones et al., Coffee and Street, and Abernathy.

Success with the summary requires the following:

1. Keep it short. It has marginal value, so don't waste time fine-tuning it.
2. Mark with quotation marks any key phrasing you cannot paraphrase.
3. Provide documentation to the author and page number. However, a page number is unnecessary when the note summarizes the entire article or book, not a specific passage.

> TV & reality   Epstein's book
>
> -----
>
> Now dated but cited by various sources, the 1973 book by Epstein seems to lay the groundwork for criticism in case after case of distorted news broadcasts.

This sort of summary might find its way into the final draft, as shown here:

> Television viewers, engulfed in the world of communication, participate in the construction of symbolic reality by their perception of and belief in the presentation. Edward Jay Epstein laid the groundwork for such investigation in 1973 by showing in case after case how the networks distorted the news and did not, perhaps could not, represent reality.

9f Writing Précis Notes

A précis note differs from a quick summary note. It serves a specific purpose, so it deserves a polished style for transfer into the paper. It requires you to capture in just a few words the ideas of an entire paragraph, section, or chapter. Use the précis for these reasons:

- To review an article or book.
- To annotate a bibliography entry.
- To provide a plot summary.
- To create an abstract.

Success with the précis requires the following:

1. Condense the original with precision and directness. Reduce a long paragraph to a sentence, tighten an article to a brief paragraph, and summarize a book in one page.
2. Preserve the tone of the original. If the original is serious, suggest that tone in the précis. In the same way, retain moods of doubt, skepticism, optimism, and so forth.
3. Write the précis in your own language. However, retain exceptional phrases from the original, enclosing them in quotation marks. Guard against taking material out of context.
4. Provide documentation.

Use the Précis to Review Briefly an Article or Book

Note this example of the short review:

> On the "Donor Initiative"   2003 Web site
>
> -----
>
> The National Community of Organ and Tissue Sharing has a Web site devoted to its initiatives. Its goal is to communicate the problem—for example, more than 55,000 people are on the waiting lists. It seeks a greater participation from the public.

With three sentences, the writer has made a précis of the entire article.

Preparing a review of literature, pages 119–126.

Use the Précis to Write an Annotated Bibliography

An annotation is a sentence or paragraph that offers explanatory or critical commentary on an article or book. It seldom extends beyond two or three sentences. The difficulty of this task is to capture the main idea of the source.

> "Top Ten Myths about Donation and Transplantation." (N.d.). October 10, 2000 <http://www.transweb.org/myths/myths.htm>. This site

dispels the many myths surrounding organ donation, showing that selling organs is illegal, that matching donor and recipient is highly complicated, and secret back room operations are almost impossible.

> "Preparing an Annotated Bibliography," pages 117–119.

Use the Précis in a Plot Summary Note

In just a few sentences, a précis summarizes a novel, short story, drama, or similar literary work, as shown by this next note:

Great Expectations by Charles Dickens describes young Pip, who inherits money and can live the life of a gentleman. But he discovers that his "great expectations" have come from a criminal. With that knowledge, his attitude changes from one of vanity to one of compassion.

Furnish a plot summary in your paper as a courtesy to your readers to cue them about the contents of a work. The précis helps you avoid a full-blown retelling of the whole plot.

Use the Précis As the Form for an Abstract

An abstract is a brief description that appears at the beginning of an article to summarize the contents. It is, in truth, a précis. Usually, it is written by the article's author, and it helps readers make decisions about reading or skipping the article. You can find entire volumes devoted to abstracts, such as *Psychological Abstracts* and *Abstracts of English Studies*. An abstract is required for most papers in the social and natural sciences. Here's a sample:

> Abstract using APA style, pages 322–323.

Abstract

The functional food revolution has begun! Functional foods, products that provide benefits beyond basic nutrition, are adding billions to the nation's economy each year. So what is their secret? Why are functional foods a hit? Functional foods are suspected to be a form of preventive medicine. This news has made the public swarm and food nutritionists salivate. Consumers hope that functional foods can calm some of their medical anxieties. Many researchers believe that functional foods may be the answer to the nation's prayers for lower health care costs. This paper goes behind the scenes, behind all the hype, in its attempt to determine if functional foods are an effective form of preventive medicine. The paper identifies several functional foods, locates the components that make them work, and explains the role that each plays in the body.

9g Writing Notes from Field Research

You sometimes will be expected to conduct field research. This work requires different kinds of notes kept on charts, cards, notepads, laboratory notebooks, a research journal, or the computer.

> The report of empirical research, section 5d, pages 84–86.

If you **interview** knowledgeable people, make careful notes during the interview and transcribe those notes to your draft in a polished form. A tape recorder can serve as a backup to your notetaking.

If you conduct a **questionnaire,** the results will become valuable data for developing notes and graphs and charts for your research paper.

If you conduct **experiments, tests,** and **measurements,** the findings serve as your notes for the results section of the report and will give you the basis for the discussion section.

▮ YOUR RESEARCH PROJECT

1. Look carefully at each of the sources you have collected so far—books, photocopies of journal articles, and Internet printouts. Try writing a summary or précis of each one. At the same time, make decisions about material worthy of direct quotation and material that you wish to paraphrase or summarize.

2. Decide how you will keep your notes—in a research journal, on handwritten note cards, or in computer files. *Note:* The computer files will serve you well because you can transfer them into your text and save typing time.

3. Write various types of notes—that is, write a few that use direct quotations, some that paraphrase, and some that summarize.

4. Conscientiously and with dedication, write as many personal notes as possible. These will be your ideas, and they will establish your voice and position. Don't let the sources speak for you; let them support your position.

5. If you have access to Take Note! or some other notetaking program, take the time to consider its special features. You can create notes, store them in folders, and even search your own files by keyword, category, and reference.

10 Drafting the Paper in an Academic Style

As you draft your paper, your voice should flow from one idea to the next smoothly and logically. You should adopt an academic style, understanding that such a style requires precision but not necessarily long, polysyllabic words pulled from a thesaurus. Therefore, treat the initial draft as exploratory, one that searches for the exact word, not just a long word. Every discipline has its own specialized words, and this matter is discussed in more detail on page 166.

Try to present a fair, balanced treatment of the subject. Do not load the paper with favorable citations at the expense of contradictory evidence. In fact, mentioning opposing viewpoints early in a report gives you something to work against and may strengthen the conclusion. Also, the claims made should be supportable. The writer who says, "Robert Frost exhibits a death wish in many of his poems," must be ready to cite both from the poems and from well-researched biographical data.

A research paper may examine a subject in depth, but it also examines *your* knowledge and the strength of *your* evidence. You may need to retrace previous steps—reading, researching, and notetaking. Ask your instructor to examine the draft, not so much for line editing but for the big picture, to see if you have met the assignment and not oversimplified the issues.

Be practical
- Write what you know and feel, not what you think somebody wants to hear.
- Write portions of the paper when you are ready, not only when you arrive there by outline sequence.
- If necessary, leave blank spots on the page to remind you that more evidence is required.
- Skip entire sections if you are ready to develop later paragraphs.

Be uninhibited
- Initial drafts must be attempts to get words on the page rather than to create a polished document.
- Write without fear or delay.
- Be conscientious about references.
- Cite the names of the sources in your notes and text.
- Enclose quotations in your notes and text.
- Preserve the page numbers of the sources.

Your early draft is a time for discovery. Later, during the revision period, you can strengthen skimpy paragraphs, refine your prose, and rearrange material to maintain the momentum of your argument. Revision techniques are examined in Chapter 13, pages 218–226.

Begin with these tasks:

1. Focus your argument (10a).
2. Refine your thesis sentence (10b).
3. Write a title that identifies your key terms (10c).
4. Begin writing from your notes and outline (10d).

10a Focusing Your Argument

Your writing style in a research paper should be factual, but it should also reflect your take on the topic. Your draft will evolve more quickly if you focus on the central issue(s). Each paragraph then amplifies your primary claim. Your aim or purpose is the key to discovering an argument. Do you wish to persuade, inquire, or negotiate?

Persuasion means convincing the reader that your position is valid and, perhaps, asking the reader to take action. For example:

> We need to establish green zones in every city of this country to control urban sprawl and to protect a segment of the natural habitat for the animals.

Inquiry is an exploratory approach to a problem in which you examine the issues without the insistence of persuasion. It is a truth-seeking adventure. For example:

> Many suburban home dwellers complain that deer, raccoons, and other wild animals ravage their gardens, flowerbeds, and garbage cans; however, the animals were there first. Thus, we may need a task force to examine the rights of each side of this conflict.

Negotiation is a search for a solution. It means you attempt to resolve a conflict by inventing options or a mediated solution. For example:

> Suburban neighbors need to find ways to embrace the wild animals that have been displaced rather than voice anger at the animals or the county government. Perhaps green zones and wilderness trails would solve some of the problems; however, such a solution would require serious negotiations with real estate developers who want to use every square foot of every development.

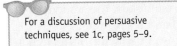

For a discussion of persuasive
techniques, see 1c, pages 5–9.

Often, the instructor's research assignment
will tell you whether you want to persuade,
inquire, or negotiate. But if it doesn't, try to
determine early in the process where your
research is heading.

Maintaining a Focus on Objective Facts and Subjective Ideas

As an objective writer, you should examine the problem, make your claim
in a thesis statement, and provide supporting evidence. As a subjective writer,
you should argue with a touch of passion; you must believe in your position on
the issues. For this reason, complete objectivity is unlikely in any research paper
that puts forth an intellectual argument in the thesis statement (see again pages
24–27). Of course, you must avoid being overly subjective, as by demanding,
insisting, and quibbling. Moderation of your voice, even during argument, suggests control of the situation, both emotionally and intellectually.

Your objective and subjective analysis alerts the audience to your point
of view in two ways:

Ethical appeal. If you project the image of one who knows and cares
about the topic, the reader will recognize and respect your deep interest
in the subject and your carefully crafted argument. The reader will also
appreciate your attention to research conventions.

Logical appeal. For readers to believe in your position, you must provide sufficient evidence in the form of statistics, paraphrases, and direct
quotations from authorities on the subject.

For example, in his examination of the world's water supply (see pages
236–247), Norman Berkowitz remained objective and logical in presenting
his evidence and statistics. Even so, the ethical problem remained close to the
surface, for he recognized the crisis as a global concern affecting most nations.

10b Refining the Thesis Sentence

A thesis statement expresses a theory you hope to support with your evidence and arguments. It is a proposition you want to maintain, analyze, and
prove. It performs three tasks:

1. It sets the argument to control and focus the entire paper.
2. It provides unity and a sense of direction.
3. It specifies to the reader the point of the research.

For example, one student started with the topic "exorbitant tuition." He narrowed
his work to "tuition fees put parents in debt." Ultimately, he crafted this thesis:

The exorbitant tuition at America's colleges is forcing out the
poor and promoting an elitist class.

This statement, a conclusion he must defend, focuses the argument on the fees and their effects on enrollment. Without such focus, the student might have drifted into other areas, confusing himself and his readers.

These same issues apply also to the use of the enthymeme or the hypothesis, as discussed earlier (see pages 24–27).

ENTHYMEME: America's colleges are promoting an elitist class because exorbitant tuition forces out the poor and limits their access to higher education.

HYPOTHESIS: This study will gather evidence on this proposition: Poor students are being locked out of higher education by the rapidly rising costs of tuition and registration fees.

Writing a thesis, enthymeme, or hypothesis, pages 24–27.

Using Questions to Focus the Thesis

If you have trouble focusing on a thesis sentence, ask yourself a few questions. One of the answers might serve as the thesis.

- What is the point of my research?

    THESIS: A delicate balance of medicine, diet, and exercise can control diabetes mellitus to offer a comfortable lifestyle for millions.

    ENTHYMEME: Because diabetes attacks the body in several ways, a person needs a careful balance of medicine, diet, and exercise.

    HYPOTHESIS: The objective of this study is to examine the effects of a balanced program of medication, diet, and exercise for a victim of diabetes.

- What do I want this paper to do?

    THESIS: The public needs to understand that advertisers who use blatant sexual images have little regard for moral scruples and ordinary decency.

- Can I tell the reader anything new or different?

    THESIS: The evidence indicates clearly that most well water in the county is unsafe for drinking.

- Do I have a solution to the problem?

  THESIS: Public support for safe houses will provide a haven for children who are abused by their parents.

- Do I have a new slant and new approach to the issue?

  THESIS: Personal economics is a force to be reckoned with, so poverty, not greed, forces many youngsters into a life of crime.

- Should I take the minority view of this matter?

  THESIS: Give credit where it is due: Custer may have lost the battle at Little Bighorn, but Crazy Horse and his men, with inspiration from Sitting Bull, *won* the battle.

- What exactly is my theory about this subject?

  THESIS: Because they have certain medicinal powers, functional foods can become an economic weapon in the battle against rising health care costs.

- Will an enthymeme serve my purpose by making a claim in a *because* clause?

  ENTHYMEME: Sufficient organ and tissue donation, enough to satisfy the demand, remains almost impossible because negative myths and religious concerns dominate the minds of many people.

- Will a hypothesis serve my purposes?

  HYPOTHESIS: An education program to dispel negative myths and religious concerns will build a greater base of organ and tissue donors.

- What are the keywords surrounding this issue that I might use in framing the thesis sentence?

  HYPOTHESIS: The objective is examination of issues with regard to supply and demand, the political power struggles that are emerging, and the ethical and perhaps even moral implication engulfing the world's scattered supply of fresh water.

Adjust or Change Your Thesis During Research if Necessary

Be willing to abandon your preliminary thesis if research leads you to new and different issues. For example, one writer began research on

---

CHECKLIST

Writing the Final Thesis

You should be able to answer "yes" to each question that follows.

Does the thesis:

1. Express your position in a full, declarative statement that is not a question, not a statement of purpose, and not merely a topic?
2. Limit the subject to a narrow focus that grows out of research?
3. Establish an investigative, inventive edge to the discovery, interpretation, or theoretical presentation?
4. Point forward to the conclusion?
5. Conform to the title and the evidence you have gathered?

---

child abuse with this preliminary thesis: "A need for a cure to child abuse faces society each day." Investigation, however, narrowed her focus: "Parents who abuse their children should be treated as victims, not criminals." The writer moved, in effect, to a specific position from which to argue that social organizations should serve abusing parents in addition to helping abused children.

10c Writing an Academic Title

A clearly expressed title, like a good thesis statement, will control your writing and keep you on course. Although writing a final title may not be feasible until the paper is written, the preliminary title can provide specific words of identification to keep you on track. For example, one writer began with this title: "Diabetes." Then, to make it more specific, the writer added another word: "Diabetes Management." As research developed and she realized the role of medicine, diet, and exercise for victims, she refined the title even more: "Diabetes Management: A Delicate Balance of Medicine, Diet, and Exercise." Thereby, she and her readers had a clear idea of what the paper was to do—that is, explore methods for managing diabetes. Note that long titles are standard in scholarly writing. Consider the following strategies for writing your title.

1. Name a general subject, followed by a colon and a phrase that focuses or shows your slant on the subject.

Organ and Tissue Donation and Transplantation: Myths, Ethical Issues, and Lives Saved

The World's Water Supply: The Ethics of Distribution

2. Name a general subject and narrow it with a prepositional phrase.

> Gothic Madness `in Three Southern Writers`

3. Name a general subject and cite a specific work that illuminates the topic.

> Analysis of Verbal Irony `in Swift's A Modest Proposal`

4. Name a general subject and follow it by a colon and a phrase that describes the type of study.

> Black Dialect in Maya Angelou's Poetry: `A Language Study`

5. Name a general subject and follow it by a colon and a question.

> AIDS: `Where Did It Come From?`

6. Establish a specific comparison.

> Religious Imagery `in N. Scott Momaday's The Names and Heronimous Storm's Seven Arrows`

As you develop a title, be sure to avoid fancy literary titles that fail to label issues under discussion.

Poor:	"Foods, Fads, and Fat"
Better:	"Nutritional Foods: A Survey"
Best:	"Nutritional Foods: A Powerful Step on the Path of Preventive Medicine"

For placement of the title, see "Title Page or Opening Page," page 221.

10d Drafting the Paper from Your Research Journal, Notes, and Computer Files

To begin writing your research essay, you may work systematically through a preliminary plan or outline. You may also begin by writing what you know at the time. Either way, keep the pieces of your manuscript under control; your notes will usually keep you focused on the subject, and your thesis statement will control the flow and direction of your argument. Yet you must let the writing find its own way, guided but not controlled by your preliminary plans. Consult also the paradigm (see pages 134–137) that best fits your design.

Writing from Your Notes

Use your notes and research journal to:

1. Transfer personal notes, with modification, into the draft.
2. Transcribe précis notes and paraphrased materials directly into the text.
3. Quote primary sources.
4. Quote secondary sources from notes.

Weave source material into the paper to support *your* ideas, not as filler. Your notes will let the essay grow, blossom, and reach up to new levels of knowledge. You can do this in several ways, and you may even have a method beyond the four mentioned here.

Method one requires separate note files within a specially named directory, as explained on page 146. During the drafting stage, you can use the Insert, Copy, or Read command to transfer your notes into your text.

Method two assumes you have placed all your notes in one file. Begin writing your paper in a new file. As you need a note, minimize this text file and maximize your file of notes, or use two windows. Find the note you wish to transfer, highlight it, copy it, and then paste it into your file.

Method three assumes you have placed all your notes within one file and labeled each with a code word or title. Begin drafting your paper at the top of this file, which will push the notes down as you write. When you need a note, find it, copy it, and paste it into your text.

Method four requires the complete outline on file so you can enter information under any of the outline headings as you develop ideas (see Chapter 8 for details on outlining). You can import your notes to a specific location of the outline. This technique allows you to work anywhere within the paper to match your interest of the moment with a section of your outline. In effect, you expand your outline into the first draft of your research paper.

In the initial draft, leave plenty of space as you write. Keep the margins wide, use double spacing, and leave blank spaces between paragraphs. The open areas will invite your revisions and additions later on. The process is simplified when you use a computer because you will keyboard the paper the first time and revise directly within the file.

When working with pages copied from articles, books, or Internet sites, use caution. You will be tempted to borrow too much. Quote or paraphrase key phrases and sentences; do not quote an entire paragraph unless it is crucial to your discussion and you cannot easily reduce it to a précis. Moreover, any information you borrow should come from a credible source that has a scholarly or educational basis.

HINT: Drafting a paragraph or two by using different methods of development is one way to build the body of your paper, but only if each part fits the purpose and design of your work. Write a comparison paragraph, classify and analyze one or two issues, show cause and effect, and ask a question and answer it. Sooner than you think, you will have drafted the body of the paper. See Chapter 12 for detailed discussion of these methods of development.

Writing with Unity and Coherence

Unity refers to exploring one topic in depth to give your writing a single vision. With unity, each paragraph carefully expands on a single aspect of the narrowed subject. *Coherence* connects the parts logically by:

• Repetition of keywords and sentence structures.

- The judicious use of pronouns and synonyms.
- The effective placement of transitional words and phrases (e.g., *also, furthermore, therefore, in addition*, and *thus*).

The next passage reads with unity (it keeps its focus) and coherence (it repeats keywords and uses transitions effectively, as shown in boldface type).

> Talk shows are spectacles and forms of dramatic entertainment; therefore, members of the studio audience are acting out parts in the drama, like a Greek chorus, just as the host, the guest, and the television viewers are actors as well. **Furthermore,** some sort of interaction with the "characters" in this made-for-television "drama" happens all the time. If we read a book or attend a play, we question the text, we question the presentation, and we determine for ourselves what it means to us.

Writing in the Proper Tense

Verb tense often distinguishes a paper in the humanities from one in the natural and social sciences. MLA style requires the present tense to cite an author's work (e.g., "Patel *explains*" or "the work of Scoggin and Roberts *shows*"). The CMS footnote style also asks for present tense.

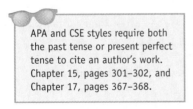

APA and CSE styles require both the past tense or present perfect tense to cite an author's work. Chapter 15, pages 301–302, and Chapter 17, pages 367–368.

MLA style requires that you use the present tense for your own comments and those of your sources because the ideas and the words of the writers remain in print and continue to be true in the universal present. Therefore, when writing a paper in the humanities, use the historical present tense, as shown here:

> "Always forgive your enemies; nothing annoys them so much," writes Oscar Wilde about adversaries and forgiveness.

> Yancy argues that sociologist Norman Guigou has a "fascination with the social causes rather than community solutions to homelessness" (64).

Use the past tense in a humanities paper only for reporting historical events. In the next example, past tense is appropriate for all sentences except the last:

> Great works of art had been created for ages, but Leonardo da Vinci was the first to paint the atmosphere, the air in which the

subject sat and which occupied the space between the eye and the thing seen. This technique continues to influence modern paintings which place subjects in lights and shadows as well as natural settings.

Using the Language of the Discipline

Every discipline and every topic has its own vocabulary. Therefore, while reading and taking notes, jot down words and phrases relevant to your research study. Get comfortable with them so you can use them effectively. For example, a child abuse topic requires the language of sociology and psychology, thereby demanding an acquaintance with these terms:

social worker	maltreatment	aggressive behavior
poverty levels	behavioral patterns	incestuous relations
stress	hostility	battered child
formative years	recurrence	guardians

Similarly, a poetry paper might require such terms as *symbolism, imagery, rhythm, persona,* and *rhyme.* Many writers create a terminology list to strengthen their command of appropriate nouns and verbs. However, nothing will betray a writer's ignorance of the subject matter more quickly than awkward and distorted technical terminology. For example, the following sentence uses big words, but it distorts and scrambles the language:

The enhancement of learning opportunities is often impeded by a pathological disruption in a child's mental processes.

The words may be large, but what does the passage mean? Probably this:

Education is often interrupted by a child's abnormal behavior.

Using Source Material to Enhance Your Writing

Blending sources into your text, Chapter 11.

Readers want to see your thoughts and ideas on a subject. For this reason, a paragraph should seldom contain source material only; it must contain a topic sentence to establish a point for the research evidence. Every paragraph should explain, analyze, and support a thesis, not merely string together a set of quotations.

The following passage cites effectively two sources.

Organ and tissue donation is the gift of life. Each year many people confront health problems due to diseases or congenital birth defects. Tom Taddonia explains that tissues such as skin, veins, and valves can be used to correct congenital defects, blindness, visual impairment, trauma, burns, dental defects, arthritis, cancer, and vascular and heart disease (23). Steve Barnill says, "More than 400 people each month receive the gift of sight through yet another type of tissue donation—corneal transplants. In many cases, donors unsuitable for organ donation are eligible for tissue donation" (356). Barnill notes that tissues are now used in orthopedic surgery, cardiovascular surgery, plastic surgery, dentistry, and podiatry (358). Even so, not enough people are willing to donate organs and tissues.

This passage illustrates four points. A writer should:

1. Weave the sources effectively into a whole.
2. Use the sources as a natural extension of the discussion.
3. Cite each source separately, one at a time.
4. Provide separate in-text citations to pages or footnote numerals.

This means you must read carefully so you can select key ideas and phrasing. It also means you should be accurate and precise.

Writing in the Third Person

Write your paper with third-person narration that avoids "I believe" and "It is my opinion." Rather than saying, "I think objectivity on television is nothing more than an ideal," drop the opening two words and say, "Objectivity on television is nothing more than an ideal." Readers will understand that the statement is your thought. However, attribute human functions to yourself or other persons, not to nonhuman sources:

WRONG: The study considered several findings.

CORRECT: The study reported the findings of several sources.

The study can report its findings, but it can't consider them.

Writing with the Passive Voice in an Appropriate Manner

Instructors often caution young writers against using the passive voice, which is often less forceful than an active verb. However, research writers sometimes need to shift the focus from the actor to the receiver, as shown here:

PASSIVE: Forty-three students of a third-grade class at Barksdale School were observed for two weeks.

ACTIVE: I observed forty-three students of a third-grade class at Barksdale school.

In the previous examples, the passive voice is preferred because it keeps the focus on the subject of the research, not the writer. Also, as a general rule, avoid the first person in research papers. Here are additional examples of the effective use of the passive voice:

The soil was examined for traces of mercury.

President Jackson was attacked repeatedly for his Indian policy by his enemies in Congress.

Children with attention disorders are often targeted for drug treatment.

As you see, the sentences place the focus on the soil, the President, and the children.

10e Using Visuals Effectively in a Research Essay

Graphics and visuals enable you to analyze trends and relationships in numerical data. Use them to support your text. Most computers allow you to create tables, line graphs, or pie charts as well as diagrams, maps, and other original designs. You may also import tables and illustrations from your sources. Place these graphics as close as possible to the parts of the text to which they relate. It is acceptable to use full-color art if your printer will print in colors; however, use black for the captions and date.

A table is a systematic presentation of materials, usually in columns. A figure is any non-text item that is not a table, such as a blueprint, a chart, a diagram, a drawing, a graph, a photo, a photostat, a map, and so on. Use graphs appropriately. A line graph serves a different purpose than does a circle (pie) chart, and a bar graph plots different information than does a scatter graph. Figures provide a visual amplification of the text. For example, a pho-

Table 2[a]

Mean Sources of Six Values Held by College Students According to Sex

All Students		Men		Women	
Pol.	40.61	Pol.	43.22	Aesth.	43.86
Rel.	40.51	Theor.	43.09	Rel.	43.13
Aesth.	40.29	Econ.	42.05	Soc.	41.13
Econ.	39.45	Soc.	37.05	Econ.	36.85
Soc.	39.34	Aesth.	36.72	Theor.	36.50

[a]Carmen J. Finley, et al. (165).

FIGURE 10.1
Sample table with in-text citation source

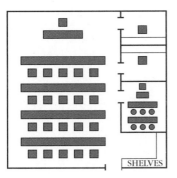

FIGURE 10.2 Sample figure with caption

Figure 4: Audio Laboratory with Private Listening Rooms and a Small Group Room

tograph of John Keats would reinforce and augment a research paper on the British poet.

Your figures, photographs, and tables should conform to the following guidelines:

- Present only one kind of information in each one, and make it as simple and as brief as possible. Frills and fancy artwork may distract rather than attract the reader.
- Place small figures and tables within your text; place large figures, sets of figures, or complex tables on separate pages in an appendix.
- Place the figure or table as near to your textual discussion as possible, but it should not precede your first mention of it.
- In the text, explain the significance of the figure or table. Describe the item so that your reader may understand your observations without reference to the item itself, but avoid giving too many numbers and figures in your text. Refer to figures and tables by number (for example, "Figure 5") or by number and page reference ("Table 4, 16"). Avoid using vague references (such as "the table above," "the following illustration," or "the chart below").
- Write a caption for the figure or table so that your reader can understand it without reference to your discussion.
- Number figures consecutively throughout the paper with Arabic numbers, preceded by "Fig." or "Figure" (for example, "Figure 4").
- Number tables consecutively throughout the paper with Arabic numerals, preceded by "Table" (for example, "Table 2").
- Insert a caption or number for each column of a table, centered above the column or, if necessary, inserted diagonally or vertically above it.
- When inserting an explanatory or reference note, place it below both a table and an illustration; then use a lowercase letter as the identifying

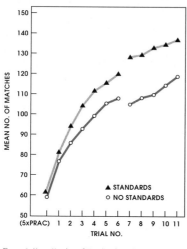

FIGURE 10.3 Sample graph with clear labels and caption

Figure 6: Mean Number of Matches by Subject with and without Standard (by Trial). Source: Lock and Bryan (289).

superscript, not an Arabic numeral. Sources are abbreviated as in-text citations, and full documentation must appear on the Works Cited page.

Note: See the paper by Norman Berkowitz, pages 236–247, for an example.

File Formats

Illustration and information graphics are usually huge files, so you will need to compress them with a compression format, either JPEG or GIF, so named for their file name extensions: ".jpg" and ".gif." In general, JPEGs work best for photographs and GIFs work best for line drawings.

Making your own graphics file is complex but rewarding. It adds a personal creativity to your research paper. Use one of the following techniques:

- *Use a graphics program*, such as Macromedia Freehand and Adobe Illustrator. With such software you can create a graphics file and save it as a JPEG or GIF. Also useful are Adobe Photoshop and JASC Paintshop Pro, which are designed primarily for working with photographs.
- *Use a scanner* to copy your drawings, graphs, photographs, and other matter.
- *Create original photographs with a digital camera.* Consult the owner's manual to learn how to create JPEGs or GIFs from your photography.
- *Create your own information graphics* in PowerPoint or Microsoft Excel.

As long as you create JPEG files or GIF files for your graphics, you can transport the entire research paper to a Web site.

10f Avoiding Sexist and Biased Language

Racial and gender fairness is one mark of the mature writer. The best writers exercise caution against words that may stereotype any person, regardless of gender, race, nationality, creed, age, or disability. If the writing is precise, readers will not make assumptions about race, age, and disabilities. Therefore, do not freely mention sexual orientation, marital status, ethnic or racial identity, or a person's disability. The following guidelines will help you avoid discriminatory language:

Age

Review the accuracy of your statement. It is appropriate to use *boy* and *girl* for children of high school age and under. *Young man* and *young woman* or *male adolescent* and *female adolescent* can be appropriate, but *teenager* carries a certain bias. Avoid *elderly* as a noun; use *older persons,* as in "Fifteen older patients suffered senile dementia of the Alzheimer's type.

Gender

Gender is a matter of our culture that identifies men and women within their social groups. *Sex* tends to be a biological factor (see below for a discussion of sexual orientation).

1. Use plural subjects so that nonspecific, plural pronouns are grammatically correct. For example, do you intend to specify that Judy Jones maintains *her* lab equipment in sterile condition or to indicate that technicians, in general, maintain *their* own equipment?
2. Reword the sentence so a pronoun is unnecessary:

   Correct: The doctor prepared the necessary surgical [not *his*] equipment without interference.

   Correct: Each technician must maintain the laboratory [not *her*] equipment in sterile condition.

3. Use pronouns denoting gender only when necessary to specify gender or when gender has been previously established.

   Larissa, as a new laboratory technician, must learn to maintain *her* equipment in sterile condition.

4. The use of *woman* and *female* as adjectives varies, as in *female athlete* and *woman athlete.* Use *woman* or *women* in most instances (e.g., *a woman's intuition*) and *female* for species and statistics, (e.g., *four female subjects, 10 males and 23 females, a female chimpanzee*). The word *lady* has fallen from favor (i.e., avoid *lady pilot*).
5. The first mention of a person requires the full name (e.g., Ernest Hemingway, Joan Didion) and thereafter requires only the use of the surname (e.g., Hemingway, Didion). At first mention, use Emily Brontë, but thereafter use

Brontë, *not* Miss Brontë. In general, avoid formal titles (e.g., Dr., Gen., Mrs., Ms., Lt., or Professor). Avoid their equivalents in other languages (e.g., Mme, Dame, Monsieur).

6. Avoid *man and wife* and *7 men and 16 females.* Keep the terms parallel by saying *husband and wife* or *man and woman* and *7 male rats and 16 female rats.*

Sexual Orientation

The term *sexual orientation* is preferred over the term *sexual preference.* It is preferable to use the terms *lesbians* and *gay men* rather than *homosexuals.* The terms *heterosexual, homosexual,* and *bisexual* can be used to describe both the identity and the behavior of subjects.

Ethnic and Racial Identity

Some people prefer the term *Black,* others prefer *African American,* and still others prefer *person of color.* The terms *Negro* and *Afro-American* are now dated and inappropriate. Use *Black* and *White,* not the lowercase *black* and *white.* In like manner, some individuals may prefer *Hispanic, Latino, Mexican,* or *Chicano.* Use the term *Asian* or *Asian American* rather than *Oriental. Native American* is a broad term that includes *Samoans, Hawaiians,* and *American Indians.* A good rule of thumb is to specify a person's nationality, tribe, or ethnic group when it is known (*Mexican, Korean, Comanche,* or *Nigerian*).

Disability

In general, place people first, not their disability. Rather than *disabled person* or *retarded child,* say *a person who has scoliosis* or *a child with Down's syndrome.* Avoid saying *a challenged person* or *a special child* in favor of *a person with _____* or *a child with _____.* Remember that a *disability* is a physical quality, while a *handicap* is a limitation that might be imposed by nonphysical factors, such as stairs, poverty, or social attitudes.

YOUR RESEARCH PROJECT

1. Examine your own thesis using the Final Thesis Checklist on page 162. Revise your thesis as necessary.

2. Consider your focus to determine if you will persuade, inquire, negotiate (see pages 158–159) or perhaps use a focus as explained in Chapter 1:

evaluation, definition, proposal, causal argument, analogy, precedence (see pages 5–9).

3. Write an academic title for your paper—one that clearly describes the nature of your work (see pages 162–163).

4. After you draft a significant portion of the paper, review it carefully for each of these items: coherence, proper tense, third-person voice, and the language of the discipline.

11 Blending Reference Material into Your Writing by Using MLA Style

Your in-text citations should conform to standards announced by your instructor. This chapter explains the MLA style, as established by the Modern Language Association. It governs papers in freshman composition, literature, English usage, and foreign languages.

> MLA style, pages 248–299
> APA style, pages 300–336
> CMS style, pages 337–365
> CSE style, pages 366–385

The MLA style puts great emphasis on the writer of the source, asking for the full name of the scholar on first mention but last name only thereafter and last name only in parenthetical citations. Other styles emphasize the year of publication as well as the author. Still other styles use merely a number in order to emphasize the material, not the author or date.

11a Blending Reference Citations into Your Text

As you might expect, writing a research paper carries with it certain obligations. You should gather scholarly material on the topic and display it prominently in your writing. In addition, you should identify each source used with the authority's name or the title of the work with a page number, except for unprinted sources and most Internet sources which will not require a page number. As a general policy, keep citations brief. Remember, your readers will have full documentation to each source on the Works Cited page (see Chapter 14).

Making a General Reference without a Page Number

Sometimes you will need no parenthetical citation.

> The women of Thomas Hardy's novels are the special focus of
> three essays by Nancy Norris, Judith Mitchell, and James Scott.

Beginning with the Author and Ending with a Page Number

Introduce a quotation or a paraphrase with the author's name and close it with a page number, placed inside the parentheses. Try always to use this standard citation because it informs the reader of the beginning and the end of borrowed materials, as shown here:

Herbert Norfleet states that the use of video games by children improves their hand and eye coordination (45).

In the following example, the reader can easily trace the origin of the ideas.

Video games for children have opponents and advocates. Herbert Norfleet defends the use of video games by children. He says it improves their hand and eye coordination and that it exercises their minds as they work their way through various puzzles and barriers. Norfleet states, "The mental gymnastics of video games and the competition with fellow players are important to young children for their physical, social, and mental development" (45). Yet some authorities disagree with Norfleet for several reasons.

Putting the Page Number Immediately after the Name

Sometimes, notes at the end of a quotation make it expeditious to place the page number immediately after the name.

Boughman (46) urges car makers to "direct the force of automotive airbags <u>upward</u> against the windshield" (emphasis added).

Putting the Name and Page Number at the End of Borrowed Material

You can, if you like, put cited names with the page number at the end of a quotation or paraphrase.

"Each DNA strand provides the pattern of bases for a new strand to form, resulting in two complete molecules" (Justice, Moody, and Graves 462).

In the case of a paraphrase, you should give your reader a signal to show when the borrowing begins, as shown next:

One source explains that the DNA in the chromosomes must be copied perfectly during cell reproduction (Justice, Moody, and Graves 462).

Use last names only within the parenthetical citation *unless your list contains more than one author with the same last name,* in which case you should add the author's first initial—for example, (H. Norfleet 45) and (W. Norfleet 432). If the first initial is also shared, use the full first name: (Herbert Norfleet 45).

> **HINT:** In MLA style, do not place a comma between the name and the page number.

11b Citing a Source When No Author Is Listed

When no author is shown on a title page, cite the title of the article, the name of the magazine, the name of a bulletin or book, or the name of the publishing organization. You should abbreviate or use an acronym (e.g., BBC, NASA).

> **HINT:** Search for the author's name at the bottom of the opening page, at the end of the article, at an Internet home page, or an e-mail address.

Citing the Title of a Magazine Article

Use a shorted version of the title when no author is listed:

> The preservation of our natural world, including green space, mountain ranges, and the seas, can only be protected with a conscious effort from all citizens. Conservation efforts are our last resort. According to a recent article in Audubon magazine, "Our world may be getting smaller, but roads less traveled still exist" ("To the Ends").

The Works Cited entry would read:

> "To the Ends of the Earth." Audubon July–August 2005: 45.

Citing the Title of a Report

> One bank showed a significant decline in assets despite an increase in its number of depositors (Annual Report, 2006, 23).

Citing the Name of a Publisher or a Corporate Body

> The report by the Clarion County School Board endorsed the use of Channel One in the school system and said that "students will benefit by the news reports more than they will be adversely affected by advertising" (CCSB 3–4).

11c Citing Nonprint Sources That Have No Page Number

On occasion you may need to identify nonprint sources, such as a speech, the song lyrics from a CD, an interview, or a television program. Since no page number exists, omit the parenthetical citation. Instead, introduce the type of source—for example, lecture, letter, interview—so readers do not expect a page number.

Thompson's lecture defined impulse as "an action triggered by the nerves without thought for the consequences."

Mrs. Peggy Meacham said in her phone interview that prejudice against young black women is not as severe as that against young black males.

11d Citing Internet Sources

Identify the Source with Name or Title

Whenever possible, identify the author of an Internet article. Usually, no page number is listed.

Hershel Winthrop interprets Hawthorne's stories as the search for holiness in a corrupt Puritan society.

If you can't identify an author, give the article title or Web site information.

One Web site claims that any diet that avoids carbohydrates will avoid some sugars that are essential for the body ("Fad Diets").

Identify the Nature of the Information and Its Credibility

As a service to your reader, indicate your best estimate of the scholarly value of an Internet source. For example, the next citation explains the role of the Center for Communications Policy:

The UCLA Center for Communication Policy, which conducted an intensive study of television violence, has advised against making the television industry the "scapegoat for violence" by advocating a focus on "deadlier and more significant causes: inadequate parenting, drugs, underclass rage, unemployment and availability of weaponry."

Here's another example of an introduction that establishes credibility:

John Armstrong, a spokesperson for Public Electronic Access to Knowledge (PEAK), states:

> As we venture into this age of biotechnology, many people predict gene manipulation will be a powerful tool for improving the quality of life. They foresee plants engineered to resist pests, animals designed to produce large quantities of rare medicinals, and humans treated by gene therapy to relieve suffering.

HINT: To learn more about the source of an Internet article, as in the case immediately above, learn to search out a home page. The address for Armstrong's article is <http://www.peak.org/~armstroj/america.html#Aims>.

By truncating the address to <http://www.peak.org/>, you can learn about the organization Armstrong represents.

If you are not certain about the credibility of a source—that is, it seemingly has no scholarly or educational basis—do not cite it, or describe the source so readers can make their own judgments:

> An Iowa non-profit organization, the Mothers for Natural Law, says—but offers no proof—that eight major crops are affected by genetically engineered organisms—canola, corn, cotton, dairy products, potatoes, soybeans, tomatoes, and yellow crook-neck squash ("What's on the Market").

Omitting Page and Paragraph Numbers to Internet Citations

In general, you should not list a page number, paragraph number, or screen number to an Internet site.

- You cannot list a screen number because monitors differ.
- You cannot list a page number of a downloaded document because computer printers differ.
- Unless they are numbered in the document, you cannot list paragraph numbers. Besides, you would have to go through and count every paragraph.

The marvelous feature of electronic text is that it is searchable, so your readers can find your quotation quickly with the Find or Search features. Suppose you have written the following:

> The Television Violence Report advices against making the television industry the "scapegoat for violence" by advocating a focus on "deadlier and more significant causes: inadequate parenting, drugs, underclass rage, unemployment and availability of weaponry."

A reader who wants to investigate further can consult your Works Cited page, find the Internet address (URL), use a browser to locate the article, and use Find for a phrase, such as "scapegoat for violence." That's much easier on you than numbering all the paragraphs and easier on the reader than counting them.

Some academic societies are urging scholars who publish on the Internet to number their paragraphs, and that practice may catch on quickly. Therefore, you should provide a paragraph number if the author of the Internet article has numbered each paragraph.

> The Insurance Institute for Highway Safety emphasizes restraint first, saying, "Riding unrestrained or improperly restrained in a motor vehicle always has been the greatest hazard for children" (IIHS, par. 13).

Provide a page number only if you find original page numbers buried within the electronic article. For example, a database like JSTOR reproduces original images of works and thereby provides original page numbers, as with the article by Harold R. Walley shown in Figure 11.1. Cite these pages just as you would a printed source.

> One source says the "moralizing and philosophical speculation" in Hamlet is worthy of examination, but to Shakespeare these were "distinctly subsidiary to plot and stage business . . . " (Walley 778).

11e Citing Indirect Sources

Sometimes the writer of a book or article quotes another person from an interview or personal correspondence, and you may want to use that same quotation. For example, in a newspaper article in *USA Today,* page 9A, Karen S. Peterson writes this passage in which she quotes two people:

> Sexuality, popularity, and athletic competition will create anxiety for junior high kids and high schoolers. Eileen Shiff says, "Bring up the topics. Don't wait for them to do it; they are nervous and they want to appear cool." Monitor the amount of time high schoolers spend working for money, she suggests. "Work is important, but school

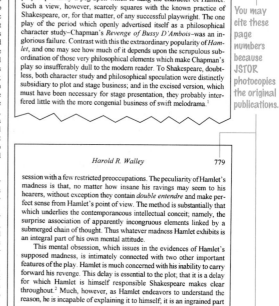

XL
SHAKESPEARE'S CONCEPTION OF *HAMLET*

What was Shakespeare's conception of *Hamlet*? That is the question. It is one which inevitably resolves itself into a reconstruction of the materials at his disposal, the dramatic problems with which he had to deal, and the means whereby he sought to satisfy contemporary dramatic taste. For such a reconstruction modern scholarship provides abundant information about both the theatrical practices and intellectual interests of the time and Shakespeare's habits as a craftsman. In particular should be noted his exceptional preoccupation with character portrayal and the scrupulous motivation of action; his conformity with changing theatrical fashion, yet at the same time his reluctance to pioneer in experiment; his sensitive, if sketchy, acquaintance with matters of contemporary interest; and his success as a skilled and inspired adapter rather than as an innovator. In the application of this knowledge two principles are fundamental. First, *Hamlet* must not be viewed as isolation, but in close conjunction with the theatrical environment which produced it. Second, Shakespeare must be recognized as primarily a practical playwright, a business man of the theater with obligations to fulfill, specific theatrical conditions to meet, and an audience to divert. For the rest, it is a pleasant exercise for the recreative imagination to try to think oneself into Shakespeare's mind, to face the problem of *Hamlet* as he faced it, and to trace the solution as he must have found it.

I

Shakespeare's *Hamlet* is a philosophical melodrama. Theatrically it is one of his most spectacular plays. For all its discursiveness it is crammed with action of the most sensational sort. Ghosts walk and cry "Revenge!" Murder is fouly done. Conspirators plot and counterplot. Two characters go mad. A queen is terrified nearly to death. A play breaks up in a near-riot. An insurrection batters the palace gates. A brawl desecrates a suicide's grave. A duel explodes into murder and general butchery. There are poison, incest, war, and debauchery. This is not closet drama for the philosopher's study; it is blood and thunder for the popular stage.

Nevertheless, *Hamlet* is also one of Shakespeare's most thoughtful plays. Permeated with moralizing and philosophical speculation, it presents in its center character a most elaborate psychological study. As for the reader these are unquestionably the most enduring elements, so to the elucidation of these criticism has devoted most of its attention.

777

778   *Shakespeare's Conception of "Hamlet"*

Indeed, not infrequently is it implied that the play exists for the express purpose of expounding Shakespeare's views on life and death, or that the play is primarily a peg upon which to hang the character of Hamlet. Such a view, however, scarcely squares with the known practice of Shakespeare, or, for that matter, of any successful playwright. The one play of the period which openly advertised itself as a philosophical character study–Chapman's *Revenge of Bussy D'Ambois*–was an inglorious failure. Contrast with this the extraordinary popularity of *Hamlet*, and one may see how much of it depends upon the scrupulous subordination of those very philosophical elements which make Chapman's play so insufferably dull to the modern reader. To Shakespeare, doubtless, both character study and philosophical speculation were distinctly subsidiary to plot and stage business; and in the excised version, which must have been necessary for stage presentation, they probably interfered little with the more congenial business of swift melodrama.[1]

You may cite these page numbers because JSTOR photocopies the original publications.

Harold R. Walley   779

session with a few restricted preoccupations. The peculiarity of Hamlet's madness is that, no matter how insane his ravings may seem to his hearers, without exception they contain *double entendre* and make perfect sense from Hamlet's point of view. The method is substantially that which underlies the contemporaneous intellectual conceit; namely, the surprise association of apparently incongruous elements linked by a submerged chain of thought. Thus whatever madness Hamlet exhibits is an integral part of his own mental attitude.

This mental obsession, which issues in the evidences of Hamlet's supposed madness, is intimately connected with two other important features of the play. Hamlet is much concerned with his inability to carry forward his revenge. This delay is essential to the plot; that it is a delay for which Hamlet is himself responsible Shakespeare makes clear throughout.[2] Much, however, as Hamlet endeavors to understand the reason, he is incapable of explaining it to himself; it is an ingrained part

FIGURE 11.1 You may cite these page numbers.

must be the priority." Parental intervention in a child's school career that worked in junior high may not work in high school, psychiatrist Martin Greenburg adds. "The interventions can be construed by the adolescent as negative, overburdening and interfering with the child's ability to care for himself." He adds, "Be encouraging, not critical. Criticism can be devastating for the teen-ager."

Suppose you want to use the quotation above by Martin Greenburg. You must quote the words of Greenburg *and* put Peterson's name in the parenthetical citation as the person who wrote the article, as shown in the following:

> After students get beyond middle school, they begin to resent interference by their parents, especially in school activities. They need some space from Mom and Dad. Martin Greenburg says, "The interventions can be construed by the adolescent as negative, overburdening and interfering with the child's ability to care for himself" (qtd. in Peterson 9A).

CHECKLIST

Using Links to Document Internet Sources

If you are publishing your project on your own Web page, you have the opportunity to send your readers to other sites via hypertext links. If you do so, follow these guidelines:

1. You may activate a hot key (hypertext link) in your document that will automatically send your reader to one of your sources.

2. Identify the linked source clearly so readers know where the link will take them.

3. Be selective; don't sprinkle your document with excessive links. You want the reader to stay with you, not wander around on the Internet.

4. The links are part of your documentation, so cite these linked sources in your Works Cited list.

On the Works Cited page, you will list Peterson's name with the bibliography entry for her article, but you will not list Greenburg's name there because he is not the author of the article.

In other words, in the text you need a double reference that introduces the speaker and includes a clear reference to the book or article where you found the quotation or the paraphrased material. Without the reference to Peterson, nobody could find the article. Without the reference to Greenburg, readers would assume Peterson spoke the words.

HINT: If you can locate the original source of the quotation, cite it rather than use the double reference.

11f Citing Frequent Page References to the Same Work

If you quote more than once from the same page within a paragraph and no other citations intervene, you may provide one citation at the end for all the references.

> When the character Beneatha denies the existence of God in Hansberry's A Raisin in the Sun, Mama slaps her in the face and forces her to repeat after her, "In my mother's house there is still God." Then Mama adds, "There are some ideas we ain't going to have in this house. Not long as I am at the head of the family" (37).

Also, when you make frequent references to the same source, you need not repeat the author's name in every instance. Note the following example:

> The consumption of "healing foods," such as those that reduce blood pressure, grows in popularity each year. Clare Hasler says that when the medicinal properties of functional food gain the support of clinical evidence, functional foods can become an economical weapon in the battle against rising health care costs. In addition, functional foods may be a promising addition to the diet of people who suffer from deadly disease. As executive director of the Functional Foods for Health Program at the University of Illinois, she claims, "Six of the ten leading causes of death in the United State are believed to be related to diet: cancer, coronary heart disease, stroke, diabetes, atherosclerosis, and liver disease" ("Western Perspective" 66).

HINT: If you are citing from two or more novels in your paper—let's say John Steinbeck's *East of Eden* and *Of Mice and Men*—provide both title (abbreviated) and page(s) unless the reference is clear: (*Eden* 56) and (*Mice* 12-13).

11g Citing Material from Textbooks and Large Anthologies

Reproduced below is a poem you might find in many literary textbooks.

> **The Red Wheelbarrow**
> so much depends
> upon
> a red wheel
> barrow
> glazed with rain
> water
> beside the white chickens
> *William Carlos Williams*

If you quote lines of the poem, and if that is all you quote from the anthology, cite the author and page in the text and put a comprehensive entry in the Works Cited list.

Text:

> For Williams, "so much depends" on the red wheel barrow as it sits "glazed with rain water beside the white chickens" (751).

Bibliography Entry:

Williams, William Carlos. "The Red Wheelbarrow." <u>An Introduction to</u>

<u>Literature</u>. 14th ed. Ed. Sylvan Barnet et al. New York: Longman,

2006. 751.

Suppose, however, that you also take quotations from other poems in the textbook.

Robert Frost calls for escape into the pleasures of nature, saying

"I'm going out to clean the pasture spring; / I'll only stop to rake the

leaves away" and invites us to join in, "You come too" (931).

T.S. Eliot describes the fog as a "yellow smoke" that "Slipped by

the terrace, made a sudden leap" (910).

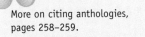

More on citing anthologies, pages 258–259.

Now, with three citations to the same anthology, you should list in your Works Cited the anthology used, as edited by Barnet et al., and also list shortened citations for Williams, Frost, and Sandburg with each referring to the lead editor's name, in this case *Barnet*.

Barnet, Sylvan, et al., eds. <u>An Introduction to Literature</u>. 14th ed. New

York: Longman, 2006.

Eliot, T.S. "The Love Song of J. Alfred Prufrock." Barnet et al. 994–997.

Frost, Robert. "The Pasture." Barnet et al. 931.

Williams, William Carlos. "The Red Wheelbarrow." Barnet et al. 926–27.

11h Adding Extra Information to In-Text Citations

As a courtesy to your reader, add extra information within the citation. Show parts of books, different titles by the same writer, or several works by different writers. For example, your reader may have a different anthology than yours, so a clear reference, such as (*Great Expectations* 81; chap. 4), will enable the reader to locate the passage. The same is true with a reference to (*Romeo and Juliet* 2.3.65–68). The reader will find the passage in almost any edition of Shakespeare's play. Here's a reference to Herman Melville's *Moby-Dick* that shows both page and chapter:

Melville uncovers the superstitious nature of Ishmael by stressing

Ishmael's fascination with Yojo, the little totem god of Queequeg

(71; chap. 16).

One of Several Volumes

These next two citations provide three vital facts: (1) an abbreviation for the title, (2) the volume used, and (3) the page number(s). The Works Cited entry will list the total number of volumes (see pages 268–269).

> In a letter to his Tennessee Volunteers in 1812 General Jackson chastised the "mutinous and disorderly conduct" of some of his troops (Papers 2: 348–49).

> Joseph Campbell suggests that man is a slave yet also the master of all the gods (Masks 2: 472).

However, if you use only one volume of a multivolume work, you need to give only page numbers in the parenthetical reference. Then include the volume number in the Works Cited entry (see page 270):

> Don Quixote's strange adventure with the Knight of the Mirrors is one of Cervantes's brilliant short tales (1,908–14).

If you refer to an entire volume, there is no need for page numbers:

> The Norton Anthology includes masterpieces of the ancient world, the Middle Ages, and the Renaissance (Mack et al., vol. 1).

Two or More Works by the Same Writer

In this example, the writer makes reference to two novels, both abbreviated. The full titles are *Tess of the D'Urbervilles* and *The Mayor of Casterbridge.*

> Thomas Hardy reminds readers in his prefaces that "a novel is an impression, not an argument" and that a novel should be read as "a study of man's deeds and character" (Tess xxii; Mayor 1).

If the author appears in the parenthetical citation, place a comma after the name: (Hardy, *Tess* xxii; Hardy, *Mayor* 1). If anything other than a page number appears after the title, follow the title with a comma: (Worth, "Computing," par. 6).

The complete titles of the two works by Campbell referenced in the following example are *The Hero with a Thousand Faces* and *The Masks of God,* a four-volume work.

> Because he stresses the nobility of man, Joseph Campbell suggests that the mythic hero is symbolic of the "divine creative and redemptive image which is hidden within us all . . . " (Hero 39). The

hero elevates the human mind to an "ultimate mythogenetic zone—the creator and destroyer, the slave and yet the master, of all the gods" (Masks 1: 472).

Several Authors in One Citation

You may wish to cite several sources that treat the same topic. Put them in alphabetical order to match that of the Works Cited page, or place them in the order of importance to the issue at hand. Separate them with semicolons.

Several sources have addressed this aspect of gang warfare as a fight for survival, not just for control of the local neighborhood or "turf" (Robertson 98–134; Rollins 34; Templass 561–65).

Additional Information with the Page Number

Your citations can refer to special parts of a page—for example, footnote, appendix, graph, table—and can also specify emphasis on particular pages.

Horton (22, n. 3) suggests that Melville forced the symbolism, but Welston (199–248, esp. 234) reaches an opposite conclusion.

However, use a semicolon to separate the page number from the edition used, a chapter number, or other identifying information: (Wollstonecraft 185; ch. 13, sec. 2).

11i Punctuating Citations Properly and Consistently

Keep page citations outside quotation marks but inside the final period, as shown here:

"The benefits of cloning far exceed any harm that might occur" (Smith 34).

In MLA style, use no comma between the name and the page within the citation (for example, Jones 16–17, *not* Jones, 16–17). Do not use *p.* or *pp.* with the page number(s) in MLA style. However, if an author's name begins a citation to paragraph numbers or screen numbers, *do* include a comma after the author's name (Richards, par. 4) or (Thompson, screens 6–7).

Commas and Periods

Place commas and periods inside quotation marks unless the page citation intervenes. The example below shows: (1) how to put the mark inside the quotation marks, (2) how to interrupt a quotation to insert the speaker, (3) how to use single quotation marks within the regular quotation marks, and (4) how to place the period after a page citation.

> "Modern advertising," says Rachel Murphy, "not only creates a marketplace, it determines values." She adds, "I resist the advertiser's argument that they 'awaken, not create desires'" (192).

Sometimes you may need to change the closing period to a comma. Suppose you decide to quote this sentence: "Scientific cloning poses no threat to the human species." If you start your sentence with the quotation, you will need to change the period to a comma, as shown:

> "Scientific cloning poses no threat to the human species," declares Joseph Wineberg in a recent article (357).

However, retain question marks or exclamation marks; no comma is required:

> "Does scientific cloning pose a threat to the human species?" wonders Mark Durham (546).

Let's look at other examples. Suppose this is the original material:

> The Russians had obviously anticipated neither the quick discovery of the bases nor the quick imposition of the quarantine. Their diplomats across the world were displaying all the symptoms of improvisation, as if they had been told nothing of the placement of the missiles and had received no instructions what to say about them.— From: Arthur M. Schlesinger, Jr., *A Thousand Days* (New York: Houghton, 1965), 820.

Punctuate citations from this source in one of the following methods in accordance with MLA style:

> "The Russians," writes Schlesinger, "had obviously anticipated neither the quick discovery of the [missile] bases nor the quick imposition of the quarantine" (820).

> Schlesinger notes, "Their diplomats across the world were displaying all the symptoms of improvisation . . . " (820).

> Schlesinger observes that the Russian failure to anticipate an American discovery of Cuban missiles caused "their diplomats across the world" to improvise answers as "if they had been told nothing of the placement of the missiles . . . " (820).

Note that the last example correctly changes the capital *T* of "their" to lower case to match the grammar of the restructured sentence, and it does not use ellipsis points before "if" because the phrase flows smoothly into the text.

Semicolons and Colons

Both semicolons and colons go outside the quotation marks, as illustrated by these three examples:

> Zigler admits that "the extended family is now rare in contemporary society"; however, he stresses the greatest loss as the "wisdom and daily support of older, more experienced family members" (42).

> Zigler laments the demise of the "extended family": that is, the family suffers by loss of the "wisdom and daily support of older, more experienced family members" (42).

> Brian Sutton-Smith says, "Adults don't worry whether their toys are educational" (64); nevertheless, parents want to keep their children in a learning mode.

The third example, immediately above, shows how to place the page citation after a quotation and before a semicolon.

Use the semicolon to separate two or more works in a single parenthetical reference:

> (Roman, Dallas 16; Manfred 345)
>
> (Steinbeck, Grapes 24; Stuben xii)

Question Marks and Exclamation Marks

When a question mark or an exclamation mark serves as part of the quotation, keep it inside the quotation mark. Put the page citation immediately after the name of the source to avoid conflict with the punctuation mark.

> Thompson (16) passionately shouted to union members, "We can bring order into our lives even though we face hostility from every quarter!"

If you place the page number at the end of the quotation, retain the original exclamation mark or question mark, follow with the page reference, and then a sentence period outside the citation.

> Thompson passionately shouted to union members, "We can bring order into our lives even though we face hostility from every quarter!" (16).

Retain questions marks and exclamation marks when the quotation begins a sentence; no comma is required.

> "We face hostility from every quarter!" declared the union leader.

Question marks appear inside the closing quotation mark when they are part of the original quotation; otherwise, they go outside.

> The philosopher Brackenridge (16) asks, "How should we order our lives?"

and

> The philosopher Brackenridge asks, "How should we order our lives?" (16).

but

> Did Brackenridge say that we might encounter "hostility from every quarter" (16)?

Single Quotation Marks

When a quotation appears within another quotation, use single quotation marks with the shorter one. The period goes inside both closing quotation marks.

> George Loffler (32) confirms that "the unconscious carries the best of human thought and gives man great dignity, but it also has the dark side so that we cry, in the words of Shakespeare's Macbeth, 'Hence, horrible shadow! Unreal mockery, hence.'"

Remember that the period always goes inside quotation marks unless the page citation intervenes, as shown below:

> George Loffler confirms that "the unconscious carries the best of human thought and gives man great dignity, but it also has the dark side so that we cry, in the words of Shakespeare's Macbeth, 'Hence, horrible shadow! Unreal mockery, hence'" (32).

11j   Indenting Long Quotations

Set off long prose quotations of four lines or more by indenting 1 inch or 10 spaces, which is usually two clicks of the tab key. Do not enclose the indented material within quotation marks. If you quote only one paragraph or the beginning of one, do *not* indent the first line an extra five spaces. Maintain normal double spacing between your text and the quoted materials. Place the parenthetical citation *after* the final mark of punctuation. As shown below, the parenthetical citation might be a title to an Internet article rather than to page numbers:

> The number of people who need transplants continues to increase, but the number of donors fails to meet these needs. Tommy G. Thompson, secretary for the Department of Health and Human Services commented on the current state of organ donation:
>
>> Citing the growing need for organ donation to save and improve lives, Tommy G. Thompson, within his first 100 days as HHS Secretary, announced his commitment to develop a new national effort to encourage organ donation. That commitment, also known as the Gift of Life Donation Initiative, led to 2004's record transplant totals through which the number of transplant candidates who died waiting for an organ fell below 6,000 for the first time in six years. ("New Record")
>
> With the ever increasing number of organ donors needed, why don't people give of themselves? The most recognized reason for the shortage of donors is directly related to the myths that are associated with organ and tissue donation.

If you quote more than one paragraph, indent all paragraphs an extra three (3) spaces or a quarter-inch. However, if the first sentence quoted does not begin a paragraph in the original source, do not indent it an extra three spaces.

> Zigler makes this observation:
>
>> With many others, I am nevertheless optimistic that our nation will eventually display its inherent greatness and successfully correct the many ills that I have touched upon here.
>>
>> Of course, much remains that could and should be done, including increased efforts in the area of family planning, the widespread implementation of Education for Parenthood programs, an increase in the availability of homemaker and child care services, and a reexamination of our commitment to doing what is in the best interest of every child in America. (42)

11k Citing Poetry

Quoting Two Lines of Poetry or Less

Incorporate short quotations of poetry (one or two lines) into your text.

> In Part 3, Eliot's "The Waste Land" (1922) remains a springtime search for nourishing water: "Sweet Thames, run softly, for I speak not loud or long" (line 12) says the speaker in "The Fire Sermon," while in Part 5 the speaker of "What the Thunder Said" yearns for "a damp gust/ Bringing rain" (73–74).

As the example demonstrates:

1. Set off the material with quotation marks.
2. Indicate separate lines by using a virgule (/) with a space before and after it.
3. Place line documentation within parentheses immediately following the quotation mark and inside the period. Do not use the abbreviations *l.* or *ll.*, which might be confused with page numbers; use *lines* initially to establish that the numbers represent lines of poetry, and thereafter use only the numbers.
4. Use Arabic numerals for books, parts, volumes, and chapters of works; acts, scenes, and lines of plays; and cantos, stanzas, and lines of poetry.

Quoting Three Lines of Poetry or More

Set off three or more lines of poetry by indenting 1 inch or 10 spaces, as shown below. Use double-spaced lines. A parenthetical citation to the lines of indented verse follows the last line of the quotation. If the parenthetical citation will not fit on the last line, place it on the next line, flush with the right margin of the poetry text.

> The king cautions Prince Henry:
>
> > Thy place in council thou has rudely lost,
> >
> > Which by thy younger brother is supplied,
> >
> > And art almost an alien to the hearts
> >
> > Of all the court and princes of my blood.
> >
> > (3.2.32–35)

Refer to act, scene, and lines only after you have established Shakespeare's *Henry IV, Part 1* as the central topic of your study; otherwise, write (1H4 3.2.32-35). If you are citing from more than one play, always add an abbreviation for the play (1H4 1.1.15-18).

Indenting Turnovers for Long Lines of Poetry

When quoting a line of poetry that is too long for your right margin, indent the continuation line 3 spaces or a quarter-inch more than the greatest indentation.

> Plath opens her poem with these lines:
>> Love set you going like a fat gold watch.
>> The midwife slapped your footsoles,
>>> and your bald cry
>> Took its place among the elements. (lines 1–3)

You may also indent less to make room for the words:

> Plath opens her poem with these lines:
>> Love set you going like a fat gold watch.
>> The midwife slapped your footsoles, and your bald cry
>> Took its place among the elements. (lines 1–3)

Retaining Internal Quotations within a Block

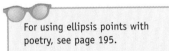

For using ellipsis points with poetry, see page 195.

While you should not use quotation marks around a block quotation, *do* retain any internal quotation marks:

> With his sonnet "Spring," Shakespeare playfully describes the cry of the cuckoo bird:
>> The cuckoo then, on every tree,
>> Mocks married men; for thus sings he, "Cuckoo!
>> Cuckoo, cuckoo!" O word of fear,
>> Unpleasing to a married ear! (524)

Providing Translations

When a quotation is run into the text, use double quotation marks for translations placed within parentheses but single quotations around a translation without the parentheses:

> Chaucer's setting is Spring, when "zephyrs ("west winds") have breathed softly all about . . . " (line 5).

> Chaucer's setting is Spring, when "zephyrs 'west winds' have breathed softly all about . . . " (line 5).

Do not place quotation marks around quotations and translations set off from the text in a block. Place the block of translation below the block of poetry.

> Ramon Magrans has translated this Lorca poem in a
> literal manner:
>
> > Alto pinar!
> >
> > Cuatro palomas por el aire van.
> >
> > Cuatro palomas
> >
> > Vuelan y tornan
> >
> > Llevan heridas
> >
> > sus cuatro sombras
> >
> > Bajo pinar!
> >
> > Cuatro palomas en la tierra están.
> >
> > Above the pine trees
> >
> > four pigeons fly through the air.
> >
> > Four pigeons
> >
> > fly and turn around
> >
> > Wounded, they carry
> >
> > their four shadows.
> >
> > Below the pine trees
> >
> > four pigeons lie on the earth.

11l   Handling Quotations from a Play

Set off from your text any dialog of two or more characters. Begin with the character's name, indented one inch and written in all capital letters. Follow the name with a period, and then start the character's lines of dialog. Indent subsequent lines of dialog an additional quarter-inch or three spaces.

> At the end of <u>Oedipus Rex</u>, Kreon chastises Oedipus, reminding him
> that he no longer has control over his own life nor that of his children.
>
> > KREON.   Come now and leave your children.
> >
> > OEDIPUS.   No! Do not take them from me!
> >
> > KREON.   Think no longer
> >
> >   That you are in command here, but rather think
> >
> >   How, when you were, you served your own
> >
> >   destruction.

11m Altering Initial Capitals in Quoted Matter

In general, you should reproduce quoted materials exactly, yet one exception is permitted for logical reasons. Restrictive connectors, such as *that* and *because,* create restrictive clauses and eliminate a need for the comma. Without a comma, the capital letter is unnecessary. In the following example, "The," which is capitalized as the first word in the original sentence, is changed to lower case because it continues the grammatical flow of the student's sentence.

> Another writer argues that "the single greatest impediment to our improving the lives of America's children is the myth that we are a child-oriented society" (Zigler 39).

Otherwise, write:

> Another writer argues, "The single greatest. . . . "

11n Omitting Quoted Matter with Ellipsis Points

You may omit portions of quoted material with three spaced ellipsis points, as shown in the examples below.

Context

In omitting passages, be fair to the author. Do not change the meaning or take a quotation out of context.

Correctness

Maintain the grammatical correctness of your sentences—that is, avoid fragments and misplaced modifiers. You don't want your readers to misunderstand the structure of the original. When you quote only a phrase, readers will understand that you omitted most of the original sentence, so no ellipsis is necessary.

> Phil Withim recognizes the weakness in Captain Vere's "intelligence and insight" into the significance of his decisions regarding Billy Budd (118).

Omission within a Sentence

Use three ellipsis points (periods) with a space before each and a space after the last.

> Phil Withim objects to the idea that "such episodes are intended to demonstrate that Vere . . . has the intelligence and insight to perceive the deeper issue" (118).

Omission at the End of a Sentence

If an ellipsis occurs at the end of your sentence, use three periods with a space before each following a sentence period—that is, you will have four periods with no space before the first or after the last. A closing quotation mark finishes the punctuation.

> R. W. B. Lewis (62) declares that "if Hester has sinned, she has done so as an affirmation of life, and her sin is the source of life. . . . "

However, if a page citation also appears at the end in conjunction with the ellipsis, use three periods with a space before each and put the sentence period after the final parenthesis. Thus, you will have three ellipsis points with a space before each, the closing quotation mark followed by a space, the parenthetical citation, and the period.

> R. W. B. Lewis declares that "if Hester has sinned, she has done so as an affirmation of life, and her sin is the source of life . . . " (62).

Omission at the Beginning of a Sentence

Most style guides discourage the use of ellipsis points for material omitted from the beginning of a source, as shown here:

> He states: " . . . the new parent has lost the wisdom and daily support of older, more experienced family members" (Zigler 34).

The passage would read better without the ellipsis points:

> He states that "the new parent has lost the wisdom and daily support of older, more experienced family members" (Zigler 34).

Another option is this one, as stipulated by the *Chicago Manual of Style:* "If a quotation that is only part of a sentence in the original forms a complete sentence as quoted, an initial lower case letter may be changed to a capital where the structure of the text suggests it."

> He states: "The new parent has lost the wisdom and daily support of older, more experienced family members" (Zigler 34).

Here's another example:

> R. W. B. Lewis declares, "If Hester has sinned, she has done so as an affirmation of life, and her sin is the source of life . . . " (62).

Omission of Complete Sentences and Paragraphs

Use a closing punctuation mark and three spaced ellipsis points when omitting one or more sentences from within a long quotation. Here's an omission in which one sentence ends, another sentence or more is omitted, and a full sentence ends the passage.

> Zigler reminds us that "child abuse is found more frequently in a single (female) parent home in which the mother is working . . . . The unavailability of quality day care can only make this situation more stressful" (42).

Here's an omission from the middle of one sentence to the middle of another:

> Zigler reminds us that "child abuse is found more frequently in a single (female) parent home in which the mother is working, . . . so the unavailability of quality day care can only make this situation more stressful" (42).

Omissions in Poetry

If you omit a word or phrase in a quotation of poetry, indicate the omission with three or four ellipsis points, just as you would with omissions in a prose passage. However, if you omit a complete line or more from the poem, indicate the omission by a line of spaced periods that equals the average length of the lines. Note that the parenthetical citation shows two sets of lines.

> Elizabeth Barrett Browning asks:
>> Do ye hear the children weeping, O my brothers,
>>> Ere the sorrow comes with years?
>> They are leaning their young heads against their mothers,
>>> And <u>that</u> cannot stop their tears.
>
> . . . .
>
>> They are weeping in the playtime of the others,
>> In the country of the free. (1–4, 11–12)

Avoid Excessive Use of Ellipsis Points

Many times, you can be more effective if you incorporate short phrases rather than quote the whole sprinkled with many ellipsis points. Note how this next passage incorporates quotations without the use of ellipsis.

> The long-distance marriage, according to William Nichols, "works best when there are no minor-aged children to be considered," the two people are "equipped by temperament and personality to spend a considerable amount of time alone," and both are able to "function in a mature, highly independent fashion" (54).

Ellipsis in the Original

If the original passage has ellipsis by the author, and you wish to cut additional words, place brackets around your ellipsis points to distinguish them from the author's ellipsis points. If the original says:

> Shakespeare's innovative techniques in working with revenge tragedy are important in *Hamlet* . . . while the use of a Senecan ghost is a convention of revenge tragedy, a ghost full of meaningful contradictions in calling for revenge is part of Shakespeare's dramatic suspense.

If you cut the middle phrase, use this form:

> One writer says, "Shakespeare's innovative techniques in working with revenge tragedy are important in <u>Hamlet</u>, . . . [. . .] a ghost full of meaningful contradictions in calling for revenge is part of Shakespeare's dramatic suspense."

11o Altering Quotations with Parentheses and Brackets

You will sometimes need to alter a quotation to emphasize a point or to make something clear. You might add material, italicize an important word, or use the word *sic* (Latin for "thus" or "so") to alert readers that you have properly reproduced the material even though the logic or the spelling of the original might appear to be in error. Use parentheses or brackets according to these basic rules.

Parentheses

Use parentheses to enclose your comments or explanations that fall outside a quotation, shown in these examples:

> The problem with airbags is that children (even those in protective seats) can be killed by the force as the airbag explodes. Boughman (46) urges car makers to "direct the force of automotive airbags <u>upward</u> against the windshield" (emphasis added).

> Roberts (22) comments that "politicians suffer a conflict with honoure" (sic).

Brackets

Use brackets for interpolation, which means inserting your own comment into a text or quotation. The use of brackets signals the insertion. Note the following rules.

Use Brackets to Clarify

This same critic indicates that "we must avoid the temptation to read it [The Scarlet Letter] heretically" (118).

Use Brackets to Establish Correct Grammar within an Abridged Quotation

"John F. Kennedy [was] an immortal figure of courage and dignity in the hearts of most Americans," notes one historian (Jones 82).

He states: "[The] new parent has lost the wisdom and daily support of older, more experienced family members" (Zigler 34).

Use Brackets to Note the Addition of Underlining

He says, for instance, that the "extended family is now rare in contemporary society, and with its demise the new parent has <u>lost the wisdom</u> [my emphasis] and daily support of older, more experienced family members" (Zigler 42).

Use Brackets to Substitute a Proper Name for a Pronoun

"As we all know, he [Kennedy] implored us to serve the country, not take from it" (Jones 432).

Use Brackets with Sic to Indicate Errors in the Original

Lovell says, "John F. Kennedy, assassinated in November of 1964 [sic], became overnight an immortal figure of courage and dignity in the hearts of most Americans" (62).

HINT: The assassination occurred in 1963. However, do not burden your text with the use of "sic" for historical matter in which outmoded spellings are obvious, as with: "Faire seemly pleasauance each to other makes."

Use Brackets with Ellipsis Points

See the example on page 196.

YOUR RESEARCH PROJECT

1. Examine your handling of the sources. Have you introduced them clearly so the reader will know when the borrowing began? Have you closed them with a page citation, as appropriate? Have you placed quotation marks at the beginning and the end of borrowed phrases as well as borrowed sentences?

2. If you have used online sources, look at them again to see if the paragraphs on the online site are numbered. If so, use the paragraph numbers in your citation(s); if not, use no numbers—not the numbers on any printout and not paragraph numbers if you must count them.

3. Look at your source material to find a table, graph, figure, or photograph you might insert into your paper as additional evidence. Be certain that you have labeled it correctly (see pages 239–241 for examples).

4. Make a critical journey through your text to be certain you have made an informed choice about the documentation style you need. Normally, instructors will inform you. In general, use MLA style for papers in freshman composition and literature classes; use APA style for papers in the social sciences; use the footnote style for papers in history and the fine arts; use CSE number style for papers in the applied sciences.

12 Writing the Introduction, Body, and Conclusion

The three parts of your paper—the introduction, the body, and the conclusion—demand special considerations. For most papers, follow the guidelines offered below. However, some scientific papers will demand different elements (see 15a, pages 300–301).

12a Writing the Introduction of the Paper

Use the first few paragraphs of your paper to establish the nature of your study. In brief, the introduction should establish the problem, the body should present the evidence, and the conclusion should arrive at answers, judgments, proposals, and closure. Most important, let the introduction and body work *toward* a demonstrative conclusion. The introduction should be long enough to establish the required elements described in the checklist on page 200.

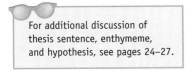

For additional discussion of thesis sentence, enthymeme, and hypothesis, see pages 24–27.

How you work these essential elements into the framework of your opening will depend on your style of writing. They need not appear in this order, nor should you cram all these items into a short opening paragraph. Feel free to write two or three paragraphs of introduction, letting it run over onto the next page, if necessary. When crafting your introduction, use more than one of the techniques described in the following approaches.

Provide the Thesis Statement, Enthymeme, or Hypothesis

Generally, the controlling statement will appear early in the introduction to establish the agenda for the paper or appear late in the introduction to set the stage for the analysis to come in the body. For example, this opening features the thesis first:

Thesis —

Created by an act of Congress in 1933 and signed into law by President Franklin D. Roosevelt, the Tennessee Valley Authority Act created stability on the waterways and in the lives of citizens in the mid-south. With its establishment of

> ### CHECKLIST
>
> ### *Writing the Introduction*
>
> **Subject** Identify your specific topic, and then define, limit, and narrow it to one issue.
>
> **Background** Provide relevant historical data. Discuss a few key sources that touch on your specific issue. If writing about a major figure, give relevant biographical facts, but not an encyclopedia-type survey. (See "Providing Background Information," page 201–202.)
>
> **Problem** The point of a research paper is to explore or resolve a problem, so identify and explain the complications you see. The examples shown below demonstrate this technique.
>
> **Thesis** Within the first few paragraphs, use your thesis sentence to establish the direction of the study and to point your readers toward your eventual conclusions.

> a series of dams, the TVA controlled the drainage of 42,000 square miles of and waterways. That same control harnessed the power of the rivers to create electricity for residents of the area.

Provide the Enthymeme

The enthymeme, as explained on pages 24–26, uses a *because* clause to make a claim. It also determines the direction your paper will take. Notice the enthymeme that closes this opening paragraph:

> Here we are, a civilized world with reasonably educated people, yet we constantly fight with each other. These are not sibling squabbles either; people die in terrible ways. We wonder, then, if there was ever a time when men and women lived in harmony with one another and with nature and the

environment. The Bible speaks of the Garden of Eden, and
the French philosopher Jean-Jacques Rousseau advanced the
idea in the 1700s of the "noble savage," and that "nothing
could be more gentle" than an ancient colony of people
(LaBlanc 15). Wrong! There has never been a "noble savage,"

Enthymeme —   as such, because even prehistoric human beings fought
frequent wars for numerous reasons.

Provide a Hypothesis

The hypothesis, as explained on pages 26–27, is a theory that needs testing in the lab, in the literature, and/or by field research to prove its validity. Writers may list it as an objective, as in this example:

Diabetes is a disease that affects approximately 11
million people in the U.S. alone. Its complications lead to
approximately 350,000 deaths per year and cost the nation
$20,373 billion per year in medical care, in the direct cost
of complications, and in the indirect costs of loss of
productivity related to the disease (Guthrie and Guthrie 1).
The condition can produce devastating side effects and a
multitude of chronic health problems. Diabetes currently
has no known cure, but it can be controlled. The objective

Hypothesis —   of this study is to examine how well diabetes can be
controlled by a combination of medication, monitoring,
diet, and exercise.

Relate to the Well Known

The next passage will appeal to the popular interest and knowledge of the reader:

Television flashes images into our living rooms, radios
invade the confines of our automobiles, and local
newspapers flash their headlines to us daily. However,

Popular
appeal —   one medium that has gained great popularity and influence
within the past decade is the specialized magazine.

Provide Background Information

Writers may trace the historical nature of a topic, give biographical data about a person, or provide a geographic description. A summary of a novel, long poem, or other work can refresh a reader's memory about details of plot, character, and so forth.

> First published in 1915, <u>Spoon River Anthology</u> by
> Edgar Lee Masters gives readers candid glimpses into the life
> of a small town at the turn of the twentieth century.
>
> Background — | Speaking from beyond the grave, the narrator of each poem
> gives a portrait of happy, fulfilled people or draws pictures
> of lives filled with sadness and melancholy.

This passage offers *essential* background matter, not information irrelevant to the thesis. For example, explaining that Eudora Welty was born in Jackson, Mississippi, in 1909 would contribute little to the following opening:

> Background — | In 1941 Eudora Welty published her first book of short
> stories, <u>A Curtain of Green</u>. That group of stories was
> followed by <u>The Wide Net</u> (1943) and <u>The Bride of the
> Innisfallen</u> (1955). | Each collection brought her critical
> acclaim, but taken together the three volumes established
> her as one of America's premier short story writers.

Review the Literature

Cite a few books and articles relevant to the specific issue to introduce literature connected with the topic. This paragraph gives distinction to your introduction because it establishes the scholarship on the subject. It also distinguishes your point of view by explaining the logical connections and differences between previous research and your work:

> Throughout his novella <u>Billy Budd</u>, Herman
> Melville intentionally uses biblical references as a
> means of presenting different moral principles by which
> people may govern their lives. | The story depicts the
> "loss of Paradise" (Arvin 294); it serves as a gospel story
> (Weaver 37-38); and it hints at a moral and solemn
> Review of literature — | purpose (Watson 319). The story explores the biblical
> passions of one man's confrontation with good and evil
> (Howard 327-328; Mumford 248). | This paper will examine
> the biblical references.

Review the History and Background of the Subject

The opening passage normally reviews the history of the topic, often with quotations from the sources, as shown below in APA style:

> Autism, a neurological dysfunction of the brain which commences before the age of thirty months, was identified by Leo Kanner (1943). Kanner studied eleven cases, all of which showed a specific type of childhood psychosis that was different from other childhood disorders, although each was similar to childhood schizophrenia. Kanner described the characteristics of the infantile syndrome as:
>
> *Background information*
>
> 1. Extreme autistic aloneness
> 2. Language abnormalities
> 3. Obsessive desire for the maintenance of sameness
> 4. Good cognitive potential
> 5. Normal physical development
> 6. Highly intelligent, obsessive, and cold parents
>
> Medical studies have reduced these symptoms to four criteria: onset within thirty months of birth, poor social development, late language development, and a preference for regular, stereotyped activity (Rutter, 1978; Watson, 1997; Waller, Smith, and Lambert, 2000). In the United States, autism affects one out of 2,500 children, and is not usually diagnosed until the child is between two and five years of age (Lambert & Smith, 2000).

Take Exception to Critical Views

This opening procedure identifies the subject, establishes a basic view taken by the literature, and then differs with or takes exception to the critical position of other writers, as shown in the following example:

> Lorraine Hansberry's popular and successful <u>A Raisin in the Sun</u>, which first appeared on Broadway in 1959, is a problem play of a black family's determination to escape a Chicago ghetto to a better life in the suburbs. There is agreement that this escape theme explains the drama's conflict and its role in the black movement (e.g., Oliver,

Archer, and especially Knight, who describes the Youngers as "an entire family that has become aware of, and is determined to combat, racial discrimination in a supposedly democratic land" [34]). Yet another issue lies at the heart of the drama. Hansberry develops a modern view of black matriarchy in order to examine both the cohesive and the conflict-producing effects it has on the individual members of the Younger family.

Exception to prevailing views — (bracketing "Yet another issue lies at the heart of the drama. Hansberry develops a modern view of black matriarchy in order to examine both the cohesive and the conflict-producing effects it has on the individual members of the Younger family.")

Challenge an Assumption

This type of introduction presents a well-known idea or general theory in order to question it, analyze it, challenge it, or refute it.

Christianity dominates the religious life of most Americans to the point that many assume that it dominates the world population as well. However, despite the denominational missionaries who have reached out to every corner of the globe, only one out of every four people on the globe is a Christian, and far fewer than that practice their faith. In truth, Christianity does not dominate religious beliefs around the globe.

Challenge to an assumption

Provide a Brief Summary

When the subject is a literary work, historic event, educational theory, or similar item, a brief summary will refresh the reader's memory.

The chief legacy of the two Bush administrations might well be one of waging war. George Bush liberated Kuwait with the 1991 war against Iraq, but he withdraw after accomplishing that mission rather than overthrow Saddam Hussein and his government in Baghdad. Later, George W. Bush retaliated against the Taliban of Afghanistan in late 2001 after the 9/11 tragedy. Then, in 2003, George W. Bush attacked Iraq again to remove Saddam Hussein from power. This study will examine the literature to confirm the hypothesis that Bush and Bush will be remembered as war presidents.

Summary

Summary

> Alice Walker's <u>The Color Purple</u> narrates the ordeal of a young black girl living in Georgia in the early years of the twentieth century. Celie writes letters to God because she has no one else to help her. The letters are unusually strong and give evidence of Celie's painful struggle to survive the multiple horrors of her life.

Define Key Terms

Sometimes an opening passage must explain difficult terminology, as in the following example:

Definition

> Occurring in one of every 3,900 babies born, cystic fibrosis remains one of the most common fatal genetic disorders in the United States. Approximately 30,000 American children and young adults have cystic fibrosis (Tariev 224). Cystic fibrosis causes the body to secrete an abnormally thick, sticky mucus that clogs the pancreas and the lungs, leading to problems with breathing and digestion, infection, and ultimately, death. Thirty years ago most infants with cystic fibrosis died in early childhood, but today more than 60 percent of babies born with cystic fibrosis reach adulthood, thanks in part to gene therapy. With continued advances in diagnosing and treating the disease, the prognosis for future generations will be significantly improved.

Supply Data, Statistics, and Special Evidence

Concrete evidence can attract the reader and establish the subject. For example, a student working with demographic data might compare the birth and death rates of certain sections of the world. In Europe, the rates are almost constant, while the African nations have birth rates that are 30 percent higher than the death rates. Such statistical evidence can be a useful tool in many papers. Just remember to support the data with clear, textual discussion. The paper by Norman Berkowitz, pages 235–247, displays a table and two maps to support his research.

Sample introduction in a student paper using these techniques, page 376.

12b   Writing the Body of the Research Paper

> Sample research papers with well-developed paragraphs, pages 235–247.

When writing the body of the paper, you should classify, compare, and analyze the issues. Keep in mind three key elements, as shown in the checklist on page 207.

The length of your paragraphs ought to be from four sentences up to twelve or even fifteen. You can accomplish this task only by writing good topic sentences and by developing them fully. The techniques described in the following paragraphs demonstrate how to build substantive paragraphs for your paper.

Relate a Time Sequence

Use *chronology* and *plot summary* to trace historical events and to survey a story or novel. You should, almost always, discuss the significance of the events. This first example traces historical events.

Time sequence established —   Following the death of President Roosevelt in April 1945, Harry S. Truman succeeded to the Presidency. Although he was an experienced politician, Truman "was ill prepared

---

CHECKLIST

Avoiding Certain Mistakes in the Introduction

Avoid a purpose statement, such as "The purpose of this study is . . . " unless you are writing reports of empirical research, in which case you *should* explain the purpose of your study (see Chapter 15, "Writing in APA Style").

Avoid repetition of the title, which should appear on the first page of the text anyway.

Avoid complex language or difficult questions that may puzzle the reader. However, general rhetorical questions are acceptable.

Avoid simple dictionary definitions, such as "Webster defines *monogamy* as marriage with only one person at a time." See page 209 for an acceptable opening that features definition.

Avoid humor, unless the subject deals with humor or satire.

Avoid hand-drawn artwork, clip art, and cute lettering unless the paper's subject matter requires it (for example, "The Circle as Advertising Symbol"). *Do* use computer graphics, tables, illustrations, and other designs that are appropriate to your subject.

CHECKLIST

Writing the Body of the Paper

Analysis   Classify the major issues of the study and provide a careful analysis of each in defense of your thesis.

Presentation   Provide well-reasoned statements at the beginning of your paragraphs, and supply evidence of support with proper documentation.

Paragraphs   Offer a variety of development to compare, show process, narrate the history of the subject, show causes, and so forth.

---

to direct a foreign policy," especially one that "called for the use of the atomic bomb to bring World War II to an end" (Jeffers 56). Consideration must be directed at the circumstances of the time, which led up to Truman's decision that took the lives of over 100,000 individuals and destroyed four square miles of the city of Hiroshima. Consideration must be given to the impact that this decision had on the war, on Japan, and on the rest of the world. Consideration must be directed at the man who brought the twentieth century into the atomic age.

The next passage shows the use of plot summary.

Quick plot summary

John Updike's "A & P" is a short story about a young grocery clerk named Sammy who feels trapped by the artificial values of the small town where he lives and, in an emotional moment, quits his job. The store manager, Lengel, is the voice of the conservative values in the community. For him, the girls in swimsuits pose a disturbance to his store, so he expresses his displeasure by reminding the girls that the A & P is not the beach (1088). Sammy, a liberal, believes the girls may be out of place in the A & P only because of its "fluorescent lights," "stacked packages," and "checkerboard green-and-cream rubber-tile floor," all artificial things (1086).

HINT: Keep the plot summary short and relate it to your thesis, as shown by the first sentence in the passage above. Do not allow the plot summary to extend beyond one paragraph; otherwise, you may retell the entire story. Your task is to make a point, not retell the story.

Compare or Contrast Issues, Critical Views, and Literary Characters

Employ *comparison* and *contrast* to show the two sides of a subject, to compare two characters, to compare the past with the present, or to compare positive and negative issues. The next passage compares and contrasts differences in forest conservation techniques.

> When a "controlled burn" gets out of hand and burns an entire town, defenders of controlled burns have a serious public relations problem. Thus, to burn or not to burn the natural forests in the national parks is the question. The pyrophobic public voices its protests while environmentalists praise the rejuvenating effects of a good forest fire. It is difficult to convince people that not all fire is bad. The public has visions of Smokey the Bear campaigns and mental images of Bambi and Thumper fleeing the roaring flames. Perhaps the public could learn to see beauty in fresh green shoots, like Bambi and Faline do as they returned to raise their young. Chris Bolgiano explains that federal policy evolved slowly "from the basic impulse to douse all fires immediately to a sophisticated decision matrix based on the functions of any given unit of land" (22). Bolgiano declares that "timber production, grazing, recreation, and wilderness preservation elicit different fire-management approaches" (23).

Comparison and contrast

Develop Cause and Effect

Write *cause-and-effect* paragraphs to develop the reasons for a circumstance or to examine its consequences. An example is shown here that not only explains with cause and effect but also uses the device of *analogy*, or metaphoric comparison—in this case, of bread dough and the uniform expansion of the universe.

> To see how the Hubble Law implies uniform, centerless expansion of a universe, imagine that you want

Analogy

> to make a loaf of raisin bread. As the dough rises, the expansion pushes the raisins away from each other. Two raisins that were originally about one centimeter apart separate more slowly than raisins that were about four centimeters apart. The uniform expansion of the dough causes the raisins to move apart at speeds proportional to their distances. Helen Write, in explaining the theory of

Cause and effect

> Edwin Powell Hubble, says the farther the space between them, the faster two galaxies will move away from each other. This is the basis for Hubble's theory of the expanding universe (369).

Define Your Key Terminology

Use *definition* to explain and expand upon a complex subject. This next example, by Katie Hebert, defines *functional foods:*

> Functional foods, as defined by the Australian National Food Authority, are:

Definition

> A class of foods that have strong putative metabolic and reulatory (physiological) roles over and above those seen in a wide range of common foods; a class of foods that achieve a defined endpoint that can be monitored (e.g., reduction in blood pressure, reduction in plasma-borne risk markers); and products referred to as special dietary foods. (Head, Record, and King S17)

Explain a Process

Draft a *process* paragraph that explains, one by one, the steps necessary to achieve a desired end:

Process — Blood doping is a process for increasing an athlete's performance on the day of competition. To perform this procedure, technicians drain about one liter of blood from the competitor about 10 months prior to the event. This time allows the "hemoglobin levels to return to normal" (Ray 79). Immediately prior to the athletic event, the blood is reintroduced by injection to give a rush of blood into the athlete's system. Ray reports that the technique produces an "average decrease of 45 seconds in the time it takes to run five miles on a treadmill" (80).

Ask Questions and Provide Answers

Framing a question as a topic sentence gives you the opportunity to develop a thorough answer with specific details and evidence. Look at how this approach is used in this example:

Question — Does America have enough park lands? The lands now designated as national and state parks, forests, and wild land total in excess of 33 million acres. Yet environmentalists call for additional protected land. They warn of imbalances in the environment. Dean Fraser, in his book, <u>The People Problem</u>, addresses the question of whether we have enough park land:

> Yosemite, in the summer, is not unlike Macy's the week before Christmas. In 1965 it had over 1.6 million visitors; Yellowstone over 2 million. The total area of federal plus state-owned parks is now something like 33 million acres, which sounds impressive until it is divided by the total number of annual visitors of something over 400 million. . . .
> (33)

Answer — We are running short of green space, which is being devoured by highways, housing projects, and industrial development.

Cite Evidence from the Source Materials

Citing evidence from authorities in the form of quotations, paraphrases, and summaries to support your topic sentence is another excellent way to build a paragraph. This next passage combines commentary by a critic and a poet to explore Thomas Hardy's pessimism in fiction and poetry.

Several critics reject the impression of Thomas Hardy as a pessimist. He is instead a realist who tends toward optimism. Thomas Parrott and Willard Thorp make this comment about Hardy in Poetry of the Transition:

Evidence from a source

> There has been a tendency in the criticism of Hardy's work to consider him as a philosopher rather than as a poet and to stigmatize him as a gloomy pessimist. This is quite wrong.(413)

The author himself felt incorrectly labeled, for he has written his own description:

> As to pessimism. My motto is, first correctly diagnose the complaint—in this case human ills—and ascertain the cause: then set about finding a remedy if one exists. The motto of optimists is: Blind the eyes to the real malady, and use empirical panaceas to suppress the symptoms. (Life 383)

Hardy is dismayed by these "optimists," so he has no desire to be lumped within such a narrow perspective.

Use a Variety of Other Methods

Many methods exist for developing paragraphs; among them are the *description* of a scene in a novel, *statistics* in support of an argument, *historical evidence* in support of a hypothesis, *psychological theory,* and others. You must make the choices, basing your decision on your subject and your notes. Employ the following methods as appropriate to your project.

- Use *classification* to identify several key issues of the topic, and then use *analysis* to examine each issue in detail. For example, you might classify several types of fungus infections, such as athlete's foot, dermatophytosis, and ringworm, and then analyze each.

- Use specific *criteria of judgment* to examine performances and works of art. For example, analyze the films of George Lucas with a critical response to story, theme, editing, photography, sound track, special effects, and so forth.
- Use *structure* to control papers on architecture, poetry, fiction, and biological forms. For example, a short story might have six distinct parts you can examine in sequence.
- Use *location* and *setting* for arranging papers in which geography and locale are key ingredients. For example, examine the settings of several novels by William Faulkner, or build an environmental study around land features (e.g., lakes, springs, sinkholes).
- Use *critical responses to an issue* to evaluate a course of action. For example, an examination of President Truman's decision to use the atomic bomb in World War II would invite you to consider several minor reasons and then to study Truman's major reason(s) for his decision.
- Dividing the body by important *issues* is standard fare in many research papers. One student examined the major issues of diabetes (see pages 375–385), and another developed the major issues about the water supplies (see pages 235–247).

12c   Writing the Conclusion of the Research Paper

The conclusion of a research paper should offer the reader more than a mere summary. Use the checklist at the bottom of the page to review your conclusion.

How you work these elements into your conclusion will depend on your style of writing. They need not appear in this order, nor should you crowd all

---

CHECKLIST

Writing the Conclusion

Thesis	Reaffirm your thesis statement.
Judgment	Reach a decision or judgment about the merits of the subject, be it a work of art, an author's writing, a historical moment, or a social position.
Discussion	Discuss the implications of your findings.
Directive	Offer a plan of action or a proposal that will put into effect your ideas. (Not required of every paper.)
Ending	Use the final paragraph, especially the final sentence, to bring the paper to closure.

the items into one paragraph. The conclusion can extend over several paragraphs and require more than one page. When drafting the conclusion, consider using several of the techniques described here.

Restate the Thesis and Reach beyond It

As a general rule, restate your thesis sentence; however, do not stop and assume that your reader will generate final conclusions about the issues. Instead, establish the essential mission of your study. In the example below, one student opens her conclusion by reestablishing her thesis sentence and then moves quickly to her persuasive, concluding judgments.

Thesis
restated
in the
conclusion

> Functional foods appear to exert a strong preventive effect on the two diseases that take most American lives than any other—coronary heart disease and cancer. High cholesterol levels cause coronary heart disease, the factor responsible for 24 percent of the fatalities that occur in the United States (Blumberg 3). Foods high in antioxidants (i.e., Vitamin C, E, and betacarotene), omega-e fatty acids, and soluble fiber, along with green and black tea have been proven to be an effective form of preventive medicine for individuals at risk of developing coronary heart disease. Second only to coronary heart disease, "cancer is the cause of death in 22 percent of Americans" (4). Functional foods have exhibited similar strength in the fight for cancer prevention. By incorporating functional foods, such as insoluble fiber, garlic, and green and black tea into the diet, an individual can lower his or her risk of being diagnosed with cancer. Although this finding does not mean one should cancel all future doctor appointments, it has shown that individuals who eat functional foods are a step ahead in the battle for disease prevention.

Close with an Effective Quotation

Sometimes a source may provide a striking commentary that deserves special placement, as shown by this example:

> W. C. Fields had a successful career that extended from vaudeville to musical comedy and finally to the movies. In his private life, he loathed children and animals, and he fought with bankers, landladies, and the police. Off screen,

he maintained his private image as a vulgar, hard-drinking cynic until his death in 1946. On the screen, he won the hearts of two generations of fans. He was beloved by audiences primarily for acting out their own contempt for authority.

Effective quotation

The movies prolonged his popularity "as a dexterous comedian with expert timing and a look of bibulous rascality," but Fields had two personalities, "one jolly and one diabolical" (Kennedy 990).

Return the Focus of a Literary Study to the Author

While the body of a literary paper should analyze characters, images, and plot, the conclusion should explain the author's accomplishments. The following closing shows how one writer focused on the author:

As to the issues of the country versus the city and the impact of a market economy,

Focus on the author

Jonathan Swift advances the conservative position of the early eighteenth century, which lamented the loss of the rural, agrarian society, with its adherence to tradition and a stable social hierarchy. His position focused on the social outcomes: unemployment, displacement, and the disenfranchisement of a significant portion of the populace. Unlike his London contemporaries, Swift resided in the economic hinterland of Ireland, so he had a more direct view of the destructive population shifts from rural to urban.

Focus on the author

Ultimately, Swift's commentary in A Modest Proposal is important because it records a consciousness of a continuing problem, one that worsens with the intensification of the urban rather than rural growth. It continues to plague the twenty-first-century world, from America to Africa and from Russia to Latin America.

Compare the Past to the Present

You can use the conclusion rather than the opening to compare past research to the present study or to compare the historic past with the contemporary scene. For example, after explaining the history of two schools of treatment for autism, one writer switches to the present, as shown in this excerpt:

Future in
contrast to
the present

> There is hope in the future that both the cause and the cure for autism will be found. For the present, new drug therapies and behavior modification offer some hope for the abnormal, SIB actions of a person with autistism. Since autism is sometimes outgrown, childhood treatment offers the best hope for the autistic person who must try to survive in an alien environment.

Offer a Directive or Solution

After analyzing a problem and synthesizing issues, offer your theory or solution, as demonstrated immediately above in the example in which the writer suggests that "childhood treatment offers the best hope for the autistic person who must try to survive in an alien environment." Note also this closing:

A directive
or solution

> All of the aspects of diabetes management can be summed up in one word: balance. Diabetes itself is caused by a lack of balance of insulin and glucose in the body. In order to restore that balance, a diabetic must juggle medication, monitoring, diet, and exercise. Managing diabetes is not an easy task, but a long and healthy life is very possible when the delicate balance is carefully maintained.

Discuss Test Results

In scientific writing (see Chapters 15 and 17), your conclusion, labeled "discussion," must explain the ramifications of your findings and identify any limitations of your scientific study, as shown:

Test results

> The results of this experiment were similar to expectations, but perhaps the statistical significance, because of the small subject size, was biased toward the delayed conditions of the curve. The subjects were, perhaps, not representative of the total population because of their prior exposure to test procedures. Another factor that may have affected the curves was the presentation of the data.

CHECKLIST

Avoiding Certain Mistakes in the Conclusion

- **Avoid** afterthoughts or additional ideas. Now is the time to end the paper, not begin a new thought. If new ideas occur to you as you write your conclusion, don't ignore them. Explore them fully in the context of your thesis and consider adding them to the body of your paper or modifying your thesis. Scientific studies often discuss options and possible alterations that might affect test results (see "Discuss Test Results," immediately above).

- **Avoid** the use of "thus," "in conclusion," and "finally" at the beginning of the last paragraph. Readers can see plainly the end of the paper.

- **Avoid** ending the paper without a sense of closure.

- **Avoid** questions that raise new issues; however, rhetorical questions that restate the issues are acceptable.

- **Avoid** fancy artwork.

The images on the screen were available for five seconds, and that amount of time may have enabled the subjects to store each image effectively. If the time period for each image were reduced to one or two seconds, there could be lower recall scores, thereby reducing the differences between the control group and the experimental group.

■ YOUR RESEARCH PROJECT

1. Review your opening to determine whether it builds the argument and sets the stage for analysis to come in the body. Consider adding paragraphs like those described on pages 200–206: Relate the well known, provide background information, review the literature, review the history of the subject, take exception to prevailing views, challenge an assumption, provide a summary of the issues, define key terms, supply statistical evidence.

2. After finishing the first draft, review the body of your paper. Has your analysis touched on all the issues? Have you built paragraphs of substance, as demonstrated on pages 206–212? Judge the draft against the checklist for the body on page 207.

3. Evaluate your conclusion according to the checklist on page 212. If you feel it's necessary, build the conclusion by these techniques: Elaborate on the thesis, use an effective quotation, focus on a key person, compare the past and the present, offer a directive or solution, or discuss test results (see pages 212–216 for a discussion of these techniques).

13 Revising, Proofreading, and Formatting the Rough Draft

Once you have the complete paper in a rough draft, the serious business of editing begins. First, revise the paper on a global scale, moving blocks of material to the best advantage and into the proper format. Second, edit the draft with a line-by-line examination of wording and technical excellence. Third, proofread the final version to ensure that your words are spelled correctly and the text is grammatically sound.

13a Conducting a Global Revision

For discussion of developing the introduction, see pages 199–205.

Revision can turn a passable paper into an excellent one and change an excellent one into a radiant one. First, revise the whole manuscript by performing the tasks in the checklist as shown on page 219.

Revising the Introduction

Examine your opening for the presence of several items:

- Your thesis
- A clear sense of direction or plan of development
- A sense of involvement that invites the reader into your investigation of a problem

Revising the Body

For discussion of building effective paragraphs, see pages 206–212.

Use the following bulleted list as a guide for revising each individual paragraph of the body of your paper.

- Cut out wordiness and irrelevant thoughts, even to the point of deleting entire sentences that contribute nothing to the dynamics of the paper.
- Combine short paragraphs with others or build one of greater substance.

CHECKLIST

Global Revision

1. Skim through the paper to check its unity. Does the paper maintain a central proposition from paragraph to paragraph?
2. Transplant paragraphs, moving them to more relevant and effective positions.
3. Delete sentences that do not further your cause.
4. As you cut, copy, and paste, remember to rewrite and blend the words into your text.
5. If your outline must be submitted with your draft, revise it to reflect these global revisions.

- Revise long, difficult paragraphs by dividing them or by using transitions effectively (see "Writing with Unity and Coherence," pages 164–168).
- For paragraphs that seem short, shallow, or weak, add more commentary and more evidence, especially quotations from the primary source or critical citations from secondary sources.
- Add your own input to paragraphs that rely too heavily on the source materials.
- Examine your paragraphs for transitions that move the reader effectively from one paragraph to the next.

Revising the Conclusion

For discussion of writing the conclusion, see pages 212–216.

Examine the conclusion to see that it meets these criteria:

- It is drawn from the evidence.
- It is developed logically from the introduction and the body.
- It expresses your position on the issues.

Participating in Peer Review

Part of the revision process for many writers, both students and professionals, is peer review. This has two sides. First, it means handing your paper to a friend or classmate, asking for opinions and suggestions. Second, it means reviewing a classmate's research paper. You can learn by reviewing as well as by writing.

Since this task asks you to make judgments, you need a set of criteria. Your instructor may supply a peer review sheet, or you can use the checklist

---

CHECKLIST

Peer Review

1. Are the subject and the accompanying issues introduced early?
2. Is the writer's critical approach to the problem presented clearly in a thesis statement? Is it placed effectively in the introduction?
3. Do the paragraphs of the body have individual unity? That is, does each one develop an important idea and only one idea? Does each paragraph relate to the thesis?
4. Are sources introduced, usually with the name of the expert, and then cited by a page number within parentheses? Keep in mind that Internet sources, in most cases, do not have page numbers.
5. Is it clear where a paraphrase begins and where it ends?
6. Are the sources relevant to the argument?
7. Does the writer weave quotations into the text effectively while avoiding long quotations that look like filler instead of substance?
8. Does the conclusion arrive at a resolution about the central issue?
9. Does the title describe clearly what you have found in the contents of the research paper?

---

shown above. Criticize the paper constructively on each point. If you can answer each question with a *yes,* your classmate has performed well. For those questions you answer *no,* you owe it to your classmate to explain what seems wrong. Make suggestions. Offer tips. Try to help!

13b Formatting the Paper to MLA Style

The format of a research paper consists of the following parts:

1. Title page
2. Outline
3. Abstract
4. The text of the paper
5. Content notes
6. Appendix
7. Works Cited

Items 4 and 7 are required for a paper in the MLA style; use the other items to meet the needs of your research. *Note:* A paper in APA style (see Chapter 15) requires items 1, 3, 4, and 7, and the order differs for items 5–7.

Title Page or Opening Page

A research paper in MLA style does not need a separate title page unless you include an outline, abstract, or other prefatory matter. Place your identification in the upper left corner of your opening page, as shown here:

1 inch from
top of page

1/2 inch in the header position   Howell 1

Pamela Howell

Professor Magrans   Identifying
                           information
English 102c

17 May 2003

Creative Marriages

Judging by recent divorce rates, it would seem that the

traditional marriage fails to meet the needs . . . .

Note: APA style requires a different setup for the title page; see page 323 for an example.

If you do include prefatory matter, such as an outline, you need the title page with centered divisions for the title, the author, and the course identification.

An Interpretation of Melville's

Use of Biblical Characters

in Billy Budd

by

Melinda Singleton

English II, Section 108b

Dr. Crampton

April 23, 2006

Follow these guidelines for writing a title page in MLA style:

1. Use an inverted pyramid to balance two or more lines.
2. Use capitals and lowercase letters without underlining and without quotation marks. Published works that appear as part of your title require underlining (books) or quotation marks (short stories). Do not use a period after a centered heading.
3. Place your full name below the title, usually in the center of the page.
4. Employ separate lines, centered, to provide the course information, institution, instructor, date, or program (e.g., Honors Program).
5. Provide balanced margins for all sides of the title page.

Outline

Print your outline with the finished manuscript only if your instructor requires it. Place it after the title page on separate pages and number these pages with small Roman numerals, beginning with ii (for example, ii, iii, iv, v), at the top right-hand corner of the page, just after your last name (e.g., Spence iii). For information on writing an outline, see section 8c, pages 138–142, and the sample outlines on pages 139–142 and pages 354–355.

Abstract

Include an abstract for a paper in MLA style only if your instructor requires it. (APA style requires the abstract; see section 15g, pages 322–323). An abstract provides a brief digest of the paper's essential ideas in about 100 words. To that end, borrow from your introduction, use some of the topic sentences from your paragraphs, and use one or two sentences from your conclusion.

In MLA style, place the abstract on the first page of text (page 1) one double-space below the title and before the first lines of the text. Indent the abstract five spaces as a block, and indent the first line an additonal five spaces. Use quadruple spacing at the end of the abstract to set it off from the text, which follows immediately after. You may also place the abstract on a separate page between the title page and first page of text.

> For more on the abstract and examples, see pages 322–323.

Remember that the abstract is usually read first and may be the *only* part read; therefore, make it accurate, specific, objective, and self-contained (i.e., it makes sense alone without references to the main text). Note this example:

Wu 1

Child Abuse: A View of the Victims

Abstract

This study examines the problems of child abuse, especially the fact that families receive attention after abuse occurs, not before. With abuse statistics on the rise, efforts devoted to prevention rather than coping should focus on parents in order to discover those adults most likely to commit abuse because of heredity, their own childhood, the economy, and other causes of depression. Viewing the parent as a victim, not just a criminal, will enable social agencies to institute

preventive programs that may control abuse and hold together
family units.

Quadruple
space

Family troubles will most likely affect the delicate members of

Text our society, the children. The recognition of

causal elements . . .

The Text of the Paper

Double-space throughout the entire paper except for the title page (page 221) and the separation of the abstract from the first line of text (page 222). In general, you should *not* use subtitles or numbered divisions for your paper, even if it becomes twenty pages long. Instead, use continuous paragraphing without subdivisions or headings. However, some scientific and business reports require subheads (see chapters 15 and 17).

If the closing page of your text runs short, leave the remainder of the page blank. Do not write "The End" or provide artwork as a closing signal. Do not start Notes or Works Cited on this final page of text.

Content Endnotes Page

Label this page with the word *Notes* centered at the top edge of the sheet, at least one double-space below your page-numbering sequence in the upper right corner. Double-space between the *Notes* heading and the first note. Number the notes in sequence with raised superscript numerals to match those within your text. Double-space all entries and double-space between them.

> For discussion of content notes, see pages 346–349.

Appendix

Place additional material, if necessary, in an appendix preceding the Works Cited page. This is the logical location for numerous tables and illustrations, computer data, questionnaire results, complicated statistics, mathematical proofs, and detailed descriptions of special equipment. Double-space appendixes and begin each appendix on a new sheet. Continue your page numbering sequence in the upper right corner of the sheet. Label the page *Appendix,* centered at the top of the sheet. If you have more than one appendix, use *Appendix A, Appendix B,* and so forth. See pages 244–245 for an example.

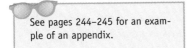

> See pages 244–245 for an example of an appendix.

See Chapter 14, "Works Cited," pages 248–299, and sample Works Cited on pages 235 and 246–247.

Works Cited

Center the heading *Works Cited* 1 inch from the top edge of the sheet. Continue the page-numbering sequence in the upper right corner. Double-space throughout. Set the first line of each entry flush left and indent subsequent lines five spaces. If your software supports it, use the hanging indent.

13c Editing before Typing or Printing the Final Manuscript

For discussion of unity, coherence, and effective writing, see pages 164–168.

The cut-and-paste revision period is complemented by careful editing of paragraphs, sentences, and individual words. Travel through the paper to study your sentences and word choice. Look for ways to tighten and condense. Below is a checklist.

Note the editing by one student in Figure 13.1. As shown, this writer conscientiously deleted unnecessary material, added supporting statements, related facts to one another, rearranged data, added new ideas, and rewrote for clarity.

CHECKLIST

Editing

1. Cut phrases and sentences that do not advance your main ideas or that merely repeat what your sources have already stated.
2. Determine that coordinated, balanced ideas are appropriately expressed and that minor ideas are properly subordinated.
3. Change most of your *to be* verbs (is, are, was) to stronger, active verbs.
4. Maintain the present tense in most verbs.
5. Convert passive structures to active if possible.
6. Confirm that you have introduced paraphrases and quotations so that they flow smoothly into your text. Use a variety of verbs for the instructions (*Winston argues, Thomas reminds, Morganfield offers*).
7. Use formal, academic style, and guard against clusters of monosyllabic words that fail to advance ideas. Examine your wording for its effectiveness within the context of your subject.

> In some cases   is   see
> ~~One critic~~ calls television "junk food" (Fransecky
>
> 717), and ~~I think~~ excessive viewing does distract
>   (see esp. Paul Witty as qtd. in Postman 41)
> from other activities, yet television can and does
>   and shows   of our best
> bring cultural programs some good novels. It does
> according to the evidence
> improve children's vocabularies, encourages their
>   and school
> reading, and inspires their writing. Television should
>   s the traditional classroom curriculum
> not be an antagonist; ~~it should complement school~~
> should seek and find harmony with the preschool television
> ~~work.~~
> curriculum.

FIGURE 13.1 Example of editing on a manuscript page.

Using the Computer to Edit Your Text

Remember to click on Tools and use the spelling and grammar checkers to spot spelling errors and to perform several tasks related to grammar and mechanics—for example, looking for parentheses you have opened but not closed, unpaired quotation marks, passive verbs, and other items. Pay attention to these caution flags. Caution: the spellchecker will not discern incorrest usage of "its" and "it's." However, you must edit and adjust your paper by *your* standards with due respect to the computer analysis. Remember, it is your paper, not the computer's. You may need to use some long words and write some long sentences, or you may prefer the passive voice to emphasize the receiver of the action, not the actor.

13d Proofreading on the Screen and on the Printed Manuscript

First, proofread your paper on the screen with a program that will check your spelling, grammar, and style, as mentioned above. Check your formatting for double-spacing, 1-inch margins, running heads, page numbers, and so forth. Check the entries in your Works Cited section for precision and completeness in the citations. Also, be sure that each is formatted with a hanging indention.

Consult Appendix A, "Glossary: Rules and Techniques for Preparing the Manuscript in MLA Style," for instructions on handling abbreviations, margins, tables, numbering, punctuation, content notes, and other matters.

After editing the text on screen to your satisfaction, print out a hard copy of the manuscript. You should proofread this final paper version with great care because the software will not have caught every error. Be sure your in-text citations are correct and confirm that you have a corresponding bibliography entry for each.

Proofreading

1. Check for errors in sentence structure, spelling, and punctuation.
2. Check for correct hyphenation and word division. Remember that *no* words should be hyphenated at the ends of lines. If you are using a computer, turn off the automatic hyphenation option.
3. Read each quotation for the accuracy of your own wording and of the words within your quoted materials. Look, too, for your correct use of quotations marks.
4. Be certain that in-text citations are correct and that each corresponding source is listed on your Works Cited page.
5. Double-check the format—the title page, margins, spacing, content notes, and many other elements, as explained on pages 220–225 and in the glossary on pages A-1–A-8.

YOUR RESEARCH PROJECT

1. Examine once again the intellectual argument of your first draft. Is it clearly established in the opening and then reaffirmed in the closing?
2. Do the paragraphs of the body develop systematically the evidence to support your claim or thesis? Examine each paragraph for relevance.
3. Examine again your title. Does it meet the criteria set forth on page 221?
4. If you participated in a peer review, consider carefully the recommendations and judgments of your reviewer. There's always a tendency to dismiss words of criticism, but you need to learn that constructive criticism exists at all levels of collegiate and professional life.
5. Read aloud to yourself a portion of the paper. Does it have an academic style? If not, read pages 164–168 and begin editing.
6. Read through the two papers that follow next in this chapter, pages 227–247, to get a feel for the academic style of writing. Try to duplicate that style.

13e Sample Papers in MLA Style

Short Literary Research Paper

Melinda Mosier's assignment was to write a literary paper on Shakespeare's play *Hamlet.* This task required her to find a focus for her work, so she chose to examine the soliloquies of the title character. In these speeches, she hoped to find a pattern that might focus the direction of her research and writing. She had read the entire play, so now she reread and studied the soliloquies. At the same time, she began her search of the source material—in the library stacks for books, on the library's electronic databases (e.g., InfoTrac), and on the Internet. Eventually, she settled her study on the settings within which the soliloquies are spoken by Hamlet. She examined each, found comparisons, cited a number of sources, and arrived at her conclusion: "Shakespeare leaves Hamlet alone on stage in the soliloquies to act out his anguish because he could not act otherwise. Each setting for each soliloquy was a pivotal but stifling moment."

Read the essay with care, noting the academic style of writing, the careful in-text citations to sources, the citations to the primary source—*Hamlet*—and the way Melinda moves carefully and methodically to her conclusion.

Mosier 1

Melinda Mosier

Professor Thompson

Humanities 1020

6 April 2006

Listening to Hamlet: The Soliloquies

A soliloquy is a dramatic form of discourse in which a person reveals inner thoughts and feelings while alone on stage or while unaware that others might be within the range of their voice. But then, the person might also deliver such a speech while knowing full well that somebody is listening. Thus, the dramatic convention has complications, and when Shakespeare uses it with a complex character like Hamlet, it appears in a variety of forms. Critical authorities have agreed that the soliloquies reveal the inner feelings of Hamlet (Auden, Bloom, and Wilson), yet they disagree somewhat in their interpretations. This study, however, will examine the settings within which the soliloquies occur and interpret the direction of Hamlet's remarks inward to himself and outward to a perceived listener.

The first soliloquy occurs in act 1, scene 2, lines 133–164, immediately after King Claudius and Queen Gertrude have left in a flourish. His mother has just admonished Hamlet for wearing black after these many days following the death of his father,

Mosier opens with a definition.

Mosier establishes the concept she will explore.

Mosier 2

and he has responded with a play on the word <u>seems</u>, indicating in lines 79–89 that his mourning clothes are "but the trappings and the suits of woe," but that he has within a mournful spirit that is so deep it "passes show." He is stricken to his core by sadness. Then he is left alone and cries out:

> Oh, that this too too sullied flesh would melt,
>
> Thaw, and resolve itself into a dew,
>
> Or that the Everlasting had not fixed
>
> His canon 'gainst self-slaughter. O God, God,
>
> How weary, stale, flat and unprofitable
>
> Seem to me all the uses of this world! (1.2.133-38)[1]

Lines of the play are indented, line breaks are maintained, and the act, scene, and lines are listed.

This opening gives its obvious nod toward suicide and to the inner darkness of his soul, which even black clothing cannot show in full force. But Shakespeare uses this soliloquy for another important purpose--the son's verbal attack on his mother, Gertrude. She has just left in a flourish with the king, her new husband. Hamlet reveals his disgust with her because she has moved with "most wicked speed" (1.2.161) to marry Claudius, her dead husband's brother. Hamlet sees the union as incest and closes the soliloquy by saying: "It is not, nor it cannot come to good: / But break, my heart, for I must hold my tongue!" (1.2.163-64). Some critics, like Ernest Jones, would suggest that Hamlet is jealous of Claudius for winning a love that he (Hamlet) wanted, but that idea is severely weakened by Hamlet's damning words against her dexterity within "<u>incestuous sheets</u>" (my emphasis).

Two lines from the play can be quoted in the text, separated by a slash.

    The second soliloquy occurs in act 2, scene 2, lines 576-634. The setting again has great relevance to Hamlet's words. An actor has just described how his company would portray the anquished and agonized cries of Hecuba, who must

This section displays the manner in which Mosier interprets one of the soliloquies, citing from it and explaining the implications in light of the drama's setting.

[1]Quotations from the text come from the Folger Library edition.

watch as her husband, Priam, the king of Troy, is hacked to death. Now, Hamlet is dismayed because a mere actor can show such passion in a fictional portrayal:

> O, what a rogue and peasant slave am I!
>
> Is it not monstrous that this player here,
>
> But in a fiction, in a dream of passion,
>
> Could force his soul so to his own conceit
>
> That from her working all his visage wanned,
>
> Tears in his eyes, distraction in his aspect,
>
> A broken voice, and his whole function suiting
>
> With forms to his conceit? And all for nothing!
>
> For Hecuba!
>
> What's Hecuba to him, or he to Hecuba,
>
> That he should weep for her? (2.2.576-86)

Comparing himself with the actor, Hamlet calls himself a "dull and muddy-mettled rascal" who "can say nothing; no, not for a king, / Upon whose property and most dear life / A damn'd defeat was made. Am I a coward?" (2.2.594-98). Hamlet is tortured in regard to his mother, who is his version of Hecuba. Next, Shakespeare uses the soliloquy to set out another comparison--one between a "pigeon-livered" (2.2.604) Prince Hamlet and an active and crafty Prince Hamlet. He recognizes his failure:

> Why, what an ass am I! This is most brave,
>
> That I, the son of a dear father murdered,
>
> Prompted to my revenge by heaven and hell,
>
> Must, like a whore, unpack my heart with words
>
> And fall a-cursing, like a very drab,
>
> A scullion!
>
> Fie upon 't! (2.2.611–16)

But suddenly, Hamlet changes his attitude, saying, "About, my brain!" This means, get busy, brain, and go to work! So now he

Mosier 4

plots the play within a play, saying, "The play's the thing /
Wherein I'll catch the conscience of the king" (2.2.633–34).

In short, this soliloquy has three parts, all tied to the
setting--praise for a performer who can act with passion, disgust
with himself for his failure to act, and then his cunning plan for
tricking the king by using the actors. Yet throughout the
soliloquy he seems to be acting, and Shakespeare scholar Harold
Bloom stresses that idea, saying:

> So histrionic is all of <u>Hamlet</u> that we need to develop
> our auditory consciousness to a new pitch, if we catch
> the prince's precise accent here. Where all is
> theatricality, our grounds for judgment must shift.
> Hamlet's hyperboles mock theater itself, in "drown the
> stage with tears." The soliloquy becomes a
> hyperparody of soliloquy . . . (30).

Mosier cites
the
authorities on
Shakespeare
in brief but
effective
ways.

The critic W. H. Auden will echo that sense of "theater" later in
this paper, and Charles Cannon argues that "<u>Hamlet</u>
is a play about the play-like deceit of much that poses for
reality" (206).

The third soliloquy, and the most famous, again has a
setting of great import. This time the king has called for Ophelia
to meet with Hamlet while he and Polonius eavesdrop nearby.
Although Shakespeare has given no stage instructions, it seems
reasonable that Hamlet knows the plot, knows Ophelia is their
foil, and knows they are listening. Thus, this suicidal monologue
could be deception on his part, not a call for Prozac or death or
any mind-altering alternative. Notice these words:

> To die, to sleep--
> To sleep--perchance to dream: ay, there's the rub,
> For in that sleep of death what dreams may come
> When we have shuffled off this mortal coil,
> Must give us pause. . . . (3.1.72–76)

He hesitates about rushing into "the undiscovered country from whose bourn / No traveler returns" (3.1.87–88), and admits that "conscience does make cowards of us all . . . " (3.1.91). He does not wish to lose his chance for action, even though some critics, like Goethe, say a call to action has been "laid upon a soul unfit for the performance of it" (154). Thereafter, he performs his own little drama with Ophelia, knowing that the king is watching. W. H. Auden has observed that Hamlet is always "conscious of acting" (161). Hamlet's words and actions convince Ophelia, the king, and Polonius that he, Hamlet, has lost his sanity:

> Ophelia: O, what a noble mind is here o'erthrown!
>
>   The courtier's, soldier's, scholar's, eye, tongue, sword:
>
>   The expectancy and rose of the fair state,
>
>   The glass of fashion and the mould of form,
>
>   Th' observed of all observers, quite, quite down!
>
>   (3.1.163–67)

Apparently insane, Hamlet can now act decisively in seeking his revenge. Youngson applies the Ganser syndrome to Hamlet, saying the prince has something "notable to gain from being thought mad" so he gives the appearance of psychiatric symptoms (1).

In the fourth soliloquy, which begins "'Tis now the very witching time of night" (3.2.419), Hamlet contrasts himself with Nero, a brutal Roman emperor, saying:

> Soft, now to my mother,
>
> O heart, lose not they nature, let not ever
>
> The soul of Nero enter this firm bosom,
>
> Let me be cruel not unnatural.
>
> I will speak daggers to her, but use none. (3.2.425–29

The ghost of his father, after all, has asked him to spare Gertrude but not Claudius. Hamlet is diverted from his task but admits, by the comparison to Nero, that he does not have the stomach for the cruel and unnatural. J. Dover Wilson says his "murderous impulses must be kept in leash. True, she deserves the worst he can find it in his heart to say to her; she may even deserve death, but it is not for him to exact it" (244).

We see Hamlet in his fifth soliloquy still motivating himself, and again Shakespeare uses a comparison to force the issue--a prince of Norway versus the prince of Denmark. The setting is a plain in Denmark where Fortinbras, the nephew of the Norwegian king, leads an army across Denmark to attack a small section of Poland, fortified by 20,000 soldiers, but in truth the piece of land is not of great value. The Norwegian Captain explains, "We go to gain a little patch of ground / That hath in it no profit but the name. / To pay five ducats, five, I would not farm it . . . " (4.4.19–21). Hamlet recognizes the irony in the contrast--Fortinbras brazenly fights for what he deems his even though it has little value, but Hamlet refuses to fight in revenge for the very real death of his father.

> Witness this army of such mass and charge,
>
> Led by a delicate and tender prince,
>
> Whose spirit, with divine ambition puffed,
>
> Makes mouths at the invisible event,
>
> Exposing what is mortal and unsure
>
> To all that fortune, death, and danger dare,
>
> Even for an eggshell. (4.4.50–56)
>
> . . . .
>
> How stand I then,
>
> That have a father killed, a mother stained,
>
> Excitements of my reason and my blood,
>
> And let all sleep, while to my shame I see
>
> The imminent death of twenty thousand men

Mosier shows how the setting on a plain in Denmark allows a comparison of Hamlet and Fortinbras.

Mosier 7

> That for a fantasy and trick of fame
>
> Go to their graves like beds, fight for a plot
>
> Whereon the numbers cannot try the cause,
>
> Which is not tomb enough and continent
>
> To hide the slain? (4.4.59–68)

Hamlet envisions 20,000 men going to slaughter and then buried on a plot of land so small it can't contain all the bodies. They will fight and die for a worthless cause while he procrastinates. "O, from this time forth," he cries, "My thoughts be bloody, or be nothing worth!" (4.4.69–70).

Thus, Shakespeare has carefully crafted a setting for each soliloquy, and the device of <u>comparison</u> plays a key role. In the first, Hamlet cries out that his soul is darker even than the black funeral garb he wears because of his mother's incestuous behavior. In the second, his behavior seems impotent (and perhaps that's a valid term) in comparison with the actor who cries so passionately for Hecuba, a distant historic figure far removed from Hamlet's recent loss of a father. In the third, he compares and contrasts the magnetism of death against "the dread of something after death, / The undiscovered country, from whose bourn / No traveler returns . . . " (3.1.86–87). In the fourth soliloquy, he reminds himself that he cannot perform cruel, unnatural acts like Nero. In the fifth, he stands ashamed of his inactivity in comparison to an aggressive Norwegian prince.

Mosier reviews briefly the elements of the five soliloquies to show how Hamlet compares himself to someone else.

In every instance Hamlet compares himself to someone else--a white knight; a passionate actor; a vibrant, throbbing human being; a Nero figure; or an aggressive soldier. Perhaps W. H. Auden expresses it best:

> Hamlet lacks faith in God and in himself.
>
> Consequently he must define his existence in terms
>
> of others, e.g., I am the man whose mother married

Mosier 8

his uncle who murdered his father. He would like to become what the Greek tragic hero is, a creature of situation. Hence his inability to act, for he can only "act," i.e., play at possibilities. He is fundamentally <u>bored</u>, and for that reason he acts theatrically. (164)

Mosier reaches her conclusion about the stifling moments that affected Hamlet.

Shakespeare leaves Hamlet alone on stage in the soliloquies to act out his anguish because he could not act otherwise. Each setting for each soliloquy was a pivotal but stifling moment. If we have only the soliloquies before us, we can see that Hamlet will fail and "prophesy the election lights / on Fortinbras" (5.2.392–93), the man of action, not a man of "acting."

Mosier 9

Works Cited

Auden, W. H. <u>Lectures on Shakespeare</u>. Ed. Arthur Kirsch.
    Princeton: Princeton UP, 2000.

Bloom, Harold. <u>Hamlet: Poem Unlimited</u>. New York: Riverhead-
    Penguin, 2003.

Cannon, Charles K. "'As in a Theater'": <u>Hamlet</u> in the Light of
    Calvin's Doctrine of Predestination." <u>Studies in English
    Literature, 1500–1600</u> 11 (1971): 203–22. <u>JSTOR</u>. 8 Apr.
    2003 <http://www.jstor.org/search>.

Goethe, Johann Wolfgang. "A Soul Unfit." <u>Wilhelm Meister's
    Apprenticeship</u>. Trans. Thomas Carlyle. <u>Hamlet: A Norton
    Critical Edition</u>. Ed. Cyrus Hoy. 2nd ed. New York:
    Norton, 1992.

Jones, Ernest. "The Oedipus-Complex as an Explanation of
    Hamlet's Mystery: A Study in Motive." <u>The American Journal
    of Psychology</u> 21.1 (1910): 72–113. <u>Shakespeare Navigators</u>.
    8 Apr. 2003 <http://www.clicknotes.com/jones>.

Shakespeare, William. <u>The Tragedy of</u> Hamlet, Prince of Denmark.
    The New Folger Library Shakespeare. Ed. Barbara A. Mowat
    and Paul Werstine. New York: Washington Square P, 1992.

Wilson, Dover. <u>What Happens in Hamlet</u>. 1935. Cambridge, UK:
    Cambridge UP, 2001.

Youngson, Robert M. <u>The Madness of Hamlet and Other
    Extraordinary States of Mind</u>. New York: Carroll
    & Graf, 1999.

Form for a book.

A citation to a database's search page.

A work in an anthology.

Citation to a Web site.

Citation to the edition used and cited in the paper.

Sample Research Paper

Norman Berkowitz decided to explore the topic of the world's pending water crisis in his research paper. His paper, on the following pages, includes a table, two maps, and an appendix.

Berkowitz 1

Norman Berkowitz

Professor Zimmerman

September 9, 2006

English 1010

A title page is
not required,
but provide
your name,
instructor's
name, date,
and course.

The World's Water Supply: The Ethics of Distribution

Opening
quotations
may be
centered, but
normally they
are indented
10 spaces
from the left
margin.

"Water, water, everywhere,

And all the boards did shrink,

Water, water, everywhere,

Nor any drop to drink"

--Samuel Taylor Coleridge, "The Rime of the Ancient Mariner"

The British poet Coleridge created a ghostly scene that might serve as a forecast for our children. The world is running out of fresh water while we, unthinking, enjoy a sip from our Evian. But wait, the bottled water craze should be a signal-- why do we need bottled water? What's happened to good, fresh tap water?

The truth is, we have a crisis on our hands, and it grows more serious all the time. In fact, some authorities now forecast world wars over water rights. It's like the old western movies with ranchers squabbling over water rights, only now the squabbling is worldwide.

The crisis has not gone unnoticed. Hundreds of articles crowd the magazines and journals in many disciplines, from economics to environmental science and from sociology to physics. The issue of water touches almost every facet of life-- religious rituals, food supply, political stability, disease, to name only a few. We might frame this hypothesis: Water will soon replace oil as the economic resource most treasured by nations of the world. However, that assertion would prove difficult to defend and may not be true at all. Rather, we need to look

Berkowitz
suggests a
hypothesis
that would
require
empirical
proof, but he
rejects it in
favor of a
theoretical
study.

Berkowitz 2

elsewhere, at human behavior, and at human responsibility for preserving the environment for our children.

Accordingly, the water crisis calls for examination of the issues with regard to supply and demand, the political power struggles that are emerging, and the ethical and perhaps even moral implications engulfing the world's scattered supply of fresh water.

A brief review of the literature reveals the extent of the complications. On one side we have the scientific community, as represented by Sandra Postel with articles in <u>BioScience</u> and her book entitled <u>Last Oasis: Facing Water Scarcity</u>, and by Mark Townsend in the journal <u>Geographical</u>. On another side we have the religious element of water, as presented by such articles as "The Liquid of the Gods" by Camille Talkeu Tounounga and "Sacred Land Film Project" by Christopher McLeod in <u>Earth Island Journal</u>.

Then there are the local environmental issues, such as Michael Misner's "Wild Wetlands of New York," which describes the urban wildlife preserve in Jamaica Bay near New York City, and "The End of Lake Powell" in <u>Earth First!</u> And in <u>International Wildlife</u>, Don Hinrichsen writes, "Down to the Last Drop—The Fate of Wildlife Is Linked to Water, But Too Many People Are Sucking It Up." As you might also expect, we have political commentators, such as Sandra K. Davis in <u>The Social Science Journal</u>, who writes on "The Politics of Water Scarcity in the Western States," and Ines Capdevila, with "Rising Population Faces Shrinking Water Supply" in <u>Insight on the News</u>.

The jungle of fragmentation seems bewildering as special interest groups advance their agenda--wildlife, irrigation, ecology, sanitation, hygiene, and so forth. Ultimately, the world community must come together, find answers, develop water resources across the entire earth, and the momentum for such a

The writer provides a brief review of the literature on the topic in the next two paragraphs.

Here Berkowitz establishes his thesis for the paper, which will be echoed in his final paragraph.

revolution may be the responsibility and the task of the youth, not the established political base.

First, we should examine the shortages of water in key places around the globe. To begin, Table 1 displays the water of the earth and its distribution. As this chart from the Department

Table 1

Water Supply of the World

	Surface area (sq mi)	Volume (cu mi)	Percentage of total
Salt water			
The oceans	139,500,000	317,000,000	97.2%
Inland seas and saline lakes	270,000	25,000	0.008
Fresh water			
Freshwater lakes	330,000	30,000	0.009
All rivers (average level)	--	300	0.0001
Antarctic ice cap	6,000,000	6,300,000	1.9
Arctic ice cap and glaciers	900,000	680,000	0.21
Water in the atmosphere	197,000,000	3,100	0.001
Groundwater within half a mile of surface	--	1,000,000	0.31
Deep-lying ground water	--	1,000,000	0.31
Total (rounded)	--	326,000,000	100.00

<u>Source:</u> Department of the Interior, Geological Survey (Washington: GPO, 2002); rpt. in <u>Science</u>. 4 May 2003 <http://www.factmonster.com/ipka/Aoo04674.html>.

For tables, type both label and caption flush left on separate lines above the table in capital letters as in a title (not in all capital letters).

Give the source of a table below the table.

Berkowitz 4

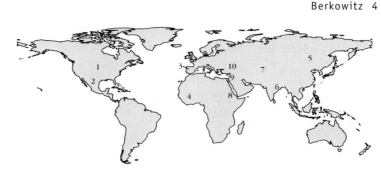

Fig. 1. Water problem Spots: My sketch that shows 10 water flashpoints around the globe.

of the Interior shows, the fresh water available for human consumption is only one-third of 1 percent of the total supply of water. The salt water of the oceans makes up the majority, 97.2 percent. The Antarctic ice cap holds an enormous amount of fresh water, 1.9 percent, but it is far removed from areas of need. BBC News warns that the "world's supply of fresh water is running out." The news bureau makes this assertion: "Already one person in five has no access to safe drinking water." Thus, we need to examine briefly ten regions that have been identified as crisis centers (BBC News, "World Water Crisis"). Figure 1 shows these locations.

1. The Ogallala, which is North America's largest aquifer (an underground bed) that stretches from Nebraska to Colorado, Kansas, Oklahoma, New Mexico, and down into Texas. According to BBC News, it is "being depleted at a rate of 12 billion cubic metres (bcm) a year" (BBC News). That equals the annual flow of the Colorado River 18 times. The High Plains of America are in trouble.

2. Mexico City, which is slowly sinking because of water pumped from under its foundations. It was at one time a land of lakes with cities built on islands, but now this large city, over

Berkowitz 5

populated, has reached a crisis--the "risk of running out of clean water" (BBC News).

3. In Cantalonia, Spain, authorities are asking France to allow a pipeline that would divert water from the Rhone River to Barcelona. It would give relief to 4.5 million people.

4. West Africa suffers massive shortages in Ghana, Mali, and Nigeria.

5. China's northern plain has three severely polluted rivers that are in danger of running dry, and the Yellow River was dry for 226 days in 1997.

6. In India, the sacred Ganges River is depleted and contains, in places, dangerous levels of arsenic.

7. The Aral Sea in Kazakhstan, Central Asia, at one time was the fourth-largest lake in the world, but its water level has dropped 16 meters, it is polluted, and the region now has high infant mortality rates.

8. The Nile River feeds Cairo and Egypt, but it also runs through Ethiopia and Sudan, two countries that could swallow the fresh water before it gets to Cairo. War looms if that happens.

9. The Middle East, already a hotbed of political differences, has tensions over fresh water usage from the River Jordan, the River Litani, and the Sea of Galilee. Any truce between the Palestine and Israel needs to include water rights.

10. Turkey has built dams along the Euphrates and Tigris rivers, to the anger of Syria and Iraq, denying those two countries of fully flowing rivers. Turkey also has plans for selling its water to parched countries in the Middle East.

Those ten spots are identified as the worst, but many others exist. The waters of the Colorado River, for example, are now totally absorbed by the basin's demand from ranches and farms, Las Vegas, and southern California. Twenty-five million people

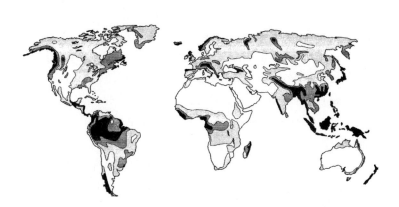

Fig. 2. The World's Renewable Water Supply showing annual precipitation minus evaporation from driest in white to the wettest in black with two degrees of gray in between, from <u>Atlas of World Water Balance</u> (Paris: UNESCO, 1977); rpt. in Postel 26.

are "plumbed into its system," more than twenty dams store its rich resources, yet at the very end of the river bed nothing is left; not even a trickle reaches the Gulf of California (Sprig 24).

After tracing that gloomy picture of the water shortages, we should also look at the supply side. Canada lucked out with about 20 percent of the world's supply of fresh water (O'Malley and Bowman), but that depends "on how one defines 'freshwater'-- whether it means 'available,' 'usable,' or merely 'existing.'" Brazil, Russia, portions of China, and the Antarctic ice cap are other rich sources of water. See Figure 2 drawn from <u>Atlas of World Water Balance</u>. The United States has an abundance, thanks to the Great Lakes. The abundance in some places and scarcity in others provokes this question: Can those with plenty somehow share with others?

Canada has become the focus of the debate on sharing water, which centers on the story of one man--Gerry White. According to reports by Martin O'Malley and John Bowman, White

Make a reference in the text to any table or figure provided nearby and on the same page if possible.

Berkowitz 7

is trying to sell water from Newfoundland's Gisborne Lake. He would skim each week from the lake 500,000 cubic meters of water that in 10 hours would be replenished. Shipped in bulk, the water would give relief to water-deprived nations. More importantly, it would "be a godsend to jobs-poor Newfoundland, especially the small community of Grand le Pierre" (O'Malley and Bowman).

Such a plan seems more than reasonable. Large tankers full of fresh water could sail the seas with the oil tankers. At least when one of them cracked open, we'd only have a "water" spill. However, like so many good ideas--and Newfoundland embraced the idea wholeheartedly--opposition quickly appeared. Environmentalists argue that water is a "vital resource" like air (but not like oil, gas, or timber) and therefore cannot be sold else it become a "commodity." As a commodity it would be subject to the terms of the General Agreement on Tariffs and Trade (GATT) and the North American Free Trade Agreement (NAFTA). At the same time, Marq de Villiers, a Canadian who won a Governor General's Award for nonfiction with his book <u>Water</u>, says the international demand for Canadian water does not exist and that collecting and shipping the water would be "far more expensive than drinkable water recovered by new-generation desalination plants" (qtd. in O'Malley and Bowman). He even declares, "Water is not an issue."

Berkowitz explores the contentious problems facing those who have water and those who do not.

While the two sides debate, the premier of Newfoundland, Roger Grimes, thinks Newfoundland might "go it alone and damn the federal torpedoes" (qtd. in O'Malley and Bowman). So while one side says water is not an issue, Mayor Fizzard of Grand Le Pierre would welcome an economic boost from Lake Gisborne's rich supply of water.

The water is needed, and it is an issue. Gar Smith in "Water Wars, Water Cures" reports that Saudi Arabia purchases half of its

Berkowitz 8

water, Israel buys 87 percent of its water, and Jordan imports 91 percent (30). Smith predicts, "In another 25 years, 48 countries with more than one-third of the world's population will suffer from water starvation."

The political implications are obvious. Each nation <u>with</u> water will resist selling even though natural resources have been sold for years. In fact, timber sales have contributed to the disappearance of rain forests. Turkey talks like it will sell water. Major corporations are moving in and may corner the market-- Bechtel (U.S.), Vivendi Universal (France), RWE/Thames (Germany/UK)--with financial help from the World Bank (Sprig). The world economy is such that a need will be met--for a price! That price may put poorer countries in peril, but the distribution is coming.

The writer explores both the political and ethical implications of water issues.

The ethical implications are something entirely different. What responsibilities do the rich nations, especially the United States, have to assure the fair and equitable distribution of water resources? Some might say that the economic forces will solve the problem, but that probably means the rich will capitalize. Meanwhile, the poor mother in Basra or New Delhi will still walk for miles in hopes of filling a jug to carry home for her children. Environmentalist Ray Dasmann puts it like this:

> We know how to solve these problems, without a doubt. To begin with, I believe we must restore a sense of individual responsibility and involvement, and get away from the idea that conservation is the responsibility of somebody else—the federal government, the state, the corporations, the rich. We must each face up to the need to develop an ecologically sustainable way of living; we need to look at our patterns of consumption and behavior, and shed those practices that contribute to the continuing destruction of nature. (48)

The page reference for an indented quotation goes outside the final period.

Berkowitz 9

Global warming is a fact, not a myth. Desertification continues and cannot correct itself without worldwide conservation. Americans consume an average of 300-plus liters of water per day per capita while the average person needs only 20 to 40 liters (O'Malley and Bowman). Postel reminds us that water is "a living system that drives the workings of a natural world we depend on" (<u>Last Oasis</u> 19). She declares: "A new water era has begun" (24). The great prairies of the world will dry up, including America's. When Americans notice the drought, then maybe something will happen. Meanwhile, a massive amount of water is locked in glaciers.

Berkowitz reaffirms his thesis in the final paragraph.

We young people have an ethical obligation to do small things now and anticipate the day when we will have political clout, maybe even by holding public office. For now, we can endorse electric automobiles, use less water, be politically active by joining conservation groups (see the Appendix, pages 10–11), and most of all by spreading the word--water is abundant in certain places but some have not a drop to drink.

Berkowitz 10

Appendix

Ways to Get Involved

1. **EarthWatch Institute** offers a rich program of activities that take small groups around the world for field research and humanitarian programs. Most teams are composed of 6 to 10 people, and the share of your cost for the trip ranges from $1,000 up to $5,000.

An appendix is the place for extra information that is not germane to the principal discussion. Begin it on a new page.

There are fifteen or so expeditions for the various continents--Africa, Asia, Central America/Caribbean, Europe,

North America, Australia/New Zealand, and South America. Most trips are for two weeks. Here are just three of 122 field trips for 2003:

- South African Penguins: Team size 4; Rendezvous site: Cape Town, South Africa; Cost $1,950; Task is to tag and monitor a threatened penguin population.
- Guatemala's Ancient Maya: Team size 10; Rendezvous site: Guatemala City, Guatemala; Cost $1,995; Task is to survey and map Mayan mounds near Chocola.
- Jackson Hole Bison Dig: Team size 12; Rendezvous site: Jackson Hole, Wyoming; Cost $1,595; Task is excavation, mapping, sorting, labeling, and documenting artifacts uncovered at the site of prehistoric bison kills. Visit EarthWatch Institute at <www.earthwatch.org>.

2. **Earth Island Journal** hosts an annual SolFest, which celebrates the sun, renewable energy, and sustainable living. It's held each year in August at the Real Goods Solar Living Center 90 minutes north of San Francisco. Check it out at <www.solfest.org>.

3. **Earth First** **magazine** sponsors numerous action camps throughout the year and all across the nation, such as nonviolent activities to protect the flora and fauna as well as the forests and wetlands. Visit this site at <www.earthfirstjournal.org>.

4. **World Water Day** is held on March 22 of each year. The United National Environment Program was the leading agency for World Water Day 2003, held in Kyoto, Japan. The goal is to inspire political and community action and encourage greater global understanding of the need for more responsible water use and conservation. Visit this site at <www.worldwaterday.org>.

Berkowitz 12

Works Cited

Capdevila, Ines. "Rising Population Faces Shrinking Water
Supply." <u>Insight on the News</u> 16 (2000): 30- . <u>Expanded
Academic ASAP</u>. InfoTrac. Vanderbilt U, Heard Lib. 3 Sept.
2006 <http://www.galegroup.com/>.

Dasmann, Ray. "Voices." Interview with David Kupfer. <u>Earth
Island Journal</u> 18 (2003): 48.

Davis, Sandra K. "The Politics of Water Scarcity in the Western
States." <u>The Social Science Journal</u> 38 (2002): 527- .
<u>Expanded Academic ASAP. InfoTrac</u>. Vanderbilt U, Heard Lib.
4 Sept. 2006 <http://www.galegroup.com/>.

Hinrichsen, Don. "Down to the Last Drop: The Fate of Wildlife Is
Linked to Water, But Too Many People Are Sucking It Up."
<u>International Wildlife</u> Nov.-Dec. 2001. <u>Expanded Academic
ASAP</u>. InfoTrac. Vanderbilt U, Heard Lib. 4 Sept. 2006
<http://www.galegroup.com/>.

McLeod, Christopher. "Sacred Land Film Project." <u>Earth Island
Journal</u> 18 (2003): 16-17.

Misner, Michael. "Wild Wetland of New York." <u>Earth Island Journal</u>
18 (2003): 46-47.

O'Malley, Martin, and John Bowman. "Selling Canada's Water."
<u>CBC News Online</u>. June 2001. 5 Sept. 2006
<http://www.cbc.ca/news/indepth/water/>.

Postel, Sandra L. <u>Last Oasis: Facing Water Scarcity</u>. New York:
Norton, 1992.

---. "Water for Food Production: Will There Be Enough in 2925?"
<u>BioScience</u> 48 (1998): 629-. <u>Expanded Academic ASAP</u>.
InfoTrac. Vanderbilt U, Heard Lib. 2 Sept. 2006
<http://www.galegroup.com/>.

"Research Expeditions 2003." <u>EarthWatch Institute</u> 21
(2003): 8-85.

Begin the Works Cited on a new page.

A source from a library's electronic database.

An interview found in a journal.

An article from an academic journal.

When a writer has two works, use three hyphens after the first in place of the name.

No author listed.

Berkowitz 13

Sprig, [no first name listed]. "The End of Lake Powell." <u>Earth</u>
    <u>First</u>! 1 May 2003: 24-25.

Smith, Gar. "Water Wars, Water Cures." <u>Earth Island Journal</u> 15
    (2000): 30-32.

Tounounga, Camile Taldeu. "The Liquid of the Gods." <u>UNESCO</u>
    <u>Courier</u> May 1993: 38-39.

Townsend, Mark. "Water Fight Is Looming: Water--Or the Lack of
    It--Threatens to Become One of the Single Biggest Factors
    Opposing World Peace." <u>Geographical</u> 74 (2002): 10- .
    <u>Expanded Academic ASAP</u>. InfoTrac. Vanderbilt U, Heard Lib.
    5 Sept. 2006 <http://www.galegroup.com/>.

"World Water Crisis." <u>BBC News</u>. 2000. 6 Sept. 2006
    <http://news.bbc.co.uk/hi/english/static/in_depth/world/
    2000/world_water_crisis/default.stm>.

"World Water Day." <u>IRC International Water and Sanitation Centre</u>.
    2003. 4 Sept. 2006 <http://www.worldwaterday.org/>.

Use brackets to insert your words.

Internet sources require the date of access preceding the URL.

14 Works Cited: MLA Style

After writing your paper, you should begin to finalize your Works Cited page to list your reference materials. List only those sources actually used in your manuscript, including works mentioned within content endnotes and in captions to tables and illustrations. Preparing the Works Cited will be relatively simple if you carefully developed your working bibliography as a computer file (see pages 57–58). It will be difficult only if you have not kept publication data on each source cited in the paper.

> Sample Works Cited pages, pages 235 and 246–247.
> Sample annotated bibliography, pages 117–119.

Keep in mind that others might use your bibliography for research of their own. A documentation system, such as the MLA style, gives all scholars in the field a consistent way to consult the sources. Inaccurate records might prevent an easy retracing of your steps.

Select a heading that indicates the nature of your list.

Works Cited for a list of works including books, articles, films, recordings, Internet sources, and so on that are quoted or paraphrased in the research paper.

Works Consulted if your list includes nonprint items such as interviews, letters, or speeches as well as printed works.

Annotated Bibliography for a list of references that includes a description of the contents of each source (see pages 117–119).

Selected Bibliography for a list of readings on the subject.

> Other bibliography forms:
> APA, Chapter 15;
> CMS footnote style, Chapter 16;
> CSE number style, Chapter 17.

Works pertinent to the paper but not quoted or paraphrased, such as an article on related matters, can be mentioned in a content endnote (see pages 346–349) and then listed in the Works Cited.

14a Formatting the Works Cited Page

Arrange items in alphabetic order by the surname of the author using the letter-by-letter system. Ignore spaces in the author's surname. Consider the first names only when two or more surnames are identical. Note how the following examples are alphabetized letter by letter.

> Bandercloth, Morgan
> Dempsey, William R.
> Lawrence, Jacob
> Lawrence, Melissa
> McPherson, James Alan
> Saint-Exupéry, Antoine de
> St. James, Christopher

When two or more entries cite coauthors that begin with the same name, alphabetize by the last names of the second authors:

> Huggins, Marjorie, and Devan Blythe
> Huggins, Marjorie, and Stephen Fisher

When no author is listed, alphabetize by the first important word of the title. Imagine lettered spelling for unusual items. For example, "#2 Red Dye" should be alphabetized as though it were "Number 2 Red Dye."

The list of sources may also be divided into separate alphabetized sections for primary and secondary sources, for different media (articles, books, Internet sources), for different subject matter (biography, autobiography, letters), for different periods (Neoclassic period, Romantic period), and for different areas (German viewpoints, French viewpoints, American viewpoints).

Place the first line of each entry flush with the left margin and indent succeeding lines one inch—which is usually one tab space on the computer or five spaces. Double-space each entry, and double-space between entries. Use one space after periods and other marks of punctuation.

Set the title "Works Cited" one inch down from the top of the sheet and double-space between it and the first entry. A sample page is illustrated below.

> **HINT:** Check your instructor's preference before using italics in place of underlining. If in doubt, use underlining because it prevents ambiguity by its distinctive marking of words and titles.

Masterson 12

Works Cited

Amato, Peter. "Hobbes, Darwinism, and Conceptions of Human Nature."

Minerva: An Internet Journal of Philosophy 6 (2002). 22 Sept.

2005 <http://www.ul.ie/~philos/vol6/hobbes.html>.

Boyd, Robert, and Joan B. Silk. How Humans Evolved. 3rd ed. New York:

Norton, 2003.

Campbell, Joseph. <u>The Hero with a Thousand Faces</u>. New York: Fine, 1996.

---. <u>The Masks of God</u>. 4 vols. New York: Viking, 1970.

Ehringhaus, Susan, and David Korn. "Conflicts of Interest in Human Subjects Research." <u>Issues in Science and Technology Online</u> 19.2 (2002). 20 Sept. 2005 <http://www.nap.edu/issues/19.2/ ehringhaus.htm>.

Jenkins, Philip. "Catch Me before I Kill More: Seriality as Modern Monstrosity." <u>Cultural Analysis</u> 3 (2002). 20 Sept. 2005 <http://socrates.berkeley.edu/%7Ecaforum/volume3/ vol_article1.html>.

Kourany, Janet A. "A Philosophy of Science for the Twenty-First Century." <u>Philosophy of Science</u> 70.1 (2005): 1-14.

Martin, Thomas R. "Religion, Myth, and Community." <u>An Overview of Classical Greek History from Homer to Alexander</u>. 3 Apr. 1999. 18 Sept. 2005 <http:// www.Perseus.tufts.edu/cgi-bin/ ptext?doc_Parsees%3Adeste%3A1999.04.0009%3Ahead%3D%2328>.

Morford, Mark P. O., and Robert J. Lenardon. <u>Classical Mythology</u>. 7th ed. New York: Oxford UP, 2002.

"North American Mythology." 20 Aug. 2002. 17 Sept. 2005 <http://www.mythome.org/NorthAm.html>.

Index to Bibliographic Models: MLA Style

(continued on page 251)

(continued from page 250)

Index to Bibliographic Models: MLA Style

(continued on page 252)

(continued from page 251)

Index to Bibliographic Models: MLA Style

(continued on page 253)

(continued from page 252)

Index to Bibliographic Models: MLA Style

(continued on page 254)

(continued from page 253)

Index to Bibliographic Models: MLA Style

14b Bibliography Form—Books

Enter information for books in the following order. Items 1, 3, and 8 are usually required; add other items according to the circumstances explained in the text that follows.

1. Author(s)
2. Chapter or part of book
3. Title of the book
4. Editor, translator, or compiler
5. Edition
6. Number(s) of volume(s) used
7. Name of the series
8. Place, publisher, and date
9. Page numbers
10. Extra bibliographic information

The following list in alphabetical order explains and gives examples of the correct form for books.

Author's Name

List the author's name, surname first, followed by given name or initials, and then a period:

Truss, Lynn. Talk to the Hand. New York: Penguin, 2006.

Always give authors' names in the fullest possible form—for example, "Grierson, Robert A." rather than "Grierson, R. A."—unless, as indicated on the title page of the book, the author prefers initials. However, APA style (see Chapter 15, pages 300-336) requires last name and initials only (e.g., Grierson, R. A.). If you spell out an abbreviated name, put square brackets around the material added:

Lewis, C[live] S[taples].

With pseudonyms you may add the real name, enclosing the addition in brackets.

Carroll, Lewis [Charles Lutwidge Dodgson].

Omit titles, affiliations, and degrees that appear with the author's name on the title page.

If the title page says:	*In the Works Cited use:*
Sir Edmund Hillary	Hillary, Edmund
Sister Margaret Nelson	Nelson, Margaret
Barton O'Connor, Ph.D.	O'Connor, Barton

However, do provide an essential suffix that is part of a person's name:

Justin, Walter, Jr.
Peterson, Robert J., III

Author, Anonymous

Begin with the title. Do not use *anonymous* or *anon.* Alphabetize by the title, ignoring initial articles, *A, An,* or *The.*

The Song of Roland. Trans. W. S. Merwin. New York: Random, 2001.

Author, Anonymous but Name Supplied

Alphabetize by the supplied name, set in square brackets.

[Madison, James.] All Impressments Unlawful and Inadmissible.
Boston: Pelham, 1804.

Author, Pseudonymous But Name Supplied

Slender, Robert [Freneau, Philip]. Letters on Various and Important
Subjects. Philadelphia: Hogan, 1799.

Author, Listed by Initials with Name Supplied

Rowling, J[oanne] K[athleen]. Harry Potter and the Half-Blood Prince.
New York: Scholastic, 2005.

Authors, Two

Middleton, Kent R., and William E. Lee Schwartz. The Law of Public Communication.
Boston: Allyn & Bacon, 2006.

Authors, Three

Be sure to list the authors in the same order they appear on the title page.

Slywotzky, Adrian, Richard Wise, and Karl Weber. How to Grow When
Markets Don't. New York: Warner, 2003.

Authors, More Than Three

Use "et al.," which means "and others," or list all the authors. See the two
examples that follow:

Garrod, Andrew C., et al. Adolescent Portraits: Identity, Relationships,
and Challenges. 5th ed. Boston: Allyn & Bacon, 2005.

Marzanno, Robert J., Jennifer S. Norford, Diane E. Paynter, Debra J.
Pickering, and Barbara B. Gaddy. Handbook for Classroom
Instruction That Works. New York: Prentice Hall, 2004.

Author, Corporation or Institution

A corporate author can be an association, a committee, or any group or
institution when the title page does not identify the names of the members.

American Medical Association. Health Professions Career and Education
Directory 2005-2006. New York: Random, 2005.

List a corporation as the author even when the organization is also the
publisher, as in this example:

Consumer Reports. Consumer Reports Electronics Buying Guide 2006.
New York: Consumer Reports, 2006.

Author, Two or More Books by the Same Author

When your works cited page includes two or more works by the same author, give the name in the first entry only. Thereafter, insert a continuous three-hyphen line flush with the left margin, followed by a period. Also, list the works alphabetically by the title (ignoring *a, an,* and *the*), not by the year of publication. In the following example, the *B* of *Bird's-Eye* precedes the *F* of *Fallen*.

Freedman, J. F. <u>Above the Law</u>. New York: Signet, 2001.

---. <u>Bird's-Eye View</u>. New York: Warner, 2001.

---. <u>Fallen Idols</u>. New York: Warner, 2004.

The three hyphens stand for exactly the same name(s) as in the preceding entry. However, do not substitute three hyphens for an author who has two or more works in the bibliography when one is written in collaboration with someone else:

Sagan, Carl. <u>Contact</u>. New York: Pocket, 1997.

---. <u>Cosmos</u>. New York: Ballantine, 1985.

Sagan, Carl, and Ann Druyan. <u>Shadows of Forgotten Ancestors: A Search</u>

<u>for Who We Are</u>. New York: Random, 1993.

If the person edited, compiled, or translated the work that follows on the list, place a comma after the three hyphens and write *ed., comp.,* or *trans.* before you give the title. This label does not affect the alphabetic order by title.

Finneran, Richard J. <u>Editing Yeats's Poems</u>. New York:

St. Martin's, 1983.

---, ed. <u>Yeats Reader</u>. New York: Scribner, 2002.

Author, Two or More Books by the Same Multiple Authors

When you cite two or more books by the same multiple authors, provide the names in the first entry only. Thereafter, use three hyphens, followed by a period.

Kennedy, X. J., and Dana Gioia. <u>Literature: An Introduction to Fiction,</u>

<u>Poetry, and Drama</u>. 9th ed. New York: Longman, 2005.

---. <u>An Introduction to Poetry</u>. 10th ed. New York: Longman, 2005.

Alphabetized Works, Encyclopedias, and Biographical Dictionaries

Treat works arranged alphabetically as you would an anthology or collection, but omit the name of the editor(s), the volume number, place of publication, publisher, and page number(s). If the author is listed, begin the entry with the author's name; otherwise, begin with the title of the article. If the article is signed with initials, look elsewhere in the work for a complete name. Well-known works, such as the first two examples that follow, need only the edition and the year of publication.

> "Kiosk: Word History." <u>The American Heritage Dictionary of the English</u>
> <u>Language</u>. 4th ed. 2004.
>
> Moran, Joseph. "Weather." <u>The World Book Encyclopedia</u>. 2005 ed.

If you cite a specific definition from among several, add *Def.* (Definition), followed by the appropriate number/letter of the definition.

> "Level." Def. 4a. <u>The American Heritage Dictionary of the English</u>
> <u>Language</u>. 4th ed. 2004.

Less-familiar reference works need a full citation, as shown in this next example:

> "Infections." <u>The American Medical Association Family Medical Guide</u>.
> Ed. Charles B. Clayman. New York: Random, 2004.

Place within quotation marks the titles of a synopsis or description of a novel or drama when that title is the name of the entry in the alphabetized reference book, even though it would normally be underscored or italicized.

> "Oedipus the King." <u>The Compact Bedford Introduction to Literature</u>.
> Ed. Michael Meyer. Boston: St. Martin's, 2006. 1049-1050.

Anthology, Component Part

In general, works in an anthology have been published previously and collected by an editor. Supply the names of authors as well as editors. Almost always cite the author first. Many times the prior publication data on a specific work may not be readily available; therefore, use this form:

> Reagon, Bernice. "Black Music in Our Hands." <u>The Conscious Reader</u>.
> Eds. Caroline Shrodes, Harry Finestone, and Michael Shugrue. 10th
> ed. New York: Longman, 2006. 345-49.

If you use several works from the same anthology, you can shorten the citation by using cross references; see "Cross-References," pages 260–261.

Provide the inclusive page numbers for the piece, not just the page or pages you cited in the text.

Use the following form if you can quickly identify original publication information. Note that the page numbers in the *The New Yorker* were unavailable in the reprint:

"Soup." The New Yorker. Jan. 1989: n.p. Rpt. in The St. Martin's Guide

to Writing. Eds. Rise B. Axelrod and Charles R. Cooper. Short 6th

ed. Boston: Bedford, 2001. 132-34.

Conform to the rules given in these examples:

Elder, Lonne. "Ceremonies in Dark Old Men." New Black Playwrights: An

Anthology. Ed. William Couch, Jr. Baton Rouge: Louisiana State

UP, 1968. 55-72.

If you cite lines from Aristophanes' drama *Lysistrata* in your paper, write this entry:

Aristophanes. Lysistrata. Trans. Douglass Parker. New York: Signet,

2006. 30–39.

If you cite material from a chapter of one volume in a multivolume set, write an entry like these:

Child, Harold. "Jane Austen." The Cambridge History of English

Literature. Ed. A. W. Ward and A. R. Waller. Vol. 12. London:

Cambridge UP, 1927.

Although not required, you may also provide the total number of volumes:

Saintsbury, George. "Dickens." The Cambridge History of Engish

Literature. Ed. A. W. Ward and A. R. Waller. Vol. 13. New York:

Putnam's, 1917. 14 vols.

The Bible

Do not underscore or italicize the word *Bible* or the books of the Bible. Common editions need no publication information, but do underscore or italicize special editions of the Bible.

The Bible. [Denotes King James version]

The Bible. The Old Testament. CD-ROM. Audio Bible, 2003.

The Bible. Revised Standard Version.

The Geneva Bible. 1560. Facsim. rpt. Madison: U of

Wisconsin P, 1961.

NIV [New International Version] Study Bible. Personal Size Rev. Ed.

n.p.: Zondervan, 2002.

A Book Published before 1900

For older books that are now out of print, you may omit the publisher. Use a comma, not a colon, to separate the place of publication from the year. If no date is listed, use "n.d." If no place of publication is mentioned, use "n.p."

Dewey, John. The School and Society. Chicago, 1899.

Chapter or Part of a Book

List a chapter or part of a book on the Works Cited page only when it is separately edited, translated, or written. For example, if you quote from a specific chapter of a book, let's say Chapter 6 of Brian Hall's book, the entry should read:

McCourt, Frank. Teacher Man: A Memoir. New York: Scribner, 2005.

> Citing individual works in an anthology: "Anthology, Component Part," pages 258–259, or "Collection, Component Part," page 260.

Your in-text citation will have listed specific page numbers, so there is no reason to mention a specific chapter, even though it is the only portion of Hall's book that you read.

Classical Works

Homer. The Odyssey. Trans. T. E. Lawrence. New York: Barnes, 2004.

You are more likely to find a classic work in an anthology, which would require this citation:

Spenser, Edmund. The Faerie Queen. The Norton Anthology of Poetry.

Ed. Margaret Ferguson, Mary Jo Salter, and John Stallworthy. New

York: Norton, 2005. 165–89.

Collection, Component Part

If you cite from one work in a collection of works by the same author, provide the specific name of the work and the corresponding page numbers. This next entry cites one story from a collection of stories by the same author:

Anderson, Mark. "The Sharp Razor of a Willing Conceit [1593–1598]."

Shakespeare by Another Name. New York: Gotham, 2005. 272–309.

Cross-References to Works in a Collection

If you are citing several selections from one anthology or collection, provide a full reference to the anthology (as explained on pages 258–259) and then provide references to the individual selections by providing the author and title of the work, the last name of the editor of the collection, and the inclusive page numbers used from the anthology.

Elbow, Peter, and Pat Belanoff. Being a Writer. Boston:

McGraw, 2003.

Koo, Eunsook. "Exploring the Writing Process." Elbow and Belanoff 181.

Spencer, Beth. "The Act of Writing as Prayer." Elbow and Belanoff 126–28.

Wilbur, Richard. "The Writer." Elbow and Belanoff 220.

Note also the following examples in which the first entry refers to the one that follows:

Eliot, George. "Art and Belles Lettres." <u>Westminster Review</u>. USA ed.

   April 1856. Partly rpt. Eliot, <u>A Writer's Notebook</u>.

---. <u>A Writer's Notebook, 1854-1879, and Uncollected Writings</u>. Ed.

   Joseph Wiesenfarth. Charlottesville: UP of Virginia, 1981.

Add an abbreviated title to the cross-reference if you list two or more works under the editor's name.

Angelou, Maya. "Uncle Willie." Axelrod and Cooper, <u>Guide</u> 82-86.

Axelrod, Rise B., and Charles R. Cooper. <u>Reading Critically, Writing</u>

   <u>Well</u>. 5th ed. New York: St. Martin's, 1999.

---. <u>The St. Martin's Guide to Writing</u>. Short 6th ed. Boston: Bedford,

   1997.

Forster, E. M. "My Wood." Axelrod and Cooper, <u>Reading</u> 111-14.

Wolff, Tobias. "On Being a Real Westerner." Axelrod and Cooper,

   <u>Guide</u> 33-35.

Edition

Indicate the edition used, whenever it is not the first, in Arabic numerals ("3rd ed."), by name ("Rev. ed.," "Abr. ed."), or by year ("1999 ed."), without further punctuation:

Agur, Anne M. <u>Grant's Atlas of Anatomy</u>. 11th ed. Philadelphia:

   Lippincott, 2004.

Indicate that a work has been prepared by an editor, not the original author:

Melville, Herman. <u>Moby-Dick</u>. Ed. with Intro. by Alfred Kazin. 2nd ed.

   Boston: Houghton, 1956.

If you wish to show the original date of the publication, place the year immediately after the title, followed by a period. *Note:* The title of an edition in a series is capitalized.

Hardy Thomas. <u>Far from the Madding Crowd.</u> 1874. Ed. Rosemarie

   Morgan and Shannon Russell. A Penguin Classic ed. New York:

   Penguin, 2003.

Editor, Translator, Illustrator, or Compiler

If the name of the editor or compiler appears on the title page of an anthology or compilation, place it first:

Mitchell, Douglas R., and Judy L. Brunson-Hadley, eds. Ancient Burial

  Practices in the American Southwest. Albuquerque: U of New

  Mexico P, 2004.

If your in-text citation refers to the work of the editor, illustrator, or translator (e.g., "The Ciardi edition caused debate among Dante scholars" or "The note by Bevington"), use this form with the original author listed after the work, preceded by the word *By*:

Birk, Sandow, and Marcus Sanders, trans. The Purgatorio. By Dante. San

  Francisco: Chronicle, 2005.

Kalman, Maira, illus. The Elements of Style. By William Strunk, Jr. and

  E. B. White. New York: Penguin, 2005.

Jowett, John, William Montgomery, Gary Taylor, and Stanley Wells, eds.

  The Oxford Shakespeare: The Complete Works. 2nd ed. Oxford:

  Clarendon, 2005.

The in-text citation should explain the editotial content cited, e.g. "(Bevington, 316n)." Otherwise, mention an editor *after* the title:

Yeats, W. B. The Poetry of W. B. Yeats. Ed. Michael Faherty. New York:

  Palgrave Macmillan, 2005.

Encyclopedia and Reference Book

Ward, Norman. "Saskatchewan." Encyclopedia Americana. 2006 ed.

See also "Alphabetized Works, Encyclopedias, and Biographical Dictionaries" on pages 257–258 and "Citing Sources Found on CD-ROM," pages 288–290.

Introduction, Preface, Foreword, Afterword

If you are citing the introduction to a work, start with the name of the person who wrote it if other than the author of the work itself. Give the name of the part being cited, neither underscored nor enclosed within quotation marks. Place the name of the author in normal order after the title, preceded by the word *By*. Follow with publication information and end with the inclusive page numbers.

Shakur, Afeni. Foreword. Thru My Eyes. By Gobi. New York: Atria, 2005.

  viii–ix.

Maisel, Eric. Introduction. A Writer's Paris. By Maisel. Cincinnati:

  Writer's Digest, 2005. 1–4.

If the author of the work is also the author of the prefatory matter, use only the last name after the word *By.*

> LaHaye, Tim, and Jerry B. Jenkins. Prologue. The Regime: Evil Advances
>
>   before They Were Left Behind. By Lahaye and Jenkins. Wheaton,
>
>   IL: Tyndale, 2005. ix–xiv.

Use the form above only if you cite from the prologue and not the main text.

Manuscript or Typescript

> Chaucer, Geoffrey. *The Canterbury Tales*. Harley ms. 7334. British
>
>   Museum, London.

> Tabares, Miguel. "Voices from the Ruins of the Aztecs." Unpublished
>
>   essay, 2006.

For more details about this type of citation, see "Chapter or Part of a Book," page 260, and "Anthologies," pages 258–259.

Page Number(s) to a Section of a Book

Cite pages to help a reader find a particular section of a book.

> Coyne, Kevin. "The Home Front, 1942-1944." Marching Home. New York:
>
>   Viking, 2003. 75-88.

Play, Classical

> Shakespeare, William. Titus Andronicus. Ed. Thomas L. Berger. Rpt. of
>
>   the 1594 ed. Shakespeare Quartos. New York: Oxford UP, 2003.

Performances of a play will include the director and, if appropriate, the actor(s).

> As You Like It. By William Shakespeare. Dir. Sir Peter Hall. Shubert
>
>   Theatre, New Haven, CT. 24 Oct. 2003.

Today, classical plays are usually found in anthologies, which will require this form:

> Shakespeare, William. The Tempest. The Longman Anthology of British
>
>   Literature. Ed. David Damrosch, et al. New York: Longman, 2003.
>
>   1292-1345.

Play, Modern

Contemporary plays may be published independently or as part of a collection.

Mamet, David. <u>Romance</u>. New York: Knopf, 2005.

Eliot, T. S. <u>The Cocktail Party</u>. <u>The Complete Poems and Plays: 1909-</u>

<u>1950</u>. New York: Harcourt, 1952. 295-387.

If you cite the translator's or editor's preface or notes to the text, put the name of the translator or editor first. See page 262.

Poem, Classical

Classical poems are usually translated, so you will often need to list a translator and/or editor. If the work is one part of a collection, show which anthology you used.

Dante. <u>The Divine Comedy</u>. Trans. John Ciardi. New York:

NAL, 2003.

Dante. <u>Inferno</u>. <u>The Divine Comedy</u>. Trans. John Ciardi. <u>The Norton</u>

<u>Anthology of World Masterpieces</u>. Ed. Sarah Lawall et al. New

York: Norton, 1999. 1303-1429.

Poem, Modern Collection

If you cite one short poem from a collection, use this form, which cites the inclusive page numbers.

Stepanek, Mattie J. T., "Splash-Adventure." <u>Reflections of a</u>

<u>Peacemaker</u>. Kansas City: Andrews McMeel, 2005. 120-21.

Use this next form if you cite from one book-length poem:

Eliot, T. S. <u>Four Quartets. The Complete Poems and Plays 1909-1950</u>.

New York: Harcourt, 1952. 115-45.

Do not cite specific poems and pages if you cite several poems of the collection. Your in-text citations should cite the specific poems and line numbers (see page 190). Your Works Cited entry would then list only the name of the collection.

Eliot, T. S. <u>The Complete Poems and Plays 1909-1950</u>. New York:

Harcourt, 1952.

Publication Information: Place, Publisher, and Date

Indicate the place of publication, the publisher, and the year of publication:

Friedman, Thomas. <u>The World Is Flat: A Brief History of the Twenty-</u>

<u>first Century</u>. New York: Farrar, 2005.

Include the abbreviation for the state or country only if necessary for clarity:

Merwin, W. S. <u>Migration: New and Selected Poems</u>. Port Townsend, WA:

Copper, 2005.

If more than one place of publication appears on the title page, the first city mentioned is sufficient. If successive copyright dates are given, use the most recent (unless your study is specifically concerned with an earlier, perhaps definitive, edition). A new printing does not constitute a new edition. For example, if the text has a 1940 copyright date and a 1975 printing, use 1940 unless other information is given, such as "facsimile printing" or "1975 third printing rev."

Bell, Charles Bailey, and Harriett P. Miller. <u>The Bell Witch: A Mysterious</u>

<u>Spirit</u>. 1934. Facsim. ed. Nashville: Elder, 1972.

If the place, publisher, date of publication, or pages are not provided, use one of these abbreviations:

n.p.   No place of publication listed
n.p.   No publisher listed
n.d.   No date of publication listed
n. pag. No pagination listed

Lewes, George Henry. <u>The Life and Works of Goethe</u>. 1855. 2 vols. Rpt.

as vols. 13 and 14 of <u>The Works J. W. von Goethe</u>. Ed. Nathan

Haskell Dole. London: Nicolls, n.d. 14 vols.

Nelson, Marilyn. "Forget Him Not. Though if I Could, I Would." <u>A</u>

<u>Wreath for Emmett Till</u>. Boston: Houghton Mifflin, 2005. N. pag.

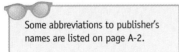

Some abbreviations to publisher's names are listed on page A-2.

Provide the publisher's name in a shortened form, such as "Bobbs" rather than "Bobbs-Merrill Co., Inc." A publisher's special imprint name should be joined with the official name, for example, Anchor-Doubleday.

Faulkner, William. "Spotted Horses." <u>Three Famous Short Stories</u>. New

York: Vintage-Random, 1963.

Republished Book

If you are citing from a republished book, such as a paperback version of a book published originally in hardback, provide the original publication date after the title and then provide the publication information for the book from which you are citing.

Vonnegut, Kurt. <u>Breakfast of Champions</u>. 1973. New York: Delta, 1999.

Although it is not required, you may wish to provide supplementary information. Give the type of reproduction to explain that the republished work is, for example, a facsimile reprinting of the text:

Hooker, Richard. <u>Of the Lawes of Ecclesiasticall Politie</u>. 1594. Facsim.

rpt. Amsterdam: Teatrum Orbis Terrarum, 1971.

Give facts about the original publication if the information will serve the reader. In this next example, the republished book was originally published under a different title:

Arnold, Matthew. "The Study of Poetry." <u>Essays: English and American</u>.

Ed. Charles W. Eliot. 1886. New York: Collier, 1910. Rpt. of the

General Introduction to <u>The English Poets</u>. Ed. T. H. Ward. 1880.

Screenplay

Linklater, Richard, Kim Krizan and Julie Delpy. <u>Before Sunrise and</u>

<u>Before Sunset</u>. Screenplay. New York: Knopf, 2005.

Series, Numbered and Unnumbered

If the work is one in a published series, show the name of the series, abbreviated, without quotation marks or underscoring, the number of this work in Arabic numerals, and a period:

Jefferson, D. W. " 'All, all of a piece throughout': Thoughts on Dryden's

Dramatic Poetry." <u>Restoration Theatre</u>. Ed. J. R. Brown and Bernard

Harris. Stratford-upon-Avon Studies 6. London: Arnold, 1965. 159-76.

Wallerstein, Ruth C. <u>Richard Crashaw: A Study in Style and Poetic</u>

<u>Development</u>. U of Wisconsin Studies in Lang. and Lit. 37.

Madison: U of Wisconsin P, 1935.

Sourcebooks and Casebooks

McGovern, Robert J. "Superior People Skills." <u>Bring Your 'A' Game</u>.

Naperville, IL: Sourcebooks, 2005. 119–33.

If you cite more than one article from a casebook, use cross-references; see pages 260–261.

If you can identify the original facts of publication, include that information also:

Ellmann, Richard. "Reality." <u>Yeats: The Man and the Masks</u>. New York:

Macmillan, 1948. Rpt. in <u>Yeats: A Collection of Critical Essays</u>.

Ed. John Unterecker. Twentieth Century Views. Englewood Cliffs:

Prentice, 1963. 163-74.

Title of the Book

Show the title of the work, underscored or italicized, followed by a period. Separate any subtitle from the primary title by a colon and one space even when the title page has no mark of punctuation or the card catalog entry has a semicolon:

> Carter, Jimmy. Our Endangered Values: America's Moral Crisis. New York:
>
> Simon & Schuster, 2005.

See Appendix A, page A-7, for additional instructions.

If an underscored title to a book incorporates another title that normally receives underscoring, do not underscore or italicize the shorter title nor place it within quotation marks. In the title below, *Absalom and Acidophil* is the shorter title; it does not receive underscoring.

> Schilling, Bernard N. Dryden and the Conservative Myth: A Reading of
>
> Absalom and Acidophil. New Haven: Yale UP, 1961.

Title of a Book in Another Language

In general, use lowercase letters for foreign titles except for the first major word and proper names. Provide a translation in brackets if you think it necessary (e.g., Étranger [The Stranger] or Praha [Prague]).

> Eco, Umberto. La Misteriosa Llama de la Reina Loana. Orlando, FL:
>
> Harcourt, 2005.
>
> Castex, P. G. Le rouge et le noir de Stendhal. Paris: Sedes, 1967.

Note: Le rouge et le noir is the shorter title within a long title, thus it does not receive underscoring; compare with the title below, which requires underscoring because there is no additional title within the title.

> Levowitz-treu, Micheline. L'amour et la mort chez Stendhal.
>
> Aran: Editions du Grand Chêne, 1978.

Translator

List the translator's name first only if the translator's work (preface, foreword, afterword, notes) is the focus of your study, for example, (Grossman note 6).

> Marquez, Gabriel Garcia. Memories of My Melancholy Whores.
>
> Trans. Edith Grossman. New York: Knopf, 2005.
>
> Jowett, Benjamin, trans. The Republic. By Plato. New York: Barnes &
>
> Noble, 2004.

Volumes

If you are citing from only one volume of a multivolume work, provide the number of that volume in the Works Cited entry with information for that volume only. In your text, you will need to specify only page numbers—for example, (Chircop and McConnell 45–46).

> Chircop, Aldo, and Moira L. McConnell, eds. <u>Ocean Yearbook</u>. Vol. 19.
>> Chicago: U of Chicago P, 2005.

Although additional information is not required, you may provide the inclusive page numbers, the total number of volumes, and the inclusive dates of publication.

> Daiches, David. "The Restoration." <u>A Critical History of English</u>
>> <u>Literature</u>. 2nd ed. Vol. 2. New York: Ronald, 1970. 537–89. 2 vols.

If you are citing from two or more volumes of a multivolume work, your in-text citation must specify volume and page (2: 320–321); then the Works Cited entry must show the total number of volumes in Arabic numerals, as shown here:

> Hersen, Michel. <u>Comprehensive Handbook of Psychological Assessment</u>.
>> 4 vols. Indianapolis: Wiley, 2003.

If you are citing from volumes that were published over a period of years, provide the inclusive dates at the end of the citation. Should the volumes still be in production, write *to date* after the number of volumes and leave a space after the hyphen that follows the initial date.

> Parrington, Vernon L. <u>Main Currents in American Thought</u>. 3 vols. New
>> York: Harcourt, 1927-32.
> Cassidy, Frederic, ed. <u>Dictionary of American Regional English</u>. 3 vols.
>> to date. Cambridge: Belknap-Harvard UP, 1985- .

Handle the republishing of volumes in this manner:

> Seivers, Harry J. <u>Benjamin Harrison: Hoosier Warrior</u>. 3 vols. 1952-68.
>> Rpt. of vol. 1. Newtown, CT: American Political Biography Press,
>> 1997.

If you are using only one volume of a multivolume work and the volume has an individual title, you can cite the one work without mentioning the other volumes in the set.

Crane, Stephen. <u>Wounds in the Rain</u>. <u>Stephen Crane: Tales of War</u>.

 Charlottesville: UP of Virginia, 1970. 95-284.

As a courtesy to the reader, you may include supplementary information about an entire edition.

Crane, Stephen. <u>Wounds in the Rain</u>. <u>Stephen Crane: Tales of War</u>.

 Charlottesville: UP of Virginia, 1970. Vol. 6 of <u>The University of</u>

 <u>Virginia Edition of the Works of Stephen Crane</u>. Ed. Fredson

 Bowers. 95-284. 10 vols. 1969-76.

14c Bibliography Form—Periodicals

For journal or magazine articles, use the following order:

1. Author(s)
2. Title of the article
3. Name of the periodical
4. Series number (if it is relevant)
5. Volume number (for journals)
6. Issue number (if needed)
7. Date of publication
8. Page numbers

These items are explained and illustrated in the following alphabetized list.

Abstract in an Abstracts Journal

If you have cited from an abstract found in a journal devoted to abstracts, not full articles, begin the citation with information on the original work and then give information on the abstracts journal. Use either item number or page number, according to how the journal provides the abstracts.

Haynie, Donald T., et al. "Polypeptide Multilayer Films."

 <u>Biomacromolecules</u> 6 (2005): 2895–2913. Chemical Abstracts 98

 (2005): item 5523.

Add the word *Abstract* if the title does not make clear that you have used an abstract, not a full article.

Gryeh, John H., et al. "Patterns of Adjustment among Children of

 Battered Women." <u>Journal of Consulting and Clinical Psychology</u>

 68 (2000): 84–94. Abstract. PsycLIT 2000–13544.

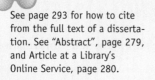

See page 293 for how to cite from the full text of a dissertation. See "Abstract", page 279, and Article at a Library's Online Service, page 280.

Use the next form when you cite from *Dissertation Abstracts International (DAI)*. The page number features A, B, or C to designate the specific series: A Humanities, B Sciences, C European dissertations. Before volume 30 (1969) the title was *Dissertation Abstracts,* so use *DA* for those early volumes.

Nicholson, Andre Wesley. "Criticisms and Critiques: An Analysis of

Proofreading Marks of College English Professors." Diss. Southern

Tech. U, 2005. DAI 66(2005): 2957D.

Author(s)

Show the author's name flush with the left margin, without a numeral and with succeeding lines indented five spaces. Enter the surname first, followed by a comma, followed by a given name or initials, followed by a period:

Burden, Barry C., and Casey A. Klofstad. "Affection and Cognition in

Party Identification." Political Psychology 26.6 (Dec. 2005):

869–86.

Author, Anonymous

"Time Capsule: 1938." *Reminisce.* July/Aug. 2005: 14–16.

Interview, Published

Skaggs, Ricky. Interview with John McManus. "Ricky Skaggs: Bluegrass

Man Conquers Cool." Oxford American Summer 2005: 26–31.

Journal, with All Issues for a Year Paged Continuously

Boardman, Jason D., et al. "Race Differentials in Obesity: The Impact of

Place." Journal of Health & Social Behavior 46.3 (2005): 229–43.

Journal, with Each Issue Paged Anew

Add the issue number after the volume number because page numbers alone are not sufficient to locate the article within a volume of six or twelve issues when each issue has separate pagination. Adding the month or season with the year will also serve the researcher.

Stiglitz, Joseph E. "The Ethical Economist." Foreign Affairs. 84.6

(Nov./Dec. 2005): 128–34.

If a journal uses only an issue number, treat it as a volume number:

Lee, Cheng Min. "China's Rise, Asia's Dilemma." The National Interest

81 (Fall 2005): 88–94.

Loose-Leaf Collection

If the article is reprinted in an information service that gathers several articles on a common topic, as part of a series, use the form shown in the following example.

> Cox, Rachel S. "Protecting the National Parks." The Environment. CQ
>
>   Researcher ser. 23 (2000): 523+.

If the service reprints articles from other sources, use this next form, which shows original publication data and then information on the SIRS booklet—title, editor, and volume number.

> Hodge, Paul. "The Andromeda Galaxy." Mercury July/Aug. 1993: 98+.
>
>   Physical Science. Ed. Eleanor Goldstein. Vol. 2. Boca Raton: SIRS,
>
>   1994. Art. 24.

Magazine

With magazines, the volume number offers little help for finding an article. For example, one volume of *Time* (52 issues) will have page 16 repeated 52 times. For this reason, you need to insert an exact date (month and day) for weekly and fortnightly (every two weeks) publications. Do not list the volume and issue numbers.

> Lim, Paul J. "The Dollar's Draw." U.S. News & World Report
>
>   28 Nov. 2005: 36.

The month suffices for monthly and bimonthly publications:

> Connell, Evan S. "Lost in Uttar Pradesh." Harper's Dec. 2005: 76–84.

Supply inclusive page numbers (202–09, 85–115, or 1112–24), but if an article is paged here and there throughout the issue (for example, pages 74, 78, and 81–88), write only the first page number and a plus sign with no intervening space:

> Awad, Mona. "If Not Winter, Then Wine." Utne Nov./Dec. 2005: 92 + .

Microform

Some reference sources, such as *NewsBank*, republish articles on microfiche. If you use such a microform, enter the original publication information first and then add the pertinent information about the microform, as shown next.

> Chapman, Dan. "Panel Could Help Protect Children." Winston-Salem
>
>   Journal 14 Jan 1990: 14. Newsbank: Welfare and Social Problems
>
>   12 (1990): fiche 1, grids A8-11.

Name of the Periodical

Give the name of the journal or magazine in full, underscored or italicized, and with no following punctuation. Omit any introductory article, such as *The*.

Marx, Gary T. "Soft Surveillance." <u>Dissent</u> Fall 2005: 36–43.

Notes, Editorials, Queries, Reports, Comments, Letters

Magazine and journals publish many pieces that are not full-fledged articles. Identify this type of material if the title of the article or the name of the journal does not make clear the nature of the material (e.g., "Letter" or "Comment").

Bly, Adam. "Science in 2006." Comment. <u>SEED</u> 2.2 (Dec./Jan. 2006):

10.

Perina, Kaja. "From the Book of Jobs." Editor's note. <u>Psychology Today</u>

38.6 (Dec. 2005): 5.

Maltby, Richard E., Jr. "Letter Drop." Puzzle. <u>Harper's</u> Dec. 2005: 99.

On occasion, an editor will reply to a reader's letter or comment. Identify such a response in this manner:

Goodman, Leisa. "A Letter from the Church of Scientology."

Reply to article of Stephen A. Kent. <u>Marburg Journal of Religion</u>

6.2 (2001): 1-4.

Reprint of a Journal Article

Vail, Kathleen. "Climate Control." <u>American School Board Journal</u> 192.6

(June 2005): 12–19. Rpt. in <u>Education Digest</u> Dec. 2005: 4–11.

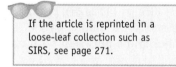

If the article is reprinted in a loose-leaf collection such as SIRS, see page 271.

Review, in a Magazine, Newspaper, or Journal

Name the reviewer and the title of the review. Then write *Rev. of* and the title of the work being reviewed, followed by a comma and the name of the author or producer. If necessary, identify the nature of the work within brackets immediately after the title.

Bowen, Peter. "Casualties of Fame." Rev. of <u>Capote</u>, by Bennett Miller.

<u>Filmmaker</u>. 14.1 (Fall 2005): 56-59.

If the name of reviewer is not provided, begin the entry with the title of the review.

"Pentax Optio WP." Rev. of Pentax Optio WP. <u>Digital Living</u> Dec. 2005:

40.

If the review has no title, omit it from the entry.

> Tappin, Nigel. Rev. of <u>Murder on the Caronia</u>, by Conrad Allen. <u>Mystery</u>
> <u>Review</u> 11.3 (Spring 2003): 15.

If the review is neither signed nor titled, begin the entry with *Rev. of* and alphabetize the entry under the title of the work reviewed.

> Rev. of <u>Anthology of Danish Literature</u>, ed. F. J. Billeskov Jansen and
> P. M. Mitchell. <u>Times Literary Supplement</u> 7 July 1972: 785.

As shown in the example above, use an appropriate abbreviation (e.g., *ed., comp., trans.*) for the work of someone other than an author.

Series

Between the name of the publication and the volume number, identify a numbered series with an ordinal suffix (2nd, 3rd) followed by the abbreviation *ser.* For publications divided between the original series and a new series, show the series with *os* or *ns*, respectively.

> Hill, Christopher. "Sex, Marriage and the Family in England." <u>Economic</u>
> <u>History Review</u> 2nd ser. 31 (1978): 450-63.
> Terry, Richard. "Swift's Use of 'Personate' to Indicate Parody." <u>Notes</u>
> <u>and Queries</u> ns 41.2 (June 1994): 196-98.

See also "Cross References to Works in a Collection," pages 260–261.

Special Issue

If you cite one article from a special issue of a journal, you may indicate the nature of this special issue, as shown next:

> Fenton, Matthew McCann. "Katrina's Last Casualty: Truth." <u>Time</u>. Spec.
> Issue of <u>Time</u> (2005): 55.

If you cite several articles from the special issue, begin the primary citation with the name of the editor:

> Knauer, Kelly, ed. Spec. Issue of <u>Time</u> (2005): 1–122.

Once that entry is established, cross-reference each article used in the following manner:

> Dworzak, Thomas. "Elysian Fields." Photograph. <u>Knauer</u>, 56–57.

Speech or Address, Published

Agnew, Karen. "Finding and Supporting Instructors in Continuing
  Education." Address to Conference on Continuing Education.
  Topeka, KS. 26 Apr. 2003. Rpt. in part <u>Continuing Education
  Review</u> 9.2 June 2003: 19–22.

United States. President. "Healthy Forests Initiative." 20 May 2003.
  Rpt. in <u>Weekly Compilation of Presidential Documents</u> 39.21 (26
  May 2003): 621–57.

Title of the Article

Show the title within quotation marks followed by a period inside the
closing quotation marks:

Tresemer, Lila Sophia. "The Magdalene Mystique: Why Her Archetype
  Matters." <u>Utne</u> (Nov./Dec. 2005): 63–64.

Title, Omitted

Jeffries, Miriam. <u>Oakleaf Journal of Conservation</u> 30.3 (2003): 393–95.

Title, Quotation within the Article's Title

Gatta, John J. "<u>The Scarlet Letter</u> as Pre-text for Flannery O'Connor's
  'Good Country People.'" <u>Nathaniel Hawthorne Review</u> 16 (1990):
  6–9.

Title, within the Article's Title

Cornils, Ingo. "The Martians Are Coming! War, Peace, Love, and
  Scientific Progress in H. G. Wells's <u>The War of the Worlds</u> and Kurd
  Labwitz's <u>Auf Zwei Planeten</u>." *Comparative Literature* 55.1 (Winter
  2003): 24–41.

Title, Foreign

Correa, Armando, and Maria Morales. "La Importancia De Ser." <u>People
  En Espanol</u> Diciembre/Enero 2006: 136–41.

Stivale, Charles J. "Le vraisemblable temporel dans <u>Le Rouge et le
  noir</u>." <u>Stendhal Club</u> 84 (1979): 299–313.

Volume, Issue, and Page Numbers for Journals

Most journals are paged continuously through all issues of an entire year,
so listing the month of publication is unnecessary. For example, page num-

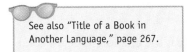
See also "Title of a Book in Another Language," page 267.

bers and a volume number are sufficient for you to find an article in *Eighteenth-Century Studies* or *English Literary Renaissance*. However, some journals have separate pagination for each issue. In this case, you will need to add an issue number following the volume number, separated by a period:

> Loranc, Roman. "Remnant Beauty." <u>Lens Work</u> 61 (Nov./Dec. 2005):
>
> 45–61.

Add the month also to ease the search for the article: "20.5 (Nov. 2005): 4–12."

14d Bibliography Form—Newspapers

Provide the name of the author; the title of the article; the name of the newspaper as it appears on the masthead, omitting any introductory article (e.g., *Wall Street Journal,* not *The Wall Street Journal*); and the complete date—day, month (abbreviated), and year. Omit volume and issue numbers.

Provide a page number as listed (e.g., 21, B-7, 13C, D4). For example, *USA Today* uses "6A" but the *New York Times* uses "A6." There is no uniformity among newspapers on this matter, so list the page accurately as an aid to your reader. If the article is not printed on consecutive pages (for example, if it begins on page 1 and skips to page 8), write the first page number and a plus (+) sign with no space before or after the (+) sign (see the entry below).

Newspaper in One Section

> Whitfield, Jeffery. "Bracing for Black Friday." <u>Clayton News Daily</u> 24
>
> Nov. 2005: 1+.

Newspaper with Lettered Sections

> Long, Bryan. "Building Brings Credibility to Projects Office Segment."
>
> <u>Atlanta Business Chronicle</u> 25 Nov. 2005: 3A+.

Newspaper with Numbered Sections

> Berger, Susan. "Animal Rescuers, Officials Clash." <u>Chicago Tribune</u> 26
>
> Nov. 2005, sec. 1: 1.

Newspaper Editorial with No Author Listed

> "New Ballparks Sporting Lots of Empty Seats." Editorial. <u>Atlanta</u>
>
> <u>Business Chronicle</u> 30 May 2003: 32A.

Newspaper Column, Cartoon, Comic Strip, Advertisement, Etc.

Add a description to the entry to explain that the citation refers to something other than a regular news story.

Donlan, Thomas G. "Fine Tuning." Column. Barron's 26 May

2003: 31.

Newspaper Article with City Added

In the case of locally published newspapers, add the city in square brackets.

Hamlin, Emily. "Famalies Grieve for Sons Killed in Iraq." Leaf Chronicle

[Clarksville, TN] 26 Nov. 2005: A1.

Newspaper Edition or Section

When the masthead lists an edition, add a comma after the date and name the edition (late ed., city ed.), followed by a colon and then the page number.

Dillon, Sam. "Students Ace State Tests, but Earn D's from U.S." New

York Times 26 Nov. 2005, national ed.: A1+.

The *New York Times* presents two types of pagination, depending on the day. On Monday through Saturday, it usually has four sections, A, B, C, D, with each having separate pagination, such as page C1 through page C24.

Myre, Greg. "A Young Man Radicalized by His Months in Jail." New York

Times 30 May 2003: A1+.

The Sunday edition of the *New York Times* has numbered sections, individually paged, to cover art, business, travel, and so forth. If you cite from one of these sections, provide the section number.

Kifner, John. "The Holiest City, the Toughest Conflict." New York Times

23 July 2000, sec. 4: 1+.

Newspaper in a Foreign Language

"Les grands de ce monde reunis a Saint-Petersbourg." Le Monde 30 mai

2003: 1.

14e Bibliography Form—Government Documents

Since the nature of public documents is so varied, the form of the entry cannot be standardized. Therefore, your goal should be to provide sufficient information for the reader to easily locate the reference. As a general rule, place information in the bibliographic entry in this order (but see below if you know the author, editor, or compiler of the document):

1. Government
2. Body or agency
3. Subsidiary body
4. Title of document
5. Identifying numbers
6. Publication facts

When you cite two or more works by the same government, substitute three hyphens for the name of each government or body you repeat:

> United States. Cong. House.
>
> ---. ---. Senate.
>
> ---. Dept. of Justice.

Congressional Papers

Senate and House sections are identified by an *S* or an *H* with document numbers (e.g., S. Res. 16) and page numbers (e.g., H2345–47).

> United States. Cong. Senate. Subcommittee on Juvenile Justice of the
>
> > Committee on the Judiciary. Juvenile Justice: A New Focus on
> >
> > Prevention. 102nd Cong., 2nd sess. S. Hearing 102-1045.
> >
> > Washington: GPO, 1992.
>
> ---. ---. ---. Violent Crime Control Act 1991. 102d Cong., 1st sess.
>
> > S. 1241. Washington: GPO, 1991.

If you provide a citation to the *Congressional Record,* you should abbreviate it and provide only the date and page numbers.

> Cong. Rec. 18 Nov. 2005: S13285-87.

Executive Branch Documents

> United States. Dept. of State. Foreign Relations of the United States:
>
> > Diplomatic Papers, 1943. 5 vols. Washington: GPO, 1943-44.
>
> ---. President. 2005 Economic Report of the President. Washington:
>
> > GPO, 2005.

Documents of State Governments

Publication information on state papers varies widely, so provide sufficient data for your reader to find the document.

2004-2005 Statistical Report. Nashville: Tennessee Board of Regents,

2005. TBR A-001-03.

Tennessee Election Returns, 1796-1825. Microfilm. Nashville: Tennessee

State Library and Archives, n.d. M-Film JK 5292 T46.

"Giles County." 2002-2003 Directory of Public Schools. Nashville: State

Dept. of Educ., n.d. 61.

Legal Citations and Public Statutes

Familiar historical documents and the United States Code can be documented with parenthetical citations in your text ("U.S. Const., art. 2, sec. 4"
or "15 U.S.C. 78, 1964). Use the following examples as guidelines for developing your citations. Laws and law cases, because of length, can be cited on
the Works Cited page.

Illinois. Revised Statutes Annotated. Sec. 16-7-81. 2005.

Noise Control Act of 1972. Pub. L. 92-574. 1972. Stat. 86.

People v. McIntosh. California 321 P.3d 876, 2001-6. 1970.

State v. Lane. Minnesota 263 N. W. 608. 1935.

U.S. Const. Art 2, Sec. 1.

14f Bibliography Form—Internet Sources

Modern technology makes it possible for you to access information at
your computer. In particular, the Internet opens a cornucopia of information
from millions of sources. Other electronic sources include e-mail and
databases.

Citing Sources Found on the Internet

Include these items as appropriate to the source:

1. Author/editor name
2. Title of the article within quotation marks, or the title of a posting to a
   discussion list or forum followed by the words *online posting*, followed
   by a period.
3. If the document has a printed version, publication information and date.
4. Information on the electronic publication, such as the title of the site, the
   date of the posting, and the sponsoring organization.
5. Date of your access, not followed by a comma or period.
6. URL (Uniform Resource Locator), within angle brackets, followed by a
   period. If you must divide the URL at the end of a line, break it only after
   a slash.

For discussion of the Internet's special format, see pages 33–44. For making judgments about the validity of Internet sources, see pages 36–37.

Note: Do not include page numbers unless the Internet article shows original page numbers from the printed version of the journal or magazine. Do not include the total number of paragraphs nor specific paragraph numbers unless the original Internet article provides them.

World Wide Web Sites

Titles of books and journals may be shown either in italics or with underlining. They are shown in this section with underlining.

Abstract

Gellis, Les A., et al. "Socioeconomic Status and Insomnia." Journal of Abnormal Psychology 114 (2005). Abstract. 10 Nov. 2005 <http://www.apa.org/journals/features/abn1141111.pdf>.

Advertisement

The Mercado. "Titanic: The Exhibition." Advertisement. 2006. 14 Feb. 2006 <http://www.titanicshipofdreams.com/>.

Anonymous Article, Nonprint Version

"What's Your PSI? Test Your Tire Safety Knowledge." National Highway Traffic Safety Administration. n.d. 31 Jan. 2006 <http://safercar.gov/Tires/pages/PSI.htm>.

Archive or Scholarly Project

British Poetry Archive. Ed. Jerome McGann and David Seaman. 2006. U of Virginia Lib. 19 Aug. 2006 <http://etext.lib.virginia.edu/britpo.html>.

Dorson, Richard M. "The Eclipse of Solar Mythology." Journal of American Folklore 68 (1955): 393-416. JSTOR 7 June 2003 <http://www.jstor.org/search>.

Article from an Online Magazine

"Controlling Anger--Before It Controls You." APA Online. 10 May 2006 <http://www.apa.org/pubinfo/anger.html>.

Koretz, Gene. "Out of Work, Out of the Loop." BusinessWeek Online 15
    May 2003. 2 Oct. 2003 <http://asia.businessweek.com/
    careers/content/may2003/ca20030515_2074_ca004.htm>.

Article from a Scholarly Journal

Bogart, L. M., et al. "Effects of Early and Later Marriage on Women's
    Alcohol Use in Young Adulthood: A Prospective Analysis." Journal
    of Studies on Alcohol 66 (2005): 729–37. 22 Mar. 2006
    <http://www.rci.rutgers.edu/~cas2/journal/march03/>.

Article Written for the Internet

"History of Elba." Elba on line. Sept. 2002. 12 April 2006
    <http://www.elba-on-line.com/Informazioni/elba.html>.

Audio Program Online

See the entry for "Television or Radio Program." page 287.

Cartoon

Parker, Brant. "My Son, the King." Cartoon. Wizard of Id. 11 May 2003.
    29 Oct. 2003 <http://umweb2.unitedmedia.com/creators/
    wizardofid/archive/wizardofid-20030511.html>.

Chapter or Portion of a Book

Add the name of the chapter after the author's name:

Dewey, John. "Waste in Education." The School and Society. Chicago:
    U of Chicago P, 1907. 4 Feb. 2006 <http://spartan.ac.brocku.ca/
    ~lward/dewey/Dewey_1907/Dewey_1907c.html>.

Article at a Library's Online Service with a Listed URL

Most libraries have converted their computer searches to online databases, such as Lexis-Nexis, ProQuest Direct, EBSCOhost, Electric Library, Info-
Trac, and others. If the source provides the URL, omit the identifying numbers
for the database or the keyword used in the search and include the URL.
Here's an example from InfoTrac:

Lee, Catherine C. "The South in Toni Morrison's Song of Solomon:
    Initiation, Healing, and Home." Studies in the Literary
    Imagination 31 (1998): 109-23. Abstract. InfoTrac. U of
    Tennessee, Hodges Lib. 19 Sept. 2005 <http://firstsearch.oclc.
    org/next=NEXTCMD>.

You will know the database is online when you see the full URL at the top or bottom of the printout.

Article with Only a Starting Page Number of the Original Print Version

Worthen, W. B. "Recent Studies in Tudor and Stuart Drama." Review.

Studies in English Literature, 1500-1900 42 (2002): 399- .

Note: Leave a space after the hypen and before the period.

Article from an Online Service to Which You Personally Subscribe

Many students research topics from their homes, where they use such services as American Online or Netscape. If the URL is provided, use the form of this next example, which shows the name of the service.

Sloan, T. A. "Pilates: Your Ticket to a Longer, Leaner You." Discovery

Health 23 Jan. 2006 <http://health.discovery.com/centers/

nutritionfitness/fitness/articles/techniques/pilates/pilates.html.

Article from an Online Service with an Unlisted or Scrambled URL

Two possible forms are available to you when the online service provides no URL.

1. *Keyword.* If you access the site by using a keyword, provide a citation that gives the name of the service, the date of access, and the keyword:

Esslin, Martin. "Theater of the Absurd." Grolier Multimedia

Encyclopedia. 1995 ed. Netscape. 22 Aug. 2005. Keyword: Theater

of the Absurd.

2. *Path.* If you follow a series of topic labels to reach the article, and no URL is provided, write the word *Path* followed by the sequence of topic labels that you followed to obtain the article. Use a semicolon to separate each topic.

Kate Chopin: A Re-Awakening. 23 June 1999. PBS. College Webivore.

Netscape. 24 Jan. 2006. Path: US Literature; 19th Century; Women

Authors; Chopin, Kate (1850-1904).

Article at a Library's Online Service with No URL Listed

On rare occasions you may access online material in the library that has no URL, or the URL on your printout is scrambled or incomplete, or the URL is so long as to make typing it difficult. In such a case, make a citation to the source, then give the name of the database, underlined (if known); the name of the service; the library; and the date of access. Provide the URL of the service's home page in angle brackets after your date of access. You can also list the site's search engine (e.g., <http://www.jstor.org/search>.)

> Brezina, Timothy. "Teenage Violence toward Parents as an Adaptation to Family Strain: Evidence from a National Survey of Male Adolescents." <u>Youth and Society</u> 30 (1999): 416-44. <u>MasterFILE Elite</u>. EBSCOhost. Clarksville Montgomery County Library, Clarksville, Tn. 23 Feb. 2006 <http://www.ebsco.com/home/>.

E-mail

> Wright, Ellen. "Online Composition Courses." E-mail to the author. 24 Mar. 2006.

Encyclopedia Article Online

> "Kurt Vonnegut, Jr." Online Vers. 2005. <u>Encarta Encyclopedia</u>. Online Vers. 2005. 19 Nov. 2005 <http://encarta.msn.com/ encyclopedia_761572520/Kurt_Vonnegut.html>.

ERIC Database

> "America's Children: Key National Indicators of Well-Being." Federal Interagency Forum on Child and Family Statistics. 1999. ERIC. University of Tennessee, Hodges Lib. 18 Sept. 2005 <http:// www.goarch.org/goa/departments/gotel/online_videos.html#LIGHT>.

Film, Video, or Film Clip Online

> "Epiphany: Festival of Lights." <u>The History of the Orthodox Christian Church</u>. 2005. GoTelecom Online. 24 Oct. 2005 <http://www.goarch.org/en/multimedia/video/>.

FTP, TELNET, and GOPHER Sites

Most ftp, telnet, and gopher sites are now found on the World Wide Web:

> "Modern Irish Language and Culture Internet FTP Site." Ed. Lisa L. Spangenberg. 4 Jan. 2003. 3 Oct. 2005 <http:// www.digitalmedievalist.com/urls/irish.html>.

Home Page for a Course

When citing a home page for a course, begin with the instructor's name and the title of the course, neither underlined nor in quotation marks. Continue with a description such as *Course Home Page,* neither underlined nor in quotation marks, the dates of the course, the department, name of the institution, date of access, and the URL.

Wilkins, John, Shelley Palmer, and Tom Barrett. Writing and Speaking
about Physics and Astronomy. Summer 2003. Dept. of Physics,
Ohio State U. 22 Mar. 2006 <http://www.physics.ohio-state.edu/
~wilkins/writing/>.

Home Page for an Academic Department

Department of Humanities. Dept. home page. Clayton College
& State U School of Arts & Sciences. 19 Sept. 2005 <http://
a-s.clayton.edu/humanities/>.

Home Page for a Personal Web Site

Nguyen, Xyin Trin. Home Page. 22 Nov. 2005. 2 Apr. 2006. <http://
www.nmt.edu/~xtnguyen>.

Home Page for an Academic Site

Since you are not citing a specific article, you can give the reader the
address of an academic site, such as the following:

Robert Penn Warren: 1905-1989. 2 April 2006 <http://
www.english.uiuc.edu/maps/poets/s_z/warren/warren.htm>.

Interview

Strassman, Marc. "Is Journalism Dead?" Interview with Pete Hamill.
Strassman Files. BookRadio 1998. 24 Nov. 2005
<http://www.bookradio.com/>.

Journal Article

Paap, Chris, and Douglas Raybeck. "A Differently Gendered Landscape:
Gender and Agency in the Web-based Personals." Electronic
Journal of Sociology. (2005). 22 Jan. 2006. <http://
www.sociology.org/content/2005/tier2/
paap_genderedlandscape.pdf>.

Letter

Peck, Ray. "Politics Played with Schools." Letter to the Editor. The
Billings Outpost Online 24 Nov. 2005. 28 Nov. 2005 <http://
www.billingsnews.com/story?storyid" = 18562&issue = 295>.

Linkage Data (An Accessed File)

"What Happens to Recycled Plastics?" Online posting. Lkd. Better World
Discussion Topics at Recycling Discussion Group nd. 18 March
2006 <http://www.betterworld.com/BWZ/9602/learn.htm>.

Manuscript

Girondo, Oliverio. <u>Scarecrow & Other Anomalies</u>. Trans. Gilbert Alter-
Gilbert. Manuscript, 2005. 24 Aug. 2006 <http://
www.xenosbooks.com/scarecrow.html>.

Map

"Virginia--1785." Map. <u>U.S. County Formation Maps 1643-Present</u>.
Genealogy, Inc. 1999. 24 Sept. 2005 <http://
www.segenealogy.com/virginia/va_maps/va_cf.htm>.

MOO, MUD, and Other Chat Rooms

"Virtual Conference on Mary Shelley's <u>The Last Man</u>." 13 Sept. 1997.
Villa Diodati at EmoryMOO. 28 Oct. 2004 <http://
www.rc.umd.edu/villa/vc97/ Shelley_9_13_97.html>.

Chat rooms seldom have great value, but on occasion you might find
something you wish to cite; if so, use this form:

"Weight Loss Support." 30 May 2006. Yahoo! Chat. 30 May 2006
<http://chat.yahoo.com/?room_Weight%20Loss%20Support%3A1%
3A%3A1602757662&identity_jfuller22&client_DHTML>.

Newsgroup, Usenet News, Forum

Kalb, Jim. "Conservatism FAQ." Online Posting. 1 June 2003.
Environment Newsgroup. 13 Oct. 2005 <http://nwww.faqs.org/
faqs/conservatism/faq/>.

Add additional data to cite a document that has been forwarded.

Kalb, Jim. "Conservatism FAQ." 1 June 2003. Fwd. by
Gwen Everett. Online posting. 16 Oct. 2005. Environment
Newsgroup. 13 June 2003 <http://nwww.faqs.org/faqs/
conservatism/faq/>.

Newsletter

"Job Market Poised to Expand." MSU News Bulletin 37.7 (23 Nov.

    2005). 28 Nov. 2005 <http://www.newsbulletin.msu.edu/

    nov2305/career_trends.html>.

Newspaper Article, Column, Editorial

Lowenthal, Alena. "Thank Goodness! We've Got Some Alternatives to

    the Mall." 25 Nov. 2005. 28 Nov. 2005 <http://www.miami.com/

    mld/miamiherald/living/13248839.htm>.

Novel or Book Online

Lawrence, D. H. Lady Chatterly's Lover. 1928. 26 Sept. 2005

    <http://bibliomania.com/0/-/frameset.html>.

Online Posting for E-mail Discussion Groups

List the Internet site, if known; otherwise show the e-mail address of the list's moderator.

Chapman, David. "Reforming the Tax and Benefit

    System to Reduce Unemployment." Online Posting. 27

    June 2005. Democracy Design Forum. 27 July 2005

    <http://www.democdesignforum.demon.co.uk/unemp.nexus.html>.

Chapman, David. "An Electoral System for Iraq." Online Posting. 21

    June 2005. Democracy Design Forum. 27 Jan. 2006

    <chapman@deodesignfor.demon.co.uk>

Photograph, Painting, Sculpture

MLA style does not require you to label the type of work, as shown in the first example of a photograph. Usually the text will have established the nature of the work. However, if you feel that clarification is necessary, as in the case of "The Blessed Damozel," which is both a painting and a poem, you may wish to designate the form.

Farrar, Ray. "Leadenhall Market." 2003. 29 Aug. 2003

    <http://www.jrfarrar.fsnet.co.uk/lon1/image17.htm>.

Rossetti, Dante. "The Blessed Damozel." 1875-78. Painting. Rossetti

    Archive. U of Virginia Lib. 9 June 1999. 3 Sept. 2003

    <http://www.engl.virginia.edu/~bpn2f/rossetti/tourf.html>.

"Leaping Gazelle, 1936." Bronze Sculpture. Marshall M. Fredericks

    Sculpture Museum. 2001. 29 Aug. 2003 <http://www.svsu.edu/

    mfsm/collections.htm>.

Poem, Song, or Story

Dylan, Bob. "Tangled Up in Blue." Song lyrics. 13 Mar. 2005.

    <http://bobdylan.com/songs/tangled.html>.

Hardy, Thomas. "To a Lady." Wessex Poems and Other Verses. 1898.

    Project Bartleby. 2000 Great Books Online. 5 Jan. 2006

    <http://www.bartleby.com/121/40.html>.

Review

Ebert, Roger. Rev. of Capturing the Friedmans, dir. Andrew Jarecki.

    Chicago Sun-Times Online 6 June 2003. 16 June 2003

    <http://www.suntimes.com/output/ebert1/

    wkp-news-friedmans06f.html>.

Report

"Pharmacy Benefit Managers: Ownership of Mail-Order Pharmacies: A

    Federal Trade Commission Report." Federal Trade Commission.

    Aug. 2005. 4 Dec. 2005 <http://www.ftc.gov/reports/

    pharmbenefit05/050906pharmbenefitrpt.pdf>.

Serialized Article

Frank, Laura. "Worker: 'I Didn't Get That at Home.'" Tennessean.com 9

    Feb. 1997. Pt. 1 of a series, An Investigation into Illnesses

    around the Nation's Nuclear Weapons Sites, begun 9 Feb. 1997. 20

    Oct. 2005 <http://www.tennessean.com/special/oakridge/part3/

    frames/html>.

Thomas, Susan. "Oak Ridge Workers Offered Medical Screening."

    Tennessean.com 21 Jan. 1999. Pt. 2 of a series, An Investigation

    into Illnesses around the Nation's Nuclear Weapons Sites, begun 9

    Feb. 1997. 20 Oct. 2005 <http://www.tennessean.com/special/

    oakridge/part3/frames/html>.

Thomas, Susan, Laura Frank, and Anne Paine. "Taking the Poison."

    Tennessean.com 9 Feb. 1997. Pt. 3 of a series, An Investigation

    into Illnesses around the Nation's Nuclear Weapons Sites, begun 9

    Feb. 1997. 20 Oct. 2005 <http://www.tennessean.com/special/

    oakridge/part3/frames/html>.

Song

See "Poem, Song, or Story."

Sound Clip or Audio Recording

See "Television or Radio Program."

Story

See "Poem, Song, or Story."

Synchronous Communication

See "MOO, MUD, and Other Chat Rooms."

Television or Radio Program

Gross, Terry. "Roseanne Cash Remembers Her Father, Johnny." <u>Fresh Air</u>.
NPR Online. 25 Nov. 2005. Audio transcript. 29 Nov. 2005 <http://
www.npr.org/templates/story/story.php?storyId_5027605>.

University Posting, Online Article

Guinane, Pat. "Uncle Sam's Pocket." Online Posting. Nov. 2005. U of
Illinois at Springfield. 6 Dec. 2005 <http://illinoisissues.uis.edu/
features/2005nov/federal.html>.

Video

See "Film, Video, or Film Clip Online."

Web Site, General Reference

As long as you are not citing a specific article but merely making reference to a site, provide the address in your text, *not* on the Works Cited page.

Further information about this program can be found at the Web site
for the Department of Psychology at the University of Wisconsin-
Parkside <http://www.uwp.edu/academic/ psychology>.

Work in an Indeterminate Medium

If the medium of a source cannot be determined, use the designation *Electronic* for the medium. For example, if you access material through a local network and cannot tell whether the work is on a CD-ROM or on the central computer's hard drive, designate it as *Electronic*. Give whatever relevant publication information you can, as well as the name of the network or of its sponsoring organization and the date of access.

Lubiano, Wahneema. "Toni Morrison." <u>African American Writers</u>. Valerie
Smith, gen. ed. 2nd ed. Vol. 2. New York: Scribner's, 1999. 321-
33. Electronic. Gale, 2001. Alabama Virtual Lib. 24 Apr. 2001.

Working Papers

Deighton, John. "The Presentation of Self in the Information Age."
Working Paper #04-059, Harvard Business School, 2004–2005. 30
Jan. 2006 <http://www.hbs.edu/units/marketing/research.htm>.

14g Bibliography Form—Sources Found on CD-ROM

CD-ROM technology provides information in four ways, each of which requires an adjustment in the form of the entry for your Works Cited page.

Full-Text Articles with Publication Information for the Printed Source

See also page 271 for citing SIRS in its loose-leaf form.

Full-text articles are available from national distributors such as Information Access Company (InfoTrac), UMI-Proquest (Proquest), Silverplatter, and SIRS CD-ROM Information Systems. (*Note:* Most of these sources are also available online.) Conform to the examples that follow:

DePalma, Antony. "Mexicans Renew Their Pact on the Economy, Retaining
the Emphasis on Stability." New York Times 25 Sept. 1994: 4. New
York Times Ondisc. CD-ROM. UMI-Proquest. Jan. 2005.

Mann, Thomas E., and Norman J. Ornstein. "Shipshape? A Progress
Report on Congressional Reform." Brookings Review Spring 1994:
40-45. SIRS Researcher. CD-ROM. Boca Raton: SIRS, 1994. Art. 57.

HINT: Complete information may not be readily available—for example, the original publication data may be missing. In such cases, provide what *is* available:

Silver, Daniel J. "The Battle of the Books." Rev. of The Western Canon:
The Books and School of the Ages, by Harold Bloom.
Resource/One. CD-ROM. UMI-ProQuest. Feb. 2005.

Full-Text Articles with No Publication Information for a Printed Source

Sometimes the original printed source of an article or report is not provided by the distributor of the CD-ROM database. In such a case, conform to the examples that follow, which provide limited data:

"Faulkner Biography." Discovering Authors. CD-ROM. Detroit:
Gale, 2001.

"U.S. Population by Age: Urban and Urbanized Areas." <u>1999 U.S. Census</u>
  <u>of Population and Housing.</u> CD-ROM. US Bureau of the
  Census. 2000.

Complete Books and Other Publications on CD-ROM

Cite this type of source as you would a book, and then provide information about the electronic source you accessed.

The Bible. Life Application Study Bible. CD-ROM. Carol Stream, IL:
  Tyndale House, 2005.
<u>English Poetry Full-Text Database</u>. Re. 2. CD-ROM. Cambridge, Eng.:
  Chadwyck, 2003.
"John F. Kennedy." <u>InfoPedia</u>. CD-ROM. n.p.: Future
  Vision, n.d.
Poe, Edgar Allan. "Fall of the House of Usher." <u>Electronic Classical</u>
  <u>Library.</u> CD-ROM. Garden Grove, CA: World Library, 1999.
Chaucer, Geoffrey. "The Wife of Bath's Tale." <u>Canterbury Tales.</u>
  CD-ROM facsimile text. Princeton: Films for the Humanities and
  Sciences, 2000.

Abstracts to Books and Articles Provided on CD-ROM by National Distributors

As a service to readers, the national distributors have members of their staff write abstracts of articles and books if the original authors have not provided such abstracts. As a result, an abstract found on InfoTrac and ProQuest may not be written by the original author, so you should not quote such abstracts. (You may quote from abstracts that say, "Abstract written by the author.") Silverplatter databases *do* have abstracts written by the original authors. In either case, you need to show in the Works Cited entry that you have cited from the abstract, so conform to the example that follows, which provides name, title, publication information, the word *abstract,* the name of the database underlined, the medium (CD-ROM), the name of the vendor, and—if available to you—the electronic publication date (month and year).

Figueredo, Aurelio J., and Laura Ann McCloskey. "Sex, Money, and
  Paternity: The Evolutionary Psychology of Domestic Violence."
  <u>Ethnology and Sociobiology</u> 14 (1993): 353-79. Abstract. <u>PsycLIT</u>.
  CD-ROM. Silverplatter. 12 Jan. 2003.

Nonperiodical Publication on CD-ROM, Diskette, or Magnetic Tape

Cite a CD-ROM, diskette, or magnetic tape as you would a book, with the addition of a descriptive word. If relevant, show edition (3rd ed.), release (Rel. 2), or version (Ver. 3). Conform to the examples that follow:

Lester, James D. Introduction to Greek Mythology: Computer Slide Show.
    12 lessons on CD-ROM. Clarksville, TN: Austin Peay State U, 2005.
"Nuclear Medicine Technologist." Guidance Information System. 17th
    ed. Diskette. Cambridge: Riverside-Houghton, 1992.
Statistics on Child Abuse--Montgomery County, Tennessee.
    Rel. 2. Magnetic tape. Clarksville, TN: Harriett Cohn Mental Health
    Center, 2006.

Encyclopedia Article

For an encyclopedia article on a CD-ROM, use the following form:

"Abolitionist Movement." Compton's Interactive Encyclopedia.
    CD-ROM. Novato, CA: The Learning Company, 2006.

Multidisc Publication

When citing a multidisc publication, follow the term *CD-ROM* with the total number of discs or with the disc that you cited from:

Parsees 2.0: Interactive Sources and Studies on Ancient Greece. CD-
    ROM. Disc 3. New Haven: Yale UP, 2000.

14h Bibliography Form—Other Electronic Sources

Citing a Source You Access in More Than One Medium

Some distributors issue packages that include several media, such as CD-ROM and accompanying microfiche or a diskette and an accompanying video-tape. Cite such publications as you would a nonperiodical publication on CD-ROM (see above, top of the page) with the addition of the media available with this product.

Franking, Holly. The Martensville Nightmare. Vers. 1.0.
    Diskette, CD-ROM. Prairie Village: Diskotech, 1997.
Jolly, Peggy. "A Question of Style." Exercise Exchange 26.2 (1982):
    39-40. ERIC. CD-ROM, microfiche. Silverplatter. Feb. 17, 1995.
    ED236601, fiche 1.

Silver, Daniel J. "The Battle of the Books." Rev. of <u>The Western Canon:</u>

<u>The Books and School of the Ages,</u> by Harold Bloom. <u>Resource/One</u>.

CD-ROM, microfiche S-637. UMI-Proquest. Feb. 1995.

Chaucer, Geoffrey. "Prologue." <u>Canterbury Tales</u>.

Videocassette, CD-ROM facsimile text. Princeton: Films for the

Humanities and Sciences, 2005.

Citing an Entire Internet Site

To cite an online database, such as Dialog, conform to the style shown in these samples:

Bronner, E. "Souter Voices Concern over Abortion Curb." <u>Boston Globe</u>

31 Oct. 1990: 1. Online. Dialog. 22 Nov. 1997.

Priest, Patricia Joyner. "Self-Disclosure on Television: The Counter-

Hegemonic Struggle of Marginalized Groups on 'Donahue.'" Diss.

New York U, 1990. <u>DAI</u> 53.7 (1993): 2147A. <u>Dissertation Abstracts</u>

<u>Online</u>. Online. Dialog. 10 Feb. 1994.

14i Bibliography Form—Other Sources

Advertisement

Provide the title of the advertisement, within quotation marks, or the name of the product or company, *not* within quotation marks, the label *Advertisement,* and publication information.

"Southern Women Writers Conference." Advertisement. <u>Oxford American</u>

Summer 2005: 111.

OnStar. Advertisement. CNNLive. 4 Aug. 2005.

Carmax. Billboard advertisement. Stockbridge, GA. Jan. 2006.

Artwork

If you actually experience the work itself, use the form shown in the next two entries:

Remington, Frederic. <u>Mountain Man</u>. Metropolitan Museum of Art, New

York.

Wyeth, Andrew. <u>Hay Ledge</u>. Private Collection of Mr. and Mrs. Joseph E.

Levine.

If the artwork is a special showing at a museum, use the form of this next example.

Michals, Duane. "The Last Rose of Summer." Pace/Macgill Gallery, New York. 3 Dec. 2005.

"Oscar Bluemner: A Passion for Color." Whitney Museum of American Art, New York. 10 Feb. 2006.

Use this next form to cite reproductions in books and journals.

Lee-Smith, Hughie. <u>Temptation</u>. 1991. <u>A History of African-American Artists: From 1792 to the Present</u>. Ed. Romare Bearden and Harry Henderson. New York: Pantheon, 1993.

Raphael. <u>School of Athens</u>. The Vatican, Rome. <u>The World Book Encyclopedia</u>. 2005 ed.

If you show the date of the original, place it immediately after the title.

Raphael. <u>School of Athens</u>. 1510-1511. The Vatican, Rome. <u>The World Book Encyclopedia</u>. 2005 ed.

Broadcast Interview

Gray, Jim. "NBA Coaching Vacancies." Interview. ESPN. 4 June 2005.

Bulletin

A bulletin is a brief publication, usually softbound, that you should treat as a book.

<u>The South Carolina Market Bulletin</u>. Columbia, SC: South Carolina Department of Agriculture, 15 May 2005.

Maryland State Bar Association's Public Awareness Committee. <u>Appointing a Guardian</u>. Baltimore: Maryland State Bar Association. 2005.

Cartoon

If you cannot decipher the name of the cartoonist and cannot find a title, use this form:

Cartoon. <u>Reminisce</u> July/Aug. 2005: 60.

Sometimes you will have the artist's name but not the name of the cartoon:

Artley, Bob. Cartoon. <u>Reminisce</u> July/Aug. 2005: 52.

Some cartoons are reprinted in magazines:

> Ramirez. "Peace." Cartoon. Rpt. in <u>Weekly Standard</u> 2 June
>
>   2005: 13.

Computer Software

> <u>Publisher Deluxe 2003</u>. CD-ROM. Redmond, WA: Microsoft, 2003.

Conference Proceedings

> Alejna Brugos, Manuella R. Clark-Cotton, and Seungwan Ha, eds.
>
>   <u>BUCLD-29: Proceedings of the Twenty-ninth Boston University</u>
>
>   <u>Conference on Language Development</u>. Apr. 2005. Somerville, MA:
>
>   Cascadilla, 2005.

Dissertation, Published

> Nordstrand, Thomas. <u>Basic Testing and Strength Design of Corrugated</u>
>
>   <u>Board and Containers</u>. Diss. Lund U, 2003. Stockholm: EFI, 2003.

Dissertation, Unpublished

> Patel-McCune, Santha. "An Analysis of Homophone Errors in the Writing
>
>   of 7th Grade Language Arts Students: Implications for Middle
>
>   School Teachers." Diss. Southern Tech. U, 2006.

> If you cite only the abstract of a dissertation, see "Abstract in an Abstracts Journal," pages 269–270 for the correct form.

Film, Videocassette, or DVD

Cite the title of a film, the director, the distributor, and the year.

> <u>Harry Potter and the Goblet of Fire</u>. Dir. Mike Newell. Warner Bros.
>
>   Video, 2005.

If relevant to your study, add the names of performers, writers, or producers after the name of the director.

> <u>The Passion of the Christ</u>. Dir. Mel Gibson. Screenplay by Benedict
>
>   Fitzgerald and Mel Gibson. Newmarket, 2004.

If the film is a DVD, videocassette, filmstrip, slide program, or videodisc, add the type of medium before the name of the distributor. Add the date of the original film, if relevant, before the name of the medium.

> <u>Citizen Kane</u>. Dir. Orson Welles. 1941. DVD. Warner, 2002.

Crimmins, Morton. "Robert Lowell: American Poet." Lecture.

Videocassette. Western State U, 2005.

If you are citing the accomplishments of the director or a performer, begin the citation with that person's name.

Mangold, James, dir. Walk the Line. Perf. Joaquin Phoenix and Reese

Witherspoon. Sony, 2005.

If you cannot find certain information, such as the original date of the film, cite what is available.

Altman, Robert, dir. The Room. Perf. Julian Sands, Linda Hunt, Annie

Lennox. Videocassette. Prism.

Interview

For an interview you conduct, name the person interviewed, the type of interview (e.g., telephone interview, personal interview, e-mail interview), and the date.

Carter, Emma. "Growing Georgia Greens." Telephone interview.

5 Mar. 2005.

For broadcast interviews, cite all relevant information, including the broadcast source.

Gray, Jim. "NBA Coaching Vacancies." Interview. ESPN.

4 June 2003.

Foote, Shelby. Interview. Shelby Foote on Faulkner.

C-SPAN. Videocassette. National Cable, 2003.

Lecture

See "Public Address," page 297.

Letter, Personal

Knight, Charles. Letter to the author. 21 Jan. 2006.

Letter, Published

Eisenhower, Dwight. Letter to Richard Nixon. 20 April 1968. Memoirs of

Richard Nixon. By Richard Nixon. New York: Grosset, 1978.

Loose-Leaf Collections

If you cite an article from *SIRS, Opposing Viewpoints,* or other loose-leaf collections, provide both the original publication data and then add information for the loose-leaf volume, as shown in these next examples:

"The Human Genetic Code." Illustration. Facts on File 29 June 2000:
    437-38.

Hodge, Paul. "The Andromeda Galaxy." Mercury July/Aug. 1993: 98+.
    Physical Science. Ed. Eleanor Goldstein. Vol. 2. Boca Raton: SIRS,
    1994. Art. 24.

Cox, Rachel S. "Protecting the National Parks." The Environment. CQ
    Researcher ser. 23 (2000): 523+. Washington: Congressional
    Quarterly Inc., 2000.

Manuscripts (ms.) and Typescripts (ts.)

Glass, Malcolm. Journal 3, ms. M. Glass Private Papers, Clarksville, TN.

Tanner. Ms. 346. Bodleian Library, Oxford, Eng.

Williams, Ralph. Notebook 15, ts. Williams Papers. Vanderbilt
    U, Nashville.

Map

Treat a map as you would an anonymous work, but add a descriptive
label, such as *map, chart, survey,* unless the title describes the medium.

County Boundaries and Names. United States Base Map GE-50,
    No. 86. Washington, DC: GPO, 2005.

Pennsylvania. Map. Chicago: Rand, 2006.

Microfilm or Microfiche

Chapman, Dan. "Panel Could Help Protect Children." Winston-Salem
    Journal 14 Jan. 1990: 14. Newsbank: Welfare and Social Problems
    12 (1990): fiche 1, grids A8-11.

Jolly, Peggy. "A Question of Style." Exercise Exchange 26.2 (1982):
    39-40. ERIC ED2336601, fiche 1.

Tuckerman, H. T. "James Fenimore Cooper." Microfilm. North American
    Review 89 (1859): 298-316.

Miscellaneous Materials (Program, Leaflet, Poster, Announcement)

"Earth Day." Poster. Louisville. 20 Mar. 2006.

"Spring Family Weekend." Program. Nashville: Fisk U
    1 April 2006.

Musical Composition

For a musical composition, begin with the composer's name, followed by a period. Underline the title of an opera, ballet, or work of music identified by name, but do not underline or enclose within quotation marks the form, number, and key when these are used to identify the instrumental composition.

Mozart, Wolfgang A. <u>Jupiter</u>. Symphony No. 41.

Wagner, Richard. <u>Lohengrin</u>.

Treat a published score as you would a book.

Legrenzi, Giovanni. <u>La Buscha</u>. Sonata for Instruments. <u>Historical</u>
<u>Anthology of Music</u>. Ed. Archibald T. Davison and Willi Apel.
Cambridge: Harvard UP, 1950. 70-76.

Pamphlet

Treat a pamphlet as you would a book.

Federal Reserve Board. <u>Consumer Handbook to Credit Protection Laws</u>.
Washington: GPO, 2006.

Westinghouse Advanced Power Systems. <u>Nuclear Waste Management: A</u>
<u>Manageable Task</u>. Madison, PA: Author, n.d.

Performance

Treat a performance (e.g., play, opera, ballet, concert) as you would a film, but include the site (normally the theater and city) and the date of the performance.

<u>Lakota Sioux Indian Dance Theatre</u>. Cherokee Heritage Center,
Tahlequah, OK. 12 May 2002.

<u>Much Ado About Nothing</u>. By William Shakespeare. Folger Elizabethan
Theatre, Washington, D.C.: 29 Oct. 2005.

<u>The Abduction of Seraglio</u>. By Mozart. Chicago Opera Theater, Chicago.
3 May 2006.

If your text emphasizes the work of a particular individual, begin with the appropriate name(s).

Hoang, Haivan, and Doug Dangler. "Getting to Know You: Database
Information for Writing Centers." Conf. on Coll. Composition and
Communication Convention. Palmer House Hotel, Chicago,
24 March, 2006.

Prégardien, Christoph. "Winterreise." Alice Tully Hall, New York.

11 Dec. 2005.

Durst, Will, comedian. Zanies, Chicago. 2 Dec. 2005.

Public Address

Identify the nature of the address (e.g., lecture, reading), include the site (normally the lecture hall and city), and the date of the performance.

Irvine, Sherry. "Migration Within the British Isles: What Genealogists

Need to Know." Lecture. St. Louis Genealogical Soc., St. Louis. 29

Oct. 2005.

Recording on Record, Tape, or Disk

If you are not citing a compact disc, indicate the medium (e.g., audio-cassette, audiotape [reel-to-reel tape], or LP [long-playing record]).

"Chaucer: The Nun's Priest's Tale." Canterbury Tales.

Narr. in Middle English by Alex Edmonds. Audiocassette.

London, 2005.

Dylan, Bob. "The Times They Are A-Changin'." Bob Dylan's Greatest

Hits. LP. CBS, 1967.

Reich, Robert B. Locked in the Cabinet: A Political Memoir.

4 audiocassettes abridged. New York: Random Audio, 1997.

Midler, Bette. "Is That All There Is?" Bette Midler Sings the Peggy Lee

Songbook. CD. Sony, 2005.

Tchaikovsky. Romeo and Juliet. Fantasy-Overture after Shakespeare.

New Philharmonia Orchestra London. Cond. Lawrence Siegel. DVD.

Classical Masters, 2000.

Do not underscore, italicize, or enclose within quotation marks a private recording or tape. However, you should include the date, if available, as well as the location and the identifying number.

Walpert, Wanda A. Folk Stories of the Smokey Mountains. Rec. Feb.

1995. Audiotape. U of Knoxville. Knoxville, TN. UTF.34.82.

Cite a libretto, liner notes, or booklet that accompanies a recording in the form shown in the following example.

Nelson, Willie. Booklet. The Great Divide. By Willie Nelson.

UMG, 2002.

Report

Unbound reports are placed within quotation marks; bound reports are treated as books:

Coca-Cola Company. 2005 Annual Report. Atlanta: Author, 2005.

Franco, Lynn. "Confidence Slips Amid Fragile Economy." Report. The

    Conference Board. New York: CBS/Broadcast Group, 23 Jan. 2006.

Reproduction, Photograph, Photocopy

Blake, William. Comus. Plate 4. Photograph in Irene Taylor. "Blake's

    Comus Designs." Blake Studies 4 (Spring 1972): 61.

Michener, James A. "Structure of Earth at Centennial, Colorado." Line

    drawing in Centennial. By Michener. New York: Random, 1974. 26.

Snowden, Mary. Jersey Pears. 1982. American Realism: Twentieth

    Century Drawings and Watercolors. New York: Abrams, 1986. 159.

Table, Illustration, Chart, Graph

Tables or illustrations of any kind published within works need a detailed label (chart, table, figure, photograph, and so on):

"Financial Indicators: Money and Interest Rates." Table. Economist 8

    July 2000: 105.

Alphabet. Chart. Columbus: Scholastic, 2006.

Television or Radio Program

If available or relevant, provide information in this order: the episode (in quotation marks), the title of the program (underscored or italicized), title of the series (not underscored nor in quotation marks), name of the network, call letters and city of the local station, and broadcast date. Add other information (such as narrator) after the title of the episode or program. Place the number of episodes, if relevant, before the title of the series.

"Distance Learning Class: The Cable Center at the Univ. of Denver."

    Host: Brian Lamb. Washington Journal. C-SPAN. 6 June 2003.

The Virgin Queen. By Paula Milne. Perf. Anne-Marie Duff. 2 episodes.

    Masterpiece Theatre. Introd. Russell Baker. PBS. WCDN, Nashville.

    13 Nov. 2005.

"Should the 22nd Amendment Be Repealed?" Crossfire. Hosts James

    Carville, Paul Begala, Tucker Carlson, and Bob Novak. CNN.

    30 May 2005.

Prairie Home Companion. NPR. WABE, Atlanta. 19 Nov. 2005.

Thesis

See "Dissertation, Unpublished," page 293.

Transparency

Sharp, La Vaughn, and William E. Loeche. <u>The Patient and Circulatory</u>
<u>Disorders: A Guide for</u> Instructors. 54 transparencies,
99 overlays. Philadelphia: Lorrenzo, 2005.

Unpublished Paper

Schuler, Wren. "Prufrock and His Cat." Unpublished essay, 2005.

Voice Mail

Nerbarger, Henry. Memo to Lester. Voice mail to the author.
6 Jan. 2006.

15 Writing in APA Style

Your instructor may require you to write the research paper in APA style, which is governed by *The Publication Manual of the American Psychological Association,* 5th edition, 2001. This style has gained wide acceptance in the social sciences, and versions similar to it are used in the biological sciences, business, and earth sciences. Research is paramount in the sciences; in fact, the APA style guide says, "No amount of skill in writing can disguise research that is poorly designed or managed." Thus, you will need to execute your project with precision.

15a Writing Theory, Reporting Test Results, or Reviewing Literature

In the sciences, you may choose between three types of articles, or your instructor will specify one of these:

- Theoretical articles
- Reports of empirical studies
- Review articles

Theoretical Article

For a sample theoretical article, see the student paper on pages 323–336, which examines some of the prevailing theories on arranged marriages through online dating services.

The theoretical article draws on existing research to examine a topic. This is the type of paper you will most likely write as a first-year or second-year student. You will need to trace the development of a theory or compare theories by examining the literature to arrive at the current thinking about topics such as autism, criminal behavior, dysfunctional families, and learning disorders. The theoretical article generally accomplishes four aims:

1. Identifies a problem or hypothesis that has historical implications in the scientific community.
2. Traces the development and history of the evolution of the theory.
3. Provides a systematic analysis of the articles that have explored the problem.
4. Arrives at a judgment and discussion of the prevailing theory.

Report of an Empirical Study

For additional details about field research, consult Chapter 5, pages 83–86.

When you conduct field research and perform laboratory testing, you must report the details of your original research. The empirical report accomplishes these four purposes:

1. Introduces the problem or hypothesis investigated and explains the purpose of the work.
2. Describes the method used to conduct the research.
3. Reports the results and the basic findings.
4. Discusses, interprets, and explores the implications of the findings.

You will need to work closely with your instructor to accomplish each of these stages.

Review Article

See pages 119–126 for a sample review of literature.

You may be required to write a critical evaluation of a published article, a book, or a set of articles on a common topic. The purpose is to examine the state of current research—and, in some cases, to determine if additional work might be in order. A review article sets out to accomplish several goals:

1. Define a problem or issue that is the subject of discussion.
2. Summarize the article(s) or book(s) under review.
3. Analyze the literature to discover strengths, weaknesses, or inconsistencies in the research.
4. Recommend additional research that might grow logically from the work under review.

15b Writing in the Proper Tense for an APA Paper

Verb tense is an indicator that distinguishes papers in the humanities from those in the natural and social sciences. MLA style, as shown in previous chapters, requires you to use present tense when you refer to a cited work ("Jeffries *stipulates*" or "the work of Mills and Maguire *shows*"). In contrast, APA style requires you to use past tense or present perfect tense ("Jeffries *stipulated*" or "the work of Mills and Maguire *has demonstrated*"). The APA style does require present tense when you discuss the results (e.g., "*the results confirm*" or "*the study indicates*") and when you mention established knowledge (e.g., "*the therapy offers some hope*" or "*salt contributes to hypertension*"). The paragraphs below, side by side, show the differences in verb tenses for MLA and APA styles.

MLA style:
The scholarly issue at work here is the construction of reality. Cohen, Adoni, and Bantz label the construction a social process "in which human beings act both as the creators and products of the social world" (34). These writers identify three categories (34–35).

APA style:
The scholarly issue at work here is the construction of reality. Cohen, Adoni, and Bantz (2002) labeled the construction a social process "in which human beings act both as the creators and products of the social world" (p. 34). These writers have identified three categories.

APA style, shown on the right, requires that you use the present tense for generalizations and references to stable conditions, but it requires the present perfect tense or the past tense for sources cited (e.g., the sources *have tested* a hypothesis or the sources *reported* the results of a test). This next sentence uses tense correctly for APA style:

> The danger of steroid use exists for every age group, even youngsters. Lloyd and Mercer (2005) reported on six incidents of liver damage to 14-year-old swimmers who used steroids.

For updates to APA style, consult the association's Internet site: http://www.apastyle.org/

As shown above in the example, use the present tense (*exists*) for established knowledge and the present perfect (*has reported*) or the past tense (*reported*) for a citation.

15c   Using In-Text Citations in APA Style

APA style uses the following conventions for in-text citations:

- Cites last names only.
- Cites the year, within parentheses, immediately after the name of the author. Include only the year in the text citation even if the reference includes a month.
- Cites page numbers with a direct quotation but not with a paraphrase.
- Uses "p." or "pp." before page numbers.

Citing Last Name Only and the Year of Publication

An in-text citation in APA style requires the last name of the author and the year of publication.

> Nguyen (2006) has advanced the idea of combining the social sciences and mathematics to chart human behavior.

If you do not use the author's name in your text, place the name(s) within the parenthetical citation.

One study has advanced the idea of combining the social sciences and mathematics to chart human behavior (Nguyen, 2006).

Providing a Page Number

If you quote the exact words of a source, provide a page number and use "p." or "pp." Place the page number in one of two places: after the year (2006, p. B4) or at the end of the quotation.

Nguyen (2006) has advanced the idea of "soft mathematics," which is the practice of "applying mathematics to study people's behavior" (p. B4).

Citing a Block of Material

Present a quotation of forty words or more as a separate block, indented five spaces or ½ inch from the left margin. (*Note:* MLA style uses ten spaces or one inch). Because it is set off from the text in a distinctive block, do not enclose it with quotation marks. Do not indent the first line an extra five spaces; however, *do* indent the first line of any additional paragraphs that appear in the block an extra five spaces—that is, ten spaces from the left margin. Set parenthetical citations outside the last period.

Albert (2003) reported the following:

> Whenever these pathogenic organisms attack the human body and begin to multiply, the infection is set in motion. The host responds to this parasitic invasion with efforts to cleanse itself of the invading agents. When rejection efforts of the host become visible (fever, sneezing, congestion), the disease status exists. (pp. 314-315)

Citing a Work with More Than One Author

When one work has two or more authors, use *and* in the text but use *&* in the citation.

Werner and Throckmorton (2006) offered statistics on the toxic levels of water samples from six rivers.

but

It has been reported (Werner & Throckmorton, 2006) that toxic levels exceeded the maximum allowed each year since 1983.

For three to five authors, name them all in the first entry (e.g., Torgerson, Andrews, Smith, Lawrence, & Dunlap, 2006), but thereafter use "et al." (e.g.,

Torgerson et al., 2006). For six or more authors, employ "et al." in the first and in all subsequent instances (e.g., Fredericks et al., 2005).

Citing More Than One Work by an Author

Use lowercase letters (a, b, c) to identify two or more works published in the same year by the same author—for example, (Thompson, 2002a) and (Thompson, 2002b). Then use "2002a" and "2002b" in your List of References (see page 310 for examples). If necessary, specify additional information:

> Horton (2001; cf. Thomas, 2005a, p. 89, and 2005b, p. 426)
> suggested an intercorrelation of these testing devices, but after
> multiple-group analysis, Welston (2006, esp. p. 211) reached an
> opposite conclusion.

Citing Indirect Sources

Use a double reference to cite a person who has been quoted in a book or article—that is, use the original author(s) in the text and cite your source for the information in the parenthetical citation.

> In other research, Massie and Rosenthal (2005) studied home
> movies of children diagnosed with autism, but determining criteria was
> difficult due to the differences in quality and dating of the available
> videotapes (cited in Osterling & Dawson, 2006, p. 248).

Citing from a Textbook or Anthology

If you make an in-text citation to an article or chapter of a textbook, casebook, or anthology, use the in-text citation to refer only to the person(s) you cite:

> One writer stressed that two out of every three new jobs in this
> decade will go to women (Ogburn 2006).

The list of references will clarify the nature of this reference to Ogburn (see page 311).

Citing Classical Works

If an ancient work has no date of publication, cite the author's name followed by n.d. within parentheses.

> Seeing psychic emotions as . . . (Sophocles, n.d.).

Cite the year of any translation you have used, preceded by *trans.*, and give the date of the version used, followed by *version.*

Plato (trans. 1963) offered a morality that . . .

Plato's _Phaedrus_ (1982 version) explored . . .

If you know the original date of publication, include it before the date of the translation or version you have used.

In his "Poetics," Aristotle (350 B.C.E.) viewed the structure of

the plot as a requisite to a good poem.

Note: Entries on your References page need not cite major classical works and the Bible. Therefore, identify in your text the version used and the book, chapter, line, verse, or canto.

In Exodus 24:3-4 Moses erects an altar and "twelve pillars

according to the twelve tribes of Israel" (King James Version).

The Epic of Gilgamesh shows, in part, the search for everlasting

life (Part 4).

In the Iliad, Homer takes great efforts in describing the shield of

Achilles (18:558-709).

Abbreviating Corporate Authors in the Text

The names of groups that serve as authors, such as corporations, associations, and government agencies, are usually spelled out each time they appear. The names of some corporate authors may be abbreviated after a first, full reference:

One source questioned the results of the use of aspirin for

arthritis treatment in children (American Medical Association

[AMA], 2005).

Thereafter, refer to the corporate author by initials: (AMA, 2001). It is important to give enough information in the text citation for the reader to locate the entry in the reference list without difficulty.

Citing a Work with No Author

When a work has no author listed, cite the title as part of the in-text citation (or use the first few words of the material).

The cost per individual student has continued to rise rapidly

("Tuition Crises," 2005, p. B-3).

Citing Personal Communications

E-mail, telephone conversations, memos, and conversations do not provide recoverable data, so APA style excludes them from the list of references. Consequently, you should cite personal communications in the text only. In so doing, give the initials as well as the last name of the source, provide the date, and briefly describe the nature of the communication.

> M. Gaither (personal communication, August 24, 2003) described the symptoms of Wilson's disease.

Citing Internet Sources in Your Text

As with MLA style, material from electronic sources presents special problems when you are writing in APA style. Currently, most Internet sources have no prescribed page numbers or numbered paragraphs. You cannot list a screen number because monitors differ. You cannot list the page numbers of a downloaded document because computer printers differ. Therefore, in most cases do not list a page number or a paragraph number. Here are basic rules.

Omit a page or paragraph number. The marvelous feature of electronic text is that it is searchable, so your readers can find your quotation quickly with the Find feature. Suppose you have written the following:

> The Internet Report presented by the University of South Carolina (2006) advised policy makers with "a better understanding of the impact the Internet is having in our society."

A reader who wants to investigate further will find your complete citation, including the Internet address of the article, in your References list. After finding the article via a browser (e.g., Netscape or Internet Explorer), the investigator can press Edit, then Find, and type in a key phrase, such as *better understanding of the impact.* The software will immediately move the cursor to the passage shown above. That is much easier than counting through forty-six paragraphs.

Provide a paragraph number. Some scholars who write on the Internet number their paragraphs. Therefore, if you find an online article that has numbered paragraphs, by all means supply that information in your citation.

> The Insurance Institute for Highway Safety (2006) has emphasized restraint first, and said, "A federal rule requiring special attachments to anchor infant and child restraints in vehicles is making installation easier, but not all child restraints fit easily in all vehicles" (par. 1).

> Recommendations for treating non-insulin-dependent diabetes mellitus (NIDDM), the most common type of diabetes, include a diet that is rich in carbohydrates, "predominantly from whole grains, fruit, vegetables, and low-fat milk" (Yang, 2005, par. 3).

Provide a page number. In a few instances, you will find page numbers buried within brackets here and there throughout an article. These refer to the page numbers of the printed version of the document. In these cases, you should cite the page just as you would a printed source. Here is the Internet source with the page numbers buried within the text to signal the break between page 17 and page 18:

> What is required is a careful reading of Chekhov's subtext, that elusive [pp17-18] literature that lingers in psychological nuances of the words, not the exact words themselves.—Ward

The page number may be included in the citation:

> One source argued the merits of Chekhov's subtext and its "psychological nuances of the words" (Ward, 2004, p. 18).

World Wide Web Site
Internet article

> Commenting on the distinction between a Congressional calendar day and a legislative day, Dove (2006) stated that "a legislative day is the period of time following an adjournment of the Senate until another adjournment."

> "Reports of abuses in the interrogation of suspected terrorists raise the question of how--or whether--we should limit the interrogation of a suspected terrorist when our national security may be at stake" (Parry & White, 2003, abstract).

HyperNews posting

> Ochberg (2005) commented on the use of algae in paper that "initially has a green tint to it, but unlike bleached paper which turns yellow with age, this algae paper becomes whiter with age."

Online magazine

> BusinessWeek Online (2006) reported that the idea of peer-to-peer computing is a precursor to new Web applications.

Government document

> The Web site *Thomas (2005)* has outlined the amendments to the *Homeland Security Act of 2002,* which will implement the READICall emergency alert system.

Other Electronic Sources
E-mail

The Publication Manual of the American Psychological Association stipulates that personal communications, which others cannot retrieve, should be cited in the text only and not mentioned at all in the bibliography.

One technical writing instructor (March 8, 2006) has bemoaned the inability of hardware developers to maintain pace with the ingenuity of software developers. In his e-mail message, he indicated that educational institutions cannot keep pace with the hardware developers. Thus, "students nationwide suffer with antiquated equipment, even though it's only a few years old" (dplattner@cscc.edu).

Listserve (e-mail discussion group)

Listserve groups have gained legitimacy in recent years, so in your text you might wish to give an exact date and provide the email address *only* if the citation has scholarly relevance and *only* if the list has an academic sponsor, such as an instructor of an online class.

R. D. Brackett (online discussion, May 7, 2006) has identified the book *Echoes of Glory* for those interested in detailed battlefield maps of the American Civil War.

A. G. Funder (January 5, 2005) argued against the "judgmental process."

FTP sites

Patel (2006) has shown in the following graph that "enrollment in radiology programs of study has increased by 67% in the past ten years."

CD-ROM

Grolier's Multimedia Encyclopedia (2005) explained that in recent decades huge swaths of the rain forest have been toppled; as the trees disappeared, so, too, did the flora and fauna that thrived under their canopy.

15d Preparing the List of References

Use the title *References* for your bibliography page. Like the body of the paper, your reference list should be double-spaced throughout. Alphabetize

Index to Bibliographic Models: APA Style

the entries letter by letter—remembering, for example, that Adkins, Y. R., precedes Adkinson, A. G., even though *o* precedes the *y* for the first entry. Every reference used in your text, except personal communications and major classical works, should appear in your alphabetical list of references at the end of the paper. Type the first line of each entry flush left and indent succeeding lines five spaces. You may italicize or underscore names of books, periodicals, and volume numbers. Underline the punctuation mark at the end of names and volume numbers.

Book

Pringle, H. (2006). *The master plan: Himmler's scholars and the*

Holocaust. New York: Hyperion.

List the author (surname first and then initials for given names), year of publication within parentheses, title of the book italicized or under-scored and with only first word of the title and any subtitle capitalized (but do capitalize proper nouns), place of publication, and publisher. In the publisher's name omit the words *Publishing, Company*, and *Inc.*, but otherwise give a full name: Florida State University Press; Addison, Wesley, Longman; HarperCollins.

List chronologically, not alphabetically, two or more works by the same author—for example, Fitzgerald's 2005 publication would precede the 2006 publication.

Fitzgerald, R. A. (2005). Crimson glow . . .

Fitzgerald, R. A. (2006). Walking . . .

References with the same author in the same year are alphabetized and marked with lowercase letters—*a, b, c*—immediately after the date:

Craighead, T. B. (2005a). Marketing trends . . .

Craighead, T. B. (2005b). Maximizing sales . . .

Entries of a single author precede multiple-author entries beginning with the same surname without regard for the dates:

Watson, S. M. (2006). Principles . . .

Watson, S. M., & Wheaton, A. F. (2003). Crimes . . .

References with the same first author and different second or third authors should be alphabetized by the surname of the second author:

Bacon, D. E., & Smithson, C. A. (2005). Arctic explorers . . .

Bacon, D. E., & Williamson, T. (2006). Seasons in . . .

If, *and only if,* the work is signed *Anonymous,* the entry begins with the word *Anonymous* spelled out, and the entry is alphabetized as if *Anonymous* were a true name. If no author is given, the title moves to the author position, and the entry is alphabetized by the first significant word of the title.

Part of a Book

List author(s), date, chapter or section title, editor (with name in normal order) preceded by "In" and followed by "(Ed.)" or "(Eds.)," the name of the book (underscored or italicized), page numbers to the specific section of the book cited (placed within parentheses), place of publication, and publisher.

> Graham, K. (2003). The male bashing stereotype. In P. Elbow & P.
> Belanoff, *Being a writer* (pp. 249-254). New York: McGraw Hill.

If no author is listed, begin with the title of the article.

> Obadiah. (2003). *Who was who in the Bible.* Nashville: Nelson.

Encyclopedia or Dictionary

> Fitch, P. T. Escrow. (2006). *Dictionary of banking terms* (5th ed.). New
> York: Barrons.
>
> Moran, J. M. (2005). Weather. *World book encyclopedia* (2005 ed., Vol.
> 21, 156–171). Chicago: World Book.

Book with Corporate Author

> American Medical Association. (2005). *American Medical Association*
> *complete medical encyclopedia.* New York: Random House.

Periodical

Journal

List author(s), year, title of the article without quotation marks and with only the first word (and any proper nouns) capitalized, name of the journal underscored or italicized and with all major words capitalized, volume number underscored or italicized, inclusive page numbers *not* preceded by "p." or "pp."

> Mather, M., & Knight, M. (2005). Goal-directed memory: The role of
> cognitive control in older adults' emotional memory. *Psychology*
> *and Aging, 20(4),* 554–570.

Article Retrieved from InfoTrac, Silverplatter, ProQuest, and Other Servers

> Galderson, J. R. & Priestly, S. L. (2006). The homeless plight: Societal views and governmental blindness. *Journal of the Social Change and Consciousness, 14*, 104–115. Retrieved April 3, 2006, from *Periodical Academic Index* database.

Magazine

List author, the date of publication—year, month without abbreviation, and the specific day for magazines published weekly and fortnightly (every two weeks)—title of the article without quotation marks and with only the first word capitalized, name of the magazine underlined with all major words capitalized, the volume number if it is readily available, and inclusive page numbers preceded by "p." or "pp." if you do not provide the volume number. If a magazine prints the article on discontinuous pages, include all page numbers.

> Dodge, C. (2006, March/April). For amber waves of grain. *Utne*, 79–83.

> Wert, J. D. (2006, March/April). Custer: Boy wonder under arms. *Civil War Times, 45*, 22–28.

Newspaper

List author, date (year, month, and day), title of article with only first word and proper nouns capitalized, complete name of newspaper in capitals and underlined, and the section with all discontinuous page numbers.

> Manasso, J. (2006, March 3). Pivotal penalty tough to take. *Atlanta Journal-Constitution*, p. F1.

Abstract

Abstract as the Cited Source

> Risch, A. C., & Frank, D. A. (2006). Carbon dioxide fluxes in a spatially and temporally heterogeneous temperate grassland [Abstract]. *Oecologia, 147*, 291–302.

Abstract of an Unpublished Work

> Darma, J. (2006). *Political institutions under dictatorship* [Abstract]. Unpublished manuscript, Knoxville: University of Tennessee.

Abstract Retrieved from InfoTrac, Silverplatter, ProQuest, or Other Servers

> Gryeh, J. H., et al. (2000). Patterns of adjustment among children of battered women. *Journal of Consulting and Clinical Psychology, 68,* 84-94. Abstract retrieved August 15, 2005 from *PsycINFO* database.

Review

> Navarro, V. J., & Senior, J. R. (2006). Current concepts: Drug-related hepatotoxicity. [rev. article]. *The New England Journal of Medicine, 354,* 731–739.

Report

> Gorman, L. (2006). Reporting insurance fraud (No. 2006–2). Hartford, CT: Insurance Institute.

Nonprint Material

Computer Program

> *Excel 2005.* (2005). [Computer program]. Redmond, WA: Microsoft.

DVD, Videotape, Film

> Ford, B., & Ford, S. (Producers). (2003). *Choreography on the Fly: Robert Royston & Lauree Baldovi* [Videotape]. Brentwood, CA: Images in Motion.

Interviews, Letters, and Memos

> Barstow, I. (2006, May 22). "Palm reading as prediction" [Interview]. Chattanooga, TN.

Unpublished Raw Data from a Study, Untitled Work

> Barstow, I. (2006, May 22). "Homophone errors in essays of 100 9th grade writers" [Unpublished raw data]. Emporia, KS.

Internet Sources

The following information conforms to the instructions of APA style. When citing sources in the References of your APA-style paper, provide this information if available:

1. Author/editor last name, followed by a comma, the initials, and a period.
2. Year of publication, followed by a comma, then month and day for magazines and newspapers, within parentheses, followed by a period.
3. Title of the article, not within quotations and not underscored, with the first word and proper nouns capitalized, followed by the total number of paragraphs within brackets only if that information is provided. *Note:* You need not count the paragraphs yourself; in fact, it's better that you don't. This is also the place to describe the work within brackets, as with [Abstract] or [Letter to the editor].
4. Name of the book, journal, or complete work, underscored or italicized, if one is listed.
5. Volume number, if listed, underscored or italicized.
6. Page numbers only if you have that data from a printed version of the journal or magazine. If the periodical has no volume number, use "p." or "pp." before the numbers; if the journal has a volume number, omit "p." or "pp.").
7. The word *Retrieved,* followed by the date of access.
8. The URL. (URLs can be quite long, but you will need to provide full data for other researchers to find the source.)

World Wide Web Sites
Article from an Online Journal

> Dixon, C. S. (2006). Faith and history on the eve of enlightenment. *The Journal of Ecclesiastical History.* Retrieved March 23, 2006, from http://journals.cambridge.org/action/displayJournal?jid_ECH.

Article from a Printed Journal, Reproduced Online

Many articles online are the exact duplicates of their print versions, so if you view an article in its electronic form and are confident that the electronic form is identical to the printed version, add within brackets *Electronic version.* This allows you to omit the URL.

> Dickerson, M. S., & Calhoun, S. L. (2003). Ability profiles in children with autism: Influence of age and IQ. [Electronic version]. *Autism, 7,* 65–80.

Add the URL and date of access if page numbers are not indicated, as shown in this next entry:

> Fluchel, R. W. (2006). For feet that never leave asphalt. *Missouri Conservationist, 67(2).* Retrieved March 13, 2006, from http://mdc.mo.gov/conmag/2006/02/10.htm.

Article from an Internet-Only Newsletter

Pyke, B. (2006). The e-health revolution: Interview with professor

Peter Yellowlees. *Telehealth News.* Retrieved August 21, 2006,

from http://www.telehealth.net/interviews/yellowlees.html.

Document Created by a Private Organization, No Date

Internet Engineering Task Force. (n.d.). *Active IETF Working Groups.*

Retrieved April 13, 2006, from

http://www.ietf.org/html.charters/wg-dir.html.

Chapter or Section in an Internet Document

Benton Foundation. (2006). *Getting to February 2009: Implementing the

digital TV transition* (sec. 1). Retrieved June 3, 2006, from

http://www.benton.org/index.php?q_node/1257.

Standalone Document, No Author Identified, No Date

Remember to begin the reference with the title of the document if the
author of the document is not identified.

Web Surveyor. (n.d.). *Learn more about surveys*. Retrieved December 2,

2005, from http://www.websurveyor.com/resources/online-survey-

resources.asp.

Document from a University Program or Department

Henry, S. (2005). *Department of language and literature writing

guidelines.* Retrieved March 2, 2006, from Clayton State

University, Department of Arts & Sciences site: http://a-

s.clayton.edu/langlit/guidelines/default.html.

Report from a University, Available on a Private Organization's Web Site

University of Illinois at Chicago, Health Research and Policy Centers.

(2006). *Partners with tobacco use research centers: Advancing

transdisciplinary science and policy studies.* Retrieved March 22,

2006, from the Robert Wood Johnson Foundation Web site:

http://www.rwjf.org/portfolios/resources/grant.jsp?id=

039787&iaid_143.

Abstract

Vasquez, M. J. T., & Jones, J. M. (2006). Increasing the number of
psychologists of color: Public policy issues for affirmative
diversity [Abstract]. *American Psychologist, 62.* Retrieved April 3,
2006, from http://www.apa.org/jounals/amp.

Article from a Printed Magazine, Reproduced Online

Allmon, J. (2003, March). Grow native! For beautifully
resilient, drought-tolerant landscapes. *Kansas City Gardener.*
Retrieved June 17, 2005, from http://www.grownative.org/
index.cfm?fuseaction=resources.articleDetail&articleID=21.

Dodge, C. (2006, March/April). Some proverbs by Sparrow. *Utne.*
Retrieved March 19, 2006, from http://www.utne.com/pub/
2006_134/promo/12003-1.html.

Article from an Online Magazine, No Author Listed

Housing market fueled by rising consumer confidence, low rates. (2006,
March 3). *Builder Online.* Retrieved March 3, 2006, from
http://www.builderonline.com/Industry-news.asp?sectionID =
27&articleID_258866.

Note: Avoid listing page numbers for online articles.

Article from an Online Newspaper

Mangan, K. S. (2006, March 3). For many students, one computer is not
enough. *Chronicle of Higher Education.* Retrieved March 3, 2006,
from http://chronicle.com/weekly/v52/i26/26a03101.htm.

Rouse, K., & Sanchez, R. (2006, March 3). Teach vs. speech.
Denver Post Online. Retrieved March 3, 2006, from
http://www.denverpost.com/frontpage/ci_3564246.

Bulletin

Bulletins are brief reports and brochures, usually printed in paperback
form, which you should treat as a book.

Murphy, F. L., (2006). *What you don't know can hurt you.* Retrieved
October 19, 2003, from the Preventive Health Center Web site:
http://www.mdphc.com/education/fiber.html.

Government Document

U.S. Cong. House. (2005, November 18). *Unlawful Internet gambling funding prohibition act.* House Resolution 4411. Retrieved April 11, 2006, from http://thomas.loc.gov/cgi-bin/query/D?c109:1:./ temp/~c109TOQn1k::.

Message Posted to an Online Discussion Group or Forum

George, D. (2005, December 30). Big Green Discussion Group [Archives]. Environmental Discussion Group. Retrieved July 18, 2006, from http://www.biggreen.org/discussion.html#archives.

Message Posted to an Electronic Mailing List

Reagle, J. (2003, April 8) Inexpensive and easy site hosting. Message posted to Fogo mailing list, archived at http://impressive.net/ archives/fogo/200304081727.55334.reagle@mit.edu.

Newsgroup, Message

Clease, G. V. (2005, November 5). Narrative bibliography [Msg. 39]. Message posted to jymacmillan@mail.csu.edu.

Virtual Conference, Report

A virtual conference occurs entirely online, so there is no geographic location. Treat a report as a book.

Ali, H., & Shou, J. (2006, May 18). *Microarray data analysis.* Paper presented at the Sixth Virtual Conference on Genomics and Bioinformatics. Retrieved July 25, 2003, from http:// midas.cs.ndsu.nodak.edu/VGAB06/overview.htm.

Symposium, Report

Eisenfeld, B. 2003, October 19). *Tutorial: CRM 101: The Basics.* Paper presented at the Gartner Symposium ITxpo, Orlando, Florida. Abstract retrieved October 22, 2003, from http:// www.gartner.com/2_events/symposium/2003/asset_46841.jsp.

Usenet, Telnet, FTP, message

Haas, H. (2004, August 5) Link checker that works with cold fusion

[Msg. 34]. Message posted to impressive.net/archives/fogo/

200000805113615.AI4381@w3.org.

Library Databases

University servers give you access to many sources stored in large databases, such as PsycInfo, ERIC, and netLibrary. Use this next form, which gives the date of your retrieval, the name of the database, and if readily available the item number within parentheses. If you cite only from the abstract, mention that fact in your reference entry (see the Kang entry below).

Colemen, L. & Coleman J. (2002). The measurement of puberty: A

review. *Journal of Adolescence, 25,* 535-550. Retrieved November

2, 2005, from ERIC database (EJ65060).

Kang, H. S. (2002). What is missing in interlanguage: Acquisition of

determiners by Korean learners of English. *Working Papers in*

Educational Linguistics, 18. Abstract retrieved November 2, 2005,

from ERIC database.

CD-ROM

Material cited from a CD-ROM requires different forms.

Abstract

Nagorra, N., et al. (2005). Light levels and the presence of vision

phenotypes of primate species [CD-ROM]. *Journal of Sociobiology,*

14, 353–79. Abstract from Silverplatter File: PsychLIT item:

94-5458.

Encyclopedia Article

African American history: Abolitionist movement [CD-ROM]. (2005).

Encarta encyclopedia. Redmond, WA: Microsoft.

Full-Text Article

Spence, D. (2005, August 10). Bible belt resistance and acceptance of

alternative lifestyles in religion [CD-ROM]. *Red River Messenger.*

p. A-11. Article from UMI ProQuest file (Item 5602-109).

15e Variations on the APA Style for Other Disciplines in the Social Sciences

Use APA style as explained in sections 15a–15d for the following disciplines:

Education
Geography
Home Economics
Physical Education
Political Science

Alternative styles may be used for papers in Linguistics and Sociology, as explained next.

Linguistics

In-Text Citation

In-text citations for linguistic studies almost always include a specific page reference to the work along with the date, separated by a colon—for example, "Jones 2003: 12–18" or "Hudson's recent reference (2006: 162)." Therefore, follow basic standards for the name and year system (see pages 302–308) with a colon to separate the year and the page number(s).

References List

As shown below, label the list as *References* and alphabetize the entries. Use full names for authors if available. Place the year immediately after the author's name. For journal entries, use a period rather than a colon or comma to separate volume and page. There is *no* underlining. Linguistic journals are abbreviated (e.g., Lg for Linguistics); others are not. A sample list follows:

References

Bauschatz, Paul. 2003. Rhyme and the structure of English consonants. [Abstract]. English Language and Lg. 7. Retrieved September 19, 2005, from the World Wide Web: http:// titles.cambridge.org/journals/journal_article.asp?mnemonic= ELL&pii=S1360674303001035.

Blot, Richard K. (Ed). Language and social identity. Westport, CT: Greenwood Publishing.

Caballero, Rosario. 2003. Metaphor and genre: The presence and role of metaphor in the building review. Applied Lg. 24.145–167.

Deutscher, Guy. The unfolding of language: An evolutionary history of mankind's greatest invention. New York: Holt, 2005.

Och, Franz, Josef., & Ney, Hermann. 2003. A systematic comparison of various statistical alignment models. Computational Lg. 29.19–51.

Unsworth, Sharon. 2000. Review of the acquisition of second language syntax, by Susan M. Braidi. Web Journal of Modern Language Lg. 4–5. Retrieved September 18, 2005, from http://wjmll.ncl.ac.uk/issue04-05/unsworth_braidi.htm.

Note: The form of these entries conforms in general to that advocated by the Linguistic Society of America, <http://www.lsadc.org/language/langstyl.html>. Updates to the language style sheet are published annually in the journal *Language* in the December issue.

Sociology and Social Work
In-Text Citation

Use the name and year system as explained above in Section 15c, pages 302–308.

References List

Use the format shown below, which duplicates the style of the *American Journal of Sociology*, or use APA style. This style is similar to MLA style, except that the date follows the author.

References

Brannen, Julia. 2003. "Towards a Typology of Intergenerational Relations: Continuities and Change in Families." *Sociological Research Online, 8.* 28 June 2003 <http://www.socresonline.org.uk/8/2/brannen.html>.

Eason, Amy. 2006. "There's a Disorder or Syndrome for Everyone." *News Daily.* [Jonesboro, GA] 11 June: 3B.

Gerteis, Joseph. 2002. "The Possession of Civic Virtue: Movement Narratives of Race and Class in the Knights of Labor." *American Journal of Sociology, 108:* 580-615. Abstract.

Sachar, Louis. 2006. *Small Steps.* New York: Delacorte.

Shilling, Chris. 2003. *The Body and Social Theory.* Thousand Oaks, CA: Sage.

15f Formatting an APA Paper

APA style applies to three types of papers: theoretical articles, reports of empirical studies, and review articles (as explained in section 15a). Each requires a different arrangement of the various parts of the paper.

Theoretical Paper

The theoretical paper should be arranged much like a typical research paper, with the additional use of centered side heads and italicized side heads to divide the sections.

The introduction should:

- Establish the problem under examination.
- Discuss its significance to the scientific community.
- Provide a review of the literature (see pages 119–126 for more information).
- Quote the experts who have commented on the issue.
- Provide a thesis sentence that gives your initial perspective on the issue.

The body of the theoretical paper should:

- Trace the various issues.
- Establish a past-to-present perspective.
- Compare and analyze the various aspects of the theories.
- Cite extensively from the literature on the subject.

The conclusion of the theoretical paper should:

- Defend one theory as it grows from the evidence in the body.
- Discuss the implications of the theory.
- Suggest additional work that might be launched in this area.

Report of Empirical Research

The general design of a report of original research, an empirical study, should conform to the following general plan.

The introduction should:

- Establish the problem or topic to be examined.
- Provide background information, including a review of literature on the subject.
- Give the purpose and rationale for the study, including the hypothesis that serves as the motivation for the experiment.

The body of the report of empirical research should:

- Provide a methods section for explaining the design of the study with respect to subjects, apparatus, and procedure.

- Offer a results section for listing in detail the statistical findings of the study.

The conclusion of a report of empirical research should:

- Interpret the results and discuss the implications of the findings in relation to the hypothesis and to other research on the subject.

Review Article

The review article is usually a shorter paper because it examines a published work or two without extensive research on the part of the review writer.

The introduction of the review should:

- Identify the problem or subject under study and its significance.
- Summarize the article(s) under review.

The body of the review should:

- Provide a systematic analysis of the article(s), the findings, and the apparent significance of the results.

The conclusion of the review should:

- Discuss the implications of the findings and make judgments as appropriate.

15g Writing the Abstract

You should provide an abstract with every paper written in APA style. An abstract is a quick but thorough summary of the contents of your paper. It is read first and may be the only part read, so it must be:

1. *Accurate,* in order to reflect both the purpose and content of the paper.
2. *Self-contained,* so that it (1) explains the precise problem and defines terminology, (2) describes briefly both the methods used and the findings, and (3) gives an overview of your conclusions—but see item 4 below.
3. *Concise and specific,* in order to remain within a range of 80 to 150 words.
4. *Nonevaluative,* in order to report information, not to appraise or assess the value of the work.
5. *Coherent and readable,* in a style that uses an active, vigorous syntax and that uses the present tense to describe results (e.g., the findings confirm) but the past tense to describe testing procedures (e.g., I attempted to identify).

For theoretical papers, the abstract should include:

- The topic in one sentence, if possible
- The purpose, thesis, and scope of the paper
- A brief reference to the sources used (e.g., published articles, books, personal observation)
- Your conclusions and the implications of the study

For a report of an empirical study (see also 5d, pages 83–84), the abstract should include the four items listed above for theoretrical papers, plus three more:

- The problem and hypothesis in one sentence if possible
- A description of the subjects (e.g., species, number, age, type)
- The method of study, including procedures and apparatus

15h Sample Paper in APA Style

The following paper demonstrates the format and style of a paper written to the standards of APA style. The paper requires a title page that establishes the running head, an abstract, in-text citations to the name and year of each source used, and a list of references. Marginal notations, below, explain specific requirements.

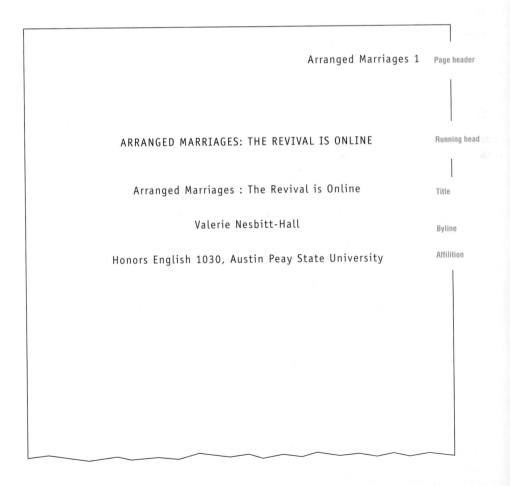

Arranged Marriages 1   Page header

ARRANGED MARRIAGES: THE REVIVAL IS ONLINE   Running head

Arranged Marriages : The Revival is Online   Title

Valerie Nesbitt-Hall   Byline

Honors English 1030, Austin Peay State University   Affilition

Abstract

Computer match making was investigated to examine the theoretical implications of marriages arranged in part by online dating. The goal was to determine the effect of Internet activity on the private lives of participants. The social and psychological implications were determined by an examination of the literature, a profile of the participants, and a case study that interviewed an affected couple. Results were mixed with failures balanced against successful matches. The social implications affect the workplace as well as the private lives of the men and women who are active in chat rooms and dating services. The psychological implications involve infidelity, damage to self-esteem, the need for psychotherapy, but—importantly—a chance for true and lasting love.

Arranged Marriages: The Revival Is Online

Arranged marriages are back, but with a twist. Online dating services provide today, among other things, an opportunity for people to meet, chat, reveal things about themselves, and—as one source has expressed it—"online dating was developed to help busy people find love with greater ease; by increasing the accuracy, efficiency, and convenience of the process" (Cohen, 2006). In addition, listserv groups by the thousands bring people together by the millions. Thus, computer match making has social and psychological implications that are being examined more and more by psychologists. This paper will examine the theoretical implications of marriages arranged in part by online dating.

Establish the topic along with social and or psychological issues that will be examined.

Arranged Marriages 4

Figures vary greatly on the amount of activity. One source (Cha, 2003) reported that 37 million people use online matchmaking annually. With 75 million singles in the United States whose time-pressed lives make them prime candidates for matchmaking services, online dating and matchmaking has become big business (Ballug, 2006). People have visited, many have found a mate, and some have even married. Match.com and America Online's dating area boast about hundreds of marriages that began as personal online messages. Can it be called a social revolution? Some have said "yes" to that question because about one-fifth of all singles in the country are online, prearranging their meetings and their lives, assuring themselves a better match than an evening's trip to a local nightclub. For example, Cooper (2002) has argued that online dating has the potential to lower the nation's divorce rate. Kass (2003) has identified the "distanced nearness" of a chat room that encourages self-revelation while maintaining personal boundaries" (cited in Razdan, 2003, p. 71). Ballug (2006) has argued that many arranged marriages, by parents or by cyberspace, have produced enduring love because of rational deliberation performed before moments of passionate impulse.

A theoretical study depends heavily upon the literature, which must be cited in correct APA form.

With the divorce rate at fifty percent, any marriage is already a role of the dice, so experts have begun to agree that online dating reverts back to the prearranged meetings of two young people whom the families have identified as compatible for economic, political, religious, and social reasons. Persons online can enjoy distance, even hiding their real names for a while, to enjoy "an intimate but protected (cyber)space" (Kass, 2003, cited in Razdan, p. 71). Participants online can erect and maintain personal fences of privacy but at the same time reveal

Arranged Marriages 5

private feelings that they might never express in face-to-face
meetings.

Method

The Internet dating services have made romance a
commodity (Ballug, 2006). Match.com, founded in 1995, and now
located in 30 countries, offers a subscription-based business
model. Subscribers may place a personal advertisement for free,
but to participate and send email they must be members and pay
about $20 per month. With several million active members,
Match.com profits greatly from its primary commodity—romance.
American Online, Yahoo!, Netscape—all the network servers offer
the search machines, for a price, of course. "If you are prepared
to pay a little—or a lot—it has never been easier to meet a
partner, Brooks (2003) has said. But Brooks has also asked, "So
why are so many people still single?" And then Brooks supplied
this answer: "Perhaps the commodification of *romance* hasn't
been as good for our hearts as it has for business."

Subjects

The people who participate in online romance run the whole
range of human subjects. Gibson (2006) identified the typical
subject as male, college educated, affluent and, contrary to
popular opinion, not a nerd. The case studies, see below in the
Results section, seem to confirm this finding, but in nine years
since the study women have crowded into cyberspace in great
numbers. Millions now consider meeting someone over the
Internet like phoning them or sending a fax. It has become an
everyday thing to send dozens of emails, so the next logical step
would be finding romance on the Internet.

High profile subjects now appear as participants, and with
success. Rush Limbaugh, the right-wing radio commentator, met his
bride, Marta Fitzgerald, on the Internet. Cyber dating for subjects

Center major
headings.

Scientific papers
demand your
explanation of
procedures used
in the study.

Suheads are
italicized and set
flush left margin.

A detailed
description of
the subjects is
a normal part
of scientific
investigation.

Arranged Marriages 6

high- or low-profile has a measure of safety while the persons conduct a typical human courtship. This courtship, according to Kass (2003), is aimed at finding and winning over an ideal mate.

Persons on both keyboards can move as quickly or as slowly as they wish to find someone. Then the process of winning understanding and affection can also be measured. Each person is involved in an arranged courtship, and it's arranged on his or her terms for the heterosexual or the homosexual, for persons of the Jewish faith, for horse lovers, and for skiing buffs.

The Internet also serves the modest person. In this age of liberated sexual activity there still exist many women, and men, who remain modest and cautious. Sexual self-restraint by a woman in this day and age may even be a magnet for men. We should witness the fact that *The Rules* by Fein and Schneider (1995) was a best seller because it offered, for example, "Rule 15: Don't Rush into Sex and Other Rules for Intimacy" or "Rule 3: Don't Stare at Men or Talk Too Much." Fein and Schneider (2002) have also targeted online dating with their *Rules for Online Dating*, which offers such rules as, "Rule 1: Don't Answer Men's Ads or E-mail Them First" and "Rule 8: Block Yourself from Instant Messages." The books are catalogs on how to be modest. Kass (1999) said in a speech:

> Modesty not only spurred a man to love; equally important, it empowered a woman by defending her against the hazards of her own considerable erotic desires. She had more at stake in sex than did the man. (In fact, even in our age of female contraception and easy abortion, pregnancy remains a concern mainly for women—indeed, arguably, more so than ever, albeit for different reasons: the law now lodges responsibility and choice regarding pregnancy and childbirth entirely with

Use present tense verbs (*serves, exist*) for what happens or can happen now.

Use the present perfect tense (*have targeted*) for actions completed and for actions continued into the present time.

Use the past tense (*was, said*) with this rule in mind—*Use the past tense to express actions that occurred at a specific time in the past, as in "Kass (1999) said."*

Indent block quotations five spaces.

Arranged Marriages 7

her; in consequence, men are no longer under social pressure to marry a woman should she become pregnant with or give birth to his child.)

The chaste or modest person can protect herself or himself by the walls of Internet protection—user names, passwords, and other security measures.

Schneider and Weiss (2001) list some of the advantages to online romance: It links people miles apart; impressions are made by words, not looks; there is time to contemplate a message; there is time to compose a well written response; and messages can be reviewed and revised before transmission (p. 66).

Procedures

The process for logging on and sending messages is similar at all the sites, but the nature of the matchmaking differs. Emode had a group of PhDs design a personality test to measure participants' styles, temperaments, independence, romanticism, importance of wealth, and other factors (Cha, 2003). Participants in a pool of 1 million are matched carefully. Emode's spokesperson said, "Our goal is for you to go into the first date knowing much more than you would after three or four dates" (C. Johnson, cited in Cha, 2003, p. A01). Emode and Match.com permit users to search by scores on various tests. Once a person puts in a profile, the search engines go to work at *Match.com* or *Yahoo!* and begin to send the participant the usernames of possible matches. Another service is eHarmony, which offers scientific matchmaking but does not permit users to search or view ads. Instead, eHarmony requires a 45-minute, 500-question compatibility test and permits the user to contact only screened, compatible people (Cha, 2003).

Procedures to access a matching partner are varied, yet each has one thing in common – to bring two compatible people

The *method* section of the paper should include a description of the study's design as well as the tools used, if appropriate, and the procedures followed by you and/or by those you cite.

together on the Web. There they can e-mail each other,
participate in IM chats, send attachments of favorite songs or
personal photographs, and eventually exchange real names, phone
numbers, and addresses. Newsgroups work in a similar fashion
with back and forth discussion, even argument, about a variety
of topics.

Case Study

Research uncovered a match that resulted in marriage. The
two subjects, Jennifer and Stephen, were interviewed on the
matter of cyber romance. What follows is a brief summary of the
interview, which is on file. The couple met online in September
of 1996 in a chat room, not on a matching service. Stephen
initiated the first contact, and they chatted anonymously for
nine months before Jennifer initiated an exchange of phone
numbers, addresses, and photographs. Stephen initiated the first
meeting in person after 11 months, inviting Jennifer to travel
from the United States to Glasgow, Scotland. Seven months later
they married; it was 1.5 years from the time they met at the
Internet newsgroup.

See pages 77–79 for more details on concluding interviews.

When asked if online romance gave her protection of her
privacy and time to prearrange things, Jennifer answered in the
affirmative with emphasis. When asked who was more aggressive
in pushing forward the romance, Stephen said it was a mutual
thing. Both agreed that when they finally met in person, they
really knew the other person—spiritually, emotionally, and
intellectually. The matter of different nationalities also played a
role on two fronts-immigration matters and the concern of
Jennifer's parents that she would fly to Scotland to see someone
she had never met.

When asked if the relationship had been excellent to this
point, both replied with affirmative answers. When asked if they

would recommend online dating to others who are seeking mates, Stephen and Jennifer said, yes, under the right circumstances—"be cautious and take your time."

Results

Results of online romance can be positive or negative. First, the negative. Cohen (2006) said:

> There's a big group of married baby boomers. When we look at ourselves in the mirror in our 40s, we wonder, "Am I still sexy?" Some women get facelifts; men get sports cars. Online infatuation can be another antidote.... From my research, only about one in four online relationships turns out happy. People get into this bodice-ripper mentality in the beginning. But after you've had "sex" with somebody in the virtual way, there's a real desire to actually be intimate. When the two do meet, the relationship can't handle the reality. Either the affair ends or it destroys their marriages.

Yet, as shown by the case studies, online romances can have happy endings.

Discussion

The effects of online romance reach into the workplace as well as the personal lives of men and women in a variety of ways, both socially and psychologically.

Social Implications

The workplace. *Business Week* (1999) reported: "There's no question cybersex is invading the workplace. A recent survey from Stanford University found that roughly 20% of those going online for sexual material use their office computers to do so" (p. 27B). What many workers fail to realize is that the computer belongs to the company, and the hard drive can be examined, even if the user thinks he or she has erased the files. In this

In many cases, the results section will include tables and charts and statistcs.

Indented paragraph headings should be italicized and end with a period.

writer's opinion, the best avenue for safety of privacy is to take out the hard drive and destroy it with a hammer.

Marital counseling. Al Cooper (2002), a psychologist at Stanford University, has explained that marital counseling because of cybersex dalliances is "exploding" (cited in *Business Week*, 27B). Cooper cited the attraction of the Web's access, anonymity, and cost as promoting sexual compulsions for married individuals, couples, and singles.

Adultery. Gibson (2006) has examined affairs on the Internet chat rooms and at dating services, and he has commented on their threat to marriages:

> Affairs [in the virtual world] often progress quickly to the point where they're considerably more intimate than a one-night stand. Are they adultery? As a writer, I think it's a gray area. It's something that lawyers and men and women of the cloth need to decide. (p. 39)

Virtual sex chat that sometimes involves the exchange of pictures has no physical contact between the two people, so can it be adultery? The courts may be deciding that question as we speak because divorces are occurring regularly as one spouse discover what's on the other's computer hard drive.

The woman's role. The woman must identify her role in a relationship to the men in her life. In that regard, Bloom (1993) said:

> Even the most independent-minded erotic man becomes dependent on the judgment of a woman, and a serious woman, one who is looking not only for an attractive man but for one who will love her and protect her, may be the best possible judge of a man's virtues and thus be regarded by even the most serious man as the supreme tribunal of his worth. (p. 104)

Cooper has observed that "the medium forces potential partners to talk, which," he says, "is something women in particular seem to want to do" (cited in "Intimacy and the Internet," 1996). Thus, although more men frequent the Web sites, the women may benefit at a higher rate, in part because they are more cautious and anonymity gives them time to prearrange any meeting.

The man's role. Times are changing. Women as much as men are cruising the Internet, and women are more serious than the men. The typical male enters the Internet dating service thinking about sex, but he encounters women thinking about a relationship. The two are not entirely antithetical, but the timing varies, and the man discovers on the Internet that the woman controls much of the timing. "They do not realize," Kass (1999) has explained, "that what they need is courtship or something like it." Perhaps that's what men have begun to learn by online romance.

Psychological Implications

It is too soon, perhaps, to understand the full ramifications of online romance. Certainly, people have been severely wounded, both psychologically and physically, by venturing onto the Internet and getting trapped into damaging and fatal liaisons. At the same time, the ability to prearrange a meeting after weeks and months of conversation has its benefits, as shown by the case study. A man or woman who ventures onto the Internet will expose themselves to some of the same dangers as a blind date, except for the built-in firewalls between a username on the Web and somebody actually knocking on the door, ready for a date.

Online infidelity. Young et al. (2000) has suggested that electronic communication can lead to marital discord, separation, and possible divorce. The ACE model (Anonymity, Convenience,

Arranged Marriages 12

Escape) has served as a driving force behind "cybersexual addiction," and it explains the dynamics for virtual adultery.

Escape and damage to self-esteem. "Affairs can be a betrayal of the self and can imply that a person is avoiding knowing himself/herself or the partner when substituting fantasy sex online for a real relationship" (Maheu, 1999). A woman at midnight escapes into her addiction with an online lover, a man she has never met who may not even be a man, and she pretends the next day as she serves breakfast to her family that all is well. The damage to her psyche is like the early morning "walk of shame" that some young women experience—that return alone to their rooms from some encounter while the man curls up in bed with a smile on his face.

Psychotherapy. Participants in the online dating game can become depressed, angry, lose self-esteem, and go in search of psychotherapy. Cooper (2002), who is director of the San Jose Marital and Sexuality Centre, has reported that marital counseling is "exploding" because of fallouts from one partner's enticement into sex on the Internet, either the pornography or the online romance or the all-night chat sessions. In addition, the machinery continues to entice more people into sexual adventures; Klaffke (2003) reported recently that software now exists that "allows singles to post personal profiles and peruse those of others through text messaging on their cell phones," and as you may know, cell phones can now transfer photographs.

In conclusion, the world of online romance is growing at a staggering rate, with millions signing on each year and with thousands finding happiness and with thousands more finding sexual chaos and dangerous liaisons. Yet little research is being done in this area. My search of the literature produced a surprisingly limited number of journal articles. Maheu (1999) has

The conclusion will often include a statement on the state of research in the area of the study.

discussed methods of helping clients, even to the point of counseling in cyberspace itself, which would establish professional relationships online. Schneider and Weiss (2001) describe it but offer little psychoanalysis. Cooper (2002) has an excellent collection of articles in his guidebook for clinicians. Counseling needs to be in place for persons who substitute fantasy sex online for a true relationship. However, numerous case studies also show that online romance can produce healthy relationships and successful marriages.

References

Ballug, M. I. (2006). Virtually yours: The world of online dating. Retrieved April 2, 2006, from http://virtualdating.tripod.com/intro.htm.

Bloom, A. (1993). *Love and friendship*. New York: Simon & Schuster.

Brooks, L. (2003, February 13). The love business. *The Guardian* (London), p. 6. Retrieved April 8, 2006, from InfoTrac database.

Cha, A. E. (2003, May 4). ISO Romance? Online matchmakers put love to the test. *Washington Post*, p. A01. Retrieved April 2, 2006, from Lexis-Nexis database.

Cohen, J. (2006). Choose the best Internet dating service for you. Retrieved April 3, 2006, from http://dating.about.com/od/onlinepersonals/qt/InternetDating.htm.

References begin on a new page.

Citation for a part of a book.

Citation for a book.

Citation for an article from a library's database.

Arranged Marriages 15

Cooper, A. (Ed.). (2002). *Sex and the Internet: A guide book for clinicians*. New York: Brunner-Routledge.

Fein, E., & Schneider, S. (1995). *The rules*. New York: Time-Warner.

Fein, E., & Schneider, S. (2002). *The rules for online dating*. New York: Pocket Books.

Gibson, R. (Ed.). (2006). *Sex, Lies, and online dating*. New York: Avon.

Intimacy and the Internet. (1996). *Contemporary Sexuality, 30*. Retrieved April 4, 2006, from http://www.sex-centre.com/InternetandSex/Index_Internt_Sex.htm.

Kass, A. A. (1999). A case for courtship. Address delivered to the Institute for American Values.

Kass, A. A., & Kass, L. R. (Eds.). (2003). *Wing to wing, Oar to oar: Readings on courting and marrying*. Notre Dame, Indiana: University of Notre Dame Press.

Klaffke, P. (2003, April 28). Never be lonely: Look dates over on a cellphone. *Calgary Herald* (Alberta, Canada), p. D3. Retrieved April 4, 2003, from Lexis-Nexis database.

Leiblum, S., & Döring. (2002). Internet sexuality: Known risks and fresh chances for women. In A. Cooper (Ed.). *Sex and the Internet: A guidebook for clinicians* pp. 263–280). New York: Brunner-Routledge.

Maheu, M. M. (1999). Women's Internet behavior: Providing psychotherapy offline and online for cyber-infidelity. Paper presented at the Annual Conference of the American Psychological Association, Boston, MA. Abstract retrieved April 9, 2003, from http://telehealth.net/articles/women/internet.html.

Miller, M. (1996, April 8). Love at first byte. *People Weekly*, 39.

Nussbaum, E. (2002, December 15). The year in ideas: Online personals are cool. *New York Times*, Sec. 6, p. 106. Retrieved April 8, 2003, from http://www.nytimes.com.

Citation for a conference pesentation.

Citation for a magazine article.

Razdan, A. (2003, May-June). What's love got to do with it?
Utne, 69–71.

Ross, M. W., & Kauth, M. R. Men who have sex with men, and the
Internet: Emerging clinical issues and their management. In
A. Cooper (Ed.). *Sex and the Internet: A guidebook for
clinicians* (pp. 263–280). New York: Brunner-Routledge.

Schneider, J., & Weiss, R. (2001). *Cybersex exposed: Simple
fantasy or obsession?* Center City, Minnesota: Hazelden.

When Cupid uses a cursor. (1999, February 22). *Business Week*.
Retrieved April 5, 2003, from InfoTrac database.

Young, K., Griffin, S., Shelley, E., Cooper, A., O'Mara, J., &
Buchanan, J. (2002). Online infidelity: A new dimension in
couple relationships with implications for evaluation and
treatment. *Sexual Addiction and Compulsivity, 7*, 59–74.
Abstract retrieved April 4, 2003, from InfoTrac database.

16 The Footnote System: CMS Style

The fine arts and some fields in the humanities (but not literature) use traditional footnotes, which should conform to standards set by *The Chicago Manual of Style* (CMS), 15th ed., 2003. In the CMS system, you must place superscript numerals within the text (like this[15]), and place documentary footnotes on corresponding pages.

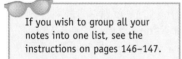
If you wish to group all your notes into one list, see the instructions on pages 146–147.

The discussion below assumes that notes will appear as footnotes; however, some instructors accept endnotes—that is, all notes appear together at the end of the paper, not at the bottom of individual pages (see pages 146-147).

There are two types of footnotes: One documents your sources with bibliographic information, but the other can discuss related matters, explain your methods of research, suggest related literature, provide biographical information, or offer information not immediately pertinent to your discussion.

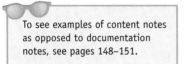
To see examples of content notes as opposed to documentation notes, see pages 148–151.

If available, use the footnote or endnote feature of your software. It will not only insert the raised superscript number but also keep your footnotes arranged properly at the bottom of each page or keep your endnotes in a correct list. In most instances, the software will insert the superscript numeral, but it will not write the note automatically; you must type in the essential data in the correct style.

16a Inserting a Superscript Numeral in Your Text

Use Arabic numerals typed slightly above the line (like this[12]). In both Microsoft Word and WordPerfect, go to Font and select Superscript or go to Insert and select Footnote. Place a superscript numeral at the end of each quotation or paraphrase, with the number following immediately without a space after the final word or mark of punctuation, as in this sample:

Steven A. LeBlanc, an archaeologist at Harvard University, along

with several other scholars, argues instead that "humans have been at

each others' throats since the dawn of the species."[1] Robin Yates, for
example, says the ancient ancestors of the Chinese used "long-range
projectile weapons" as long ago as 28,000 BC for both hunting and
"intrahuman conflict."[2] Arthur Ferrill observes, "When man first learned
how to write, he already had war to write about."[3] Ferrill adds, "In
prehistoric times man was a hunter and a killer of other men. The killer
instinct in the prehistoric male is clearly attested by archaeology in
fortifications, weapons, cave paintings, and skeletal remains."[4]

The footnotes that relate to these in-text superscript numerals will appear at
the bottom of the page, as shown here:

> 1. See Steven A. LeBlanc, *Constant Battles: The Myth of the
> Peaceful, Noble Savage* (New York: St. Martin's Press, 2004), 15, and
> also L. D. Cooper, *Rousseau, Nature, and the Problem of the Good Life*
> (University Park: Pennsylvania State Univ. Press, 2000).
>
> 2. Steven A. LeBlanc, "Prehistory of Warfare," *Archaeology*
> (May/June, 2003): 18.
>
> 3. Robin Yates, "Early China," in *War and Society in the Ancient
> and Medieval Worlds*, ed. Kurt Raaflaub and Nathan Rosenstein
> (Cambridge, Massachusetts: Center for Hellenic Studies, 2001), 9.
>
> 4. Arthur Ferrill, "Neolithic Warfare," http://eserver.org/history/
> neolithic-war.txt (accessed 6 April 2006).

However, you may place the notes at the back of your paper, so you should
usually include a source's name in your text. The first example below implies
a source that will be found in the footnote; the second expresses the name in
the text. Some writers prefer the first approach, others the second.

Implied reference:

The organic basis of autism is generally agreed upon.
Three possible causes for autism have been identified: behavioral
syndrome, organic brain disorder, or a range of biological and
psychosocial factors.[9]

Expressed reference:

Martin Rutter has acknowledged that the organic basis of autism
is generally agreed upon. Rutter named three possible causes for
autism: behavioral syndrome, organic brain disorder, or a range of
biological and psychosocial factors.[10]

Index to Footnote Models

Writing Full or Abbreviated Notes

MLA style permits you to omit a bibliography page as long as you give full data to the sources in each of your initial footnotes.

> 1. Edward Rutherfurd, *The Rebels of Ireland* (New York: Doubleday, 2006), 49.

However, you may provide a comprehensive bibliography to each source and abbreviate all footnotes entries, even the initial ones, since full data will be found in the bibliography.

> 1. Rutherfurd, *The Rebels of Ireland*, 49.

The bibliography entry would read this way:

> Rutherford, Edward. *The Rebels of Ireland*. New York: Doubleday, 2006.

Consult with your instructor on this matter if you are uncertain about the proper format for a specific course.

16b Formatting and Writing the Footnotes

Place footnotes at the bottom of pages to correspond with superscript numerals (see immediately above). Some papers will require footnotes on almost every page. Follow these conventions:

1. **Spacing.** In academic papers not intended for publication, footnotes are commonly typed single-spaced and placed at the foot of the page, usually

with a line space between each note. Drafts and manuscript intended for publication in print or on the Web should have all notes double-spaced and placed together on one page at the end of the paper. The student example on page 356 shows single-spaced footnotes. A Notes page with double spacing can be found on pages 345–346.

2. **Indention.** Indent the first line of the note five spaces or one inch (usually one click of the tab key).

3. **Numbering.** Number the footnotes consecutively throughout the entire paper with an indented number, a period, and space, as shown in the examples throughout this chapter.

4. **Placement.** Collect at the bottom of each page all footnotes to citations made on that page.

5. **Distinguish footnotes from text.** Separate footnotes from the text by triple spacing or, if you prefer, by a twelve-space bar line from the left margin.

6. **Footnote form.** Basic forms of notes should conform to the following styles.

Book

List the author, followed by a comma, the title underlined or in italics, the publication data within parenthesis (city: publisher, year), followed by a comma and the page number(s). Unless ambiguity would result, the abbreviations *p.* and *pp.* may be omitted.

> 1. Craig Clunas, *Pictures and Visuality in Early Modern China* (Chicago: Reaktion Press, 2006), 20–23.

List two authors without a comma:

> 2. Steven D. Levitt and Stephen J. Dubner, *Freakonomics: A Rogue Economist Explores the Hidden Side of Everything* (New York: HarperCollins Publishers, 2006), 18.

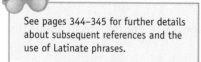

See pages 344–345 for further details about subsequent references and the use of Latinate phrases.

List three authors separated by commas. *Note:* Publisher's names are spelled out in full, but the words *Company* and *Inc.* are omitted. Reference to an edition follows the title or the editors, if listed (see footnote 6 on the next page).

> 3. Buzz Bissinger, H. G. Bissinger, and Tony Larussa, *Three Nights in August: Strategy, Heartbreak, and Joy inside the Mind of a Manager* (New York: Houghton Mifflin, 2005), 140–41.

For more than three authors, use *et al.* after mention of the lead author:

> 4. Dean H. Hepworth et al., eds., "Introduction," *Direct Social Work Practice*, 7th ed. (New York: Wadsworth, 2005), 3.

For a subsequent reference to an immediately preceding source, use "Ibid." in the roman typeface, not in italics and not underscored:

> 5. Ibid.

Collection or Anthology

> 6. Sandra Leiblum and Nicola Döring, "Internet Sexuality: Known Risks and Fresh Chances for Women," in *Sex and the Internet: A Guidebook for Clinicians*, ed. Al Cooper (New York: Brunner-Routledge, 2002), 20-21.

Journal Article

> 7. B. Corenblum and Christian A. Meissner, "Recognition of Faces of Ingroup and Outgroup Children and Adults," *Journal of Experimental Child Psychology* 93 (2006): 187.

Note: Use a colon before the page number of a journal but a comma before page numbers for magazines and books.

Magazine Article

> 8. Keith Kloor, "Secrets of the Range Creek Ranch," *Smithsonian,* March 2006: 70.

Newspaper Article

> 9. Kelly Yamanouchi, "Airports in Dogfight to Host Heroes," *Denver Post*, 9 March 2006, 1A.

> 10. John Kirkenfeld, "Digging for More Dirt," *Riverton Daily Observer*, 23 July 2006, sec. 4, 1.

Note: The abbreviations *sec.* and *p.* are necessary to distinguish the 4 and the 1.

Review Article

> 11. Chris Dodge, review of *Arborsculpture: Solutions for a Small Planet*, by Richard Reames, *Utne* March–April 2006, 24.

Nonprint Source: Lecture, Sermon, Speech, Oral Report

12. Dick Weber, "The Facts about Preparing Teens to Drive" (lecture, Morrow High School, Morrow, GA, April 16, 2006).

Encyclopedia

13. *The World Book Encyclopedia,* 2005 ed., s.v. "Raphael."

Note: "s.v." means *sub verbo,* "under the word(s)."

Government Documents

14. United States. Dept. of the Treasury, "Financial Operations of Government Agencies and Funds," *Treasury Bulletin*, Washington, DC (June 2005): 134–141.

15. U.S., *Constitution*, art. 1, sec. 4.

16. United Kingdom, *Coroner's Act, 1954*, 2 & 3 Eliz. 2, ch.31.

Television

17. Bob Schieffer, *CBS News*, September 13, 2006.

Film on DVD

18. *Walk the Line*, DVD, directed by James Mangold (Beverly Hills, CA: Twentieth Century Fox, 2005).

Musical Work on VHS

19. Hanel, George Frederic, *Messiah*, selections, VHS, Atlanta Symphony Orchestra and Chamber Chorus, Robert Shaw, conductor (Atlanta, GA: Video Imaging, 2005).

Biblical Reference

20. Matt. 10:5.

21. 1 Pet. 5:1-3 (New Revised Standard Version)

16c Writing Footnotes for Electronic Sources

To cite electronic sources, *The Chicago Manual of Style* includes a publication date and the URL but not the date of access. The models below show these requirements. Adjust your sources accordingly.

Scholarly Project

22. *British Poetry Archive*, ed. Jerome McGann and David Seaman (University Of Virginia Library, 2006), http://etext.lib.virgina.edu/britpo.html.

Article Online, Limited Information

23. Arthur Ferrill, "Neolithic Warfare Frontline Educational Foundation," http://eserver.org/history/neolithic-war.txt.

Magazine Article Reproduced Online

24. John Roach, "Mars Gravity Captures NASA Spacecraft," *National Geographic News*, March 10, 2006, http://news.nationalgeographic.com/news/2006/03/0310_060310_mars_orbit.html.

Journal Article Reproduced Online

25. Kimberly A. Tyler and Katherine A. Johnson, "Pathways In and Out of Substance Use Among Homeless—Emerging Adults," *Journal of Adolescent Research* 21 (2006): 133–57, http://jar.sagepub.com/cgi/content/abstract/21/2/133.

Journal Article Online with No Author Listed

26. "Business Methods and Professional Morals," *Journal of the American Medical Association,* March 10, 2006, http://jama.ama-assn.org/cgi/content/extract/295/10/1196.

Article from a Scientific Database

At a minimum, show in this order the name of the database, the URL, a descriptive phrase or record locator (such as a number) to indicate the part of the database being cited, and an access date.

27. NASA/IPAC Extragalactic Database, http://nedwww.ipac.caltech.edu/ (object name IRAS F004000+4059; accessed July 13, 2006).

Article Accessed from a Database through the Library System

28. Victor Davis Hanson, "War Will Be War: No Matter the Era, No Matter the Weapons, and the Same Old Hell." *National Review,* 54 (2002); InfoTrac database, Art. A84943306.

Book Online

29. D. H. Lawrence, *Lady Chatterly's Lover*, 1928, http://
bibliomania.com/fiction/dhl/chat.html.

CD-ROM Source

Place of publication and date may be omitted unless relevant.

30. The Old Testament, The Bible, CD-ROM, Bureau Development.

31. *Oxford English Dictionary*, 2nd ed. CD-ROM, version 2.0, Oxford
University Press.

Electronic Mailing List, Archived

32. Warren Watts, e-mail to Victorian Association for Library
Automation mailing list, September 23, 2006, http://www.vala.org.au/
conf2004.htm.

Article from an Online Service

33. "Nutrition and Cancer," *Discovery Health*, May 1, 2000,
http://www.discoveryhealth.com/Sc000/8096/164609.html.

E-mail

Since e-mail is not retrievable, do not document with a footnote or bibliography entry. Instead, mention the nature of the source within your text by saying something like this:

Walter Wallace argues that teen violence stems mainly from the
breakup of the traditional family (e-mail to the author).

16d Writing Subsequent Footnote References

After a first full footnote, references to the same source should be shortened to the author's last name and page number. When an author has two works mentioned, employ a shortened version of the title, e.g., "3. Jones, *Paine*, 25." In general, avoid Latinate abbreviations such as *loc. cit.* and *op. cit.*; however, whenever a note refers to the source in the immediately preceding note, you may use "Ibid." alone or "Ibid." with a page number, as shown on the next page. If the subsequent note does not refer to the one immediately above it, do not use "Ibid." Instead, repeat the author's last name (note especially the difference between notes 2 and 4):

1. Robert E. Slavin, *Educational Psychology: Theory and Practice*, 8th ed. (New York: ASCD, 2005), 23.

2. Ibid., 27.

3. Grant P. Wiggins and Jay McTighe, *Understanding by Design*, 2nd ed. (Alexandria, VA: ASCD, 2005), 91.

4. Slavin, 24.

5. Ibid., 27.

Note: Single-space footnotes but double-space between each note.

16e Writing Endnotes Rather Than Footnotes

With the permission of your instructor, you may put all your notes together as a single group of endnotes to lessen the burden of typing the paper. Most computer software programs will help you with this task by inserting the superscript numerals and by allowing you to type the endnotes consecutively at the end of the text, not at the bottom of each page. Follow these conventions:

1. Begin notes on a new page at the end of the text.
2. Entitle the page "Notes," centered, and placed two inches from the top of the page.
3. Indent the first line of each note one-half inch or five spaces. Type the number of the note followed by a period.
4. Double-space the endnotes.
5. Triple-space between the heading and the first note.

Conform to the following example:

Notes

1. Dan Kindlon, Too Much of a Good Thing: Raising Children of Character in an Indulgent Age (New York: Hyperion, 2003), 24.

2. Ibid., 27.

3. Jean Illsley Clark, Connie Dawson, and David Bredehoft, How Much Is Enough? Everything You Need to Know to Steer Clear of Overindulgence and Raise Likeable, Responsible, and Respectful Children (New York: Avalon, 2004), 221.

4. Michele Borba, "10 Tips for Raising Moral Kids," http://www.moralintelligence.com/Pages/ArtBMI13.htm.

5. Kindlon, 28.

6. Abraham J. Heschel, *Man Is Not Alone: A Philosophy of Religion* (New York: Farrar, Straus, and Young, 1951), 221.

7. Ibid., 222.

8. Borba.

9. Kindlon, 28.

10. Borba.

16f Writing Content Footnotes or Content Endnotes

See the sample paper on pages 353–365 for its use of two content footnotes: number 1, page 356, and number 26, page 363.

As a general rule, put important matters in your text. Use a content note to explain research problems, conflicts in the testimony of the experts, matters of importance that are not germane to your discussion, interesting tidbits, credit to people and sources not mentioned in the text, and other matters that might interest readers.

HINT: After you have embedded most of your computer files in your draft, check the remaining files to find appropriate material for a few content endnotes.

Content notes should conform to these rules:

1. Content notes are *not* documentation notes; a full citation to any source mentioned in the note will appear elsewhere—in a documentation note or on the References page (see item 4.)
2. Content notes may be placed on a separate page(s) following the last page of text, but generally they appear as footnotes mixed among the documentation footnotes.
3. Content footnotes should be single-spaced, like your documentation footnotes. Content endnotes should be double-spaced, as shown in the next few examples.
4. Full information on sources mentioned in content notes must appear elsewhere in a footnote or in a separate Works Cited page at the end of the paper.
5. Unless ambiguity might result without them, do not use *p.* or *pp.* with page numbers.

The following samples demonstrate various types of content endnotes.

Related Matters Not Germane to the Text

1. The problems of politically correct language are explored in Adams, Tucker (4-5), Zalers, and also Young and Smith (583). These authorities cite the need for caution by administrators who would impose new measures on speech and behavior. Verbal abuse cannot be erased by a new set of unjust laws. Patrick German offers several guidelines for implementing an effective but reasonable program (170-72).

Blanket Citation

2. On this point see Giarrett (3-4), de Young (579), Kinard (405–07), and Young (119).

3. Cf. Campbell (*Masks* 1: 170–225; *Hero* 342-45), Frazer (312), and Baird (300–44).

Note: Cf. means *compare*.

Literature on a Related Topic

4. For additional study of the effects of alcoholics on children, see especially the *Journal of Studies on Alcohol* for the article by Wolin et al. and the bibliography on the topic by Orme and Rimmer (285-87). In addition, group therapy for children of alcoholics is examined in Hawley and Brown.

Major Source Requiring Frequent In-Text Citations

5. All citations to Shakespeare are to the Fogler Library edition.

6. Dryden's poems are cited from the California edition of his *Works* and documented in the text with first references to each poem listing volume, page, and lines and with subsequent references citing lines only.

Reference to Source Materials

7. See also James Baird, who argues that the whiteness of Melville's whale is "the sign of the all-encompassing God" (257). Baird states: "It stands for what Melville calls at the conclusion of the thirty-fifth chapter of *Moby-Dick* 'the inscrutable tides of God'; and it

is of these tides as well that the great White Whale himself is the quintessential emblem, the iconographic representation" (257).

> **NOTE:** Either list Baird in the bibliography or include full bibliographic information with this footnote.

8. On this point see also the essay by Patricia Chaffee in which she examines the "house" as a primary image in the fiction of Eudora Welty.

Explanation of Tools, Methods, or Testing Procedures

9. Water samples were drawn from the identical spot each day at 8 a.m., noon, 4 p.m., and 8 p.m., with testing done immediately on site.

10. The control group continued normal dietary routines, but the experimental group was asked to consume nuts, sharp cheeses, and chocolates to test acne development of its members against that of the control group.

11. The initial sample was complete data on all twins born in Nebraska between 1920 and 1940. These dates were selected to provide test subjects 60 years of age or older.

> **NOTE:** A report of an empirical study in APA style would require an explanation of tools and testing procedures in the text under "Methods." See section 15f, pages 321–322.

Statistics

See also "Using Visuals," pages 168–171.

12. Database results show 27,000 pupil-athletes in 174 high schools with grades 0.075 above another group of 27,000 non-athletes at the same high schools. Details on the nature of various *reward structures* are unavailable.

Acknowledgments of Assistance or Support

13. Funds to finance this research were graciously provided by the Thompson-Monroe Foundation.

14. This writer wishes to acknowledge the research assistance of Pat Luther, graduate assistant, Physics Department.

Variables or Conflicts in the Evidence

15. Potlatch et al. included the following variables: the positive acquaintance, the equal status norm, the various social norms, the negative stereotypes, and sexual discrimination (415-20). However, racial barriers cannot be overlooked as one important variable.

16. The pilot study at Dunlap School, where sexual imbalance was noticed (62 percent males), differed sharply with test results of other schools. The male bias at Dunlap thereby caused the writer to eliminate those scores from the totals.

16g Using the Footnote System for Papers in the Humanities

Several disciplines in the humanities—history, philosophy, religion, and theology—use footnotes. The following list demonstrates the format for the types of notes you might need to write for papers on religion or history. They are shown as endnotes, which should be double-spaced.

Sample Page of Notes to a Paper on a Religious Topic

Notes

1. Elaine Pagels, *Beyond Belief: The Secret Gospel of Thomas* (New York: Random House, 2003), 23–27.

2. Rob Brezsny, Promoia Is the Antidote for Paranoia: How the Whole World Is Conspiring to Shower You with Blessings (Berkeley, CA: Frog, 2005), 214–17.

3. Claude Levi-Strauss, *The Savage Mind* (Chicago: University of Chicago Press, 1966), chap. 9, esp. p. 312.

4. Ibid., 314.

5. E. E. Evans-Pritchard, *Theories of Primitive Religion* (Oxford: Clarendon Press, 1965), chap. 2.

6. Evans-Pritchard, *Nuer Religion* (Oxford: Clarendon Press, 1956), 85.

7. Evans-Pritchard, *Primitive Religion*, 46.

8. Humphries, P. T., "Marriage as Inspiration," Sermon (Bowling Green, KY: Primitive Baptist Church, 2006).

9. Romans 6:2.

10. *The Church and the Law of Nullity of Marriage*, Report of a Commission Appointed by the Archbishops of Canterbury and York in 1949 (London: Society for Promoting Christian Knowledge, 1955), 12–16.

Sample Page of Notes to a History Paper

Notes

1. Bill Bryson, *A Short History of Nearly Everything* (New York: Broadway Books, 2003), 34.

2. Thomas Jefferson, "Notes on the State of Virginia" (1784), http://www.yale.edu/lawweb/avalon/jevifram.htm.

3. Darren Staloff, *Hamilton, Adams, Jefferson: The Politics of Enlightenment and the American Founding* (New York: Farrar, Straus, and Giroux, 2005), 56–60.

4. *Encyclopedia Britannica*, 2005 ed., s.v. "Declaration of Independence."

5. Henry Steele Commager, *The Nature and Study of History*, Social Science Seminar Series (Columbus, Ohio: Merrill, 2006), 10.

6. Dept. of the Treasury, "Financial Operations of Government Agencies and Funds," Treasury Bulletin (Washington, D.C.: GPO, June 1974), 134–41.

7. Constitution, Art. 1, sec. 4.

8. Great Britain, Coroner's Act, 1954, 2 & 3 Eliz. 2, ch. 31.

9. *State v. Lane*, Minnesota 263 N. W. 608 (1935).

10. Papers of Gen. A. J. Warner (P-973, Service Record and Short Autobiography), Western Reserve Historical Society.

16h   Using the Footnote System for Papers in the Fine Arts

Several disciplines in the fine arts—art, dance, music, theater—use footnotes. The following list demonstrates the format for the types of footnotes you might need to write for topics that treat the fine arts.

Notes

1. Carolyn Damstra, "The Freer Gallery of Art," *Michigan History Magazine* 86 (2002): 46.

2. Rafael Lomas, "Ignatius of Loyola's 'Music of the Heart' and His Impact on Early-Modern Spanish Musical Theatre," http://www.fmcs.us/2005/11lamas.htm.

3. Damstra, 47.

4. Sarah Dunant, *In the Company of the Courtesan* (New York: Random House 2005), 286.

5. Aristophanes, *The Birds*, in *Five Comedies of Aristophanes*, trans. Benjamin B. Rogers (Garden City, N.Y.: Doubleday, 1955), 1.2.12–14.

6. Jean Bouret, *The Life and Work of Toulouse Lautrec*, trans. Daphne Woodward (New York: Abrams, n.d.), 5.

7. Cyrus Hoy, "Fathers and Daughters in Shakespeare's Romances," in *Shakespeare's Romances Reconsidered*, ed. Carol McGinnis Kay and Henry E. Jacobs (Lincoln: Univ. of Nebraska Press, 1978), 77–78.

8. Lionello Venturi, *Botticelli* (Greenwich, Conn.: Fawcett, n.d.), plate 32, p. 214.

NOTE: Add "p." for page only if needed for clarity.

9. Cotton Vitellius MSS, A., 15. British Museum.

10. *Ham*. 2.3.2.

11. George Henry Lewes, Review of "Letters on Christian Art," by Friedrich von Schlegel, *Athenaeum* No. 1117 (1849), 296.

12. Carter Dodgson, "Comments on the Carriage House Museum," *The Monitor* (23 August 2006): 8.

13. The World Book Encyclopedia, 2005 ed., s.v. "Raphael."

14. *Last Tango in Paris*, United Artists, 1972.

15. Wolfgang A. Mozart, *Jupiter*, Symphony No. 41.

16. William Blake, *Comus*, A photographic reproduction in Irene Taylor, "Blake's *Comus* Designs," *Blake Studies* 4 (Spring, 1972): 61, plate 4.

17. Lawrence Topp, *The Artistry of Van Gogh* (New York: Matson, 2004), transparency 21.

16i Writing a Bibliography Page for a Paper That Uses Footnotes

In addition to footnotes or endnotes, you may be requested to supply a separate bibliography page that lists sources used in developing the paper. Use a heading that represents its contents, such as Selected Bibliography, Sources Consulted, or Works Cited.

> See pages 364–365 for a sample of a complete bibliography for a research paper.

If your initial footnotes are completely documented, the bibliography is redundant. Check with your instructor before preparing one because it may not be required. Separate the title from the first entry with a triple space. Type the first line of each entry flush left; indent the second line and other succeeding lines five spaces or one inch. Alphabetize the list by last names of authors. Double-space the entries as shown below. List alphabetically by title two or more works by one author. The basic forms are:

Book

Greenberg, David Lawrence. *Treehouse in Paradise*. New York: Harry N. Abrams, 2006.

Journal Article

Muller, Valerie. "Film as Film: Using Movies to Help Students Visualize Literary Theory." *English Journal* 95 (January 2006): 32–38.

Newspaper

Vecchio, Rick. "Traffickers of Babies Still Abound in Peru." *Denver Post* March 12, 2006, 1A.

Internet Article

"Biography." Paul Laurence Dunbar Website. http://www.dunbarsite.org/biopld.asp.

16j Sample Research Paper in the CMS Style

The essay that follows demonstrates the format and documentation style you should use for a research paper when the instructor asks that you use "footnotes," the Chicago style, or the CMS style, all of which refer to *The Chicago Manual of Style*. If permitted, notes may be placed at the end of the paper as double-spaced endnotes rather than at the bottom of the pages.

In the paper that follows, Jamie Johnston has researched the history of war back into prehistoric times. The student offers substantial evidence to prove that early tribes had a history of warfare and even brutality toward captives. The tools of war are reviewed, and then Johnston poses the crucial question: Why did early civilizations fight? He lists many reasons, such as fights for resources, slaves, precious metals, revenge, and honor. Ultimately, he poses the key issue: Was human behavior motivated by biology or culture? Johnston reaches an interesting conclusion, so read on.

Prehistoric Wars: We've Always Hated Each Other

Title page is required only when you have an outline or other prefatory material.

By

Jamie Johnston

English Composition 1010

Professor Sandiford

11 April 2006

Johnston i

Prehistoric Wars

For information on writing an outline, see pages 138–142.

I. We are a civilized people, yet we love a good fight.

    A. Prehistory shows that we have always fought.

    B. The wars were often savage affairs.

    C. Evidence shows the truth about our love of fighting:

        1. Executions in Peru

        2. Wars among the Mayans

        3. Massacres in Europe

        4. Savagery in the Southwestern United States

II. We have always had weapons of mass destruction.

    A. Early tribes used clubs, arrows, spears, and slings.

    B. They made use of horses, mules, and even elephants.

    C. They developed large armies for aggression and protection.

    D. They left evidence of defensive barriers, such as walls and moats.

III. The crucial question that must be examined is, Why did we fight?

    A. Early humans used war in their search for several things:

This writer uses a combination of sentences and phrases for the outline. See pages 139–141.

        1. Food

        2. Women

        3. Slaves

        4. Sacrificial victims

        5. Gold and treasures

    B. Early humans also fought for these reasons:

        1. Revenge

        2. Defense of their honor

        3. Protection of trade routes

        4. Honor God and their religion

Johnston ii

IV. Ultimately, the cause for our warlike nature boils down to
two primary causes.

   A. One group advances the theory that culture dictates our
aggression.

      1. A desire for freedom demands war at times.

      2. Capitalism and world markets affect aggressive
actions.

      3. Government and official control promote
aggression.

   B. A second group advances the theory that biology is the
motivating factor.

      1. Humans love a good fight.

      2. Tempers are explosive and sometimes uncontrollable.

      3. People want power over others.

      4. Civil law and moral behavior cannot be dictated to
others.

One advantage of sentence outline is that the material can launch the drafting of the paper itself. See page 140.

Johnston 1

Prehistoric Wars: We've Always Hated Each Other

Here we are, a civilized world with reasonably educated
people, yet we constantly fight with other. These are not sibling
squabbles either; people die in terrible ways. We wonder, then, if
there was ever a time when men and women lived in harmony
with one another and with nature and the environment. The Bible
speaks of the Garden of Eden, and the French philosopher
Jean-Jacques Rousseau advanced the idea in the 1700s of the

Repeat the title on the opening page of text.

Johnston 2

"noble savage," and that "nothing could be more gentle" than an ancient colony of people.[1] Wrong!

Steven A. LeBlanc, an archaeologist at Harvard University, along with several other scholars, argues instead that "humans have been at each others' throats since the dawn of the species."[2] Robin Yates, for example, says the ancient ancestors of the Chinese used "long-range projectile weapons" as long ago as 28,000 B.C. for both hunting and "intrahuman conflict."[3] Arthur Ferrill observes, "When man first learned how to write, he already had war to write about."[4] Ferrill adds, "In prehistoric times man was a hunter and a killer of other men. The killer instinct in the prehistoric male is clearly attested by archaeology in fortifications, weapons, cave paintings, and skeletal remains."[5]

Evidence proves that savage fighting occurred in the ancient history of human beings. We have evidence of the types of weapons employed. We can also list reasons for the prehistoric fighting. This paper will examine those items, but the crux of the debate centers on the inducement or instinct. Were early

The writer uses the introduction to discuss historical evidence.

This section opens with the writer's thesis, and discusses reasons for prehistoric wars.

---

1. See Steven A. LeBlanc, *Constant Battles: The Myth of the Peaceful, Noble Savage* (New York: St. Martin's Press, 2003, 15, and also L. D. Cooper, *Rousseau, Nature, and the Problem of the Good Life* (University Park: Pennsylvania State Univ. Press, 1999.

2. Steven A. LeBlanc, "Prehistory of Warfare," *Archaeology* (May/June, 2003), 18.

3. Robin Yates, "Early China," in *War and Society in the Ancient and Medieval Worlds*, ed. Kurt Raaflaub and Nathan Rosenstein (Cambridge, Massachusetts: Center for Hellenic Studies, 1999), 9.

4. Arthur Ferrill, "Neolithic Warfare," Frontline Educational Foundation, http://eserver.org/history/neolithic-war.txt.

5. Ibid.

Citation for a magazine.

Citation for a book.

Citation for an Internet source.

humans motivated by biological instincts or by cultural
demands for a share of limited resources? That's the issue
this paper will address.

First, we need to look briefly at the evidence. Ben Harder
has reported on the work of one forensic anthropologist, John
Verano, who has investigated a series of "grisly executions" in
the valleys of Peru during the Moche civilization.[6] Victims "were
apparently skinned alive. Others were drained of blood,
decapitated, or bound tightly and left to be eaten by vultures."[7]
Verano has the proof of the executions, but not the reason,
although speculations center on religious ceremonies. UCLA
anthropologist Christopher B. Donnan has studied Moche art and
suggests "the suffering of the losers may have had a ritualistic
meaning in Moche society much as the pain of Christ does in
Christianity."[8] At the same time, Verano thinks the victims were
prisoners of war and not the losers of ritual combat. In either
case, the ancients were less than noble savages.

LeBlanc's book *Constant Battles* is a catalog of prehistoric
fighting, David Webster describes the savage fighting of the
ancient Mayans,[9] and Nick Thorpe in *British Archaeology* describes
massacres that occurred in Europe over 8,500 years

---

6. Ben Harder, "Ancient Peru Torture Deaths: Sacrifices or
War Crimes?" *National Geographic News*, 29 April 2002,
http://news.nationalgeogrphic.com/news/2002/ 04/
0425_020426_mochekillings.html.

7. Ibid.

8. Christopher Donnan, cited in Harder.

9. David Webster, "Ancient Maya Warfare," in *War and
Society in the Ancient and Medieval Worlds*, ed. Kurt Raaflaub and
Nathan Rosenstein (Cambridge, Massachusetts: Center for
Hellenic Studies, 1999), 333-60.

The word
Ibid. refers
to the
immediately
preceding
note.

Johnston 4

ago—decapitation, scalping, axe blows, and other nasty methods.[10] Indeed, articles are now available on wars in ancient Japan, Egypt, Greece,[11] and the Southwestern areas of the United States.[12]

The weapons, too, have been uncovered: clubs, arrowheads, bows, slings, daggers, maces, and spears. Each weapon graduated upon the previous and served new purposes as armies gathered for combat. One source points out that "the bow and the sling were important for hunting, but the dagger and mace were most useful for fighting other humans."[13] The spear required close combat. The bow and arrow had a range of about 100 yards. The sling was a significant weapon because in the right hands it was accurate from long distances and very powerful with stones that could crush skulls. The mace gave way to the battle axe to cut through armor. Then with copper, bronze, and finally iron, the sword gained great popularity and remains a weapon of choice even today.[14]

Horses, mules, and even elephants gave primitive armies mobility. Ultimately, however, the primary weapon was the soldier, and over time the ragged fighting groups were organized into armies that could march in columns and lay siege to other villages and cities. Accordingly, archeologists have examined

---

10. Nick Thorpe, "Origins of War: Mesolithic Conflict in Europe," *British Archaeology* 52 (2000), http://www.birtarch.ac.uk/ba/ba52/ba52feat.html.

11. See Donald Kagan and David Webster.

12. See LeBlanc, "Prehistory of Warfare," and also *Constant Battles*.

13. "Prehistoric Warfare," http://digilander.libero.it/tepec/prehistoric_warfare.htm.

14. Ibid.

Johnston 5

walls, pits, ditches, moats, and barriers of all sorts, even villages
with all the rooms built against each other, with access only
from the roof.[15] Fortress cities were built on mountaintops, as
with the Acropolis at Athens. And researchers have found an
ancient Peruvian city high atop a mountain peak in the Andes.[16]
Thus, archeologists have uncovered many offensive weapons but
also gigantic earthen defenses, and the Great Wall of China
springs forward as one great example.

Why fight? Many reasons have been advanced by different
researchers, and we can take our pick from quite a list as armies
went out in search of:

- Food, resources, water, and cattle
- Women for concubines and wives
- Slaves
- Sacrificial victims
- Gold, bronze, copper, and other valuable metals

And they fought to:

- Seek revenge.
- Protect and secure the best trade routes.
- Honor their God and their religion.
- Defend their honor.

John Shy argues that early people, like today, fought to protect
their culture and way of life.[17] Michael Adams says the four

> This section of the paper examines the causes for prehistoric wars.

---

15. LeBlanc, "Prehistory of Warfare," 20.

16. D.L. Parsell, "City Occupied by Inca Discovered on
Andean Peak in Peru," *National Geographic News*, 21 March 2002,
http://news.nationalgeographic.com/news/2002/03/0314_0318_v
ilcabamba.html.

17. John Shy, "The Cultural Approach to the History of War,"
Abstract, *The Journal of Military History* 57 (1993),
http://web4.infotrac.galegroup.com.

Johnston 6

principles used by the Allies in World War II would serve all armies of all times—"freedom from want, freedom from fear, freedom of speech, freedom of religion."[18] Thorpe offers this theory:

> My own belief is that warfare, in earliest prehistory, arose over matters of personal honour—such as slights, insults, marriages going wrong, or theft. In a small hunter-gatherer community, everyone is related. An attack on one group member is an attack on the whole family. A personal feud may quickly involve the whole community. From there it is a small step to war.[19]

Donald Kagan echoes that concept with his focus on the word *honor*: "If a state finds that its honor is at risk, that it is treated with contempt, the other two elements of the triad immediately become part of the story. Men get fearful that in light of this contempt others will take advantage and damage their real interests."[20] Yet I recall reading *Beowulf* for one of my classes, and Beowulf fought for *wergild* (money and riches), and he made no bones about it. Victory brings economic bonanzas. LaBlanc shows that ancient battles shifted from total annihilation of the enemy to economic control of villages, cities, and even large states. Conflict waged by complex societies results in a new twist. Warfare was controlled by the elite, and wealth and prestige began

Use the computer's standard indention for block quotations.

---

18. Michael Adams, "The 'Good War' Myth and the Cult of Nostagia," *The Midwest Quarterly* 40 (1998), http://web4.infotrac.galegroup.com.

19. Thorpe.

20. Donald Kagan, "History's Largest Lessons" [interview by Fredric Smoler], *American Heritage* 48 (1997), http://web4.infotrac.galegroup.com.

to play a role. The commoners became valuable as a means to supply wealth to the elite, so warfare began to include conquest instead of annihilation as a goal.[21] Thus, we must add "the search for wealth" as a prime reason for war in primitive times and also the present because it was whispered about George W. Bush's conquest of Iraq—he did it for the oil.

Ultimately, the key question about the cause of war, whether ancient or current, centers on one's choice between biology and culture. On the one side we have the historian, like Victor Hanson, who argues, "Culture largely determines how people fight. The degree to which a society embraces freedom, secular rationalism, consensual government, and capitalism often determines—far more than its geography, climate, or population—whether its armies will be successful over the long term."[22] Hanson adds, "No nation has ever survived once its citizenry ceased to believe that its culture was worth saving."[23]

The society as a whole wants to preserve its culture, in peace if possible. In 500 B.C. Herodotus said, "No one is so foolish that he prefers war to peace. In peace sons bury their fathers, in war fathers their sons."[24]

Yet, in my opinion (I have to reach my own conclusion here), the biological history of men and women suggests that we love a good fight. I recall reading an article that said twins

---

21. LeBlanc, *Constant Battles*, 194.

22. Victor Davis Hanson, "War Will Be War: No Matter the Era, No Matter the Weapons, and the Same Old Hell," *National Review* 54 (2002), http://web4.infotrac.galegroup.com.

23. Ibid.

24. Qtd. in Peter Jones, "Ancient and Modern," *Spectator* 291 (2003), http://web4.infotrac.galegroup.com.

Johnston 8

inside the womb actually fight, and one fetus might actually
devour or absorb the other one. Siblings just naturally fight, as I
did with my older sister and younger brother. His anger exploded
one time, and he broke my arm by hitting me with a shovel. We
all have witnessed the terrible fights at sporting events, and
recently at Glenbrook North High School in Northbrook, Illinois,
hazing turned into a terrible beating for some girls. Oh sure, we
can give reasons for our eagerness to fight--to preserve our
honor ("Don't diss me!"), to preserve our freedom ("Don't
encroach!"), or because of fear ("Don't hit me 'cause I'll be
hitting back even harder!"). Yet in a final analysis, people want
power over others--men beat their wives, mothers overly spank
their children, the better team overpowers an opponent, and,
yes, a larger, stronger nation will demolish another if self-
interest prevails.

The writer's conclusion connects his thesis to the modern emphasis on war and terrorism.

    This is human nature. The men of Al Queda who flew their
suicide missions into the World Trade Center and the Pentagon
knew exactly what they were doing—exercising their power. In
effect, they said, "We'll show the United States that we can
inflict great damage." Professor Donald Kagan observes:

> In the end what people really go to war about is power, by
> which I simply mean the ability to have their will prevail. . . .
> Every being and every nation requires power for two purposes.
> The first is to be able to do what it wishes to and must do,
> some of which will be good and perfectly natural things.
> Second, one needs power to keep others from imposing their
> will, to prevent evil things from being done.[25]

The sport of boxing continues to thrive, despite attempts to end
it because of its brutality. The fans have a vicarious thrill as one

---

25. Kagan.

Johnston 9

boxer gets pounded to the canvas. At NASCAR races the greatest shouts occur as the fenders crash and cars go tumbling topsy-turvy down the asphalt. The aggressive behavior of humans is not always a pretty sight, such as the eager willingness of some to loot and pilfer a neighborhood that has been hit by a tornado or other natural disaster.

At the same time, a country like ours governs itself, imposing order by law and moral behavior by religion.[26] Our government, our culture, and our sense of honor have prevailed in a world of nations gone berserk and lawless. Whether we should use our power to impose our sense of democracy on other countries is an international question without a clear answer. My brother, with the shovel in his hand, would say "yes."

---

26. When chaos develops, as in Baghdad during the 2003 war, lawless looting and violence emerge because neither the religious leaders nor an absent police force can maintain order. The breakdown of the culture opens a vacuum filled quickly by primitive behavior.

Bibliography

A separate bibliography is not required if you write initial footnotes with full data.

Adams, Michael. "The 'Good War' Myth and the Cult of Nostagia." *The Midwest Quarterly*, 40 (1998). http://web4.infotrac.galegroup.com.

Cooper, L. D. *Rousseau, Nature, and the Problem of the Good Life.* University Park: Pennsylvania State Univ. Press, 1999.

Ferrill, Arthur. "Neolithic Warfare," Frontline Educational Foundation. http://eserver.org/history/neolithic-war.txt.

Hanson, Victor Davis. "War Will Be War: No Matter the Era, No Matter the Weapons, and the Same Old Hell." *National Review*, 54 (2002). http://web4.infotrac.galegroup.com.

Harder, Ben. "Ancient Peru Torture Deaths: Sacrifices or War Crimes?" *National Geographic News*, 29 April 2002. http://news.nationalgeographic.com/news/2002/04/0425_020426_mochekillings.html.

Jones, Peter. "Ancient and Modern." *Spectator* 291 (2003). http://web4.infotrac.galegroup.com.

Kagan, Donald. "History's Largest Lessons." Interview by Fredric Smoler. *American Heritage* 48 (1997). http://web4.infotrac.galegroup.com.

LeBlanc, Steven A. *Constant Battles: The Myth of the Peaceful, Noble Savage.* New York: St. Martin's Press, 2004.

---. "Prehistory of Warfare," *Archaeology* May/June, 2003.

Parsell, D. L. "City Occupied by Inca Discovered on Andean Peak in Peru." *National Geographic News*, 21 March, 2002. http://news.nationalgeographic.com/news/2002/03/0314_0318_vilcabamba.html.

"Prehistoric Warfare." http://digilander.libero.it/tepec/prehistoric_warfare.htm.

Johnston 11

Shy, John. "The Cultural Approach to the History of War." *The Journal of Military History*, 57 (1993). http://web4.nfotrac.galegroup.com.

Thorpe, Nick. "Origins of War: Mesolithic Conflict in Europe." *British Archaeology* 52 (2000). http://www.birtarch.ac.uk/ba/ba52/ba52feat.html.

Webster, David. "Ancient Maya Warfare." In *War and Society in the Ancient and Medieval Worlds*. Ed. Kurt Raaflaub and Nathan Rosenstein. Cambridge, Massachusetts: Center for Hellenic Studies, 1999.

Yates, Robin. "Early China." In *War and Society in the Ancient and Medieval Worlds*. Ed. Kurt Raaflaub and Nathan Rosenstein. Cambridge, Massachusetts: Center for Hellenic Studies, 2001.

17 CSE Style for the Natural and Applied Sciences

The Council of Science Editors who produced the *CBE Style Manual* has established two forms for citing sources in scientific writing. One is the **citation-sequence** system for writing in the applied sciences, such as chemistry, computer science, mathematics, physics, and medicine. The second is the **name-year** system for use in the biological and earth sciences.

Citation-Sequence

> The original description (3) contained precise taxonomic detail that differed with recent studies (4-6).

Name-Year

> The original description (Roberts 1999) contained precise taxonomic detail that differed with recent studies (McCormick 2005a, 2005b, and Tyson and others 2004).

There are advantages and disadvantages to each system. The citation-sequence system saves space, and the numbers make minimal disruption to the reading of the text. But this system seldom mentions names, so readers must refer to the bibliography for the names of authors. Also, any disruption in the numbering sequence late in the composition may necessitate a renumbering of all references in the text and the bibliography.

The name-year system mentions authors' names in the text with the year to show timely application and historical perspective. Citations can be deleted or added without difficulty. But a long string of citations in the text can be more disruptive than numbers. In truth, the decision is usually not yours to make. The individual disciplines in the sciences have adopted one form or the other, as shown in the chart on page 367.

Guide by Discipline

Agriculture, Name-Year, 17c–17d
Anthropology, Name-Year, 17c–17d

Archaeology, Name-Year, 17c–17d
Astronomy, Name-Year, 17c–17d

Index to Bibliographic Models: CSE Style

17a Writing In-text Citations Using the CSE Citation-Sequence System

This system employs numbers to identify sources. Use this style with these disciplines: chemistry, computer science, mathematics, physics, and the medical sciences (medicine, nursing, and general health). In simple terms, the system requires an in-text *number,* rather than the year, and a list of References that are numbered to correspond to the in-text citations.

After completing a list of references, assign a number to each entry. Use one of two methods for numbering the list: (1) arrange references in alphabetical order and number them consecutively (in which case the numbers will appear in random order in the text), or (2) number the references consecutively as you put them into your text, interrupting that order when entering references cited earlier.

The number serves as the key to the source, as numbered in the References. Conform to the following regulations:

1. Place the number within parentheses (1) or brackets [2] or as a raised index numeral, like this.[5] A name is not required and is even discouraged, so try to arrange your wording accordingly. Full information on the author and the work will be placed in the references list.

   It is known (1) that the DNA concentration of a nucleus doubles during interphase.

   A recent study [1] has raised interesting questions related to photosynthesis, some of which have been answered [2].

   In particular, a recent study[1] has raised many interesting questions related to photosynthesis, some of which have been answered.[2]

2. If you include the authority's name, add the number after the name.

   Additional testing by Cooper (3) included alterations in carbohydrate metabolism and changes in ascorbic acid incorporation into the cell and adjoining membranes.

3. If necessary, add specific data to the entry:

   "The use of photosynthesis in this application is crucial to the environment" (Skelton,[8] p 732).

   The results of the respiration experiment published by Jones (3, Table 6, p 412) had been predicted earlier by Smith (5, Proposition 8).

17b   Writing a References Page

Supply a list of references at the end of your paper. Number the entries to correspond to sources as you cite them in the text. An alternate method is to alphabetize the list and then number it. Label the list *References*. The form of the entries should follow the examples shown below.

Book

Provide a number and then list the author, title of the book, place of publication, publisher, year, and total number of pages (optional).

1. Goldschneider G. The precision approach to charting your life, career, and relationships. Philadelphia: Running; 2005. 928 p.

Article in a Journal

Provide a number and then list the author, the title of the article, the name of the journal, the year and month if necessary, volume number and issue number if necessary, and inclusive pages. The month or an issue number is necessary for any journal that is paged anew with each issue (see item 3).

2. Christensen P. Burying the dead. Antioch Review 2005;63:697–718.

3. Monhanty S, Jayawardhana R. The mystery of brown dwarf origins. Scientific American 2006 Jan;294(1):38–45.

Internet Articles and Other Electronic Publications

Add at the end of the citation an availability statement as well as the date you accessed the material. Use the form in number 4 for an article published on the Web. Use the form in number 5 for a periodical article reproduced on the Web.

4. Shane-McWhorter L. Complementary and alternative medicine (CAM) in diabetes. Complementary and Alternative Medicine [article online] 2005. Available from http://www.childrenwithdiabetes. com/clinic/alternative. Accessed 2006 Feb 8.

5. Wade R, Vande Pol S. Minimal features of paxillin that are required for the tyrosine phosphorylation of focal adhesion kinase. Biochem J. [serial online] 2005;393:565–573. Available from http://www. biochemj.org/bj/393/0565/bj3930565.htm. Accessed 2006 May 18.

Magazine or Newspaper Article

Add a specific date and, for newspapers, cite a section letter or number.

6. Rosenwald M. The flu hunter. Smithsonian 2006 Jan:36–46.

7. [Anonymous]. Diesel fumes may cause harm to circulation. The [Nashville] Tennessean 2005 Dec27;Sect D:3.

Proceedings and Conference Presentations

After supplying a number, give the name of the author or editor, the title of the presentation, name of the conference, type of work (report, proceedings, proceedings online, etc.), name of the organization or society, the date of the conference, and the place. If found on the Internet, add the URL and the date you accessed the information.

> For a sample of a "References" page using the number system, see pages 384–385.

8. Sneden GG, Gottlieb-Nudd A, Gottlieb NH. Linking real data to a program assessment and feedback model in state tobacco prevention and control programs [abstract online]. In: Abstracts: 19th National Conference on Chronic Disease Prevention and Control; 2005 Mar 1–3; Atlanta(GA). Available from http://www.cdc.gov/nccdphp/ conference/pdf/ AbstractBook.pdf. Accessed 2006 Feb 18.

Article from a Loose-Leaf Collection

9. [Anonymous]. Mariculture: Farming on the coastal plains. HRRS Research Collection 2006;2:287.

17c Writing In-text Citations with Name and Year

The CSE Name-Year style applies to these disciplines:

Agriculture	Anthropology	Archaeology
Astronomy	Biology	Botany
Geography	Geology	Zoology

When writing research papers in accordance with the Name-Year system, conform to the following rules:

1. Place the year within parentheses immediately after the authority's name:

    Stroyka (2004) ascribes no species-specific behavior to man.

    However, Adamson (2005) presents data that tend to be contradictory.

2. If you do not mention the authority's name in your text, insert the name, year, and page numbers within the parentheses:

    One source found some supporting evidence for a portion of the questionable data (Marson & Brown 2005, pp 23-32) through point bi-serial correlation techniques.

3. For two authors, employ both names in your text and in the parenthetical citation:

> Torgerson and Andrews (2003)

or

> (Torgerson and Andrews 2003)

Note: Unlike APA style, the CSE style does not use the ampersand (&). For three or more authors, use the lead author's name with "and others." *Note:* CSE style prefers English terms and English abbreviations rather than Latin words and abbreviations, such as *et al.*

In the text: Torgerson and others (2005)
In the parenthetical citation: (Torgerson and others 2005)

4. Use lowercase letters (a, b, c) to identify two or more works published in the same year by the same author—for example, "Thompson (2003a)" and "Thompson (2006b)." Then use "2006a" and "2006b" in your List of References.
5. If necessary, supply additional information:

> Alretta (2004a, 2004b; cf. Thomas, 2005, p 89) suggests an
> intercorrelation of these testing devices. But after multiple-group
> analysis, Welston (2006, esp. p 211) reached an opposite conclusion.

6. In the case of a reference to a specific page, separate the page number from the year with a comma and a space. Do not use a period after the "p."
   a. A quotation or paraphrase in the middle of the sentence:

> Jones stated, "These data of psychological development
> suggest that retarded adolescents are atypical in maturational
> growth" (2005, p 215), and Jones attached the data that were
> accumulated during the study.

   b. A quotation or paraphrase that falls at the end of a sentence:

> Jones (2005) found that "these data of psychological
> development suggest that retarded adolescents are atypical in
> maturational growth" (p 215).

   c. A long quotation, indented with the tab key and set off from the text in a block (and therefore without quotation marks):

> Tavares (2004) found the following:
>> Whenever these pathogenic organisms attack the human
>> body and begin to multiply, the infection is set in motion.

> The host responds to this parasitic invasion with efforts to cleanse itself of the invading agents. When rejection efforts of the host become visible (fever, sneezing, congestion), the disease status exists. (pp 314–315)

7. Punctuate the citations according to the following stipulations:
   a. Use a comma followed by a space to separate citations of different references by the same author or authors in same-year or different-year references:

   > Supplemental studies (Johnson 2002a, 2002b, 2003) have shown. . . .

   > Supplemental studies (Randolph and Roberts 2002, 2003) have shown. . . .

   b. Use a comma to separate two authors of the same work who have the same surname.

   > (Ramirez SL, Montoya CB, and others 2005)

   Use commas with three or more authors:

   > (Smith, Jones, Thompson, and others 2003)

   c. Use a semicolon followed by a space to separate citations to different authors:

   > Supplemental studies (Smith, 2004; Barfield 1999, 2002; Barfield and Smith 2005; Wallace 2006) have shown. . . .

17d   Using Name-Year with Bibliography Entries

Alphabetize the list and label it *References*. Double-space the entries and use the hanging indention. When there are two to ten authors, all should be named in the reference listing. When there are eleven or more authors, the first ten are listed, followed by "and others." If the author is anonymous, insert "[Anonymous]." Place the year immediately after the author's name.

Article in a Journal

List the author, year, article title, journal title, volume number, and inclusive pages. Add an issue number for any journal that is paged anew with each issue.

Winickoff JP, Hillis VJ, Palfrey JS, Perrin JM, Rigotti NA. 2003. A smoking cessation intervention for parents of children who are hospitalized for respiratory illness: The Stop Tobacco Outreach

Program. Pediatrics 111:140–146.

Book

List the author, year, title, place of publication, publisher, and total number of pages (optional).

Winchester S. 2005. A crack in the edge of the world. New York:

HarperCollins. 464 p.

Internet Articles and Other Electronic Publications

Add at the end of the citation an availability statement as well as the date you accessed the material.

Schiber M. 2005 Dec 23. Building a better chemical trap. ScienceNOW

[online]. Available from http://sciencenow.sciencemag.org/cgi/

content/full/2005/1223/2. Accessed 2006 Jan 17.

Journal Article Reprinted on the Internet

Provide original publication data as well as the Internet address and the date you accessed the material. Label it as *serial online.*

Linker D. 2006. Heidegger's revelation: The end of enlightenment

[abstract]. American Behavioral Scientist. [serial online]; 49:

733–749. Available from http://abs.sagepub.com/cgi/content/

abstract/49/5/733. Accessed 2006 Apr 3.

Magazine or Newspaper Article

Add a specific date and, if listed, a section letter or number.

McDaniel A. 2006 Jan–Feb. The three R's of ecofashion. Utne 133:81.

Human K. 2005 Dec 27. Scientists leaping to make time. Denver Post A1.

Proceedings and Conference Publications

Give author, date, title of the presentation, name of conference, type of work (report, proceeding, proceedings online, etc.), name of the organization or society, and place of the conference. If found on the Internet, add the URL.

Sneden GG, Gottlieb-Nudd A, Gottlieb NH. 2005 Mar 1–3. Linking real

data to a program assessment and feedback model in state

tobacco prevention and control programs [abstract online]. In:

Abstracts: 19th National Conference on Chronic Disease

Prevention and Control; Atlanta(GA). Available from http:// www.cdc.gov/nccdphp/conference/pdf/AbstractBook.pdf. Accessed 2006 Feb 18.

Article from a Loose-Leaf Collection

[Anonymous]. 2006. Mariculture: Farming on the coastal plains. HRRS Research Collection 2:287.

Arranging the References List

The list of references should be placed in alphabetical order, as shown next.

References

[Anonymous]. 2006. Myths and facts about Perchlorate. Council on Water Quality. Available from http://www.councilonwaterquality. org/know/myths.html. Accessed 2006 Feb 22.

[Anonymous]. 2005. Perchlorate in California drinking water: Overview and links. California Department of Health Services. Available from http://www.dhs.ca.gov/ps/ddwem/chemicals/perchl/ perchlindex.htm. Accessed 2006 Feb 22.

Hogue C. 2005. Federal policy on perchlorate evolves. Chemical and Engineering News. Available from http://pubs.acs.org/cen/news/ 83/i39/8339perchlorate.html. Accessed 2006 Feb 21.

Logan BE, 2005. Simultaneous wastewater treatment and biological electricity generation. Water Science and Technology 52(1–2): 31–37.

Sanchez CA, Crump KS, Kreiger RI, Khandaker NR, Gibbs JP. 2005. Perchlorate and nitrate in leafy vegetables of north America. Environmental Science and Technology 39(24):9391–9397.

17e Sample Paper Using the CSE Citation-Sequence System

Student Sarah Bemis has researched problems with managing diabetes and presented the paper using the CSE citation-sequence system. As she cites a source in the text, she uses a number that also reappears on her References page. Accordingly, the references are not in alphabetical order. As is standard with writing in the sciences, an abstract is provided.

Diabetes Management:

A Delicate Balance

Balance the
title, name,
and
affiliation.

By

Sarah E. Bemis

English 103: College Writing

Sister Winifred Morgan, O.P.

5 March 2005

Bemis ii

Abstract

An abstract of
100–200
words states
the purpose,
scope, and
major
findings of
the report.

Diabetes affects approximately 11 million people in the U.
S. alone, leading to $350 billion in medical costs. Two types, I
and II, have debilitating effects. The body may tolerate
hyperglycemia for a short time, but severe complications can
occur, such as arterioscleroses, heart disease, nerve damage, and
cerebral diseases. New drugs continue to improve the life style of
a person with diabetes, but controlling blood sugar requires
three elements working together—medication, diet, and exercise.
This study examines the importance of each of the three. Patients
need a controlled balance of the medication, diet, and exercise
program.

Bemis 1

Diabetes Management: A Delicate Balance

Use a number to register the use of a source.

Diabetes is a disease that affects approximately 11 million people in the U.S. alone (1), and its complications lead to hundreds of thousands of deaths per year and cost the nation billions in medical care for the direct cost of complications and for indirect costs of lost productivity related to the disease. The condition can produce devastating side effects and a multitude of chronic health problems. For this reason, it can be very frightening to those who do not understand the nature and treatment of the disease. Diabetes currently has no known cure, but it can be controlled. Diabetes research has made great advancements in recent years, but the most important insights into the management of this disease are those which seem the most simplistic. By instituting a healthy, balanced lifestyle, most persons with diabetes can live free of negative side effects.

The thesis or hypothesis is expressed at the end of the introduction.

Scientific writing requires careful definition, as shown here.

More than one source can be listed for one idea or concept.

Diabetes mellitus, according to several descriptions, is a disorder in which the body cannot properly metabolize glucose or sugar. The body's inability to produce or properly use insulin permits glucose to build up in the bloodstream. The excess sugar in the blood, or hyperglycemia, is what leads to the side effects of diabetes (2,3,4).

There are actually two types of diabetes. Type 1, or juvenile diabetes, is the name given to the condition in which the pancreas produces very little or no insulin. It is normally discovered during childhood, but can occur at any age (3). Adult onset, or Type II diabetes, occurs when the pancreas produces usable insulin, but not enough to counteract the amount of glucose in the blood. This often results from obesity or poor diet.

In both Type I and Type II diabetes, the problem has been identified as hyperglycemia (5). This buildup of glucose in the

Bemis 2

bloodstream leads to a number of dangerous side effects. The initial effects and indicators of hyperglycemia are frequent urination, intense thirst, increased hunger and fatigue. When glucose begins to build up in the blood, the kidneys begin to filter out the excess sugar into the urine. The amount of glucose the kidneys can filter varies with each person. In this process, all the water in the body's tissues is being used to produce urine to flush glucose from the kidneys. This is what leads to the intense thirst and frequent urination associated with hyperglycemia (5).

Causal analysis, as shown here, is a staple of scientific writing.

Because the body lacks the insulin needed to allow glucose into the cells, the glucose cannot be processed to produce energy. The cells signal the brain that they are not getting sugar and this causes hunger. However, no matter how much a victim of hyperglycemic diabetes eats, the cells will not be producing energy (6).

It has been shown (4) that with hyperglycemia the kidneys try to compensate for the excess of sugar and lack of energy. While the kidneys attempt to filter the sugar from the blood, the liver tries to produce energy by burning fat and muscle to produce ketones, a protein that the body attempts to burn in place of glucose. Ketones do not provide the energy the body requires but do produce chemicals toxic to the body. When too many ketones are present in the blood, kentoacidosis occurs (4).

Refer to the sources with the past tense verb or the present participle.

Guthrie and Guthrie (1) have demonstrated that ketoacidosis is a condition caused by high levels of hydrogen in the blood. This leads initially to a high blood pH, depleted saline fluids and dehydration. If untreated it can lead to a shut down of the central nervous system, coma or even death. In fact, many diabetes-related deaths are caused by ketoacidosis that has reached a comatose state. Ketoacidosis is characterized by

In addition to the number, you may mention the name(s) of your sources.

Bemis 3

frequent urination, dry mouth, extreme thirst, headache, rapid and deep respiration, increased heart rate, nausea, vomiting, disorientation. and lethargy (1).

The American Academy of Family Physicians (4) has reported that hyperglycemia can cause other, more subtle, side effects. Because the body is not receiving the nourishment it requires, a victim of hyperglycemic diabetes often experiences poor tissue growth and repair. This can cause problems with growth and development in children and wound healing in adults as well as children. It has also been reported (7) that the immune system is also affected and that victims experience infection more often and more severely than a person without diabetes. Other conditions that frequently occur in conjunction with hyperglycemia in its early stages are depression and chronic fatigue (8). Many patients who experience hypoglycemia have difficulties controlling gain and loss of weight as well.

It has been shown (Guthrie and Guthrie 1) that the body may tolerate hyperglycemia over a short time period. However, if untreated, it leads to other chronic and often fatal health conditions. Arterioscleroses occurs in hyperglycemic diabetics over time, resulting in decreased circulation and eyesight. This also may lead to heart disease, angina and heart attack, the most prevalent causes of death among diabetics (1). Also common is diabetic neuropathy, a degeneration of the nerves. This condition causes pain and loss of function in the extremities (1).

A person with diabetes is also at risk for many cerebral diseases. Both the large and small cerebral arteries of victims are prone to rupture, which can cause cerebral hemorrhage, thrombosis or stroke. Blockages in the carotid arteries can decrease blood flow to the brain, causing episodes of lightheadedness and fainting (1, p 201-202).

You may add page numbers to the reference as a courtesy to the reader.

Diabetic nephropathy occurs when the kidneys are overloaded with glucose. Eventually, they begin to shut down. The kidneys of a person with uncontrolled diabetes are also susceptible to infection, resulting in decreased kidney function (1).

With all the complications victims experience, the outlook for a long and healthy life does not seem good for those diagnosed with the disease. However, all of these effects can be reduced, delayed, and even prevented with proper care and control. By monitoring blood sugar and reacting accordingly with medication, by special diets, and by exercise and a controlled lifestyle, persons with diabetes can avoid these serious health conditions (Hu and others 9).

The first aspect of diabetes care is blood sugar monitoring and medication. The two go hand in hand in that the patient must have the appropriate type and dosage of medication and must know blood sugar values and patterns in order to determine the correct regimen. Two main types of monitoring are necessary for diabetes control. Patients must perform home glucose monitoring on a daily basis. Advancements in this area in recent years have made this relatively effortless. Several glucose monitoring kits are available to the general public. These consist of a small, electronic machine that measures the amount of glucose in the blood, as well as the equipment necessary to obtain a small sample. With such equipment, patients can test and record blood sugars several times per day. This gives both short-term and long-term information by which they and their physicians can determine insulin dosages and meal plans.

Process analysis, as shown here, is often a staple of scientific writing.

In addition to daily monitoring, victims should visit their physician regularly. Doctors usually perform a test called a hemoglobin AIC, which gives a better indication of blood sugar control over a longer period of time than a home test. This

Bemis 5

should be done approximately every ninety days, as that is the time period over which blood cells are renewed. This test along with consideration of daily glucose values can help the physician determine overall control and effectiveness of the patient's routine. Regular visits also give the physician an opportunity to monitor the general health of the patient, including circulation, eyesight, infections, and organ infections.

The treatment of diabetes usually involves medication. Since Type I diabetics produce very little or no insulin, insulin injections will always be necessary. For Type II, the treatment may be strictly dietary, dietary with oral hypoglycemic agents, or insulin therapy.

The writer explores control element number one: methods of administering medication.

When insulin therapy is required, it is very important that the appropriate type and dosage is implemented. Many types of insulin are available. The main distinction among these types is in their action time, onset, peak-time, and duration. Different types of insulin begin to act at different rates. They also continue to act for different periods of time and hit peak effectiveness at different intervals (1). This is why it is important to have records of blood sugars at regular intervals over several weeks. From this it can be determined when and what type of insulin is needed most. Once it is determined what insulin regimen is appropriate, the patient must follow it closely. Routine is very important in controlling diabetes.

Patients with diabetes now have a few options when it comes to injection method. One may chose traditional manual injection, an injection aid, or an insulin pump. Injection aids can make using a needle easier and more comfortable or actually use air pressure to inject. The insulin pump is a device that offers convenience as well as improved control. The pump is a small battery-operated device that delivers insulin 24 hours a day through a small needle worn under the skin. The pump contains a computer chip which controls the amount of insulin delivered according to the wearer's personalized plan (10). The pump is meant for patients who do not wish to perform multiple injections, but are willing to test blood sugars frequently. The pump can help patients who have some trouble controlling their blood sugars by providing insulin around the clock. It also provides an element of freedom for persons with busy schedules.

Some type II patients can control the disease with a combination of diet, exercise and an oral hypoglycemic agent. These drugs themselves contain no insulin. They traditionally lower blood glucose levels by stimulating the pancreas to produce insulin (1). Therefore, they are only appropriate for patients whose pancreas is still producing some insulin. Diabetes research has advanced in recent years, however. Some new drugs may be coming available in the new millennium. Creators of the pharmaceuticals are able to increase sensitivity to insulin and suppress the secretion of hormones that raise blood sugar. A number of new drugs that are aimed at taking the place of insulin therapy are currently in the final stages of research and development. Glucovance has been advanced as a valuable new medication (11). For now, the oral medications that are available can aid in keeping better control when properly paired with an effective diet and exercise plan.

While it is important to have the proper medication, the backbone of diabetes management is the meal plan. By making wise choices in eating, persons with diabetes can reduce stress on the body and increase the effectiveness of their medication. The basis of a good meal plan is balanced nutrition and moderation. Eating a low fat, low sodium, low sugar diet is the best way for a diabetic to ensure longevity and health. It is important for everyone to eat balanced meals on a routine

The writer now explores control element number two: methods of diet management.

schedule. For victims of diabetes, it can help in blood sugar control and in preventing heart disease and digestive problems.

Two established meal plans are recommended for patients: the Exchange Plan and carbohydrate counting (12, 13). Both are based on The Diabetes Food Pyramid (Nutrition). The Food Pyramid divides food into six groups. These resemble the traditional four food groups, except that they are arranged in a pyramid in which the bottom, or largest, section contains the foods that should be eaten most each day. The top, or smallest, section contains the foods that should be eaten least, if at all. With any diabetic meal plan, the patient should eat a variety of foods from all the food groups, except the sweets, fats, and alcohol group. New directives by the American Diabetes Association offer helpful and authoritative guidance to help victims cope with their meal planning (14, 15).

The Exchange Plan provides a very structured meal plan. Foods are divided into eight categories, which are more specific than those of the Food Pyramid are. A dietician or physician determines a daily calorie range for the patient and, based on that range, decides how many servings she or he should eat from each category per meal. Portion sizes are determined and must be followed exactly. The patient then has the option to either choose foods that fit into the groups recommended for each meal or exchange foods from one group for foods from another.

Another meal plan patients can utilize is carbohydrate counting. This plan is less structured and gives the patient more flexibility in making meal choices. It also involves less planning. Once again, food is categorized, but into only three groups. The largest food group, carbohydrates, encompasses not only starches, but dairy products, fruits, and vegetables as well. The dietician or physician again assigns a calorie range. With this plan, however,

Bemis 8

only the number of carbohydrates per meal are assigned, and even this is flexible. This plan is recommended for those who know how to make balanced meal choices, but need to keep track of their food intake. Once again, portion sizes are important, and the patient must remember to eat the recommended amount of foods from each pyramid category (5, 11, 12).

The final element in successfully managing diabetes is exercise. It has been shown (16) that exercise can help stimulate the body to use glucose for energy, thus taking it out of the blood. Diabetic patients need regular exercise programs that suit their personal needs. Something as simple as a walking routine can significantly reduce blood glucose levels (16). Some patients may require as little as a fifteen-minute per day walk, where some may need a more involved workout. In each case, an exercise schedule works with meal plans, medication, and lifestyle. Also crucial to the success of an exercise routine is close monitoring of blood sugar. If glucose levels are too high or too low, exercise will have negative effects.

All of the aspects of diabetes management can be summed up in one word: balance. Diabetes itself is caused by a lack of balance of insulin and glucose in the body. In order to restore that balance, a person with diabetes must juggle medication, monitoring, diet, and exercise. Managing diabetes is not an easy task, but a long and healthy life is very possible when the delicate balance is carefully maintained.

The writer now explores control element number three: methods of exercise.

References

Citations on this page demonstrate the citation-sequence method, as explained on pages 368–370. For details on the name-year system, see pages 372–374.

1. Guthrie DW, Guthrie RA. Nursing management of diabetes mellitus. New York: Springer, 2002. 500 p.

2. [Anonymous]. Diabetes insipidus. American Academy of Family Physicians. Available from http://www.aafp.org/patientinfo/ insipidu.html. Accessed 2006 Feb 20.

3. Clark CM, Fradkin JE, Hiss RG, Lorenz RA, Vinicor F, Warren-Boulton E. Promoting early diagnosis and treatment of type 2 diabetes. JAMA 2000;284:363–365.

4. [Anonymous]. Diabetes: Monitoring your blood sugar level. American Academy of Family Physicians. Available from http://familydoctor.org/355.xml. Accessed 2006 Feb 19.

5. Peters AL. Conquering diabetes. New York: Penguin, 2005. 368 p.

6. Schlosberg S. The symptoms you should never ignore. Shape 2000 Aug;19:136–142.

7. Inzucchi S. Diabetes Mellitus Manual. New York: McGraw-Hill, 2004. 360 p.

8. Roberts SS. The diabetes advisor. Diabetes Forecast 2005;58(11):41–42. Available from http://www.diabetes.org/ diabetes-forecast/nov2005/toc.jsp. Accessed 2006 Feb 18.

9. Hu FB, Li TY, Colditz GA, Willett WC, Manson JE. Television watching and other sedentary behaviors in relation to risk of obesity and type 2 diabetes mellitus in women. JAMA 2003; 289:1785–91.

10. [Anonymous]. Insulin pump therapy. Children with Diabetes 2005. Available from http://www.childrenwithdiabetes.com/pumps/. Accessed 2006 Feb 21.

11. [Anonymous]. Glucophage. Diabetes Healthsource. 2005. Available from http://www.glucophage.com. Accessed 2006 Feb 23.

12. McDermott MT. Endocrine Secrets. New York: Elsevier, 2004. 448 p.

13. Eades MR, Eades MD. Protein Power. New York: Warner, 2001. 464 p.

Bemis 10

14. American Diabetes Association. The American diabetes association complete guide to diabetes. New York: McGraw-Hill; 2005. 518 p.

15. American Diabetes Association. Magic Menus for people with diabetes. Alexandria, VA: ADA; 2003. 244 p.

16. [Anonymous]. Exercise. American Diabetes Association [article online] 2006. Available from http://www.diabetes.org/weightloss-and-exercise/exercise/overview.jsp. Accessed 2006 Feb 22.

18 Creating Electronic Research Projects

This chapter suggests ways to create and publish your research project electronically. It begins with the easiest—putting a word-processed research paper on a disk for your instructor—and moves to the most difficult—designing a Web site and releasing the paper onto the Internet. This chapter will give you a sense of the possibilities of electronic research papers.

Creating your research paper electronically has a number of advantages:

- **It is easy.** Creating electronic research projects can be as simple as saving your paper in a computer file and publishing your paper electronically.
- **It offers multimedia potential.** Unlike paper documents, electronic documents enable you to include anything available in a digital form—including text, illustrations, sound, and video.
- **It can link your reader to more information.** Your readers can click a hyperlink to access additional sources of information. (A **hyperlink** or link is a highlighted word or image that, when clicked, lets readers jump from one place to another—for example, from your research paper to a Web site on your subject.)

18a Beginning the Electronic Project

Before you decide to create your research paper electronically, consider three questions to assist the development of the presentation:

1. **What support is provided by your school?** Most institutions have made investments in technology and the personnel to support it. Investigate how your college will help you publish in an electronic medium.
2. **Is electronic publishing suitable for your research topic?** Ask yourself what your readers will gain from reading an electronic text rather than the traditional paper version. Will an electronic format really help you get your ideas to readers?
3. **What form will it take?** Electronic research papers appear generally in one of the following forms:
   - A word processed document (see section 18b)
   - An electronic slide show (see section 18c)
   - A Web site (see section 18d)

Each of these forms can be researched and produced using traditional methods, but the writing and presentation will differ.

18b Using Word Processing

The easiest way to create an electronic document is by using word processing programs such as Microsoft Word or Corel Word Perfect and then distributing your report in its electronic form rather than printing it out.

Most popular word processing programs include tools for handling features that will enhance your presentation:

- **Graphics.** Word processors can accommodate graphics in a variety of formats, including .gif and .jpg (see section 18f for more information on graphic formats).
- **Sound and Video.** Word processors can include several common audio and video clip formats. Usually, the reader has to click on an icon to activate the clip.
- **Hyperlinks.** Readers can click to go to a Web site on the Internet for further reading.

There are unique advantages when using a word processor to create an electronic research paper. Using a word processor is familiar; you probably already use one to create your traditional research papers. It is also flexible; word processors give you more control over format and design.

However, using a word processor to create your electronic research paper has two disadvantages: The computer file created by your word processor can become quite large if you include graphics, sound, and video. Also, to view your paper, readers must own the same word processing software and sometimes even the same version of the software. Nevertheless, a word processor works well in a classroom or computer laboratory that shares the same software.

18c Building Electronic Presentations

If you plan an oral presentation, an electronic slide show can help illustrate your ideas. Electronic presentations differ from word-processed documents in that each page, or slide, comprises one computer screen. By clicking, you can move to the next slide.

The most common programs for creating electronic presentations are Microsoft PowerPoint and Corel Presentations. Both help you create a series of slides for presentation on your computer screen or through a projector to a large screen. These programs allow you to include graphics, sound, and other elements. More complex, stand-alone presentations with multimedia animation—designed for distribution on CD-ROM or through the Internet—can be created with programs such as Macromedia Director and Hyperstudio.

For small audiences you can usually present the show on a computer screen. For larger audiences, you may need a wide-screen television or a data projector. Check with your instructor or school technology specialist to find out what presentation equipment is available.

As you create your electronic presentation, consider the following suggestions:

- Because each slide can hold only limited information, condense the content of each slide to key points and fill in the details orally.
- Use the slide show to support your oral presentation.
- If appropriate, include graphics from your research project in your slide show.
- End the slide show with a carefully designed closing slide or an empty slide so that people will know the presentation is finished.

If you distribute the slide show by disk, CD, or the Web, you will probably need to adjust the presentation by adding more information to the slides because your oral commentary will be unavailable to the viewer—or you can record your audio commentary for inclusion with the presentation.

18d Research Paper Web Pages and Sites

A Web site can be an exciting and flexible way to convey your research. It is also the easiest way to get your work out to a large audience. Like an electronic presentation, a research paper Web site can include graphics, sound, and video.

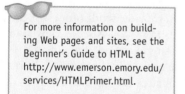

For more information on building Web pages and sites, see the Beginner's Guide to HTML at http://www.emerson.emory.edu/services/HTMLPrimer.html.

Creating a Web page or a Web site involves collecting or making a series of computer files— some that contain the basic text and layout for your pages, and others that contain the graphics, sounds, or video that goes in your pages. These files are assembled together automatically when you view them in a Web browser.

Creating a Single Web Page

If you want to create a single Web page from your research paper, the easiest but most limited method is to save your word-processed research paper in HTML (Hyper Text Markup Language, the computer language that controls what Web sites look like). Different word processing programs perform this process differently; so consult your software's help menu for specific instructions.

When the word processing software converts your document to HTML, it also converts any graphics you have included to separate graphics files. Together, your text and the graphics can be viewed in a Web browser like any other Web page.

Your research paper will look somewhat different in HTML format than in its word-processed format. In some ways, HTML is less flexible than word processing, but you can still use word processing software to make changes to your new HTML-formatted paper.

NOTE: The reader will need to scroll down the screen to continue to read the document.

Creating a Web Site with Multiple Pages

A multiple-page Web site allows you to assemble a large number of shorter pages, which are easy for readers to access and read. It requires careful planning and organization.

Creating a multipage Web site means creating one Web page after another—you repeat the basic process to create each page, and you add links between pages so readers can navigate easily from one to the next. Start with a home page that includes a title, a basic description of your project, and an index with hyperlinks to the contents of your site. Navigational elements, like links to the home page and other major pages of your site, provide a way for readers to "turn the pages" of your report.

Using an Editor to Create Web Pages

The easiest way to create your pages is with a Web page editor such as Microsoft FrontPage, Adobe Page Mill, or Netscape Composer. These programs work differently, but they all do the same thing—create Web pages. Using them is like using a word processor: you enter or paste in text, insert graphics or other multimedia objects, and save the file.

Importing, Entering, and Modifying Text

You can create your text within the Web page editor or outside it. To import text, simply copy it from your word processor and paste it into your Web page editor. You can also specify fonts, font sizes, font styles (such as bold), alignment, lists with bullets, and numbered lists. Here are a few tips for entering text into a Web page:

- **Use bold rather than underlining for emphasis and titles.** On a Web site, links are underlined, so any other underlining will cause confusion.
- **Do not use tabs.** HTML does not support tabs for indenting the first line of a paragraph. You also will not be able to use hanging indents for your bibliography.
- **Do not double space.** The Web page editor automatically single spaces lines of text and double spaces between paragraphs.
- **Make all lines flush left** on the Works Cited Page; HTML does not support the hanging indentions.

Citing Your Sources in a Web Research Paper

If you are using MLA, APA, or CSE styles, include parenthetical citations in the text itself and create a separate Web page for references. Remember to include such a page in your plans. Do not put footnotes at the bottom of each of your Web pages. Instead, use endnotes and create a separate page that holds all of the notes, just as you would have a separate page for the Works Cited or References pages. Create each note number in the text as a link to the notes page so readers can click on the number to go to the note. Remember to have a link on the notes page or Works Cited page to take the reader back again to the text.

18e Planning Electronic Research Papers

Because creating an electronic research paper can be more complicated than creating a traditional paper, it's important to plan your project carefully.

Creating a Plan for Your Research Paper

The following questions will help you think through the planning of your project.

- **Assignment.** Does your instructor have specific requirements for this assignment you should keep in mind?
- **Project description.** What topic will you be writing on?
- **Purpose.** What are your reasons for creating an electronic project? Are you going to blend photographs of the 1960s with an essay on the Civil Rights Movement? Or provide audio examples in an essay on John F. Kennedy's speeches?
- **Audience.** Are you writing for the instructor, or will there be a broader audience, such as classmates or readers on the Web?
- **Format.** Will your research paper be a word-processed document, an electronic presentation, or a Web site?
- **Multimedia content.** What information, other than text, will you present? Do you have the tools available to scan or import multimedia?
- **Structure.** How will you organize your document?

Designing Your Electronic Research Paper

Reading any kind of electronic document can be difficult for the reader unless you take special care in designing it. Aim for the following:

- **A consistent look and feel.** Make your research paper look very consistent throughout. Presentation software usually includes ready-made templates that help you to create a consistent look and feel.
- **A subtle design.** It is easy to create a Web site or presentation that includes all the bells and whistles—but such documents are hard to navigate and even harder to read. Avoid distractions like blinking text, garish colors, or unnecessary animations.
- **Ease of navigation.** Include consistent navigation tools so readers can see where they are and where they can go next.
- **Legibility.** Because readers often access electronic documents through a computer screen, legibility is important. Make

For more information on Web site design, see the Yale C/AIM WWW Style Guide at http://cal. bemidjistate.edu/webtraining/ YaleManual/contents.html.

the contrast between your text and background colors strong enough that readers can see the text easily. Avoid using the italic fonts, which are difficult to see on a computer screen.

18f Using Graphics in Your Electronic Research Paper

Graphics will give your electronic text some exciting features that are usually foreign to the traditional research paper. They go beyond words on a printed page to pictures, sound, video clips, animation, and a vivid use of full-color art.

Decorative graphics make the document look more attractive but seldom add to the paper's content. Most clip art, for example, is decorative.

Illustration graphics provide a visual amplification of the text. For example, a picture of Thomas Hardy would reinforce and augment a research paper on the British poet and novelist.

Information graphics, such as charts, graphs, or tables, provide data about your topic.

Graphic File Formats

Graphics usually take up a lot of space, but you can save them as either JPEG or GIF files to make them smaller. In fact, Web sites can use only graphics saved in these formats. Both formats compress redundant information in a file, making it smaller while retaining most of the image quality. You can recognize the file format by looking at the extension to the file name—GIFs have the extension .gif, and JPEGs have the extension .jpg or jpeg. GIF stands for Graphical Interchange Format, which develops and transfers digital images. JPEG stands for Joint Photographic Experts Group, which compresses color images to smaller files for ease of transport.

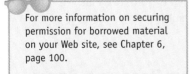

For more information on JPEG and GIF files, go to one of these sites:
Wide Area Communications at http://www.widearea.co.uk/designer/compress.html
Graphics 101 at About.com, at http://graphicdesign.about.com/

For more information on securing permission for borrowed material on your Web site, see Chapter 6, page 100.

In general, JPEGs work best for photographs and GIFs work best for line drawings. To save a file as a GIF or JPEG, open it in an image-editing program like Adobe Photoshop and save the file as one of the two types (for example, thardy.jpg or thardy.gif).

When the graphic is ready, you can insert it into your electronic research paper. Programs usually have specific menu commands for inserting graphics; refer to your user documentation to find out how to do so.

You can also borrow images from clip art or other Web sites (with proper documentation, of course). To borrow an image, go to the site with your Web browser, right-click on the image that you want, and left-click on "Save image as . . ." to put it on your hard drive. You can then insert the image into your research paper.

Creating Your Own Digital Graphics

Making your own graphics file is complex but rewarding. It adds a personal creativity to your research paper. Use one of the following techniques:

- **Use a graphics program**, such as Macromedia Freehand or Adobe Illustrator. With such software you can create a graphic file and save it as a JPEG or GIF.
- **Use a scanner** to copy your drawings, graphs, photographs, and other matter. Programs such as Adobe Photoshop and JASC Paintshop Pro are useful for modifying scanned photographs.
- **Create original photographs with a digital camera.** Digital cameras usually save images as JPEGs, so you will not need to convert the files into a usable format.

As long as you create JPEG files or GIF files for your graphics, you can transport the entire research paper to a Web site.

18g Using Sound and Video in Your Electronic Research Paper

Because it usually requires additional hardware and software, working with sound and video can be complicated. It also makes your research paper large and difficult to compress and transfer. Before attempting to use digital audio or video, check into your own resources as well as that of your instructor and school. Many institutions have invested heavily in multimedia technology, while others have not.

> For information on digital audio and video, consult the following Web sites:
> Builder.com, at http://www.builder.com/graphics
> Webmonkey's multimedia tutorial for audio and video resources, at http://www.webmonkey.com/multimedia/

A detailed discussion of digital audio and video is beyond the scope of this chapter, but the Web holds a wealth of information on the subject.

18h Delivering Your Electronic Research Paper to Readers

Follow your instructor's requirements for delivering your electronic research paper or use one of the techniques in the following checklist.

CHECKLIST

Delivering Your Electronic Research Paper

- **Disk.** Disks are a convenient way to share information. However, they are unreliable, and papers with graphics, sound, or video may not fit on a disk.

- **Zip disk.** A Zip disk or other proprietary format will hold much larger files, but your reader/professor must own a drive that can read it.

- **CD-ROM disks.** These disks hold large amounts of data and thus work well for transmitting graphics, sound, or video files. However, you must own or have access to a CD-R (Compact Disk Recordable) or CD-RW (Compact Disk Recordable/Writeable) drive. Most readers will have regular CD-ROM drives that can read your disks, but you might want to confirm this beforehand.

- **High-Speed USB Flash Drive.** These devices hold large amounts of data, so they work well for transmitting graphics, sound, or video files. Its compact size and plug and play operation allows easy access to your instructor's laptop or desktop computer with a USB port.

- **E-mail.** E-mailing your file as an attachment is the fastest way to deliver your electronic research paper; however, it works best if you have a single file, like a word-processed research paper, rather than a collection of related files, like a Web site.

- **Web site.** If you have created a Web site or Web page, you can upload your work to a Web server, and readers can access your work on the Internet. Procedures for uploading Web sites vary from school to school and server to server; work closely with your instructor and Webmaster to perform this process successfully. Regardless of what method you choose, be sure to follow your instructor's directions and requirements.

18i Presenting Research in Alternative Formats

Current technology provides various options for presenting your research project. Desktop publishing programs such as Microsoft Publisher, Adobe PageMaker, or Broderbund Print Shop provide templates for the effective design of newsletters and brochures. Consider an alternative format for your findings when information inform or assist a broad array of readers.

Often printed on both sides of a sheet of paper, **newsletters** usually contain multiple pages. **Brochures** are formatted with columns or "panels" that are designed to fit on the front and back of one single sheet of paper so that it can easily be folded. Both newsletters and brochures follow certain conventions of style:

- Place your information in a logical order.
- Use a type size, font style, and color of text that is easy to read.
- Use a left justified formatting that leaves a "ragged" right-hand margin. This is a style that is easier for readers to follow.
- Avoid distracting gaps between words and awkward hyphens dividing words at the end of lines.
- Keep paragraphs short when information is presented in columns.

For most class projects, newsletters and brochures can be printed from your personal computer. For documents in the workplace or for a social group, you may choose to consider using a professional printer; however, remember that a print agency will charge for its services.

Alternative formats for the presentation of your research, such as newsletters and brochures, should stimulate interest and highlight the key components of the project.

CHECKLIST

Publishing Alternative Documents

- Decide on the purpose of the document and the response that your want the audience to have about the information.
- Sketch out or visualize how each section or panel will look.
- Select a paper size, binding, or folding that presents your research in a straightforward, clear method.
- Consider graphics, colors, and formatting that add to the clarity of your document.
- Use a distinctive font in the masthead or title as well as headlines for the sections of the document that emphasize their importance.
- Make each section or panel an independent item that can be understood if the brochure is folded or turned to a secondary page.
- Limit information to what readers can comprehend in a brief reading, while informing them where more information can be found.

YOUR RESEARCH PROJECT

1. If you are interested in producing an electronic research paper, consult with your instructor for advice and to learn about institutional support.

2. Begin by building a basic model with word processing, one that might include graphics and other elements as described in section 18f.

3. If the assignment includes an oral presentation, consider building a slide show as described in 18c.

4. Try building a Web page and then a Web site. Consult with your instructor before uploading it to the Web.

5. Make yourself comfortable about your knowledge of technical terms such as Zip disk, CD-ROM, USB flash drive, e-mail, and Web site.

Glossary

Rules and Techniques
for Preparing the Manuscript
in MLA Style

The alphabetical glossary that follows will answer most of your questions about matters of form, such as margins, pagination, dates, and numbers. For matters not addressed below, consult the index, which will direct you to appropriate pages elsewhere in this text.

Abbreviations

Employ abbreviations often and consistently in notes and citations, but avoid them in the text. In your citations, but not in your text, always abbreviate these items:

- technical terms and reference words (anon., e.g., diss.).
- institutions (acad., assn., Cong.).
- dates (Jan., Feb.).
- states and countries (OH, CA, U.S.A.).
- names of publishers (McGraw, UP of Florida).
- titles of well-known religious and literary works.

See also "Names of Persons," page A-5, for comments on abbreviations of honorary titles.

A few general rules apply:

1. With abbreviations made up of capital letters, use neither periods nor spaces:
   MS   JD   CD-ROM   AD
2. Do use periods and a space with initials used with personal names:
   J. K. Rowlings   T. S. Eliot

Abbreviations Commonly Used for Technical Terms and Institutions

abr.	abridged
anon.	anonymous
art., arts.	article(s)
bibliog.	bibliography, bibliographer, bibliographic
bk. bks.	book(s)
ca., c.	*circa* 'about'; used to indicate an approximate date, as in "ca. 1812"
cf.	*confer* 'compare' (one source with another); not, however, to be used in place of "see" or "see also"
ch., chs.	chapter(s), also shown as chap., chaps.
col., cols.	column(s)
doc.	document
ed., eds.	editor(s), edition, or edited by
et al.	*et alii* 'and others'; "John Smith et al." means John Smith and other authors
f., ff.	page or pages following a given page
ibid.	*ibidem* 'in the same place,' i.e., in the immediately preceding title, normally capitalized and underlined as in "<u>Ibid.</u>, p. 34"
i.e.	*id est* 'that is'; preceded and followed by a comma
loc. cit.	*loco citato* 'in the place (passage) cited'
ms., mss.	manuscript(s) as in "(Cf. the mss. of Glass and Ford)"

narr.	narrated by
n.d.	no date (in a book's title or copyright pages)
n.p.	no place (of publication)
n. pag.	no page
ns	new series
op. cit.	*opere citato* 'in the work cited'
p., pp.	page(s); do not use "ps." for "pages"
proc.	proceedings
qtd.	quoted
rev.	revised, revised by, revision, review, or reviewed by
rpt.	reprint, reprinted
ser.	series
sic	'thus'; placed in brackets to indicate an error has been made in the quoted passage and the writer is quoting accurately.
supp.	supplement(s)
trans., (tr.)	translator, translated, translated by, or translation
vol., vols.	volume(s) (e.g., vol. 3)

Abbreviations of Publishers' Names

Use the shortened forms below as guidelines for shortening all publishers names for MLA citations (but *not* for APA, CMS, or CSE styles).

Abrams	Harry N. Abrams, Inc.
Barnes	Barnes and Noble Books
Farrar	Farrar, Straus and Giroux
MIT P	The MIT Press
U of Chicago P	University of Chicago Press

Abbreviations of Biblical Works

Use parenthetical documentation for biblical references in the text—that is, place the entry within parentheses immediately after the quotation. For example:

> He hath shewed thee, O man, what is good; and what doth the LORD
> require of thee, but to do justly, and to love mercy, and to walk humbly with thy
> God? (Mic. 6:8).

Do not italicize or underline titles of books of the Bible. Abbreviate books of the Bible, except some very short titles, such as Ezra and Mark, as shown in these examples.

Acts	Acts of the Apostles	Matt.	Matthew
1 and 2 Chron.	1 and 2 Chronicles	Num.	Numbers
1 and 2 Cor.	1 and 2 Corinthians	Obad.	Obadiah
Deut.	Deuteronomy	Ps. (Pss.)	Psalm(s)

Abbreviations for Literary Works

Shakespeare

In parenthetical documentation, use italicized or underscored abbreviations for titles of Shakespearean plays, as shown in this example:

MIRANDA O, wonder!
How many goodly creatures are there here!
How beauteous mankind is! O brave new world,
That has such people in't! (*Tmp.* 5.1.181–184).

Abbreviate as shown by these examples:

Ant.	*Antony and Cleopatra*	*JC*	*Julius Caesar*
AWW	*All's Well That Ends Well*	*Lr.*	*Lear*
F1	*First Folio Edition (1623)*	*Mac*	*Macbeth*
H5	*Henry V*	*MND*	*A Midsummer's Night Dream*

Chaucer

Abbreviate in parenthetical documentation as shown by these examples. Italicize the book but not the individual tales:

CkT	The Cook's Tale	NPT	The Nun's Priest's Tale
CT	*The Canterbury Tales*	PardT	The Pardoner's Tale

Other Literary Works

Wherever possible in your in-text citations, use the initial letters of the title. A reference to page 18 of Melville's *Moby-Dick: The White Whale* could appear as: (*MD* 18). Use the following italicized abbreviations as guidelines:

Aen.	*Aeneid* by Vergil	*Lys.*	*Lysistrata* by Aristophanes
Beo.	*Beowulf*	*Med.*	*Medea* by Euripides

Accent Marks

When you quote, reproduce accents exactly as they appear in the original. You may need to use the character sets embedded within the computer software. Write the mark in ink on the printout if your typewriter or word processor does not support the mark.

> "La tradición clásica en españa," according to Romana, remains strong and vibrant in public school instruction (16).

Acknowledgments

Generally, acknowledgments are unnecessary. Nor is a preface required. Use a superscript reference numeral to your first sentence and then place any obligatory acknowledgments or explanations in a content endnote (see pages 346–349). Acknowledge neither your instructor nor typist for help with your research paper, though such acknowledgments are standard with graduate theses and dissertations.

Ampersand

MLA Style

Avoid using the ampersand symbol "&" unless custom demands it (e.g., "A&P"). Use *and* for in-text citations in MLA style (e.g., Smith and Jones 213–14).

APA Style

Use "&" within citations (e.g., Spenser & Wilson, 2006, p. 73) but not in the text (Spenser and Wilson found the results in error.)

Annotated Bibliography

An annotation describes the essential details of a book or article. Place it just after the facts of publication. Provide enough information in about three sentences for a reader to have a fairly clear image of the work's purpose, contents, and special value. See pages 117–119 for a complete annotated bibliography.

Arabic Numerals

Both the MLA style and the APA style require Arabic numerals whenever possible: for volumes, books, parts, and chapters of works; acts, scenes, and lines of plays; cantos, stanzas, and lines of poetry.

Bible

Use parenthetical documentation for biblical references in the text (e.g., 2 Chron. 18.13). Do not underline the books of the Bible. For abbreviations, see page A-2.

Clip Art

Pictures, figures, and drawings are available on many computers, but avoid the temptation to embed them in your document. Clip art, in general, conveys an informal, sometimes comic effect, one that is inappropriate to the serious nature of most research papers.

Copyright Law

"Fair use" of the materials of others is permitted without the need for specific permission as long as your purpose is noncommercial for purposes of criticism, scholarship, or research. Under those circumstances, you can quote from sources and reproduce artistic works within reasonable limits. The law is vague on specific amounts that can be borrowed, suggesting only the "substantiality of the portion used in relation to the copyrighted work as a whole." In other words, you should be safe in reproducing the work of another as long as the portion is not substantial.

To protect your own work, keyboard in the upper-right-hand corner of your manuscript, "Copyright © 20__ by _____." (Fill the blanks with the proper year and your name.) Then, to register a work, order a form from the U. S. Copyright Office, Library of Congress, Washington, D.C. 20559.

Covers and Binders

Most instructors prefer that you submit manuscript pages with one staple in the upper left corner. Unless required, do not use a cover or binder.

Definitions

For definitions and translations within your text, use single quotation marks without intervening punctuation. For example:

The use of <u>et alii</u> 'and others' has diminished in scholarly writing.

Electronic Presentations

If you have the expertise, many instructors will allow you to submit the research paper in electronic form. See Chapter 18 for more information.

Endnotes for Documentation of Sources

An instructor or supervisor may prefer traditional superscript numerals within the text and documentation notes at the end of paper. If so, see Chapter 16, pages 345–349.

Footnotes for Documentation

If your instructor requires you to use footnotes, see Chapter 16, pages 337–365, for discussion and examples.

Fonts

Most computers offer a variety of typefaces. Use a nonserif typeface like Ariel (**Ariel**) or a serif typeface like Times Roman (**Times Roman**). Use the same font consistently throughout for your text. Use 12-point type size.

Foreign Cities

In general, spell the names of foreign cities as they are written in original sources. However, for purposes of clarity, you may substitute an English name or provide both with one in parentheses:

Köln (Cologne)   Braunschweig (Brunswick)
München (Munich)   Praha (Prague)

Foreign Languages

Underscore or italicize foreign words used in an English text:

> Like his friend Olaf, he is <u>aut Caesar, aut nihil</u>, either overpowering
> perfection or ruin and destruction.

Do not underscore or italicize quotations of a foreign language:

> Obviously, he uses it to exploit, in the words of Jean Laumon, "une
> admirable mine de themes poetiques."

Do not underscore or italicize foreign titles of magazine or journal articles, but *do* underline the names of the magazines or journals themselves:

> Arrigoitia, Luis de. "Machismo, folklore y creación en Mario Vargas Llosa." <u>Sin</u>
> <u>nombre</u> 13.4 (1983): 19-25..

Headings

Begin every major heading on a new page (title page, opening page, notes, appendix, Works Cited or references). Center the heading in capital and lowercase letters one inch from the top of the sheet. Use a doublespace between the heading and your first line of text. Number *all* text pages, including those with major headings.

Indention

Indent paragraphs five spaces or a half-inch. Indent long quotations (four lines or more) ten spaces or one inch from the left margin.

Italics

If your word processing system and your printer can reproduce italic lettering, use it in place of *underscoring* if you prefer that style.

Margins

A one-inch margin on all sides of each page is recommended. Place your page number one-half inch down from the top edge of the paper and one inch from the right edge. Your software will provide a ruler, menu, or style palette that allows you to set the margins. *Tip:* If you develop a header, the running head may appear one inch from the top, in which case your first line of text will begin 1 1/2 inches from the top.

Names of Persons

As a general rule, the first mention of a person requires the full name (e.g., Ernest Hemingway, Margaret Mead) and thereafter requires only usage of the surname (e.g., Hemingway, Mead). *Note:* APA style uses last name only in the text. Omit formal titles (Mr., Mrs., Dr., Hon.) in textual and note references to distinguished persons, living or dead.

Numbering

Pagination

Use a header to number your pages in the upper right-hand corner of the page. Depending on the software, you can create the head with the Numbering or Header feature. It may appear one-half inch or a full inch down from the top edge of the paper and one inch from the right edge. Precede the number with your last name unless anonymity is required, in which case you may use a shortened version of your title rather than your name, as in APA style (see page 323). Otherwise, type the heading and then double-space to your text.

Use lowercase Roman numerals (ii, iii, iv) on any pages that precede the main portion of your text. If you have a separate title page, count it as page i, but do not type it on the page. You *should* put a page number on your opening page of text, even if you include course identification (see page 221).

Paper

Print on one side of white bond paper, sixteen- or twenty-pound weight, 8 1/2 by 11 inches. Use the best-quality paper available; avoid erasable paper. Staple the pages of your manuscript together with one staple in the top left corner. Do not enclose the manuscript within a cover or binder unless your instructor asks you to do so.

Proofreader Marks

Be familiar with the most common proofreading symbols so you can correct your own copy or mark your copy for a typist or keyboarder. Some of the most common proofreading symbols are shown next.

Common Proofreading Symbols

✓	error in spelling (mistake) with correction in margin
lc	lowercase (mistake)
⌒	close up (mis take)
ℐ	delete and close up (misstake)
⊢⊣	delete and close up more than one letter (the mistakes and errors continue)
∧	insert (mitake)
∿ tr	transpose elements (their)
⌒	material to be corrected or moved, with instructions in the margin, or material to be spelled out, (corp.)
caps or ≡	capitalize (Huck finn and Tom Sawyer)
¶	begin a paragraph
No¶	do not begin a paragraph
∧	insert
_e	delete (a mistakes)
#	add space
⊙	add a period
⌃	add a comma
⌃	add a semicolon
⌄	add an apostrophe or single closing quotation mark
⌄	add a single opening quotation mark
⌄ ⌄	add double quotation marks
bf	change to boldface
stet	let stand as it is; ignore marks

Roman Numerals

Use capital Roman numerals in titles of persons as appropriate (Elizabeth II) and major sections of an outline (see pages 138–142). Use lowercase Roman numerals to number the preliminary pages of a text or paper, as for a preface or introduction (iii, iv, v). Otherwise, use Arabic numerals (e.g., Vol. 5, Act 2, Ch. 17, Plate 21, 2 Sam. 2.1–8, or *Iliad* 2.121–30), *except* when writing for some instructors in history, philosophy, religion, music, art, and theater, in which case you may need to use Roman numerals (e.g., III, Act II, I Sam. ii.1–8, *Hamlet* I.ii.5–6).

Running Heads

Repeat your last name in the upper right corner of every page just in front of the page number (see the sample paper, pages 227–235). APA style differs, see page 323.

Short Titles in the Text

Use abbreviated titles of books and articles mentioned often in the text after a first full reference. For example, after initially citing *Backgrounds to English as Language,* shorten the title to *Backgrounds* in the text, notes, and in-text citations (see also pages 184–185), but not in the bibliography entry. Mention *The Epic of Gilgamesh* and thereafter use *Gilgamesh* (*Note:* Be certain to italicize it when referring to the work).

Slang

Avoid the use of slang. When using it in a language study, enclose in double quotation marks any words to which you direct attention. Words used as words, however, require underlining.

Spacing

As a general rule, double-space the body of the paper, all indented quotations, and all reference entries. Footnotes, if used, should be single-spaced, but endnotes should be double-spaced (see pages 345–346). APA style (see Chapter 15) requires doublespacing after all headings and before and after indented quotes and figures.

Spelling

Spell accurately. Always use the computer to check spelling if the software is available. When in doubt, consult a dictionary. If the dictionary says a word may be spelled two ways, employ one way consistently (e.g., theater *or* theatre).

Statistical and Mathematical Copy

Use the simplest form of equation that can be made by ordinary mathematical calculation. If an equation cannot be reproduced entirely by keyboard, type what you can and fill in the rest with ink on the printout. As a general rule, keep equations on one line rather than two:

$$(a + b)/(x + y)$$

APA style requires quadruple line spacing above and below an equation.

Theses and Dissertations

The author of a thesis or dissertation must satisfy the requirements of the college's graduate program. Therefore, even though you may use MLA style or APA style, you must abide by certain additional rules with regard to paper, typing, margins, and introductory matter such as title page, approval page, acknowledgment page, table of contents, abstract, and other matters. Use both the graduate school guidelines and this book to maintain the appropriate style and format.

Titles within Titles

For an article title within quotation marks that includes a book title, as indicated by underlining, retain the underlining or use italic lettering.

> "<u>Great Expectations</u> as a Novel of Initiation"

For an article title within quotation marks that includes another title indicated by quotation marks, enclose the internal title within single quotation marks.

> "A Reading of O. Henry's 'The Gift of the Magi' "

For an underscored book title that incorporates another title that is normally underscored, do not underscore or italicize the internal title nor place it within quotation marks.

> *Interpretations* of Great Expectations
> <u>Using Shakespeare's</u> Romeo and Juliet <u>in the Classroom</u>

Typing

Submit the paper in typed 12-point form. Use no hyphens at the ends of lines. Avoid widows and orphans, which are single lines at the top of a page and single words at the bottom of a paragraph, respectively; some computers will help you correct this problem. Use special features—boldface, italics, graphs, color—with discretion. Your writing, not your graphics, will earn the credits and the better grades. You are ultimately responsible for correct pagination and accuracy of the manuscript. See also "Revising, Proofreading, and Formatting the Rough Draft," pages 218–226.

Underscoring (Italicizing)

Do not underscore sacred writings (Genesis, Old Testament); series (The New American Nation Series); editions (Variorum Edition of W. B. Yeats); societies (Victorian Society); courses (Greek Mythology); divisions of a work (preface, appendix, canto 3, scene 2); or descriptive phrases (Nixon's farewell address or Reagan's White House years).

Underscoring Individual Words for Emphasis

Italicizing words for emphasis is discouraged. A better alternative is to position the word in such a way as to accomplish the same purpose. For example:

Graphical emphasis: Perhaps an answer lies in <u>preventing</u> abuse, not in makeshift remedies after the fact.

Linguistic emphasis: Prevention of abuse is a better answer than makeshift remedies after the fact.

Some special words and symbols require underlining.

- Species, genera, and varieties:

    <u>Penstemon caespitosus</u> subsp. <u>thompsoniae</u>

- Letters, words, and phrases cited as a linguistic sample:

    the letter <u>e</u> in the word <u>let</u>

- Letters used as statistical symbols and algebraic variables:

    trial <u>n</u> of the <u>t</u> test or <u>C</u>(3, 14) = 9.432

Word Division

Avoid dividing any word at the end of a line. Leave the line short rather than divide a word.

Finding Reference Works for Your General Topic

We have tried to make this list as user-friendly as possible, which will enable you to select rather quickly a few basic references from one of nine general categories. Three of four items from a list will be more than sufficient to launch your investigation. Each category has two lists:

1. *Library reference books and electronic databases.* The books will require you to make a trip to the library, but the academic databases can be accessed anywhere by logging into your library's network—from your dorm room, computer lab, or at the library itself.
2. *Reputable Internet sources accessed by a browser,* such as Google, Lycos, AltaVista, and others, as listed on pages 34–35.

Remember, too, that the library gives you an electronic catalog to all books in the library as well as access to general-interest databases, such as:

> InfoTrac
> FirstSearch
> NewsBank
> Lexis-Nexis Academic
> netLibrary
> Online Books Page
> Oxford Reference Online

Here are the ten sections and the page number that begins each:

1. Historic Issues of Events, People, and Artifacts, page A-9
2. Scientific Issues in Physics, Astronomy, and Engineering, page A-10
3. Issues of Health, Fitness, and Athletics, page A-11
4. Social and Political Issues, page A-11
5. Issues in the Arts, Literature, Music, and Language, page A-12
6. Environmental Issues, Genetics, and the Earth Sciences, page A-12
7. Issues in Communication and Information Technology, page A-13
8. Issues in Religion, Philosophy, Psychology, page A-14
9. Issues in Business and Economics, page A-14
10. Popular Culture, Current Events, and Modern Trends, page A-15

By no means are the nine lists definitive, but one of them should serve as your launching pad at the beginning of the project. These works will carry you deeper and deeper toward specific material for collecting your summaries, paraphrases, and quotations.

Historic Issues of Events, People, and Artifacts

If you are interested in events of the past, classical architecture, famous people, and ancient artifacts, you need sources in history, biography, art history, architecture, anthropology, and similar sources. Listed below are important reference works in the library and on the Internet that can launch your investigation.

At the library, investigate these books and academic databases:

Abstracts in Anthropology. Farmingdale: Baywood, 1970–date. This reference book gives brief descriptions of thousands of articles on the cultural development of human history.

American National Biography. 24 vols. New York: Oxford, 1999. This set of books is the place to start for a study of most historical figures in American history.

Dictionary of American History. 3rd ed. 10 vols. New York: Scribner's, 2003. This set of books offers a well-documented, scholarly source on the people, places, and events in U.S. history and includes brief bibliographies to recommended sources.

Historical Abstracts. Santa Barbara, CA: ABC-CLIO, 1955–date. This set of printed abstracts provides a quick overview of historical issues and events worldwide.

Illustrated Encyclopedia of Mankind. 22 vols. Freeport, NY: Marshall Cavendish, 1989. This massive work has been a standard in the field for some time.

Lexis-Nexis Primary Sources in U.S. History. This academic database is wide-ranging and gives, for example, excellent sources on American women's studies.

Recently Published Articles. Washington: American Historical Association, 1976–date. These printed volumes provide an effective index to articles in *American Historical Review, Journal of American History, Journal of the West,* and many others.

On the Internet, investigate these sites:

Annual Reviews: Anthropology, at <http://anthro.AnnualReviews.org>

Anthropology Internet Resources, at <http://www.wcsu.edu/socialsci/antres.html>

Archiving Early America, at <http://earlyamerica.com>

History Best Information on the Net (BIOTN), at <http://library.sau.edu/bestinfo/Majors/History/hisindex.htm>

Scientific Issues in Physics, Astronomy, and Engineering

If you are interested in the heavens (the stars, moon, and planets), the laws of supersonic flight, nuclear energy, plasma television screens, and similar topics, you need to begin your investigation with some of the reference works listed below, which you will find in the library and on the Internet.

At the library, investigate these books and academic databases:

American Chemical Society Publications (ACS). This database offers searchable access to online archives of chemistry journals dating back to 1879.

Astronomy Encyclopedia. Ed. Patrick Moore. New York: Oxford UP, 2002. This source suggests possible topic ideas for research in the field; good starting point for students.

Applied Science and Technology Index. New York: Wilson, 1958–date. This major reference work indexes recent articles in all areas of the applied sciences, engineering, and technology.

Current Physics Index. New York: American Institute of Physics, 1975–date. This book indexes most articles in physics journals such as *Applied Physics, Journal of Chemical Physics, Nuclear Physics,* and *Physical Review*.

Engineering Index. New York: Engineering Index Inc., 1884–date. This work is available in versions ranging from books to electronic databases; check the academic library to locate which version is available locally.

General Science Index. New York: Wilson, 1978–date. This index covers about 100 science periodicals, including many in the applied sciences.

Physics Abstracts. Surrey, England: Institute of Electrical Engineers, 1898–date. Using keywords, this reference helps you choose a topic and find abstracts to articles on that topic.

On the Internet, investigate these sites:

American Astronomical Society, at <http://www.aas.org>

Extrasolar Planets Encyclopaedia, at <http://cfa-www.harvard.edu/planets/>

Mount Wilson Observatory, at <http://www.mtwilson.edu>

National Academy of Sciences, at <http://www.nas.edu>

PhysicsWeb, at <http://physicsweb.org/resources/search/phtml>

Issues of Health, Fitness, and Athletics

If you have an interest in sports medicine, jogging, dieting, good health, nutrition, and similar topics, you should begin your investigation with some of the reference works listed below, which you will find in the library and on the Internet.

At the library, investigate these books and academic databases:

Atlas of Human Anatomy. 3rd ed. Frank H. Netter. Teterboro, NJ: ICON, 2003. This reference work contains wonderful illustrations of the human body, extensively labeled.

Consumer Health and Nutrition Index. Phoenix: Oryx , 1985–date. This reference work contains an index, published quarterly, to sources for consumers and scholars.

Cumulated Index Medicus. Bethesda, MD: U.S. Department of Health and Human Services, 1959–date. This reference work is an essential starting point for most papers in medical science.

Cumulated Index to Nursing and Allied Health Literature. Glendale, CA: CINAHL, 1956–date. This reference work offers nursing students an index to *Cancer Nurse, Journal of Practical Nursing, Journal of Nursing Education*, and many more journals; may be listed as *CINAHL*.

Encyclopedia of Human Nutrition. 3 vols. San Diego, CA: Academic, 1999. This reference work offers a good starting point for a paper on nutrition.

Miller-Keane Encyclopedia and Dictionary of Medicine, Nursing, and Allied Health. 6th ed. Philadelphia: Saunders, 2003. This reference work offers practical applications as well as explanations of concepts and terminology. The reference is now offered in an electronic version also.

Physical Education Index. Cape Giradeau, MO: BenOak, 1978–date. This reference work indexes most topics in athletics, sports medicine, and athletics.

On the Internet, investigate these sites:

Healthfinder, at <http://www.healthfinder.gov>

Medweb: Medical Libraries, at <http://www.medweb.emory.edu/MedWeb/>

National Institutes of Health, at <http://www.nih.gov>

PubMed, at <http://www.ncbi.nlm.nih.gov/PubMed>

SPORTQuest, at <http://www.sportquest.com>

Social and Political Issues

If you have an interest in social work at nursing homes, current events such as rap music or rave parties, congressional legislation on student loans, education, and the SAT examinations, gender issues, and similar topics, you should begin your investigation with some of the reference works listed below, which you will find in the library and on the Internet.

At the library, investigate these books and academic databases:

ABC: Pol Sci. Santa Barbara: ABC-CLIO, 1969–date. This reference work indexes the tables of contents of about 300 international journals in the original language.

CQ Researcher. This reference work provides access to a database containing documents covering hundreds of hot-topic issues such as abortion, child abuse, election reform, and civil liberties.

Education Abstracts. New York: Wilson, 1994. This reference work provides short descriptions of hundreds of articles.

Education Index. New York: Wilson, 1929–date. This reference work indexes articles in such journals as *Childhood Education, Comparative Education, Education Digest*, and *Journal of Educational Psychology*.

Encyclopedia of Sociology. Ed. Edgar F. Borgatta et al. 2nd ed. 5 vols. Detroit: Macmillan, 2000. This encyclopedia offers a starting point for research, giving you terms, issues, and theories to motivate your own ideas.

Social Sciences Index. New York: Wilson, 1974–date. This reference work provides a vital index to all aspects of topics in sociology, social work, education, political science, geography, and other fields.

Westlaw. This database contains federal and all state court cases and statutes (laws).

Women's Studies Index. Boston: Hall, 1989–date. This reference work offers an annual index considered by many librarians the best source for immediate information on women's issues.

On the Internet, investigate these sites:

Internet Legal Resources Guide, at <http://www.ilrg.com/>

Online Educational Resources, at <http://quest.arc.nasa.gov/>

Political Science Resources on the Web, at <http://www.lib.umich.edu/govdocs/polisci.html>

Thomas, at <http://thomas.loc.gov>

Issues in the Arts, Literature, Music, and Language

If you have an interest in Greek drama, the films of Mel Gibson, the postcolonial effects on languages in the Caribbean, the music of Andrew Lloyd Webber, the poetry of Dylan Thomas, and similar topics, you should begin your investigation with some of the reference works listed below, which you will find in the library and on the Internet.

At the library, investigate these books and academic databases:

Art Index. New York: Wilson, 1929–date. This reference work indexes most art journals, including *American Art Journal, Art Bulletin*, and *Artforum*.

Avery Index to Architectural Periodicals. Boston: Hall, 1973–date. This reference work is a good source for periodical articles on ancient and modern edifices.

Bibliographic Guide to Art and Architecture. Boston: Hall, 1977–date. Published annually, this reference work provides bibliographies on most topics in art and architecture—an excellent place to begin research in this area.

Bibliographic Guide to Music. Boston: Hall, 1976–date. This reference work provides an excellent subject index to almost every topic in the field of music and gives the bibliographic data for several articles on most topics in the field.

Contemporary Literary Criticism (CLC). This database provides an extensive collection of full-text critical essays about novelists, poets, playwrights, short story writers, and other creative writers who are now living or who died after December 31, 1959.

Humanities Index. New York: Wilson, 1974–date. This reference work indexes all of the major literary magazines and journals; it may be listed as *Wilson Humanities Index*.

Music Index. Warren, MI: Information Coordinators, 1949–date. This reference work indexes music journals such as *American Music Teacher, Choral Journal, Journal of Band Research*, and *Journal of Music Therapy*.

On the Internet, investigate these sites:

The English Server, at <http://eserver.org/>

Project Gutenberg, at <http://promo.net/pg>

Voice of the Shuttle: Art and Art History, at <http://vos.ucsb.edu/>

World Wide Arts Resources, at <http:/wwar.world-arts-resources.com>

Worldwide Internet Music Resources, at <http://theme.music.indiana.edu/music_resources/>

Environmental Issues, Genetics, and the Earth Sciences

If you have an interest in cloning, abortion, the shrinking rain forest in Brazil, sinkholes in Florida, the Flint Hills grassland of Kansas, underground water tables in Texas, and similar topics, you should begin your investigation with some of the reference works listed below, which you will find in the library and on the Internet.

At the library, investigate these books and academic databases:

AGRICOLA. This database, produced by the National Agricultural Library, provides access to articles, books, and Web sites in agriculture, animal and plant sciences, forestry, and soil and water resources.

Bibliography and Index of Geology. Alexandria, VA: American Geological Institute, 1933–date. Organized monthly, with annual indexes, this reference work indexes excellent scholarly articles.

Biological and Agricultural Index. New York: H.W Wilson. 1916-date. This reference work is a standard index to periodicals in the field.

Biological Abstracts. Philadelphia: Biosis, 1926-date. This reference work contains abstracts useful to review before locating the full articles at the library's computer.

Ecological Abstracts. Norwich, UK: Geo Abstracts, 1974-date. This reference work offers a chance to examine the brief abstract before finding and reading the complete article.

The Environmental Index. Ann Arbor, MI: UMI, 1992-date. This reference work indexes numerous journals in the field, including *Environment, Environmental Ethics,* and *Journal of Applied Ecology.*

Geographical Abstracts. Norwich, UK: Geo Abstracts, 1972-date. This reference work provides a quick overview of articles that can be searched for full text later.

On the Internet, investigate these sites:

The Academy of Natural Sciences, at <http://www.acnatsci.org/library/link.html>

Agricola, at <http://www.nalusda.gov/ag98>

BioOnline, at <http://www.bio.com/os/start/home.html>

BIOSIS, at < http://www.biosis.org/>

Envirolink, at <http://envirolink.org>

Issues in Communication and Information Technology

If you have an interest in talk radio, television programming for children, bias in print journalism, developing computer software, the glut of cell phones, and similar topics, you should begin your investigation with some of the reference works listed below, which you will find in the library and on the Internet.

At the library, investigate these books and academic databases:

Computer Abstracts. London: Technical Information, 1957-date. This work provides short descriptions of important articles in the field.

Computer Literature Index. Phoenix: ACR, 1971-date. This index identifies articles on computer science in a timely fashion, with periodic updates.

Encyclopedia of Computer Science and Technology. Ed. J. Belzer. 22 vols. New York: Dekker, 1975-91. Supplement 1991-date. This reference work provides a comprehensive source for launching computer investigations.

Information Technology Research, Innovation, and E-Government. Washington, DC: National Press Academy, 2002. This site focuses on the use of the Internet in government administration.

The Elements of Style. William Strunk, Jr., and E. B. White. Boston: Allyn and Bacon, 1999. A classic book that teaches and exhorts writers to avoid needless words, urges them to use the active voice, and calls for simplicity in style.

On Writing Well. 25th anniversary ed. William K. Zinsser. New York: HarperResource, 2001. This book is a well-written text on the art of writing, especially on the best elements of nonfiction prose.

Style: Ten Lessons in Clarity and Grace. 7th ed. Joseph M. Williams. New York: Longman, 2003. This book provides an excellent discussion of writing style and the means to attain it.

On the Internet, investigate these sites:

Computer Science, at <http://library.albany.edu/subject/csci.htm>

Information Technology Association of America, at <http://www.itaa.org/index.cfm>

Journalism and Mass Communication Resources on the Web, at <http://www.lib.iastate.edu/collections/eresourc/journalism.html>

Technical Communication Online, at <http://www.techcomm-online.org/>

Virtual Computer Library, at <http://www.utexas.edu/computer/vcl/>

Issues in Religion, Philosophy, Psychology

If you have an interest in human values, moral self-discipline, the ethics of religious wars, the power of religious cults, the behavior of children with single parents, the effect of the environment on personality, and similar topics, you should begin your investigation with some of the reference works listed below, which you will find in the library and on the Internet.

At the library, investigate these books and academic databases:

Cambridge Dictionary of Philosophy. 2nd ed. Ed. R. Audi. New York: Cambridge, 1999. This reference work provides an excellent base for launching your investigation into philosophical issues.

Encyclopedia of Psychology. Ed. Alan E. Kazdin. 8 vols. New York: Oxford, 2000. This reference work contains the most comprehensive basic reference work in the field; published under the auspices of the American Psychological Association.

Humanities Index. New York: Wilson, 1974–date. This reference work indexes religious journals such as *Church History, Harvard Theological Review,* and *Muslim World*.

Philosopher's Index: A Retrospective Index. Bowling Green, OH: Bowling Green U, 1967–date. This reference work indexes philosophy articles in journals such as *American Philosophical Quarterly, Humanist, Journal of the History of Ideas, and Journal of Philosophy*.

Psychological Abstracts. Washington, DC: APA, 1927–date. This reference work provides brief abstracts to articles in such psychology journals as *American Journal of Psychology, Behavioral Science, and Psy-* *chological Review*. On the library's network, look for *PsycINFO*.

Religion: Index One: Periodicals, Religion and Theological Abstracts. Chicago: ATLA, 1949–date. This reference work indexes religious articles in such journals as *Biblical Research, Christian Scholar, Commonweal,* and *Harvard Theological Review*.

Routledge Encyclopedia of Philosophy. 10 vols. Ed. E. Craig. New York: Routledge, 1999. This work is the most comprehensive, authoritative, and up-to-date reference work in the field. A condensed version is available in some libraries.

On the Internet, investigate these sites:

The American Philosophical Association, at <http://www.amphilsoc.org/>

Episteme Links: Philosophy Resources on the Internet, at <http://www.epistemelinks.com/> .

Humanities: Religion Gateway, at <http://www.academicinfo.net/religindex.html>

PsycREF: Resources in Psychology on the Internet, at <http://maple.lemonyne.edu/~hevern/psychref.html>

Vanderbilt Divinity School, at <http://divinity.library.vanderbilt.edu/lib/>

Issues in Business and Economics

If you wish to write about the impact of rising tuition costs, the effect of credit cards for college students, the marketing success of Wal-Mart stores, the economic impact of federal tax cuts, the stock market's effect on accounting practices, and similar topics, you should begin your investigation with some of the reference works listed below, which you will find in the library and on the Internet.

At the library, investigate these books and academic databases:

Business Abstracts. New York: Wilson, 1995–date. This reference work provides short descriptions of business, economic, and marketing articles.

Business Periodicals Index. New York: Wilson, 1958–date. This reference work indexes most journals in the field, such as *Business Quarterly, Business Week, For-* *tune,* and *Journal of Business*. See also on the library's network *Reference USA, Business Dateline,* and *Business and Company*.

Business Publications Index and Abstracts. Detroit: Gale, 1983–date. This reference work provides a place to launch searches on almost any topic related to business.

General Business File. This database lists citations and summaries of articles and the entire text of some articles in business, management, and economic periodicals.

Index of Economic Articles. Nashville: American Economic Association, 1886–date. This reference work, arranged as both a topic and an author index, provides a good start for the student and professional alike.

Journal of Economic Literature. Nashville: American Economic Association, 1886–date. This reference work offers articles followed by bibliographies for further research.

World Economic Survey. 1945–date. An annual publication originally from the League of Nations and currently from the United Nations, this reference work offers varying topics each year to researchers.

On the Internet, investigate these sites:

All Business Network, at <http://www.all-biz.com>

Finance: The World Wide Web Virtual Library, at <http://www.cob.ohio-state.edu/dept/fin/overview.html>

FinWeb, at <http://www.finweb.com>

International Resources in Business Economics, at <http://www.lib.berkeley.edu/BUSI/bbg18.html>

Popular Culture, Current Events, and Modern Trends

If you are interested in current events and popular culture as well as modern trends, consult sources that provide recent facts and details about famous people, developments in society, and changes in human customs. Listed below are important reference works in the library and on the Internet that can launch your investigation.

At the library, investigate these books and academic databases:

American National Biography. 24 vols. New York: Oxford, 1999. This set of books provides the place to start for a study of most historical figures in American history.

CQ Researcher. This reference works provides access to a database containing documents covering hundreds of "hot topic" issues such as abortion, child abuse, election reform, or civil liberties.

Illustrated Encyclopedia of Mankind. 22 vols. Freeport, NY: Marshall Cavendish, 1989. This massive work has been a standard in the field for some time.

NewsBank. NewsBank provides searchable full text articles appearing in local publications.

Recently Published Articles. Washington: American Historical Association, 1976–date. These printed volumes provide an effective index to articles in *American Historical Review, Journal of American History, Journal of the West,* and many others.

On the Internet, investigate these sites:

Center for Study of Popular Culture, at <http://www.cspc.org/>

Gallup Organization, at <http://www.gallup.com>

The Internet Movie Database, at <http://www.us.imdb.com>

Multi-Channel News, at <http://www.multichannel.com>

Popular Culture: Resources for Critical Analysis, at <http://www.wsu.edu/~amerstu/pop/tvrguide.html>

Credits

Index

Note: Page numbers followed by the letters *f* and *t* indicate figures and tables, respectively. **Bold** page numbers indicate main discussions.

(continued)

I–6

I–8